Investigating Terrorism

Praise for *Investigating Terrorism: Current Political, Legal and Psychological Issues*

'How can we be more effective in bringing terrorists to justice in ways that uphold our legal traditions? This book provides crucial clues drawn from highly experienced prosecution and defence lawyers, detectives, security experts and forensic psychologists. I highly recommend it for all who want to understand and respond to the serious threat from jihadist terrorism over the years to come.'

Professor Sir David Omand, former UK Security and Intelligence Coordinator, Permanent Secretary of the Home Office and Director GCHQ

'The threat of terrorism is a dark shadow which affects all citizens throughout the world. In this well constructed book a group of eminent experts with extensive experience in the field provides valuable discussion of the causes and wider consequences of terrorism as well as its circumvention, investigation and prosecution. It comprises a substantial body of precious insight and guidance which will be of unquestionable value to policy and law makers, police investigators, judges and legal practitioners. Those who are active in this sphere would be well advised to familiarize themselves with its contents. I very strongly recommend it.'

Anthony Heaton-Armstrong, practising barrister at 9–12 Bell Yard

'Edited and written by experts in their fields and with a plethora of experience, the authors know what they are talking about. This book is a must for those who need to know, those who are interested to know, and those who think they know it all already.'

Susan Young, Professor of Forensic Clinical Psychology, Broadmoor Hospital, West London Mental Health Trust

'First-rank expertise on the detection, investigation and prosecution of terrorist crime accompanies insights into the motives of its perpetrators. The combination is unusual, welcome and thought-provoking.'

David Anderson, QC, Independent Reviewer of Terrorism Legislation

'A collection of very informative papers from many of the experts in the front line of confronting, analyzing, detecting and dealing with terrorism and terrorist suspects. It confirms that we have no room for complacency, that we are still learning and there is still much to be done.'

Alastair Logan, OBE, LLB, solicitor and member of The Law Society's Human Rights Committee

Investigating Terrorism

Current Political, Legal and Psychological Issues

Edited by

John Pearse

WILEY Blackwell

This edition first published 2015
© 2015 John Wiley & Sons, Ltd.

Registered Office
John Wiley & Sons Ltd, The Atrium, Southern Gate, Chichester, West Sussex, PO19 8SQ, UK

Editorial Offices
350 Main Street, Malden, MA 02148-5020, USA
9600 Garsington Road, Oxford, OX4 2DQ, UK
The Atrium, Southern Gate, Chichester, West Sussex, PO19 8SQ, UK

For details of our global editorial offices, for customer services, and for information about how to apply for permission to reuse the copyright material in this book please see our website at www.wiley.com/wiley-blackwell.

The right of John Pearse to be identified as the author of the editorial material in this work has been asserted in accordance with the UK Copyright, Designs and Patents Act 1988.

Library of Congress Cataloging-in-Publication Data

Investigating terrorism : current political, legal, and psychological issues / edited by John Pearse.
    pages cm
 Includes bibliographical references and index.
  ISBN 978-1-119-99415-2 (cloth) – ISBN 978-1-119-99416-9 (pbk.) 1. Terrorism – Law and legislation – Great Britain. 2. Terrorism – Prevention – Law and legislation – Great Britain.
3. Terrorism investigation – Great Britain. 4. Terrorism – Political aspects – Great Britain.
5. Terrorism – Great Britain – Psychological aspects. 6. Suicide bombers. 7. Domestic terrorism – Law and legislation. I. Pearse, John Joseph, 1954– editor.
  KD8039.I58 2015
  363.325 – dc23

                                                                                    2014020564

A catalogue record for this book is available from the British Library.

Cover image: © Marco Prati / Shutterstock
Cover design by Design Deluxe

Typeset in 10.5/13pt MinionPro by Laserwords Private Limited, Chennai, India
Printed and bound in Malaysia by Vivar Printing Sdn Bhd

1   2015

In memory of Tom, Andrew and John Mc – who achieved so much.

Contents

About the Editor

John Pearse, PhD, C. Psychol, AFBPsS, is Vice President of the Paul Ekman Group (paulekman.com) and Director of Forensic Navigation Services Ltd, an independent company that combines forensic consultancy and investigation with psychological training and empirical research. He has provided counter-terrorist advice and training around the world and has designed and delivered a number of acclaimed international multi-agency counter-terrorism seminars. John has undertaken a confidential national review of police interviewing with terrorist suspects in the UK and has designed and delivered a specialist national interview course for terrorist investigators combining essential interpersonal skills and cultural awareness with effective questioning techniques, strategic awareness and tactical measures. John has been researching and publishing on interviewing and interrogation and terrorist-related issues since 1991, and is a visiting lecturer at a number of colleges within the University of London.

About the Contributors

Lord Carlile of Berriew, CBE, QC, was called to the Bar in 1970. He became a Queen's Counsel in 1984, is a Master of the Bench of Gray's Inn and sits as a deputy High Court judge. From 2001 to 2011 he was the UK Independent Reviewer of Terrorism Legislation. He now advises in a professional capacity on terrorism and compliance matters.

Peter Carter, QC, was called to the bar in 1974, made Queen's Counsel in 1995 and is a Master of the Bench of Gray's Inn. From 2003 to 2005 he was chair of the Bar Human Rights Committee. He is ranked as a leading criminal silk by Chambers Guide to the Legal Profession, with an emphasis on fraud, terrorism, homicide and trafficking. He is an expert in international human rights law. He appears pro bono in appeals to the Privy Council. He has appeared in domestic and regional human rights courts outside the UK and participated in *amicus* briefs in overseas jurisdictions. He was one of the team instructed on behalf of both Houses of Parliament to present an *amicus* brief for the US Supreme Court in the Guantanamo Bay case of *Rasul v. Bush* which successfully challenged the US government's denial of constitutional and international human rights to the detainees.

Peter Clarke, CVO, OBE, QPM, joined the Metropolitan Police in 1977 after graduating in Law from Bristol University. After attending the Royal College of Defence Studies, in May 2002 he became the head of the Anti-Terrorist Branch and for nearly six years led all terrorist investigations in the UK and against British interests overseas, including the London bombings (2005), the transatlantic airliners 'liquid bomb' plot (2006) and attacks in Bali, Saudi Arabia, Turkey, Qatar and elsewhere. He retired in 2008 and in 2009 he was appointed by the prime minister to the UK National Security Forum to advise government on the implementation of the UK National Security Strategy. From 2009 to 2013 he was a non-executive director of the Serious

Organised Crime Agency in the United Kingdom. In 2014 he was appointed by the Secretary of State for Education to investigate allegations of Islamist infiltration into schools in the city.

John G. D. Grieve, MPhil, CBE, QPM, served as a detective throughout London in roles that varied from undercover officer to intelligence policy chair. He was the first Director of Intelligence and led the Anti-Terrorist Squad as National Co-ordinator during the 1996–1998 bombing campaigns before becoming the first Director of the Racial and Violent Crime Task Force. He retired in 2002. He holds a number of academic posts including Senior Research Fellow at the University of Portsmouth; Professor Emeritus at London Metropolitan University; Honorary Fellow at Roehampton Institute, Surrey University; and Honorary Doctor at London Metropolitan University. In 2004 he was appointed as a Commissioner of the International Independent Monitoring Commission for the Peace Process in Northern Ireland, in which role he served until 2011. He is the independent chair of the Home Office/Ministry of Justice Independent Advisory Group on Hate Crime. He has published extensively on policing issues including investigation, counter-terrorism, intelligence, crisis management, community engagement, prevention and cultural changes.

Gisli H. Gudjonsson is an Emeritus Professor of Forensic Psychology at the Institute of Psychiatry, King's College London, and an honorary consultant clinical and forensic psychologist at Broadmoor Hospital. Prior to his retirement from King's College on 1 January 2012, he was the head of Forensic Psychology Services for the Lambeth Forensic Services and Medium Secure Unit at the South London and Maudsley NHS Trust (SLaM). Professor Gudjonsson is a chartered psychologist and a Fellow of the British Psychological Society. A registered practitioner (clinical and forensic) with the Health & Care Professions Council (HCPC), he has been awarded two lifetime achievement awards and was appointed a Commander of the Order of the British Empire (CBE) in the Queen's Birthday 2011 Honours List for services to clinical psychology.

Max Hill, QC, is Head of Red Lion Chambers in London, chair of the Kalisher Trust and a Bencher of Middle Temple. He is a former chairman of the Criminal Bar Association of England and Wales. He has unrivalled experience prosecuting terrorism trials, from *R v. Hulme and others* 2003 (Real IRA), to *R v. Ibrahim and others* 2007 (21 July 2005 London bombers) and *R v. Faraz* 2011 (terrorist publications). He represented the Metropolitan Police Service at the Coroner's Inquests into the London bombings of 7 July 2005. He has a broad practice in general crime, spanning homicide to fraud and money laundering, as well as regulatory proceedings. He is also a Crown Court Recorder, authorized to sit at the Central Criminal Court.

Robert Lambert divides his time between two part-time teaching posts at the Handa Centre for the Study of Terrorism and Political Violence, University of St Andrews, and at the John Grieve Policing Centre, London Metropolitan University. At both centres he teaches postgraduate and undergraduate modules based on his research and publications on terrorism, counter-terrorism, far right political violence and anti-Muslim hate crimes. In addition, he supervises and examines PhD research in the same arena. He is the author of *Countering al-Qaeda in London: Police and Muslims in Partnership* (Hurst, 2011).

Simon McKay, LLB, LLM, is a solicitor advocate (all proceedings) and an honorary fellow of the School of Law, University of Leeds. He specializes in human rights and criminal law with a particular interest in state-based crimes (terrorism, Official Secrets Act, etc.), covert policing and surveillance issues. Until he resigned in 2012, he was the only solicitor advocate on the Attorney General's panel of special advocates in terrorist cases. He is the author of *Covert Policing Law and Practice* (Oxford University Press, 2011) and *Undercover Cop* (McKay Law, 2013).

Amy McKee, BSc, MSc, DClinPsy, is a clinical psychologist based in the north west of England providing risk assessments, management advice, consultancy and treatment interventions with forensic populations. She has extensive experience of working with offenders who present with complex forensic and mental health needs and provides training to specialist investigation and interviewing courses with a focus on understanding the offender, particularly child offenders and female offenders. She has provided advice on media appeals, investigative interview strategies and downstream monitoring support to police forces throughout the United Kingdom on a number of major inquiries, and has worked closely for a number of years with the North West Counter Terrorism Unit, providing consultation services, risk and threat assessments, training and research. Currently she is working on Project Regulus examining pathways of lone actor terrorists by bringing together academic, practitioner and clinical perspectives to enhance counter-terrorism practice. This research is being carried out in collaboration with NWCTU, SO15 and University College London.

Geraldine Noone is a sergeant in An Garda Síochána with over 30 years' service. She has considerable operational and training experience and specializes in investigative interviewing with An Garda Síochána and other European law enforcement agencies. She is a senior interview adviser and is responsible for the design and delivery of advanced interview and interview adviser courses. In addition, she is the business leader in the development of the Garda Síochána Interviewing Model (GSIM) and the *Manual of Guidance and Training* which supports this model. She is currently researching the psychological and background factors associated with 'no comment' interviews for a PhD at Liverpool University.

Carys Owen was called to the Bar in 2002 following a short career in the British Army as an Intelligence Corps officer. Since 2009 she has specialized in terrorism cases, both civil and criminal. Her civil terrorism cases have included Guantanamo Bay litigation (involving a novel use of the Norwich Pharmacal disclosure regime: *Shaker*

Aamer v. Secretary of State for Foreign and Commonwealth Affairs [2009] EWHC 3316 (Admin)), Abu Hamza (deprivation of British citizenship: *Abu Hamza v. Secretary of State for the Home Department* SC/23/2003), various exclusion, deportation, and terrorist asset freeze cases, as well as control order and TPIM cases involving suspected members of the transatlantic bomb plot, among others. Her criminal terrorism cases have involved bomb plotting in the UK as well as terrorist training abroad and possession of terrorism materials.

Karl Roberts is a forensic psychologist and is Professor and Chair of Policing and Criminal Justice at the University of Western Sydney in Sydney, Australia. He is also an Adjunct Professor of Criminology and Criminal Justice at the University of Massachusetts. His areas of expertise are within the field of interpersonal violence and law enforcement investigation with a focus on the behavioural assessment of offenders, investigative interviewing by law enforcement, and risk assessment and risk management. He works closely with law enforcement and other agencies throughout the world, providing training and advice to investigations, and has advised over 400 major police investigations worldwide.

Andrew Silke is Head of Criminology and Director for Terrorism Studies at the University of East London. He has a background in forensic psychology and criminology and has worked both in academia and for government. He has written extensively on terrorism and counter-terrorism and is frequently invited to speak at international conferences. Professor Silke serves by invitation on the UN Roster of Terrorism Experts and the European Commission's Network of Experts on Radicalisation. He is a member of the UK Cabinet Office National Risk Assessment Behavioural Science Expert Group. He has provided research advice to both the Royal Society in the UK and the National Academy of Sciences in the US and briefings to select committees of the House of Commons, and he was appointed in 2009 as a specialist adviser to the House of Commons Communities and Local Government Committee. In 2010 he gave invited oral testimony before the Canadian Special Senate Committee on Anti-Terrorism.

Clive Walker is Professor of Criminal Justice Studies at the School of Law, University of Leeds, where he has served as the Director of the Centre for Criminal Justice Studies (1987–2000) and as Head of School (2000–2005, 2010). He has been a visiting professor at many universities, including George Washington and Stanford in the United States, and Melbourne and New South Wales in Australia. He has published extensively on terrorism issues. His most comprehensive work on terrorism is his book *Terrorism and the Law* (Oxford University Press, 2011). He is currently the special adviser to the Home Office's Independent Reviewer of Terrorism Legislation and has served as a special adviser to the parliamentary select committee which scrutinized what became the Civil Contingencies Act 2004. That experience resulted in another book, *The Civil Contingencies Act 2004: Risk, Resilience and the Law in the United Kingdom* (Oxford University Press, 2006).

Simon Wells completed 30 years with the Metropolitan Police, and for 20 years he promoted the principles and practices of behavioural science for the benefit of law enforcement. Between 2003 and 2008 Simon was the course director of the National Negotiators Course and the operation head of the Hostage and Crisis Negotiation Unit. He was engaged in communicating and negotiating on behalf of the UK government, often with al-Qaeda, the Taliban and other 'insurgent' groups. He continues to interact with those involved in terrorism threatening national security, as well as training, coaching and mentoring support for the United Nations, and the US and UK governments. He is a co-director of Acacia 17, a company set up to provide expertise in communication skills, and has published on a wide range of issues, most recently on 'Crisis Negotiation: From Suicide to Terrorism', in *Handbook of Research in Negotiation* (Edward Elgar, 2013).

Adrian West is a forensic clinical psychologist working in the National Health Service. During the past 20 years, he has also advised the police service on many serious crime investigations. His contribution to risk assessment in relation to the diverse forms of violent extremism is founded on a commitment to evidence-based practice, alongside the hope that future generations will find a way of living with each other that is more tolerant of difference.

Introduction

When this book was just a fledgling proposal it was sent to a number of anonymous reviewers to critique and one of the questions they were asked to address was:

To whom will this book be useful?

I am told that one of the responses was simply 'al-Qaeda'. Under such circumstances I must start by outlining what this book is not about. It will not be revealing law enforcement or security service working practices and methodologies or any details of sensitive operational activity in the terrorist field. Rather, its purpose is to look at all of the very practical problems that those entrusted with investigating terrorism have been confronted with since the world order, and our perception of that world order, was drastically changed following the attacks on the Twin Towers and the Pentagon in the United States on September 11, 2001 – universally known as 9/11.

I am using the term 'investigate' in a very elastic fashion, given that I include in it not only law enforcement officers engaged in this field but also the lawyers tasked with prosecuting and defending terrorist suspects and the psychologists who have been challenged to explain and help us try to understand the motivation and belief systems that allow individuals to engage in such extreme behaviour: what drives a suicide bomber to carry out his or her mission, for example?

Prior to 9/11, the United Kingdom had endured three decades of terrorist conflict and unrest emanating principally from Northern Ireland, where one of the protagonists, the Provisional Irish Republican Army (PIRA), had repeatedly shown itself capable of detonating explosive devices throughout the British Isles. Such outrages led to the loss of many lives and many more people injured by such attacks, but over time the negative impact and press coverage they received, together with notable enforcement operations against them, led to a substantial change in

Investigating Terrorism: Current Political, Legal and Psychological Issues, First Edition. Edited by John Pearse.
© 2015 John Wiley & Sons, Ltd. Published 2015 by John Wiley & Sons, Ltd.

strategy: advance warning with coded telephone messages replaced random attacks, allowing the police to evacuate the target areas and, while this '10 pence' tactic resulted in considerable damage and disruption to services, there was a substantial reduction in the number of people killed or injured.

In a strange way, this became accepted as the norm: there was an expectation of attack and people needed to remain alert and vigilant; essential infrastructure received additional protection; civil and military contingencies were drawn up, but intentional large-scale loss of life was no longer part of the equation. In addition, as the population of the British Isles neared the concluding years of the twentieth century, there was an expectation of peace, brought about by the successful political peace process which culminated in the signing of the Good Friday Agreement in April 1998. All augured well for the twenty-first century – but 9/11 changed that.

So much has been written on this subject that it will serve no useful purpose to describe the events here, and indeed it was a day where our individual memories of the unfolding events will be indelibly etched in our minds, our thoughts and our feelings as an episode of unforgettable atrocity. We will all remember where we were that day.

It changed our perceptions of terrorism and it changed how we responded to terrorism, and that, in many ways, is one of the motivations behind this book. To what extent has the investigation of such offences changed? Has it matured and evolved to be able to deal with the new dimensions brought about by increased communication and travel opportunities, by the globalization process? What are the problems and practical difficulties that are now presented to the police or security services? Are there new legal and constitutional challenges as a result of this new terrorist paradigm and, if so, how have we responded to them over the course of the last 13 years?

The subtitle of the book is 'Current Political, Legal and Psychological Issues', and there is no doubt that the legal landscape has changed considerably in the UK since 9/11, with the introduction of many new specialist pieces of terrorist legislation. We know it remains an explicit goal of Western governments to charge and prosecute and to bring to justice those responsible for terrorist acts, but in the UK we have witnessed successive governments facing repeated legal challenges and many instances where they have been defeated in their attempts to respond to this new terrorist threat (detention without trial, extended pre-charge detention, and control orders are just a few examples). Does this suggest that they have legislated in haste and failed to understand the complex nature of international terrorism and the threat it poses to the traditional laws and political values of the country? Indeed, there are those that have interpreted recent legislation as heralding a success for the terrorist specifically because the new laws seek to undermine such tradition and values: hasty legislation represents the real threat to the life of a nation.

We shall explore this shifting political and legal landscape but also attend to the many emerging psychological issues. Where better to start than to examine the meaning and power of the word itself? In psychological research it is important to establish a personal or group baseline, how people normally respond in a given situation, because it is any departure or change from this that is so informative. So, whether I am speaking to the business community, police officers on a terrorist senior investigators' course, or delegates at legal conferences, I often ask them to complete the following sentence:

To me, terrorism means …

Just reflect on this question. While many countries and their legislators often disagree on an acceptable definition for this term, individuals from all walks of life have no such difficulty. Initially, references are often made to acts demonstrating extreme levels of violence, loss of life, and attempts to influence the political debate by violent means. A more personal dimension is often revealed when people consider their own safety (or lack of it) and the extreme levels of fear engendered by terrorist acts and terrorist groups. The notion of the 'mad' terrorist or suicide bomber sometimes permeates the debate. Interestingly, as the debate broadens and the emotional membrane is removed, terrorist acts can be seen as a form of communication, albeit communication *in extremis*. The removal of these emotional shrouds is very important, as it provides for a more informed and efficient decision-making environment. It also represents another goal of this book – to provide a critical analysis, devoid of unhelpful emotional rhetoric, of a number of thorny issues that psychologists working in this field have to contend with on a regular basis.

This book in divided into three sections. Part I provides the reader with an insight into the political, legal and policing context that has dominated events for the past 13 years. Given that nothing takes place in a vacuum, it is so important to set the scene in order to understand the true impact of terrorism in these critical arenas. Part II examines the impact of terrorist acts on the criminal justice process, and we have chosen to explore the implications and consequences on the legal, policing and prison systems following the failed suicide bombing attempts on the London Underground system in July 2005. In Part III we bring together individual and group perspectives in trying to make sense of terrorist acts. Can we better understand the motivation of suicide acts or the dynamics that underpin terrorist groups? In this section we also examine where widespread anti-terrorist measures actually disrupt established community cohesion, and we conclude by examining the crucial importance of intelligence in contributing to and securing an enduring peace.

Part I: Political, Legal and Policing Context

In Chapter 1 we examine the legal and political landscape of the last 13 years, a period of considerable activity and intense debate including the rather turbulent passage of the Justice and Security Act 2013 through both Houses of Parliament. Lord Carlile of Berriew, who was appointed by the UK government as the independent reviewer of terrorist legislation only a few hours before the 9/11 attacks (a position he held for almost 10 years), and his colleague Carys Owen provide the necessary insight and gravitas to illuminate this landscape. Their review covers many of the contentious legal issues of the decade that often exposed in a very public manner the tensions between the executive and the judiciary. Such issues included the vexed question of stop and search, detention without trial, extended pre-charge detention, control orders and, most recently, the notion of secret courts. They debate the extent to which our legal system has managed to respond effectively to the ever-changing and global aspects of modern terrorism in a manner and form that is acceptable and proportionate and that upholds the fundamental principle of the rule of law.

In Chapter 2 Peter Clarke draws on his considerable experience as a former National Coordinator of Terrorist Investigations to provide an authoritative yet objective overview of the evolving landscape that sets terrorist investigations apart from traditional major crime. In his six years as head of terrorist investigations in the UK he had ultimate responsibility for numerous terrorist plots on a scale and magnitude never previously experienced. These included the 'liquid bomb' attack destined for airlines departing from the UK, the 'fertilizer' case and the dreadful 7 July suicide attacks in London and the arrest and prosecution of the failed suicide attackers of 21 July 2005. He explains why, in the post-9/11 world, there had to be a complete recalibration of terrorist investigations if the UK is to remain successful in the fight against such attacks.

Part II: The Criminal Justice Process

In Chapter 3 John Pearse provides a critical overview of the history and application of the current police interview model and provides details of confidential research findings relating to counter-terrorism police practice undertaken by him. Importantly, he is also able to provide a unique insight with an in-depth examination of the urgent interviews with the first detained suicide bomber (Omar). This represents the first time that a ticking bomb scenario has unfolded in Western Europe, and he is able to focus in some detail on the first series of interviews with the terrorist, which are designed to establish the location of other bombs, bomb-making equipment or other bombers – where public safety is the overriding consideration rather than obtaining prosecution evidence. In terrorist cases such interviews can lead to lengthy legal challenge and this case remains a prime example.

In Chapter 4 Max Hill, as prosecution counsel in the Omar case, tackles the thorny issue of the extent to which police officers can conduct urgent or public safety interviews at times and under circumstances not allowed within conventional legislation. This is a rarely used tactic and as such has been challenged through the UK legal system up to the Court of Appeal and has yet to be settled in the European Court. In a clear and forthright manner, this chapter outlines the special requirements and appropriate conduct necessary to ensure that investigating officers remain within the letter and spirit of the law when engaged in this potentially life-saving interaction.

Chapter 5 by Peter Carter, the defence counsel in the Omar case, is much more than an insight into a single terrorist case. It includes a lively introduction that sets out the fundamental roles and responsibilities of both defence and prosecution counsel in a clear and uncluttered exposure that dispenses with much of the arcane 'legal speak' that often adorns such texts. It also provides an insight from the defence perspective into how to undermine the prosecution case legitimately, as well as highlighting some of the little-known difficulties faced by defence counsel in the run-up to major terrorist trials. He is able to provide a clear and cogent legal argument in relation to why the urgent interviews with Omar should not have been allowed in evidence – a decision that has yet to be scrutinized in the European Court.

In Chapter 6 Geraldine Noone provides the first published version of a new police interviewing model, the An Garda Síochána Interviewing Model (GSIM), which she and her colleagues developed for use by the police in Ireland. Following the critical review of the established UK interviewing model (PEACE) by Pearse (in Chapter 3), this represents a refreshing opportunity to examine the evolution of a new model some two decades after the nationwide introduction of PEACE in the UK. The utility of the model, developed against a rapidly changing political, legal and cultural backdrop, is predicated on identifying the personal characteristics of the person to be interviewed (whether as victim, witness or suspect, or indeed a combination) rather than the labels themselves. Its introduction has been timed to complement the roll-out of advanced interview training in Ireland, and both the model and the training are currently under evaluation.

In Chapter 7 we welcome the collaborative efforts of Gisli Gudjonsson, Adrian West and Amy McKee who tackle the complex issues surrounding the imprisonment of terrorist offenders and the subsequent need for risk assessments not only while they are in detention but, more crucially, for a parole board that may consider their release. Undertaking risk assessments for the prison population is now established practice but that is not the case for terrorists, and the practice of psychologists conducting risk assessments with this population in the absence of empirically validated risk assessment tools has proved to be a contentious issue within the normally urbane psychological society. The authors succeed in illuminating this rather impenetrable domain with an incredibly well-researched and up-to-date review of the issues from around the globe and a clear exposé of the professional issues for all practitioners.

We close Part II with a chapter that is dedicated to hostage negotiation and communication skills in terrorist cases. The author, Simon Wells, is an extremely experienced detective from New Scotland Yard who for many years was the Director of the famous Hostage Negotiation Course, which was recognized worldwide as the benchmark in this area. He provides an insight into the skills and knowledge required to direct and deal with a range of incidents including hijacking, kidnapping and siege or barricade situations. In this wide-ranging chapter he provides a valuable insight into the key psychological processes and vulnerabilities that can assist negotiators in understanding the terrorist personality and how to convert this knowledge into tangible and productive resolutions.

Part III: Individual and Group Perspectives

In Chapter 9 Andrew Silke provides a succinct and layperson's insight into the historic and psychological aspects of the phenomenon of suicide bombers. The threat of suicide attacks anywhere in the world is very real and the fear generated by this activity extends across all borders. The chapter confronts many of the widespread misconceptions and ingrained stereotypes about suicide bombers: that suicide bombers are mad, deranged individuals, that suicide attacks are a uniquely Islamic phenomenon and that, apart from momentary publicity, such tactics achieve very little. This chapter succeeds in removing much of the myth and innuendo around the issue and allows the reader an opportunity to analyse and reflect on the debate from a well-informed position.

We move in Chapter 10 to focus on the activities of the recent 'spree killer' Anders Breivik who in July 2011 carried out the worst criminal atrocities witnessed in Norway in modern times. Robert Lambert provides a detailed and critical analysis of Breivik's motivation and deeply held beliefs and political commitment. He explores Breivik's unusually long period of planning and preparation and, as a starting point, examines Breivik's own detailed account written prior to the atrocities as a gateway to understanding his motivation, strategy and, importantly, his state of mind. Lambert succeeds in placing the Breivik case in the wider context of political terrorism in general, and of extremist nationalist political violence in particular.

In Chapter 11 Karl Roberts identifies and discusses the importance and highly influential impact of groups on individuals and their behaviour, often providing justification and the motivation to carry out extremist acts. Where timing is crucial, prior knowledge of such dynamics is essential for investigators if they are to create a means to disrupt terrorist activity. Such information will also contribute to improved decision-making and more robust risk analysis, especially where concepts such as groupthink have taken hold. From the group perspective, this chapter then moves on to the question of individual identity and its fundamental role in allowing people to make sense of who they are. Roberts then draws out the impact of competing identities and the possible consequences for extremists and crucially for the investigating and interviewing officers.

In Chapter 12 the considerable expertise of Clive Walker and Simon McKay is brought to bear on the nature and the implications arising from the deployment of mass community surveillance for the purpose of gathering intelligence about terrorism. They examine in detail the controversial surveillance project in Birmingham, Project Champion, which itself became the subject of a full and revealing official investigation. As Project Champion is not a unique example of community surveillance, the chapter also provides the context and overview for other relevant surveillance tactics within the counter-terrorism strategy. This analysis is set within the framework of 'all risks' policing, in which mechanisms such as stop and search and dataveillance also perform major functions. Crucially, they also evaluate some of the dilemmas and consequences which flow from community surveillance in general and which did arise in the particular scenario of Project Champion.

Finally, how better to conclude than with a chapter on peace! Chapter 13 draws on the considerable experience of its author, John Grieve, to analyse and identify what actually works in the relentless and unending quest to 'win the peace' in the aftermath of decades of armed conflict in Northern Ireland. This is clearly a multifaceted phenomenon but the chapter concentrates on an impressive strategic architecture influenced by and integral to the UK government's CONTEST strategy. Another dimension is the robust tactical doctrine outlining the implementation of an effective investigative philosophy and a comprehensive resilience infrastructure. In addition, this chapter examines the extent to which communities defeat terrorism and, in particular, the role of intelligence and decision-making in crisis.

The genesis for this book arose from empirical research designed to examine the effectiveness of the police response to international terrorism in the United Kingdom in the first decade of the twenty-first century (see Chapter 3) and, as ever, such issues demand a broader appreciation of the political, legal and social psychological aspects at work to facilitate understanding. It is hoped that this eclectic compilation has gone some way to illuminate an increasingly complex phenomenon that continues to dominate our global news consumption and threaten the peace and stability of the world order. One thing is certain: any response to the global terrorist threat will have to be multifaceted in nature and flexible enough to evolve and adapt to the ever-changing challenges we may face.

I remain eternally grateful to all the authors for their time, patience and intellectual generosity in compiling this volume and for their valuable contributions to the UK Police Training Programme that emerged from the original research.

John Pearse
August 2014

Part I

Political, Legal and Policing Context

1

The Impact and Consequences of Terrorist Legislation in the United Kingdom Since 2001

A Review

Lord Carlile of Berriew, QC, and Carys Owen

This chapter is designed to provide a historical and current political context for established and developing counter-terrorism law in the United Kingdom. It focuses principally on events since the attack on the World Trade Center in New York on 11 September 2001. Since that time every step in counter-terrorism law has been the subject of intense debate in the UK Parliament, a feature exemplified, as we shall examine, by the debates in both the House of Commons and the House of Lords on the Justice and Security Act 2013. This was legislation dealing with two important but limited areas of national security law and policy: first, the objective and empirical scrutiny of national security activity by a committee made up of parliamentarians and, secondly, the protection or disclosure of national security information in civil proceedings brought against the state by claimants alleging unlawful activity by the state in the name of national security.

The legislation illustrates an increasing tension. On the one hand, the state has to be able to take appropriate action founded on the best available methods to disrupt, prevent, detect and discourage terrorist activity. State actors may find the intervention of the law and the courts to be an inhibiting irritant in this difficult task, especially as the extent of action by the security agencies and the expectation of accountability have expanded since the early 2000s. On the other hand, the protection of the rule of law is seen as the essential protection against arbitrary action by the state even when there is a veneer of statutory or common law justification. The overarching question is the extent to which the action of the state to keep its citizens safe has been subject to 'juridification' (see also Walker, 2011).

Other very recent factual examples can be given. The detention of David Miranda at London Heathrow Airport on 18 August 2013 gave rise to a deeply contentious

Investigating Terrorism: Current Political, Legal and Psychological Issues, First Edition. Edited by John Pearse.
© 2015 John Wiley & Sons, Ltd. Published 2015 by John Wiley & Sons, Ltd.

discussion about the freedom of the media to disclose questioned intelligence activity which may directly or indirectly disclose national security information (see *R (Miranda) v. Secretary of State for the Home Department and others*, 2013, and Blair, 2013). This is exactly the kind of dispute likely to attract intense scrutiny of the provisions and effectiveness of the Justice and Security Act.

Another example is the parliamentary debate and ubiquitous media comment on action falling short of war against Syria, following the use of chemical weapons against the civilian population in August 2013. The focus on legality in the parliamentary debates of 29 August 2013 exceeded that in the parliamentary settings of France and the United States on the same issue. As the Chilcot Inquiry into the war in Iraq (set up in July 2009 but still to report at the time of writing) has shown in its proceedings, the role of the Attorney General has for the time being become of paramount importance (as well as politically exposed for the individual concerned), in his or her capacity as legal adviser to Her Majesty's Government, and therefore indirectly to Parliament.[1]

As a result of the situation in Northern Ireland, the statute book in the UK thickened. There were seven material Acts of Parliament between 1974 and 2001, and 62 statutory instruments (secondary legislation that allow the provisions of an Act to come into force or be revised without the need to pass another Act). Between 2001 and the end of 2013 there were an additional nine terrorist-related Acts and an astonishing 67 statutory instruments. The post-2000 legislation, after the enactment of the Terrorism Act 2000, has been mainly a reaction to 9/11 and the onset of violent extremism linked to al-Qaeda. Though it has existed as a movement since 1988 and carried out terrorist attacks well before 2001, al-Qaeda became deeply ingrained in the British consciousness after 9/11. As with all legislation enacted in haste or fear, or both, counter-terrorism legislation has been inadequately debated and scrutinized in Parliament.

The frequent and profound political controversy and argument about the legislation has been supported by representatives of the legal professions. Accusations have been levelled at the British government that, in pursuing policies designed to simplify the detection of terrorism, they have sought to diminish the rule of law by breaching the rights of the individual, thereby increasing the risk that innocent people, especially associates of genuine terrorism suspects, will be unjustly affected. It is noteworthy that these accusations have now been levelled at each major political party in the UK (Gearty, 2013).

The political debates and clashes surrounding the proliferation of legislative action represent the UK's struggle to balance the aims of protecting the public from terrorism while protecting the individual's rights. There has been no declaration of 'war on terror', as in the United States, which depicted terrorism suspects as 'enemy combatants', thereby circumventing the norms of criminal justice. Here, the battle has been a very British one, informed by difficult lessons learned during the Northern Ireland conflict.

Lord Macdonald, QC, a past Director of Public Prosecutions and now a Liberal Democrat member of the House of Lords, pointedly opposed the rhetoric of the 'war on terror' by characterizing the issue in the following terms:

> the fight against terrorism on the streets of Britain is not a war. It is the prevention of crime ... a culture of legislative restraint in the area of terrorist crime is central to the existence of an efficient and human rights compatible process. (Macdonald, 2007)

Challenges on both sides have pushed boundaries, provoked thought and divided opinion, generally depicted simplistically as a difference between those charged with the protection of the nation's security and those protecting the rights of the individual. Without the robust legal challenges mounted by and on behalf of some of these individuals, the rule of law would most certainly have been eroded significantly.

Whether the rule of law has prevailed is a matter of opinion. However, a conclusion which these authors draw is that almost all state agencies have recognized the importance of keeping within the rule of law, albeit with subjective elasticity sometimes being applied to that phrase.

The Changing Legal Landscape

Al-Qaeda is described by the British Security Service (MI5) on their website in the following terms:

> an ideology that unites a variety of grievances ... into a 'single narrative' of a global conspiracy against the Muslim world ... Al Qaida's members adopt an extreme interpretation of Islamic teaching which they believe places an obligation on believers to fight and kill to achieve their aims. Most Muslims and the world's leading Islamic scholars reject this position. (MI5, n.d.)

The emergence of al-Qaeda and terrorism linked with Islamic extremism created a new dimension to terrorism in the UK. No longer were terrorist attacks preceded by advance warning to minimize civilian casualties; in fact, suicide bombers were deployed in order to maximize the same. The threat from this type of attack has created a need for the executive to find means to intervene early enough to disrupt such plots. Terrorists seeking to harm British interests include foreign nationals and British citizens alike, and therefore greater coordination between intelligence and enforcement agencies has been required to deal with these threats. According to the former head of MI5, the main terrorism threat to the UK comes from (1) the tribal areas of Pakistan, where the senior al-Qaeda leadership is based; (2) Somalia; (3) Yemen; (4) home-grown terrorists; (5) Syria (Evans, 2007). The legislature has responded with a stream of controversial legal measures.

The foundations for the major piece of legislation the Terrorism Act 2000 (the 2000 Act) originate from a report into counter-terrorism legislation produced for the then government in 1996 by Lord Lloyd of Berwick with Sir John Kerr, although it is to be noted that the legislation in a number of respects did not follow all or with precision the recommendations made in the Lloyd report (Lloyd & Kerr, 1996).

The legal landscape may be examined from the perspective of: (1) changes to the criminal justice system to prosecute terrorism as crime; (2) the expansion of executive powers to deal with suspected terrorists who may not be prosecuted because of difficulties of evidence and disclosure; and (3) procedural constraints (intelligence sharing, disclosure, closed hearings and torture). Each has struggled to find the balancing point between protection of the public from terrorist attacks and protection of the individual's rights.

Criminal Justice System: Prosecuting Terrorism

Successive governments have asserted that prosecution is the preferred approach when dealing with suspected terrorists. Consistent with this policy, many offences charged against terrorists are provided for in counter-terrorism legislation, but many charges have been of non-specialty offences such as homicide, offences against the person and offences under the Explosive Substances Act 1883. A lesson from the experience of Northern Ireland is that the use of 'normal' criminal legislation is generally to be preferred to specialty legislation.

What follows is a short review of the terrorist specialty legislation as it affects the criminal jurisdiction.

The Terrorism Act 2000

An offence of terrorism as such does not exist. But several offences related to terrorism are created by this Act, including membership of, support for and the wearing of the uniform of a proscribed organization; fund-raising and offences related to money laundering. The Act also created offences of omission (where certain individuals fail to report their suspicions) relating to terrorist financing, training for terrorism, directing terrorism, possession of items for terrorist purposes and collecting information for terrorist-related purposes. The last two are the most commonly used.

The above offences are directed to protect the public, the government would say, without any irrationality or oppressiveness attached to them and as such are within the rule of law.

Stop and search powers

Sections 41 and 44 of the 2000 Act have created sufficient interest to warrant separate treatment. They provided the stop and search powers of people and vehicles within zones permitted by the Home Secretary on application by the police, and without the otherwise normal requirement of reasonable suspicion.

Section 44 ran foul of the truism that terrorism-related powers should be used only for terrorism-related purposes, otherwise their credibility is severely damaged, and the damage to community relations if they are used incorrectly can be considerable. Its purpose and deployment were poorly understood and examples of poor or unnecessary use of section 44 have abounded (Carlile, 2007). For example, the authors are aware of numerous uses against individuals who could not conceivably be seen to be potential terrorists, including a retired military chief and a middle-aged and highly regarded solicitor travelling in his large car who happens to be Asian.

Guidance on stop and search in relation to terrorism, created on behalf of the Association of Chief Police Officers (ACPO), failed to produce the necessary effect. In the year 2008, 250,000 individual section 44 searches were made in Great Britain; in 2009 this figure reduced significantly, but was still very high – 148,798. Of the 43 territorial police forces in England and Wales, only a minority ever used section 44. Only a single territorial force in Scotland used it, in very limited and special circumstances. The Metropolitan Police and the British Transport Police accounted for 96.4 per cent of all section 44 stop and searches during that year; 16 per cent of those stopped in 2009 were Asian or Asian British (Home Office, 2012a).

In March 2010 the Home Office published the findings of an Occasional Paper it had commissioned into public perceptions of the impact of counter-terrorism legislation (Home Office, 2010). Its conclusions showed a mixed reaction from the public but it is clear that there are perceptions that

- the process was discriminatory;
- it was based on stereotypes and racial profiling and,
- importantly, the difficulties were not necessarily linked to the measure itself, but to the way it was implemented.

The report was careful to accept that there were significant limitations to the surveys conducted and relied on in the paper. It remains, however, the most comprehensive compilation of studies and provides some community insights of value.

The executive responded to calls for change. The Home Secretary, the Right Honourable Teresa May, MP, responded to the European Court of Human Rights' judgment in the case of *Gillan and Quinton v. The United Kingdom* (2010) in a statement to Parliament in July 2010:

> This judgment found that the stop and search powers granted under section 44 of the Terrorism Act 2000 amount to the violation of the right to a private life … I am introducing a new suspicion threshold. Officers will no longer be able to search individuals using section 44 powers; instead, they will have to rely on section 43 powers, which require officers to reasonably suspect the person to be a terrorist. And officers will only be able to use section 44 in relation to searches of vehicles. I will only confirm these authorisations where they are considered to be necessary and officers will only be able to use them when they have 'reasonable suspicion'. (May, 2010)

This view has gained traction, not just in relation to counter-terrorism measures but also in respect of non-terrorism-related powers of stop and search under section 60 of the Police and Criminal Evidence Act (PACE) 1984. Sir Bernard Hogan-Howe, Metropolitan Police Commissioner, announced in January 2012, shortly after the verdicts in the third Stephen Lawrence trial, his intention to halve the number of stop and searches being conducted by his officers in recognition of the damaging effect that random and unfair searches of members of certain communities had on community relations (Hughes, 2012).

The issue was followed up in the government's 2010–2011 counter-terrorism review, which advocated the repeal of the stop and search provisions under the 2000 Act (Macdonald, 2011). The Protection of Freedoms Act 2012 (the 2012 Act) at sections 59–62 amended the grounds for stop and search of persons and vehicles based on the new 'reasonable suspicion' test and, furthermore, a code of practice was created in 2012 (Home Office, 2012b).

The authors suggest that the section 44 powers were the product of an honest mistake, in that ministers did not estimate accurately the extensive and sometimes inappropriate use the police would make of them, and were shown by successive reviews to be disproportionate and of no clear use against Islamist terrorism. It may have been thought that their effective use in Northern Ireland could be transferred across to Great Britain: however, the circumstances were barely comparable.

Pre-charge detention

The second significant aspect meriting special mention relates to the period of detention between arrest and charge or release. In his seminal 1996 report on terrorism legislation Lord Lloyd of Berwick considered that the pre-emptive power of arrest under the then existing legislation was useful because it enabled the police to intervene before a terrorist act was committed. If the police had to rely on their general powers of arrest, he argued, they would be obliged to hold back until they had sufficient information to link a particular individual with a particular offence, and in some cases this would be too late to prevent the prospective crime. However, Lord Lloyd expressed concern that the power contravened a fundamental principle that a person should be liable to arrest only when he or she was suspected of having committed, or being about to commit, a specific crime (Lloyd & Kerr, 1996, ch. 8). He was particularly mindful of the reference to 'an offence' (meaning a specific offence) in Article 5(1)(c) of the European Convention on Human Rights (ECHR), on the right to liberty and security. The amendment to section 41 of the 2000 Act was the government's response to the concerns expressed by Lord Lloyd and others.

Detention under section 41 and under Schedule 7 (port detention) of the 2000 Act was subject to codes of practice issued pursuant to Schedule 8 of the Act. By section 306 of the Criminal Justice Act 2003, Schedule 8 of the 2000 Act was amended to allow up to 14 days' detention for the purposes of questioning and associated investigation. This was extended to 28 days by sections 23–24 of the Terrorism Act 2006 (the 2006 Act) and could have been increased had Tony Blair's tabled extension of pre-charge detention up to 90 days not been defeated in Parliament. Senior circuit judges supervised the 14- to 28-day period of detentions, pursuant to the 2006 Act. Of the 106 relevant people arrested in 2009, 21 were released after 8 days had passed. None were held for more than 14 days. The use of these provisions must be seen in the context of the shock felt after the events in London on 7 and 21 July 2005: in the first of the incidents 52 people were killed by suicide bombers in three underground stations and on a bus in London.

Arguments in support of detaining suspects for longer than 14 days related to the nature of the evidence seized during the initial arrest phase, which often requires lengthy analysis of digital media. By extending the period of detention without charge, the police are provided with more time to analyse seized devices, which requires the assistance of technical experts. Given the international nature of terrorism offences, the police may need to undertake overseas enquiries and may have to liaise with security and intelligence services. Such enquiries may be complex and take a long time to yield results.

Following political debate in both Houses of Parliament, in particular differences between the coalition partners, and intense scrutiny by lawyers in the House of Lords, the coalition government enacted section 57 of the 2012 Act, which reduces the maximum period of detention from 28 days to 14 days, with an unusual power, arguably tautologous with normal parliamentary procedure, to bring in emergency legislation for exigencies. In other words, in the wake of a major terrorist attack in the UK, the police would not be able to detain suspects for longer than 14 days, notwithstanding that the number of suspects might be very large and the evidence complicated, unless Parliament intervened and allowed for an extension of detention.

Home Office statistics reveal that, between 25 July 2006 and 25 January 2011 (when the maximum period of pre-charge detention was 28 days), six individuals were held for more than 27 days (in 2006–2007), of whom three were charged and three were released without charge. Of those charged, two were convicted and the remaining individual was not proceeded against (Home Office, 2012a). It is clear that, when it was available, the police sometimes made good use of the extended pre-charge period available to them, by gathering evidence and intelligence from abroad, translating material found and penetrating electronic protections.

Time will tell whether this dilution of detention powers will affect investigations. The likelihood is that terrorism plots will be allowed by the authorities to run closer to fruition, to ensure that they have evidence capable of securing convictions. The more counter-terrorism investigations are equated with other investigations of organized and serious crime, the easier it will be to demonstrate that normal rule of law standards are being fulfilled.

Civil Jurisdiction: Expansion of Executive Powers

The Anti-Terrorism, Crime and Security Act 2001: Indefinite detention without trial

Shortly after 9/11, the government introduced the Anti-Terrorism, Crime and Security Act 2001 (the 2001 Act), which provided for the certification of 'terrorist suspects' based on evidence from secret national security sources and the detention in prison of 'foreign terrorism suspects' pending deportation for an indefinite period. These are often referred to as the 'Belmarsh Provisions'. The bill attracted little scrutiny in either the House of Commons or House of Lords. It was treated as emergency legislation and received royal assent in under four weeks, having passed through all legislative stages in both Houses. Legislation in emergency runs the risk of serious flaws and consequent difficulty in the higher courts: this was no exception. The government, in passing the 2001 Act, became the first European state to derogate from Article 5 of the ECHR (the right to liberty and security) in order to detain foreign suspects indefinitely without trial. (For an erudite analysis of legal issues arising in relation to counter-terrorism legislation across the world, see Arden, 2006.) Civil liberties campaigners were outraged by these proposals, likening the provisions to the policy of 'internment' (detention without charge) exercised by the government during both the First and the Second World Wars, and challenged them in the courts on the basis that such extreme measures undermined the rule of law.

The 2001 Act conferred rights of appeal in lieu of the right to apply for habeas corpus. The Secretary of State issued certificates in respect of a number of foreign nationals he considered to be suspected terrorists. These certificates were subject to an appeal to the Special Immigration Appeals Commission (SIAC) which upheld the Belmarsh Case appeal on the ground that the order was discriminatory and contrary to Article 14, which prohibits discrimination. The Secretary of State appealed to the Court of Appeal, which allowed the appeal, holding that the discrimination was justified because the detainees had no right to be in this country and were free to leave if they wished to.

This reasoning did not withstand a further appeal to the House of Lords. In their decision given on 16 December 2004, the system of detention was struck down by the House of Lords (*A v. Secretary of State for the Home Department*, 2004). Lord Hoffman, in a characteristically robust critique of the 2001 Act, stated:

> 86 ... This is one of the most important cases which the House has had to decide in recent years. It calls into question the very existence of an ancient liberty of which this country has until now been very proud: freedom from arbitrary arrest and detention. The power which the Home Secretary seeks to uphold is a power to detain people indefinitely without charge or trial. Nothing could be more antithetical to the instincts and traditions of the people of the United Kingdom ...

97 … The real threat to the life of the nation, in the sense of a people living in accordance with its traditional laws and political values, comes not from terrorism but from laws such as these. That is the true measure of what terrorism may achieve. It is for Parliament to decide whether to give the terrorists such a victory.

Eight out of the nine Law Lords held that the derogation was justified, holding that the question involved a political judgement with which they should not interfere. On the main question, seven Law Lords held that Part 4 was incompatible with the UK's obligations under the ECHR. They ruled that the measure did not rationally address the threat to security, was not a proportionate response, was not required by the exigencies of the situation and unjustifiably discriminated against foreign nationals on grounds of their nationality.

This landmark decision posed a choice to Parliament: to repeal Part 4 of the 2001 Act and institute an alternative regime or to sit tight and hope they would not be defeated in Strasbourg. Parliament elected to repeal and further legislate. This was enacted as the Prevention of Terrorism Act 2005 (the 2005 Act) and created the control order regime, enabling closed hearings with the use of special advocates. Arguably, the speed with which the control order regime was created resulted in one flawed system being replaced with another ill-thought-out scheme. The disclosure regime applied under the control order system suffered much challenge and ultimately radical change, and the system itself was abolished in 2012 when a system of far 'lighter' measures was imposed, as we shall discuss.

The Prevention of Terrorism Act 2005

The Prevention of Terrorism Act 2005 (the 2005 Act) was enacted to replace the Belmarsh Provisions with control orders. It was a type of executive order which imposed strict obligations on the controlled person for an indefinite term, so long as there was reasonable suspicion that they had been engaged in terrorism-related activity, and the order and the obligations remained necessary and proportionate.

The 2005 Act came into force on 11 March 2005, only three months after the earlier critical decision of the House of Lords. The enactment of the 2005 Act occurred before the fatal London suicide bombings of 7 July 2005 and the unsuccessful bombing attempts of 21 July 2005. The control order system was the object of fierce and continuous controversy, derided by civil liberty campaigners but supported by the public at large and by independent review. Detractors characterized the regime as a wholly disproportionate encroachment on civil liberties by the executive powers. For example, Liberty (2013) has consistently opposed control orders, and ran a campaign for their repeal. Parliament, on the other hand, sought to tackle a deepening problem of home-grown Islamist extremism against which the criminal law failed to provide the necessary protection.

The main conclusions of the 2011 report of the independent reviewer of terrorism legislation noted that:

> The control orders system, or an alternative system providing equivalent and proportionate public protection, remains necessary, but only for a small number of cases where evidence is available to the effect that the individual in question presents a considerable risk to national security, and conventional prosecution is not realistic.
>
> The control order system continued to function reasonably well in 2010, despite some challenging Court decisions and unremitting political controversy. (Carlile, 2011, p. 1)

In parliamentary debates, concern was expressed about judges becoming involved in what was really an executive activity; this could affect their independence and breach the principle of the separation of powers. There was judicial discomfort. The former Lord Chief Justice, Lord Phillips, questioned whether the 2005 Act was compatible with ECHR obligations, and further queried whether the restrictions might amount to a deprivation of liberty contrary to Article 5 and whether the provisions for review by the court satisfied the requirements of a fair trial, under Article 6. In a lecture at the University of Hertfordshire he commented:

> The proceedings fall some way short of guaranteeing the equality of arms, in so far as they include in camera hearings, the use of secret evidence and special advocates, unable subsequently to discuss proceedings with the suspect … Quite apart from the obvious flouting of the presumption of innocence, the review proceedings described can only be considered to be fair, independent and impartial with some difficulty. Substituting 'obligation' for 'penalty' and 'controlled person' for 'suspect' only thinly disguises the fact that control orders are intended to substitute the ordinary criminal justice system with a parallel system run by the executive. (Phillips, 2006)

The activities intended to be disrupted as a result of control orders have included the planning of mass casualty attacks in the UK; providing financial, material or other logistical support for terrorism-related activity; travelling overseas to attack British or allied military forces; and travelling to attend a terrorist training camp. A range of obligations that were considered necessary and proportionate could have been imposed on the controlees according to the exigencies of the case.

There were two distinct potential species of control orders – derogating and non-derogating. A *derogating* order contained obligations incompatible with the right to liberty under Article 5 of the ECHR. In reality, there was only a remote possibility of derogating control orders and none were ever made: a very serious series of events would have been required to trigger derogation. *Non-derogating* control orders imposed conditions intended to be short of a deprivation of liberty under Article 5.

Critics of the regime argue that the system was far from successful. The first batch of control orders imposed by the Home Secretary required the controlees to stay in their homes, in some cases for 18 hours a day, and placed restrictions on where they could go and whom they could see in the remaining six hours. These orders were challenged and, where terrorist suspects were subject to such stringent conditions, it was found to amount to a deprivation of liberty (see *Secretary of State for the Home Department v. JJ and others*, 2007). However, as the system responded to legal challenge and matured, it could be argued the regime enjoyed a measure of success in that fewer appeals against control orders were upheld.

Disclosure

The use of closed evidence given in control order proceedings was highly controversial. The government sought to limit disclosure to terrorist suspects so that they were not even given the gist of the allegations they faced and to apply a 'what difference' test to disclosure, namely, assessing how any failure in disclosure would have affected the suspect's ability to contest the factual basis for the control order (see *Secretary of State for the Home Department v. MB*, 2007). The system itself was challenged domestically in a series of decisions that culminated in the legal test for disclosure being redefined by the leading House of Lords decision of *Secretary of State for the Home Department v. AF* (2009, also referred to as 'AF (No. 3)').

In AF (No. 3), Lord Philips, at paragraph 59, set out the legal test for disclosure to be satisfied: 'the controlee must be given sufficient information about the allegations against him to enable him to give effective instructions in relation to those allegations'. It was inadequate for full information merely to be provided to the special advocate representing the controlee's interests during the closed sessions.

Control orders caused legal challenge in numerous areas, with mixed results. In the two years between 2009 and 2011 it was held that it was not an abuse of the court's power to impose a control order where a criminal prosecution had failed (*Secretary of State for the Home Department v. AY*, 2010); it was lawful to relocate individuals away from their homes to another city with which they had no connection (*Secretary of State for the Home Department v. BX*, 2010; *Secretary of State for the Home Department v. CD*, 2011), and there were findings that a control order remained necessary even though the alleged terrorism-related activity had occurred some years earlier (*Secretary of State for the Home Department v. AM*, 2009; *Secretary of State for the Home Department v. AY*, 2010).

Anonymity was usually granted to controlees, which was of advantage both to the controlee and to the government. In particular, for the controlee it avoided publicity that might have led to harassment of the individual and his or her family in the community, or it might have prejudiced a fair trial if criminal charges were later brought.

The nexus between control orders and their replacement, Terrorism Prevention and Investigation Measures (TPIMs), reflected considerable movement by both of the governing parties forming the coalition government of the UK. To a greater or lesser extent, they had both been opposed to the orders in any form. One can assume that the material they were shown after entering government changed their views.

The coalition sought to change the previous system which, according to their view, involved oppressive prohibitions, and instead preferred to impose measures that could facilitate further investigation as well as prevent terrorist activities. Additional investigatory resources were provided to complement the new regime of lighter-touch prohibitive measures. It was accepted, by the nature of the two strands of measures (prohibitive and investigatory) sought, that covert investigative techniques, including surveillance, cannot themselves control terrorist suspects, but can help to do so and may produce evidence for use in a prosecution. This was used as justification for the new system.

Terrorism Prevention and Investigation Measures Act 2011

The Terrorism Prevention and Investigation Measures Act 2011 (the 2011 Act) represents a major shift in approach by the executive, giving prominence to the rights of the individual suspected of involvement in terrorism-related activity. In accordance with the coalition's stated intentions, the 2005 Act was repealed on 15 December 2011 and replaced by a system of TPIMs. Transitional provisions were contained in Schedule 8. Control orders, in force immediately before commencement, were to remain in force until 42 days after commencement (Schedule 8, paras. 1 and 9). Thus no control order could be made or renewed after 15 December 2011 or continued after 26 January 2012, other than in respect of hearings relating to pre-existing reviews, appeals and damages claims (Schedule 8, para. 3).

In order for a TPIM to be imposed, the higher test of 'reasonable belief' by the Secretary of State, and the court on a review, must be satisfied that the individual is or has been involved in terrorism-related activity. This higher threshold test was imposed following its recommendation by Lord Macdonald of River Glaven, QC, in his review of counter-terrorism and security powers (Macdonald, 2011).

The TPIM notice itself and the associated measures must be both proportionate and necessary (replicating the test that applied to control orders). The disclosure process and appeal procedure were also similar to that which went before and, as before, criminal prosecutions were to be preferred to civil proceedings.

The key differences between the two regimes are:

- The two-year limit: A TPIM notice is in force for the period of one year but may be extended by an additional year only once if certain conditions are satisfied, for example, the suspect is or has been involved in terrorism-related activity (condition A); a TPIM is necessary (condition C); and the measures are necessary (condition D). Subsequent TPIM notices may be imposed but only if the individual has engaged in terrorism-related activity since the imposition of the last notice. The effect has been that all TPIMs have lapsed.
- The TPIM may be extended beyond the second year if new terrorism activity is undertaken (condition B).

- Under a TPIM, there is no power to relocate the individual to an area away from those with whom he or she may engage in terrorism-related activity.
- The curfew obligation has not been replaced, although a similar measure of 'overnight residence' exists, imposing something similar to the 'doorstop' curfew familiar in criminal bail conditions. Verification of location is possible by electronic tagging with GPS.
- Exclusion zones: The boundary imposed by control orders is no longer permitted, thereby allowing greater freedom of movement.
- Communication and association: Individuals subject to a TPIM are entitled to one computer with Internet access and one mobile phone (previously neither Internet-enabled telephones nor computers were permitted).

The two-year limit creates a problem as to what to do with individuals who, after two years, have not changed their terrorist mind-set but who have not, during the TPIM, re-engaged in terrorism-related activity. It may be that they have decided to put terrorism behind them. Alternatively, it may be that they are simply biding their time and intending to re-engage in terrorism-related activity once the order has been lifted.

One practical problem is illustrated in the case of AM and AY, suspected of involvement in a transatlantic airline plot involving a conspiracy to murder hundreds of innocent travellers, for which sentences of up to 40 years were imposed. They were at liberty and free from all statutory controls by early 2014. No further measures may be imposed on them under the TPIM regime. The police may, of course, devote resources to watching them and monitoring their activities using personal and technical surveillance methods, but how effective can they really be?

It has been suggested that the extra threat may be neutralized by the provision of additional resources to the Security Service. This formed a central plank of the justification for the TPIM regime. However, taking as an example the murder of Drummer Lee Rigby in 2013, some regard it as unrealistic to expect the authorities to be capable of anticipating street-based terrorist crime, committed by individuals acting with limited direction and with little planning and preparation. The authorities have been criticized for failing to recognize that one of the suspects posed a threat to life which could have led to the imposition of a control order or TPIM on him, following the accusation by Kenyan authorities in 2010 that he led a group of youths to join the terrorist group Al Shabbab (Flood, 2013).

Nevertheless, the TPIM system enables the security services to prioritize the application of their limited resources to individuals who are perceived at any given time to pose the greatest threat. That threat in part may be neutralized by these orders. The cases of AM and AY raise interesting issues that are not legal in nature but reflect the difficulties faced in seeking to change mind-set and to prevent destructive belief systems which attract minute but disproportionately dangerous support in some communities. This is the challenge of the Prevent strand of the government's counter-terrorism policy (Home Office, 2011).

Procedural Constraints

Pervading much legislation on counter-terrorism and connected litigation are concerns with torture, closed material proceedings, intelligence sharing and disclosure. There has been tension politically between the desire to maintain good standards of disclosure and public hearings on the one hand, and, on the other, the need to protect national security and the public purse from paying damages to claimants who were properly judged to be terrorists.

Torture

Torture is the subject of an absolute ban under ECHR Article 3 and the United Nations Convention against Torture and Other Cruel, Inhuman or Degrading Treatment or Punishment:[2] it is illegal. Following the case of *A and others v. Secretary of State for the Home Department* (2005), the question arose, when determining the legality of a certificate given by the Secretary of State that a person was a suspected terrorist and could therefore be detained (pursuant to the now repealed 2001 Act), whether SIAC could rely on evidence which the appellant suspected had been obtained from overseas governments who had obtained it by torture of other persons. The House held that, while the executive would not act unlawfully if in its decision-making it took account of evidence provided by foreign states which was likely to have been obtained by the use of torture, evidence obtained by torture was inadmissible in a court of law.

Whether Her Majesty's Government engaged in such activity has become a matter of legal challenge in Guantánamo Bay litigation, including civil damages claims and Norwich Pharmacal disclosure cases, in which detainees have sought to challenge the UK and US governments on the basis that their detention at Guantánamo Bay was unlawful and that alleged confessions were obtained from them by torture, evidence of which is purportedly held by the British authorities (see *Mohamed, R (on the application of) v. Secretary of State for Foreign & Commonwealth Affairs*, 2010; Gardham & Rayner, 2010). A Norwich Pharmacal order is an order granted against a third party, which has been innocently caught in wrongdoing, forcing the disclosure of documents or information. By identifying individuals, the documents and information sought are disclosed in order to assist the applicant for such an order in bringing legal proceedings against individuals who are believed to have wronged the applicant.

While the UK courts do not allow evidence obtained from torture to be relied on, thereby upholding the rule of law, what is unclear is how the British authorities deal with other countries that do use torture. Put simply, and in context, how should UK authorities react to a piece of information obtained after torture by another country, but which demonstrates the possibility of a suicide bomber at a major public event? The answer under English law is probably that the authorities must use the information to protect the public, could not use the foreign intelligence as part of a prosecution, but could use as evidence the 'fruits of the poisoned tree', that is, the evidence gathered by UK authorities following the receipt of the tainted intelligence.

Justice and Security Act 2013: Disclosure and closed material procedures

The most recent and contentious issue relating to terrorism cases has involved the extension of cases where 'secret' hearings may take place. The term 'secret' to describe these hearings is a misnomer; all parties to the litigation are aware of the closed proceedings, in which evidence relating to national security is heard by the judge in the presence of the party holding the confidential material and of special advocates who represent the interests of the individual concerned. The Justice and Security Act 2013 (the 2013 Act) creates, for the first time, statutory provision for the protection of national security sensitive material in generic civil litigation where it is in the public interest.

Closed material procedures (CMPs) allow courts to hear national security evidence within a controlled environment to ensure that the tribunal hears the relevant evidence and that there is no damaging disclosure of national security information to the public at large. Their use has been extended to a restricted range of civil proceedings following the 2013 Act (see below).

Historically, closed material procedures were exercised in immigration appeals concerning foreign nationals suspected of terrorism and, with respect to British nationals, in the High Court in control order/TPIM cases. The government was keen to extend the use of CMPs. Without them, their options were limited to either seeking to strike out claims or settling them, often for large sums of money, even where they believed that the case had no merit.

The government sought to rely on CMPs in civil claim cases. The Supreme Court judgment in *Al-Rawi and others v. Security Service and others* (2011) held that there is no power at common law to impose a CMP in such cases. Al-Rawi and others claimed compensation for their alleged detention, rendition and mistreatment by foreign authorities in various locations, including Guantánamo Bay, in which, they claimed, the Security Service had been complicit. The court held there was no power at common law to replace public interest immunity (PII, whereby a judge decides whether, in the public interest, certain material should be excluded from a hearing) with a CMP (designed to allow the national security material to be included in the hearing but not to be revealed to a party to the litigation).

In response, the government enacted the 2013 Act, which introduced closed material procedures in civil trials relating to national security where it had been intended that the executive would decide when to deploy 'secret' hearings into all relevant civil litigation (see above). In its passage through Parliament several amendments were tabled, led by Lord Pannick, QC, among others (Pannick, 2013). Section 6 was amended, significantly, to ensure that a CMP is a procedure of last resort, imposed at the discretion of the court. The court will conduct a PII exercise, disclosing material where possible prior to deciding whether a CMP applies to the remaining material. The background to and perceived needs for the Act can be found ubiquitously.[3]

Lord Pannick, QC, was strongly opposed to the introduction of CMPs to civil litigation in general as the proposals were of constitutional significance, namely, (1) it was contrary to the principle of open justice which required evidence to be given in public; and (2) it was contrary to the principle of natural justice that each of the disputing parties must have the opportunity to respond to the evidence on which the other relies.

The debate produced opposition from many quarters that included a hefty riposte from Peto and Tyrie (2013) which suggested that it risked damaging Britain's system of open justice and the reputation and effectiveness of the security agencies in the struggle against terrorism. They claimed three major areas of concern in the bill: (1) the expansion of 'secret justice' through the introduction of CMPs to civil cases, enabling the government to present its evidence in secret session in the absence of the other party or his or her lawyers, the press or the public; (2) blocking the use of the information-gathering principle known as Norwich Pharmacal in cases deemed to be 'sensitive', making it harder to uncover official wrongdoing in matters such as extraordinary rendition (the kidnap and torture of individuals by the state); and (3) inadequate proposals to strengthen the Intelligence and Security Committee (ISC), which is supposed to oversee the intelligence services but which failed to uncover the truth about rendition.

David Anderson, QC, Independent Reviewer of Terrorism Legislation since 2011, advised that there was a case for extending the use of CMPs, although he was convinced that the decision was one for the judge to make and not, as tabled by the government, a decision for the executive.

Lord Phillips of Worth Matravers when contributing to the Lords debate concluded:

> I am reluctantly persuaded of the need, in the interests of justice, for a closed material procedure in exceptional cases where the Government would otherwise have no alternative but to submit to a civil claim for damages because to defend it would necessarily involve putting into the public domain material that would cause disproportionate harm to national security. It is for that reason that I support the batch of amendments tabled by the noble Lord, Lord Pannick, and the other noble Lords in relation to Clauses 6 and 7 (relating to the election of CMP by the judge hearing the case and not the Executive). (Phillips, 2012)

The House of Lords voted for major amendments to the bill, seeking to introduce more discretion for judges, and not the executive, to make use of CMPs as a device of last resort. Debate raged for months on these and other related issues and finally resulted in the shift of power to elect whether a case merited the CMP process, from the executive to the judiciary, marking a significant change of direction for the government.

Following significant amendments to the bill, arguably the greatest remaining flaw in the Act relates to the limited role played by special advocates who generally may not take instructions from the claimant once they have read the sensitive material. Plainly, the CMP system would be strengthened were measures adopted to enable special advocates routinely to take instructions from the individual whose interests they protect.

Following the contentious Guantánamo Bay litigation, the 2013 Act provides a statutory regime, pursuant to section 17, prohibiting disclosure of sensitive information, thereby protecting the agreement of confidentiality between the US and the UK described as the 'control principle', the principle that the UK does not have permission to reveal any intelligence that the US passes on in confidence, a principle at the heart of foreign intelligence sharing.

Additionally, oversight of intelligence and security activities has been strengthened by amending the nature and role of the Intelligence and Security Committee (ISC) to increase its independence of the executive. It will now report to Parliament rather than the prime minister. The committee is further empowered to oversee the expenditure, administration, policy and (most significantly) operations (albeit not ongoing intelligence operations) of the Security Service, Secret Intelligence Service and Government Communications Headquarters.

While criticism is still made about this Act, it has benefited from a protracted and vigorous debate in both Houses of Parliament. It complies well with the rule of law as described earlier in this chapter.

Conclusions

Conflicts have abounded as each successive measure has been taken to tackle the unique problems posed by terrorism. While the executive seeks to prevent major incidents by imposing measures to prevent attacks, the libertarian backlash against infringements of liberty have largely been played out in the courts, often after hasty legislation, rather than in lengthy debate resulting in consensual legislation. That said, in a sometimes febrile parliamentary setting, consent would be a tall order. Perhaps the 2013 Act demonstrates a maturing of terrorism legislation. It took many months of critical debate to create an Act which, while not welcomed by liberty campaigners, at least may claim some consensus, having adopted many of the amendments tabled by Lord Pannick, QC, and others, who shored up the rule of law by removing the decision to elect a CMP from the executive and putting it into the hands of the judiciary as a measure of last resort.

The post-2010 coalition government appears to have taken on board past criticism. The two-year limit to TPIMs appears to be a response to the outcry against the control order regime. The executive perhaps has come to recognize that the problem of home-grown terrorists may not be solved proportionately by containment with draconian measures.

Intense scrutiny applies to the imposition and application of terrorism legislation and is a result of the chequered history of legislation in this field. While critics of terrorism legislation in the UK still condemn various aspects, as a whole the UK's approach has gained international respect and even emulation (Roach, 2011).

It is our view that, broadly, what most objective commentators interpret as the rule of law has prevailed in this area of the law. That is to say, proportionate laws falling within accepted human rights norms have been devised and operated. There have been some failures, but it must be accepted that this is an exceptionally difficult, asymmetric and fluid area of the law and of public policy, given the changing nature of the threat.

The increased scrutiny now afforded to legislation in this field is valuable and important, scrutiny not just by the Independent Reviewer of Terrorism, but also by the intense debate in Parliament in relation to measures that seek to balance protection of the public with protection of individual freedoms and further in court by the judiciary who will have increased jurisdiction over national security matters under the extended closed material procedures.

The case law reviewed in this chapter reveals how specific cases have led to significant changes to policy and legislation. It is as if the legislators have grown up with the practitioners and judiciary in this field and, while there are diametrically opposed views as to approach, there is an increasing harmony to the law governing terrorism.

It would appear that the intense scrutiny applied by civil liberties campaigners, the courts, the media and the public is having a significant impact on the manner in which the UK legislates in this field. The democratization of terrorism laws in this way has resulted in increased legislative restraint. Such legislation is an art, not a science: the rule of law is probably the winner as matters stand at the time of writing, but the quality of legislation deserves eternal vigilance, as of course does the continuing struggle against terrorism of all kinds.

Notes

1   See www.iraqinquiry.org.uk (retrieved 21 May 2014).
2   At http://www.hrweb.org/legal/cat.html (retrieved 21 May 2014).
3   For example, HM Government, 2011; House of Lords Select Committee on the Constitution, 2012; Joint Committee on Human Rights, 2012.

References

Arden, M. (2006). Meeting the challenge of terrorism: The experience of English and other courts. *Australian Law Journal, 80*, 818–838.

Blair, Ian (2013, 25 August). David Miranda row: New law 'needed to protect secrets'. Retrieved 28 May 2014 from http://www.bbc.co.uk/news/uk-23832492

Carlile, A. (2007). *The definition of terrorism.* Cm 7052. London: Stationery Office.

Carlile, A. (2011). *Sixth Report of the Independent Reviewer pursuant to section 14(3) of the Prevention of Terrorism Act 2005*. London: Stationery Office. Retrieved 20 May 2014 from http://www.homeoffice.gov.uk/publications/counter-terrorism/independent-reviews/lord-carlile-sixth-report?view=Binary

Evans, J. (2007, 5 November). Full text of MI5 Direct-General's speech. *Telegraph*. Retrieved 28 May 2014 from http://www.telegraph.co.uk/news/uknews/1568360/Full-text-of-MI5-Director-Generals-speech.html

Flood, Z. (2013, 25 May). Woolwich attack: Soldier's 'killer' in dock on terror link three years ago. *Telegraph*. Retrieved 20 May 2014 from http://www.telegraph.co.uk/news/editors-choice/editors-picks/10080958/Woolwich-attack-soldiers-killer-in-dock-on-terror-link-three-years-ago.html

Gardham, D., & Rayner, G. (2010, 10 February). MI5 'knew Guantanamo detainee Binyam Mohamed was being tortured'. *Telegraph*. Retrieved 20 May 2014 from http://www.telegraph.co.uk/news/uknews/terrorism-in-the-uk/7204741/MI5-knew-Guantanamo-detainee-Binyam-Mohamed-was-being-tortured.html

Gearty, C. (2013). *Liberty and security*. Cambridge, UK: Polity.

HM Government. (2011, October). *Justice and security green paper*. Cm. 8194. London: Stationery Office. Retrieved 21 May 2014 from https://www.gov.uk/government/uploads/system/uploads/attachment_data/file/228860/8194.pdf

Home Office. (2010, March). *What perceptions do the UK public have concerning the impact of counter-terrorism legislation implemented since 2000?* Occasional Paper 88. London: Home Office.

Home Office. (2011, June). *Prevent strategy*. Cm 8092. London: Home Office. Retrieved 20 May 2014 from https://www.gov.uk/government/uploads/system/uploads/attachment_data/file/97976/prevent-strategy-review.pdf

Home Office. (2012a). *Operation of police powers under the Terrorism Act 2000 and subsequent legislation: Arrests, outcomes and stops and searches*. Home Office Statistical Bulletin (HOSB) 11/12. London: Home Office. Retrieved 20 May 2014 from https://www.gov.uk/government/uploads/system/uploads/attachment_data/file/116756/hosb1112.pdf

Home Office. (2012b). Code or practice for the exercise of stop and search powers. Retrieved 20 May 2014 from https://www.gov.uk/government/publications/code-of-practice-for-the-exercise-of-stop-and-search-powers

House of Lords Select Committee on the Constitution. (2012). *Justice and Security Bill (HL): Report*. London: Stationery Office. Retrieved 21 May 2014 from http://www.publications.parliament.uk/pa/ld201213/ldselect/ldconst/18/18.pdf

Hughes, M. (2012, 13 January). Random stop and search to be halved, Met chief orders. *Telegraph*. Retrieved 20 May 2014 from http://www.telegraph.co.uk/news/uknews/crime/9011490/Random-stop-and-search-to-be-halved-Met-chief-orders.html

Joint Committee on Human Rights. (2012). *Legislative scrutiny: Justice and Security Bill*. HL Paper 59. HC 370. London: Stationery Office. Retrieved 21 May 2014 from http://www.publications.parliament.uk/pa/jt201213/jtselect/jtrights/59/59.pdf

Liberty. (2013). Unsafe unfair. Retrieved 20 May 2014 from http://www.liberty-human-rights.org.uk/campaigning/other-campaigns/unsafe-unfair

Lloyd, A., & Kerr, J. (1996). *Inquiry into legislation against terrorism*. Cm 3420. London: Stationery Office.

Macdonald, K. D. J. (2007, 23 January). *Security and rights*. Speech given to the Criminal Bar Association. Retrieved 20 May 2014 from http://www.cps.gov.uk/news/articles/security_rights/

Macdonald, K. D. J. (2011). *Review of counter-terrorism and security powers*. Cm 8003. London: Stationery Office.

May, T. (2010). Stop and search powers under the Terrorism Act 2000 (section 44): Home Secretary's statement. Retrieved 20 May 2014 from https://www.gov.uk /government/speeches/stop-and-search-powers-under-the-terrorism-act-2000-section -44-home-secretarys-statement

MI5. (n.d.). Al Qaida's ideology. Retrieved 20 May 2014 from https://www.mi5 .gov.uk/home/the-threats/terrorism/international-terrorism/the-nature-of-the-threat /al-qaidas-ideology.html

Pannick, D. P. (2013, 14 March). Secret courts: Balancing justice and security. *Times*. Retrieved 20 May 2014 from http://www.thetimes.co.uk/tto/law/article3712643.ece

Peto, A., & Tyrie, A. (2013). *Neither just nor secure*. London: Centre for Policy Studies.

Phillips, N. A. (2006, 19 October). *Terrorism and human rights*. Law lecture at the University of Hertfordshire.

Roach, K. (2011). *The 9/11 effect: Comparative counter-terrorism*. Cambridge, UK: Cambridge University Press.

Walker, C. (2011). The judicialisation of intelligence in legal process. *Public Law, 235*, 235–237.

Legal Cases

A v. Secretary of State for the Home Department [2004] UKHL 56

A and others v. Secretary of State for the Home Department [2005] UKHL 71

Al-Rawi and others v. Security Service and others [2011] UKSC 34

Gillan and Quinton v. The United Kingdom [2010] ECHR 28

Mohamed, R (on the application of) v. Secretary of State for Foreign & Commonwealth Affairs [2010] EWCA Civ 65 (10 February 2010)

R (Miranda) v. Secretary of State for the Home Department and the Commissioner of Police for the Metropolis [2013] EWHC 2609 (Admin)

Secretary of State for the Home Department v. JJ and others [2007] UKHL 45, 920080 1 AC 385

Secretary of State for the Home Department v. MB [2007] UKHL 46

Secretary of State for the Home Department v. AM [2009] EWHC 3053

Secretary of State for the Home Department v. AF (FC) [2009] UKHL 28 ('AF (No. 3)')

Secretary of State for the Home Department v. AY [2010] EWHC 1860 (Admin)

Secretary of State for the Home Department v. BX [2010] EWHC 990 (Admin)

Secretary of State for the Home Department v. CD [2011] EWHC 1273 (Admin)

2

Investigating Terrorism in the First Decade of the Twenty-First Century

A Different Sort of Crime

Peter Clarke

I very much doubt that many of us who were involved in the investigation of terrorist crime in the aftermath of 9/11 had any idea what the next few years would bring. For my own part, I certainly didn't foresee the revolution that was to take place in the way the British police and intelligence agencies would approach the subject. Although it was obvious that there were going to be some fundamental changes to the way we worked, I don't think anyone could have predicted the scale and pace of those changes.

For much of the decade after 9/11 there was a seemingly inexorable pattern of unfolding plots, attacks, failed attacks and trials. There was rarely an opportunity to step back and try to understand what was happening on a broader front. I made an attempt to take stock when invited to give the inaugural Colin Cramphorn Memorial Lecture in 2007. I deliberately chose the title 'Learning from Experience: Counter Terrorism in the UK Since 9/11' to try to reflect the reality that, by and large, we had been reacting to events, rather than shaping them (Clarke, 2007). This is not to say that our reaction had not been strategic in its scope and ambition, as by 2007 the new structure of British police counter-terrorism (CT) was maturing and the objective of having capable CT units outside London had been achieved. Regional units were established, and new ways of working with the Security Service were by then firmly embedded. Nevertheless, the operational response to the jihadist terrorist threat was still being developed, driven by events and shaped by those at every level who played a part in counter-terrorist investigations in those sometimes frantic years. In describing some of the main themes that have had an impact on counter-terrorist investigations, I trust that none of the wonderful leaders and innovators that I was privileged to work with will feel that their own

Investigating Terrorism: Current Political, Legal and Psychological Issues, First Edition. Edited by John Pearse.
© 2015 John Wiley & Sons, Ltd. Published 2015 by John Wiley & Sons, Ltd.

personal contributions have been ignored or diminished in my description of the broad sweep of events – that is certainly not my intention.

Despite the fact that by 2001 the United Kingdom had endured some 30 years of a domestic terrorist campaign, the events of the first decade of this century taught us that counter-terrorism now operates in a changed and very different context. And, if the police service is to meet these new challenges, it is absolutely vital that practitioners have a thorough understanding of the evolution and background to the new operating environment. It needs to be alive not only to new terrorist methodology, but also to the changed operational dynamics in terms of community interactions, the law, media, the international dimension and the political landscape. No one could or should claim to have a monopoly of wisdom. Indeed it seems to me that an essential prerequisite for success is to have the humility to admit mistakes, to learn from experience and to remember that seamless teamwork at all levels is vital.

Irish versus Islamist

So what has changed? Because of the Northern Ireland experience, the UK had well-developed structures, skills and capabilities to deal with a terrorist threat. But the simple fact remains that, in the wake of the attacks in the United States in September 2001, there had to be a complete recalibration, not only of the resources available to deal with counter-terrorism, but in the mind-set that governed the deployment of those resources. I firmly believe that gaining an understanding of why there had to be change, and of the nature of that change, is essential for anyone who aspires to be a student of what has occurred in the UK, or to be a practitioner in the future.

The terrorist campaign pursued by Irish terrorists was, of course, deadly and enduring. Terrible atrocities were carried out, and the pain and suffering they caused were immense. However, the campaign was actually carried out within a set of parameters. In saying this, I do not intend to suggest that Irish terrorism was not viciously ferocious and demanding of the highest levels of skills and courage to counter it. However, there were some defining characteristics. By and large, it was a domestic campaign, carried out within the confines of the UK, with occasional excursions abroad. As a general rule, investigators did not have to leave the UK to carry out their work. The attacks themselves, although deadly, were frequently preceded by warnings, often coded and frequently misleading. Nevertheless, the existence of the warnings did serve to restrict the number of casualties, with the attack in Omagh in 1998 having the worst death toll of 29. The weaponry used by Irish terrorists was for the most part conventional, in the sense that the bomb and the gun were the weapons of choice, and there was always a determination on the part of the terrorists to avoid capture. Indeed, the return of prisoners was a key part of the negotiations during the peace process. The whole campaign was, as we have seen, underpinned by a negotiable political agenda. It could well have been the wish to maintain a degree of popular support and therefore a voice within the political process that caused the terrorists to limit the carnage they inflicted.

The terrorist acts carried out by those claiming to do so in the name of Islam have been entirely different in many ways from those practised during the Irish campaigns. For instance, the attacks have been global in their origins and impact. Every continent has been affected to a greater or lesser extent, and investigations into plots and attacks in the UK have frequently spanned the globe. As an example, the 2002–2003 investigation into the plot to use the poison ricin in the UK (Operation Springbourne) took investigators to some 25 countries. There has been a much less obvious wish to avoid capture, and of course suicide has been used as a frequent method of attack. There has certainly been no wish to restrict casualties, either for political or any other reason; on the contrary, we have frequently seen a simple determination to kill as many people as possible. The weaponry used by jihadist terrorists has been both conventional and unconventional. Along with the bombs and the guns, there have been poisons and aspirations towards radiological weapons, both here and overseas. But perhaps most important of all has been the lack of a political agenda around which governments can negotiate. People may argue that there are political approaches that can be made to many of the issues that underpin the sense of grievance felt by many in the Muslim world, and that may well be true. It is still too early to understand the long-term impact of the 2011 upheavals in the Arab world, or that of the conflicts in Syria and Iraq, on the strategies and influence of terrorist groups. However, for the time being investigators will have to work on the basis that a terrorist's ability and desire to cause death and destruction will not be tempered by political aspirations. In the absence of specific intelligence to the contrary, the only safe assumption is that a modern terrorist will wish to inflict the maximum possible loss of life.

A New Concept of Operations

So what does this mean for the law enforcement practitioner in practical terms? In reality, it has led to a complete reappraisal of the concept of operations that under-pins police counter-terrorism efforts. It used to be the case that law enforcement, in the shape of the detective looking for evidence to support a criminal prosecution, was to an extent divorced from the work of the intelligence agencies or police Special Branches. The disciplines of intelligence gathering, collation and assessment tended to operate separately from the evidential investigator. This usually worked well enough in the context of the times, although I have heard of instances where it was not without its difficulties. There were occasions when senior investigating officers (SIOs) struggled to understand the context in which an operation had developed. They were frequently left in the dark in respect of the role of intelligence sources in investigations, or other important aspects of the enquiry of which it was vital that they should have been aware.

Since the early 1990s every major terrorist investigation on the mainland of the UK has been coordinated through an Executive Liaison Group (ELG), chaired by the National Co-ordinator of Terrorist Investigations, and composed of senior representatives from the Security Service, Special Branch and the affected police forces. And yet the SIO was excluded. He or she was not entitled to attend or be part of the process of setting the strategy for the investigation. This was usually explained as being in his or her best interests, so that he or she did not experience difficulty when giving evidence in court. There may have been other reasons as well, but it was nevertheless a conscious act of policy to separate the intelligence and evidential strands of investigation. Extraordinary as it may seem, the SIO formally gained admittance to the ELG only when a policy decision was taken by the Association of Chief Police Officers in 2005. In practice, SIOs had been attending ELGs, with the full support of the National Co-ordinator and the Security Service, since 2002. For legal reasons alone the status quo had to change as the disclosure regime in criminal prosecutions took hold in England and Wales. But it also had to change for even more compelling reasons connected to public safety, and the rationale for this is easy to demonstrate.

Traditionally, the objective of the evidential investigator was to intercept the terrorist as close as possible to the point of attack – to capture him or her with the bomb or gun, and thereby have the strongest possible evidence to put before a court. The arrest of Rab Friars, a Provisional Irish Republican Army bomber on his way into central London, with his bomb, at a bus stop in Cricklewood in 1993 was a prime example of this. I cannot imagine a similar operation being considered as either desirable or permissible today. It is inconceivable, in the age of the suicide bomber, that a suspect would be allowed to travel into a city, carrying his bomb, before being challenged by the police. We have seen all too clearly the enormous, indeed well-nigh impossible, challenges that are presented by trying to find a safe and appropriate way of interdicting potential suicide bombers. This one example clearly demonstrates the changed approach to managing risk that has to be mastered by the modern terrorist investigator. The obvious conclusion is that evidential opportunities have to be sought at every stage of an investigation, and it is no good relying on the traditional operational denouement to provide the unequivocal evidence of terrorism needed for a successful prosecution.

Another key change in the operational environment has been the extent to which the conduct of an operation sits within the sole control of the police officer in charge. The complex and often international web of stakeholders in a modern counter-terrorist operation has to be taken into account. The scale of the threat and the potential impact if an attack were successfully mounted are so great that the traditional operational independence of the police, while not yet directly under challenge, has to be attuned to the wider environment. The operational commander, while bearing risks on behalf of his or her own operation, must be sensitive to events, fears, influences and legal considerations in, as has often been the case, multiple jurisdictions. Many of those jurisdictions have very different law enforcement traditions from the UK, in which political influence or even direction may have an acknowledged and entirely proper impact on the conduct of an investigation. By way of contrast, I can honestly say that in the six years during which I held the role of National Co-ordinator of Terrorist Investigations my operational decision-making was never subject to any domestic political pressure. However, on several occasions I was aware of concerns and questions that were raised by foreign governments about the conduct of UK operations. This is entirely proper and inevitable, and needs to be acknowledged as part of the operating context by senior investigators. I can recall one or two cases in which there was considerable external pressure to move an investigation towards the executive action phase, and was grateful that the concept of the independence of the office of constable, long recognized in UK law and supported by constitutional convention, allowed the evidence gathering to continue uninterrupted. This was not about maintaining an arrogant aloofness but more about keeping a clear focus on the operational objectives at the same time as explaining the operational strategy to, and discussing it with, a whole range of interested partners.

Police and Security Service

There has also been a fundamental change in the nature of the relationship between the Security Service and the police. No longer are the evidential investigators reliant on whatever information the intelligence world chooses to share with them as an investigation reaches the critical phase. Nowadays, the police and the Security Service are working partners from a much earlier stage in an investigation than ever used to be the case. Because of the increased scale of risk to the public, there now needs to be the collective capacity for a full range of intervention options to be open at every stage of a terrorist conspiracy. So, instead of focusing on the attack itself, we now look to be able to disrupt it, through either arrest and prosecution or other means, at every stage of terrorist planning. This in turn means that, as far as possible, every aspect of the investigation needs to be carried out to evidential standards from the very beginning. This does not mean that there are no longer any secrets, or that the Security Service and others are not able to protect from public scrutiny those things that should properly remain secret. What it does mean is that when an investigation is started, all parties will work to a rebuttable presumption that information will be gathered in a way that will allow it to be admitted as evidence in a criminal court. The system of revelation and disclosure in criminal cases, supported by the application of public interest immunity (PII) orders to protect information that needs to be protected, has worked well. There have been determined attempts by defence teams to break down the walls of PII and force the prosecution to abandon cases rather than disclose material that could harm national security, but so far these attempts have failed. They have probably failed because of the faith that the judiciary have in the integrity of the revelation and disclosure regime adopted by the prosecution in such cases. The process, by which the trial judge, through counsel, will have had sight of all relevant material, enjoys widespread confidence. It is of course vital that secret information and methodology can be protected, so that the intelligence agencies can have confidence in being able to work closely with law enforcement.

Legislation

In the UK the approach has always been that terrorism is a crime, that terrorists are criminals and should be treated as such. This means that, as far as possible, they should be subject to the criminal law and put on trial by a judge and jury in the normal criminal courts. From the perspective of maintaining the confidence of Muslim communities in the means by which terrorists have been brought to justice, the transparency of the criminal trial process has been vitally important. In the years since 9/11, terrorist trials in the UK have generated comparatively little controversy or suspicion of unfairness in terms of doubts as to the integrity of the evidence being presented or whether due process has been followed at all stages.

Public scepticism has been much greater where there has been a perceived departure from recognized judicial process. This has been clearly evident when the focus has been on the use of Control Orders or TPIMs, or when individuals have been detained under the auspices of the Special Immigration Appeals Commission or extradited from the UK under the provisions of the US–UK Extradition Treaty of 2003 or a European Arrest Warrant. However, if the normal criminal courts are to be able to deal with twenty-first-century terrorism, there must be legislation that supports the ability to intervene at early stages of an investigation if necessary. Finding the right balance to strike between individual liberties and collective security has proved to be immensely challenging, as legislators find themselves in a 'perfect storm' of sensitivities linked to ethnicity, nationality, ideology and religion. The experience of the past few years shows, I believe, that the arguments put forward by those who say there is no need for specific legislation to deal with terrorism are wide of the mark. What experience should be teaching us is that we need a proper legal strategy to deal with terrorism, based as far as possible on existing and well-recognized due process, but robust enough to provide judicial outcomes in the vast majority of cases. It is undoubtedly a difficult balance to strike, but the balance needs to be found and to enjoy public confidence, if we are to maintain a model of counter-terrorism that has criminal justice at its heart.

In the years immediately following 9/11 it became obvious that there were serious gaps in the existing legal framework. On occasion there was clear evidence of terrorist activity, but difficulty in framing specific charges that would give the courts sufficient powers of sentencing to reflect the criminality of what the terrorists were actually doing. I very much hope that in the future dedicated international terrorists who wish to poison or irradiate the public will not have to be charged with the nineteenth-century common law offence of 'Conspiracy to Cause a Public Nuisance' for want of anything more suitable. The offence under section 5 of the Terrorism Act 2006 of 'Preparation of terrorism acts' should help to prevent this, and gives investigators and prosecutors the opportunity to develop an investigative strategy that complements the desire to minimize risk to the public.

We also now have the ability to prosecute, in front of the normal courts of law, offences ranging from propagandizing and recruitment, through fund-raising and hostile reconnaissance, to acquiring terrorist-related material and of course the attack itself. But the legislation would be wasted if legally admissible evidence were not available to support prosecutions. Inevitably this has meant far-reaching changes to the way in which the Security Service and Special Branches work. Their exposure to the evidential arena has been an enormous challenge, and I think the way in which those engaged in the collection of intelligence have adapted to play their role in the criminal trial process has been a great credit to all concerned. I firmly believe that the combination of an updated body of counter-terrorist law, together with the change in relationship and working arrangements between the police and the Security Service, has given the UK a counter-terrorist machinery that is second to none, and as well placed to defend the public from the threat as any in the world.

Counter-Terrorism versus Ordinary Decent Crime

Terrorist investigations can be distinguished from traditional criminal investigations, and it is absolutely vital that practitioners, senior officers, politicians, commentators and others understand this. They all need to grasp the essential differences between terrorist investigations and what is sometimes referred to as 'ordinary decent crime'.

The priority for any investigator operating in the world of counter-terrorism will always be the safety of the public. However, the scale of the potential harm means the CT investigator is managing an entirely different scale of risk. There can never be any compromise on this, given the nature of the threat that is presented by Islamist terrorists. This in turn means that the decision as to when to intervene is frequently governed by the level of knowledge that the investigators have of the terrorists' ambitions – how advanced they are in their attack planning and so on. Frequently this knowledge will only come from the surveillance that can be mounted against the targets. If a case is to be allowed to 'run long', so that there can be unequivocal evidence of terrorist planning and intention to attack, the investigator must be satisfied that the terrorists are not in a position to mount an unexpected or sudden attack. This frequently means that the scale of the surveillance operation will exceed anything that would have been contemplated in the past. In 2006, during the closing stages of Operation Overt, the investigation of a plot to attack commercial aircraft in flight, no fewer than 27 surveillance teams were deployed at one stage. There are other cases that illustrate this point. In 2004 Operation Crevice, the investigation into a plot to build and detonate a large bomb in the South East, the so-called Fertilizer Plot, was allowed to run for many weeks because we could be sure that there was no imminent danger to the public. There came a moment at which it was not entirely clear whether we were still in complete control of the threat to the public, and so the decision was made to move to immediate executive action and make the arrests. Fortunately, by then there was clear evidence to support serious charges against the terrorists.

By contrast, in August of that same year, another case brought into stark relief the difficulties of taking what could be called a risk management approach to terrorist investigation. Operation Rhyme was the investigation into a group of terrorists led by Dhiren Barot, a long-standing and dedicated terrorist. He and his network were very difficult targets to control through surveillance. We could not be sure how advanced their attack planning was, and so the decision was made to arrest the members of the network. At the time of their arrests there was plenty of intelligence about their activities, more than sufficient grounds to make the arrests, but not one single shred of admissible evidence. There then began something of a race against time to find the evidence, which turned out to be buried deep in the mass of encrypted digital data that was seized during the arrests and subsequent searches. The evidence was found just in time, and, three years later, the entire network had been convicted of serious terrorist offences. But at the time it was touch and go, and there were some in the media who were queuing up to offer criticism of the operation, if the evidence had not been forthcoming.

This is not the place to explore this theme in depth, but it is an excellent example of why there needs to be a wider understanding that counter-terrorism is a matter of managing extreme risks, and that success in protecting the public can rest in outcomes other than a successful prosecution. This is not, I think, understood by the public, the media, or indeed many in the police service. It is certainly not widely understood within communities, and the inability to explain publicly the intelligence background that has given rise to the decision to mount operations has caused some real difficulties in gaining understanding and acceptance of police actions. One only has to think back to cases such as the deployment of military support at Heathrow in 2003, the Manchester United plot that same year or the controversial police operation at Forest Gate in 2006 to see the difficulties.

The Forest Gate case illustrates this point very neatly. The intelligence that sat behind the operation was investigated at great length in an effort to prove or disprove its veracity. Eventually the point was reached at which it was agreed across the relevant agencies that the investigation could be taken no further without executive action – in other words, a search and arrest operation. The potential risk to the public as described in the intelligence could not be left unresolved. During the subsequent operation an innocent man was accidentally shot by police, and no evidence of terrorist activity was found. Nevertheless, the investigation by the Independent Police Complaints Commission concluded that the police operation had been 'necessary and proportionate' in the light of the intelligence picture (Independent Police Complaints Commission, 2007).

It really boils down to this. If there is intelligence about a threat to the public which, however long and hard you investigate, cannot be proved or disproved, what do you do? Do you hope for the best and do nothing, or do you take further action in the form of searches or arrests to bottom it out? If you choose the latter, and evidence of terrorism is not forthcoming, the implications in terms of community confidence in the police are obvious, particularly when one is not able to explain the full intelligence background, even to trusted community partners. The origins and ownership of much counter-terrorist intelligence frequently make this impossible, and this is a key distinguishing feature from mainstream crime. In my experience this distinction is rarely understood. If one is investigating traditional crime, the results of failing to stop an individual criminal act will rarely be catastrophic. A drug shipment may get through, property might be stolen and indeed, in some cases, serious injury or death may result. However, the balance of risk never includes mass murder – but that is what the counter-terrorist investigator must consider.

In the British policing and legal system, the SIO has a range of specific procedural and legal responsibilities. In exercising these responsibilities, he or she has a huge amount of discretion and independence. In any major investigation, the SIO sets the strategy and the policies to deliver that strategy. This is much less clear-cut in counter-terrorism. The partnerships at local, national and international level that play a role in major terrorist investigations have to be taken account of by the SIO. He or she cannot ride roughshod over intelligence equities or sensitive international arrangements. In major cases, the overall strategy for the investigation will have been set at the ELG (referred to above). Frequently the intelligence itself will not be 'owned' by the police service and careful negotiation will be required to understand what may and may not be used in support of a prosecution. In short, in a counter-terrorist operation the SIO is not in complete control of the risk that he or she is attempting to manage, and certainly not to the extent that a colleague in a major crime investigation would be. I have seen experienced investigators come into the world of counter-terrorism and really struggle with this concept. But it is an operational reality, and has to be managed.

Aside from the structural and partnership issues, counter-terrorism in the modern context demands the deployment of assets on a scale that would have been unimaginable only a few years ago. I have already mentioned the immensity of a surveillance operation to control a threat while investigation continues, but it goes beyond this. As the various inquiries into the attacks on London in July 2005 showed, there is an expectation that every piece of information that is available at any given time will be recorded, compared with all the other data held by the police and intelligence agencies, contextualized, analysed and understood. The resources that are necessary to achieve this are, of course, immense.

The advent of the National Crime Agency in 2013 has inevitably opened a debate as to whether counter-terrorism should become part of its remit in due course. Indeed, there have already been views expressed from various quarters. Some of the opinions have been based on an idea that the supposed linkages between CT and serious crime, in terms of both those involved and the operational response, could lead to savings. Others have based their views on a belief that the Metropolitan Police, currently the leader and coordinator of the national CT law enforcement effort, should revert to being a municipal police force. To date, I have seen little in the way of properly informed discussion or much that goes beyond a superficial appreciation of the issues. Whatever emerges from this debate, it is vital that it is properly informed by a thorough understanding of the operational realities of counter-terrorism and that, while it quite properly should be a *political* decision, it is not one that should be *politicized*.

The Politics of Counter-Terrorism

This is not the place for an exhaustive analysis of the relationship between operational counter-terrorism and the political process, except to say that the two disciplines have not always been happy bedfellows in the recent past. The debate about
pre-charge detention which led to the Blair government suffering its first parliamentary defeat in 2005, and the subsequent defeat for the Brown administration on an
alternative 42-day detention proposal, stands as a clear warning of the difficulties
when political consensus in matters of counter-terrorism breaks down and party politics intervene. The difficulty for practitioners when this happens is that there have
been occasions when the integrity of their operational decision-making has been
called into question and suggestions made that they were influenced by a wish to
support the government for political reasons. This happened over the deployment
of military assets to Heathrow in support of the police in 2003, and again over the
length of time some suspects were detained before being charged or released in 2006
as part of Operation Overt (the so-called Airlines Plot). These types of allegations are
easily made and potentially massively damaging in terms of the relationship between
the police and the Muslim communities whose trust and support they need.

So far the police have not been too deeply drawn into a political debate over the
implementation of the new Prevent strand of the government's CT strategy, CON-
TEST, published in July 2011. The strand is intended to counter the forces of radicalization within society and, although its scope has broadened to include non-Islamist
radicalization, its focus has narrowed. There is an explicit intention to challenge
extremist ideology, and not to work with extremist groups. This is a distinct change
from the tone of the previous strategy, and has been characterized by some critics as
being itself driven by a distinct political ideology. All this inevitably leaves the police
at risk of being caught between two political standpoints which at the moment seem
irreconcilable. The police have a clear right (and duty, it can be argued) to engage with
whoever they wish as part of either community outreach or intelligence-gathering
activity. This can be uncomfortable, either in reality or in perception, but the bigger
risk for the police is being drawn into a political argument about it. I am not putting
forward any solution to the problem here, but simply warning of the consequences
of what has become an ideological discussion getting in the way of effective intelligence and evidence gathering, and of effective community interventions to counter
extremists.

Conclusion

There is no more complex area of policing than the investigation of terrorism. Those
who choose to practise their professional skills in this area will meet challenges
unlike any they will encounter in other parts of policing. The complex interplay

of community influences, partnership working, legal obligations, international relations, media scrutiny and the overriding obligation to preserve public safety will test the most skilful, knowledgeable and experienced of practitioners to the full. There is a real need to capture what has gone before, to learn from it and to move forward with a sense of real purpose to protect the safety of the British public. That there have been so few successful terrorist attacks in the United Kingdom in recent years has nothing to do with any diminution in the lethal intent of terrorists. The reason is quite simply that the UK, through long experience and a level of cooperation across agencies, the law, government and public that is unmatched anywhere else in the world, has built its defences against the enduring threat of political violence.

References

Clarke, P. (2007). *Learning from experience: Counter terrorism in the UK since 9/11.* Inaugural Colin Cramphorn Lecture. London: Policy Exchange. Retrieved 21 May 2014 from http://www.policyexchange.org.uk/images/publications/learning%20from%20experience%20-%20jun%2007.pdf

Independent Police Complaints Commission. (2007, February). IPCC independent investigations into complaints made following the Forest Gate counter-terrorist operation on 2 June 2006. Retrieved 21 May 2014 from http://webarchive.nationalarchives.gov.uk/20100908152737/ipcc.gov.uk/forest_gate_2_3report.pdf

Part II
The Criminal Justice Process

3

Challenge, Compromise and Collaboration

Part of the Skill Set Necessary for Interviewing a Failed Suicide Bomber

John Pearse

This chapter examines what took place in the urgent interviews conducted with a failed suicide bomber in London at the height of the terrorist bombing campaign in 2005. Urgent (or public safety) interviews are undertaken by police at very short notice when they have arrested a failed suicide bomber and urgently need to find and make safe bombs or bomb-making equipment in order to protect the public. The author will analyse the type of tactics used and the nature of the responses in this the first example of a ticking bomb scenario in Western Europe. The views and opinions of serving counter-terrorism police officers who are regularly tasked with interviewing terrorist detainees will be discussed with reference to the nature and type of tactics they currently employ, and the author will examine the extent to which the current police training paradigm is able to adapt to meet the needs of a rapidly changing policing environment.

Following the introduction of audio taping for all police interviews, which had been implemented across the United Kingdom by 1992, and the findings of subsequent psychological research, it was apparent that police officers required a comprehensive training package to educate them in the skills and knowledge necessary to conduct effective and ethical interviews (see Gudjonsson, 2003; Williamson, 1993, 1994).

The resulting training package has become known by its mnemonic, PEACE: planning and preparation; engagement and explanation; account and clarification; closure; evaluation. PEACE was introduced to provide an ethical framework to guide officers towards a more information-gathering and non-coercive approach rather than seeking to extract a confession per se (Gudjonsson, 2003; Williamson 1993, 1994). More recently, a national interviewing strategy has been developed to promote awareness of and support for this concept with the introduction of a

Investigating Terrorism: Current Political, Legal and Psychological Issues, First Edition. Edited by John Pearse.
© 2015 John Wiley & Sons, Ltd. Published 2015 by John Wiley & Sons, Ltd.

well-defined tier system that will allow police officers to progress from an initial awareness programme (level 1) to an advanced level of operational expertise (level 3) and beyond as they progress through their police career (Griffiths & Milne, 2006).

However, a number of criticisms have been published in relation to the training paradigm and strategy. In 1996 the author and a colleague reviewed police interviews at two south London police stations and found little evidence of any probing or challenging questions, and it was suggested that the C in PEACE ought to include and promote appropriate 'challenge' (Pearse & Gudjonsson, 1996). In 2001 a major review of PEACE was critical of the training and supervisory elements of the programme and, in particular, of the limited communication skills exhibited by the officers (Clarke & Milne, 2001). Interestingly, in one of his last publications the late Tom Williamson, arguably the man responsible for nurturing and delivering the PEACE training regime, acknowledged the need for 'challenge' in his summary 'C – Clarify, challenge and conclude', but this has not been taken up by other parties (Williamson, 2006, p. 154).

More recently Shaw (2012) has reinforced the challenge component as a vital part of the interview process and noted how it seems to have lost its focus and that officers lack confidence with regard to its use. With some irony, he points to the historic criticism by the courts of the police for their use of challenge and notes the current judicial complaint of the lack of challenges! Hawkins (2012), a senior prosecutor, eloquently articulates the essence of a good interviewer as someone who has the ability to think on his or her feet and to adapt accordingly, and he is critical of some investigators who stick so rigidly to the PEACE model that they often do not apply their own common sense to the situation.

It remains a distinct possibility that the PEACE training process has imposed on the officers a quite rigid framework, stifled the opportunity for spontaneity and flexibility and provided limited support for appropriate and challenging questioning regimes. It seems that changes have been made to support the infrastructure surrounding PEACE but the question remains: To what extent have the concept and philosophy evolved to meet the changing needs and climate of modern policing? (Gudjonsson & Pearse, 2011; see also Chapter 6 by Geraldine Noone in this volume).

One such important contextual change for police officers in the UK has been the increase in the number of terrorist suspects arrested and interviewed as the impact of international terrorism has taken effect (Pearse, 2006, 2009) and this has highlighted the need for officers, often at short notice and without a great deal of time to prepare, to undertake urgent or public safety interviews (the legal aspects of these interactions from a prosecution and defence perspective are dealt with in the following chapters by Max Hill, QC, and Peter Carter, QC, respectively). Such interviews may take place at the time of arrest or subsequently at the police station, and are designed to try and locate bombs, bomb-making equipment or other potential bombers in order to save lives. Urgent interviews are not the exclusive domain of terrorist investigations and could apply to the kidnapping of a child, for instance, where the suspect has been detained but the location of the child is unknown. In terrorism the term 'ticking bomb scenario' has been applied to the potential for this set of circumstances and, until 2005, it had remained a hypothetical discussion in Western Europe.

The UK experienced a series of deadly suicide bomb attacks on the London Underground transport system on 7 July 2005 (also known as 7/7) and also a number of failed suicide bomb attacks two weeks later (21/7), which gave rise to a massive nationwide police hunt for the five would-be suicide bombers. The arrest of the first bomber provided the investigating police with a real-life ticking bomb scenario, where, in order to save lives, they needed urgently to locate the other bombers and to recover and make safe any other bombs or bomb-making equipment. This was, therefore, like no other police interview – the consequences were potentially extreme, with considerable pressure on the whole investigating team.

In the UK the police interview is recognized as the only inquisitorial element in an otherwise overtly accusatorial legal system, but the urgent public safety interview can add yet other dimensions that might depart from the traditional prosecution route. Given that the overarching responsibility is public safety, the officer in charge can direct his or her staff to use any number of tactics; for example, the instruction might include the freedom for officers to step outside the constraints of their training and make a deal with the detainee, in order to negotiate the location of bombs or other bombers in return for a guarantee that the information will not be used in evidence against him or her.

In the first instance, this chapter will examine this question from the perspective of serving police officers. It will then provide an analysis of the nature and type of tactics actually employed by the police in the real-life 2005 case. This case was heard at the Central Criminal Court (the Old Bailey) and the convictions subsequently reviewed and upheld at the Court of Appeal, but the debate over the use in evidence of the product from the urgent interview has yet to be heard in the European Court. This is the first time that a psychological analysis of the interaction between the police officers and the unsuccessful suicide bomber has been published.

Counter-Terrorism Police Study

The author was granted access to analyse a number of terrorist cases and to conduct face-to-face interviews with a range of serving counter-terrorism (CT) officers. This in turn led to the distribution of a questionnaire to other CT officers containing questions relating to a ticking bomb scenario (Pearse, 2006), and so we can now examine this as a hypothetical issue from the CT officers' perspective.

The actual research was divided into three sections: an analysis of 30 CT cases within which there were 187 interview sessions; a survey of the views of a range of officers from senior investigators (SIOs) and managers to detective inspectors, sergeants and constables; and finally a customized questionnaire distributed randomly to investigating officers (detective sergeants and detective constables).

To place this CT review in context we need first to explore the main hypothesis behind the research: that interviews with terrorist suspects would be treated by police in the same manner as they would treat serious criminal offences, and that police officers would engage in a range of coercive and manipulative interviewing tactics in order to influence the decision-making process of the suspect, in order to obtain a confession or an admission (Pearse & Gudjonsson, 1999). It makes sense to understand the 'normal' tactics used by CT officers before moving to the specific ticking bomb scenario.

The author has analysed many hundreds of police interviews and has developed a robust methodology for understanding and interpreting what takes place within this particular interaction. Essentially, the nature and type of tactics employed by the police in serious criminal cases can be captured within a specially designed coding frame predicated on a multidimensional typology including delivery (or context); maximization; and manipulation (Pearse, 2011; Pearse & Gudjonsson, 1999).

Delivery is very much an overlapping category that is present throughout the process and is designed to capture *what type of questions* are asked (closed, leading, open, etc.), *how* they are put (in hushed, lowered tones, or harshly and aggressively), as well as any relevant contextual features, that is, *where* the questioning takes place (i.e., the custodial environment). It is designed to capture all relevant contextual features.

Maximization is a 'hard sell' technique by which the interrogator tries to scare and intimidate the suspect into confessing by making claims (false or otherwise) about evidence and exaggerating the seriousness and/or the magnitude of the charges. This includes any tactic designed to increase a suspect's internal anxiety. Finally, *manipulation* relates to the more subtle and insidious form of questioning that attacks a suspect's perception of the crime, or the consequences of his or her actions; it includes manipulating the details or significant others, flattery, making unrealistic promises, as well as attacking a suspect's self-esteem or stature.

To examine this hypothesis the author analysed 187 interview sessions. Table 3.1 provides an insight into the type of tactics employed. The most immediate finding is the limited use of many of the categories. 'Use of evidence' (83%) was the most popular tactic, covering the production of exhibits, photographs and other materials, but it tended to occur in a rather sterile and perfunctory atmosphere. The limited use of 'challenges' is indicative of the polite and non-confrontational nature of these interactions, even though the use of silence by important terrorist suspects was prevalent. Given previous research that showed that in serious criminal cases police officers would resort to coercive and manipulative tactics (Pearse & Gudjonsson, 1999), it was unexpected to find such limited use of maximization tactics (emphasizing the serious nature of the offence), minimization (reducing the suspect's perception of consequences) or manipulation (use of themes, flattery), and some of the reasons behind the passive nature of these tactics will be discussed later on.

We can now turn our attention to the type of tactics that might be employed in a ticking bomb scenario. In this section the officers were provided with a realistic scenario that would require them to interview a terrorist suspect arrested *after he had placed his bomb in a busy public area*. Here the immediacy of a likely detonation with mass casualties has been emphasized.

Table 3.1 Extent of the use of CT police interviewing tactics (Pearse, 2006)

Tactics	Never used	Infrequent use	Average use	Frequent use	Very frequent use
Open question	0	3 (1.5%)	75 (40%)	104 (56%)	5 (2.5%)
Closed question	4 (2%)	54 (29%)	105 (56%)	21 (11%)	3 (2%)
Leading question	84 (45%)	73 (39%)	27 (14.5%)	2 (1%)	1 (.5%)
Repeat question	159 (85%)	20 (11%)	8 (4%)	0	0
Multiple question	165 (88%)	14 (7.5%)	7 (4%)	1 (.5%)	0
Multiple officers	175 (94%)	7 (3.5%)	5 (2.5%)	0	0
Challenges	56 (30%)	42 (22.5%)	63 (34%)	19 (10%)	7 (3.5%)
Improper tactics	184 (98%)	3 (2%)	0	0	0
Manipulative tactics	150 (80.5%)	17 (9%)	19 (10%)	1 (.5%)	0
Minimization	170 (91%)	12 (6.5%)	5 (2.5%)	0	0
Maximization	123 (66%)	18 (9.5%)	39 (21%)	7 (3.5%)	0
Use of evidence	10 (5%)	23 (12%)	51 (27%)	63 (34%)	40 (22%)

Note: N = 187.

Table 3.2 Counter-terrorist police tactics in a hypothetical ticking bomb scenario (Pearse, 2006)

Tactics	Agree	Disagree	Not selected
Direct accusatorial style	38 (76%)	2 (4%)	10 (20%)
Open, then challenge	45 (90%)	0	5 (10%)
Suspend human rights	38 (76%)	4 (8%)	8 (16%)
Incommunicado	43 (86%)	0	7 (14%)
No access to legal advice	42 (84%)	2 (4%)	6 (12%)
Psychological pressure	35 (70%)	6 (12%)	9 (18%)
Physical pressure	12 (24%)	19 (38%)	19 (38%)
Medical pressure	22 (44%)	12 (24%)	16 (32%)
Manipulation	26 (52%)	10 (20%)	14 (28%)
Information gathering	36 (72%)	1 (2%)	13 (26%)
Other	10 (20%)	0	40 (80%)

Note: N = 187.

Table 3.2 shows the type of tactics officers indicate they would be prepared to engage in (or sanction as a SIO) if they were required to interview a person suspected of placing an explosive device in a busy public area. The tactic categories were selected as a result of pilot work during the development of the questionnaire, and represent a summary of CT officers' views. 'Physical pressure' relates to the threat of physical assault and 'medical pressure' relates to threatening to call a medical professional to administer the 'truth drug' (it is accepted that this is something of a misnomer, this suggested tactic owing more to fiction than fact: see Bimmerle (1993) for an informative and historical review).

With regard to the general style or approach to the tactics to be used, 76 per cent considered a direct and accusatorial style and 90 per cent also indicated that they would resort to a challenging style if open-ended questions failed. The removal of a suspect's rights – 86 per cent favour incommunicado (not allowing the suspect to speak to anyone) and 84 per cent not permitting access to legal advice – is clearly a dominant theme. There is also an indication that the officers were more likely to use a variety of coercive and manipulative tactics (psychological pressure, manipulation, medical and physical pressure) than was previously found in an analysis of earlier terrorist cases. There is no mention of the use of negotiation by the officers.

These findings represent a departure from the actual tactics used (see Table 3.1) and this may well reflect the hypothetical nature of the exercise and the weakness behind such 'what if' scenarios. To overcome these weaknesses, we now turn our attention to the actual failed suicide bomber case involving Yassin Hassan Omar, who was the first bomber arrested in July 2005.

Failed Suicide Bomber: Interview Analysis

To set the context for this series of interviews, it makes sense to repeat the words of the Court of Appeal in giving judgment in April 2008, dismissing the appeals of the four men convicted of conspiring to murder commuters on 21 July 2007:

> Without minimising the personal impact on those who were using the transport system at the time when the bombs were detonated, it is sufficient for present purposes to note that all five men made their escapes. They were then at large for some days. It is virtually impossible to imagine the pressure and concerns which must have been felt by the police investigating teams. Two weeks earlier four bombs had been successfully detonated with the dreadful consequences with which we are familiar, and they were now faced with four more bombs, again in the transport system, which had been detonated, but failed to explode. The bombers involved on 7th July had perished, but the perpetrators of the second intended atrocity were at large, free to repeat their murderous plans, and to do so more effectively. They had to be found and detained, and the immediate objective of the investigation, including interviews of those arrested in connection with these incidents, was directed to public safety. (*R v. Ibrahim and others* [2008] 2 Cr App R 23 at para. 5)

Yassin Hassan Omar was arrested by CT officers at 5.20 a.m. at an address in Birmingham on Wednesday 27 July 2005 and transferred to a London police station. There he was subjected to five taped interviews which lasted a total of three hours and four minutes, starting at 10.25 in the morning with the last one recorded at 4.19–4.21 in the afternoon.

Although the written transcripts from the second interview onwards suggest that a solicitor was present throughout, the solicitor was in fact only present for the final very brief (three-minute) interview of the day. The presence of both the audio tape of the interview and the transcript provided the author with a valuable insight into what actually took place, as well as a reference document to annotate. In previous research, access to this combination has proved invaluable in correcting a large number of sometimes very serious errors in the court transcripts (Pearse, 1997), although no major typographical errors were uncovered in this case. All transcript reproduction in this chapter remains faithful to the original document produced at court and has not been corrected. The exception to this is if the transcript has failed to reproduce part of the dialogue or does not allude to any noticeable change and I have inserted it in brackets, for example, [crying, raised voices].

Tape 1

Omar was interviewed from 10.25 until 11.11 a.m. by a detective sergeant (DS) and a detective constable (DC). He had been assessed by a doctor as fit for interview, as he reported feeling unwell, although this is not elaborated on further. In the interviews Omar describes himself as a 24-year-old Somali who at some time had been in foster care in the UK, and in the very last interview on the day of his arrest, at 4.19 p.m., there is a reference to his receiving further medical attention – to have stitches in his leg.

The officers were keen to progress the interview and it started at quite a fast pace, with questions designed to identify who else was involved in the attempted bombing.

DS:	Right. Okay then. Let's start off quickly. Tell me who else is involved?
OMAR:	Who else is involved?
DS:	Right. There was four, four and perhaps five incidents yeah
OMAR:	Yeah
DS:	Warren Street. The one at Warren Street that was you. Is that right?
OMAR:	I was in Warren Street yes.
DS:	Right okay then. Who else is involved?
OMAR:	As far as I know …
DS:	No, no, Yasin, not as far as you know. Who else was involved. A couple of weeks ago, over 50 people were killed alright.
OMAR:	Yes
DS:	There's at least three people out there, if not four, that are willing to die in order to kill others. Let's not prat about. Who else is involved? Let's start with The Oval then. Who was that?
OMAR:	The Oval?
DS:	Yeah
OMAR:	I don't know. The Oval. I don't know because I wasn't there.
DS:	Right. Look we'll show you a photograph.

In many respects, this brief dialogue is quite representative of the pace and tactics throughout the entire interview process. The officers were keen to move matters on quickly to establish the names and locations of other bombers, while Omar adopted a general policy of avoidance – initially repeating back the question, for example: 'Tell me who else is involved?'; 'Who else is involved?'; 'The Oval then. Who was that?'; 'The Oval?' Although Omar made a number of admissions early on in the interview, over time the vagueness of his responses left the officers frustrated, and a number of challenges emerged especially in relation to the lack of substance and credibility in the answers given. For example, he introduced the suggestion that he was to be married:

> DS: On the day when you did it yeah? Who else was there. Tell us the story about that.
>
> OMAR: All I know is I, I was told, what happened is, I was told I, because I was supposed to get married, so I was told to meet up with my friend Hasm, one of my friend's Hasm. So I went …
>
> DS: Right hold on. You're supposed to meet up with your friend Hassan. Who told you that?

And then shortly after:

> DS: I'll remind you yet again, as far as I'm concerned, you're a suicide bomber and you were prepared to die on Thursday
>
> OMAR: But I didn't know there was something in it.
>
> DS: You were prepared to die for the cause on Thursday
>
> OMAR: How could I be prepared and, and I was supposed to be getting married that day.

And shortly after:

> OMAR: I don't mind saying anything to you but what it is is I don't want to say anything which is gonna make things worse for me. Because if I'm, if I giving you …
>
> DS: I tell you what's, I'll tell you what's going to make things worse for you. What's going to make things worse for you, if these three and the others, they went back to get materials to do further bombings, actually succeed next time and kill people. That's what's going to be the worst thing that's going to happen. So don't worry about what's going to make it worse for you. You're in it already right. But you're not dead and other people aren't dead. You never killed anyone but these might. Alright. I want to know the story Yasin, and I want to start, and I want you to start telling me the truth now. We're trying to save lives yeah?
>
> OMAR: Yes.
>
> DS: You were prepared to die on Thursday [actually said last Thursday], you're not now you're safe. These are still out there and they're prepared to die. Don't give me this about I don't know what was in the bag. Don't give me this about I don't know who was involved and I don't know I might have met him here, there and everywhere. Tell me who these other three are and tell me how you met up and tell me you were going to do.

The challenges from the officers about lack of credibility or the unbelievable nature of the answers continued, often in a normal tone of voice, although there were a number of interruptions and raised voices from the officers. It was noticeable that quite early on Omar indicated that he didn't 'want to say anything which is gonna make things worse' for himself, although the officer interrupted him before he actually finished. The first tape concluded with an insightful exchange that reveals something of Omar's physical and emotional state and also the officer's view of Omar's story to date.

DS: So the reason for you being interview [said interviewed] now, under these circumstances is that we are trying to find these blokes alright.
OMAR: Yeah
DS: You're shaking, you're scared and I can appreciate you're scared.
OMAR: Yeah
DS: But man to man I want you to tell me the story, who these other people are, what you were going to do, what was the plan, who taught you? Everything like that.
OMAR: Okay firstly, firstly I told you
DS: Yeah
OMAR: Firstly I'll tell you the truth
DS: I don't want to hear, I don't want to hear any more lies
OMAR: No I'm not telling lies
DS: I don't want to hear any lies
OMAR: I'm not telling lies.

Omar went on to provide a lengthy response which included denials, a claim that a 'guy used my house', and talk about his girlfriend and his arrest, at which point he said:

OMAR: Today after I got arrested everything, that's when it hit me. Because the guys, the way they spoke to me, the way they treated me, I realised this was one of the biggest mistake ever happened you know. Because I have lived here, they have treated me well, even though I had hard times in foster care, but the people in this country, they don't deserve this.

The second interview session resumed after a gap of 15 minutes, at 11.26 a.m., and finished at 12.11 p.m. This second exchange was characterized by further examples of avoidance and some denials from Omar, with the officers getting increasingly exasperated as they set out to examine separate topic areas – flat location, associates and a car journey with the other suspected bombers – only for Omar to suggest that he had fallen asleep at crucial times, with the result that no topic area was ever satisfactorily resolved. For example:

DS: Right. Did you meet up with him Hasm, last Thursday
OMAR: Did I meet up with him? – Yeah I met up with him
DS: Right. And did you meet up with Hassan you were at his flat?
OMAR: Yeah. I, in, in my area I met, I met this guy
DS: No on the day, on the day
OMAR: No, no, no. On that day?

DS: On that day?
OMAR: On what …
DC: Thursday 21st,
DS: On the day that your bag went bang
OMAR: Thursday or Wednesday what, what.
DS: [In a raised and annoyed tone] Look don't give Wednesday what, what. The
           day your bag went bang

And in relation to another suspect's address, where Omar stayed the night before the failed attack:

DS: Right okay. Can we describe it then. Is it in a block of flats or is it a house on
           its own or what is it?
OMAR: It's like a house
DS: It's like a house, it's either a house or it's not a house. What is it?
OMAR: It's not a block of flats
DS: Right. So it's like, is it like a terraced house?
OMAR: What's a terraced house?
DS: Right is it lots of houses together?
OMAR: No. No. No.
DC: Do you want to draw it on that? Draw it on that piece of paper
OMAR: I can't really tell you. It's like a, it's like a …
DC: Try
OMAR: It's like umm … it's like two, two floor house.
DS: Oh right.
OMAR: It's on two floors.
DS: Okay then.
OMAR: What's that one terrace?
DS: Right. No okay that's alright. Just two floor house. Does he live downstairs
           and upstairs or is there different people live upstairs?
OMAR: No. No. He lives upstairs.
DS: He lives upstairs. What, what colour is the front door? Is there anything you
           can tell me about this address that might help us identify it?
OMAR: I can't tell you. I'm not, I'm not very good at that.
DS: You're not very good at a lot of things but we must sort out now

We do learn that the property was about a five-minute car journey from a hospital, and then questions focused on the time of arrival and other parties who may have been present.

OMAR: Then afterwards some couple of faces came but I, I did not get to see.
DC: Is this in the evening or the morning, the following morning?
OMAR: I'm not sure now. No I think it's in the evening, yeah evening, I think.
DC: Did they stay the night?
OMAR: Not as far as I, 'cos I, I went to sleep straight away I was …
DC: Where did you sleep in the house?

OMAR: I slept in the sitting room.
DC: Where on the floor on the sofa?
OMAR: On the floor.
DC: Okay.
DS: Right okay then. So you said earlier that in the morning a couple of guys came and spoke to him, but you now think it might be the evening.
OMAR: I think it's in the, it's in the morn … it's morning, it's morning. It's morning.

Having settled on morning, and that the owner of the flat was the person responsible for running out of the Oval tube station, as shown in a photograph exhibit number JET/10, Omar was asked:

DS: JET/10 is Hassan, that's right. Okay. So you've, so you've slept there the night. You've woke up in the morning now I want you, this is where I need you to be as detailed as you can because we're trying to not only identify the people that are out there planning to kill people now, but we're also after information that might help us about the bombs.
OMAR: Lead, yeah lead to them.
DS: Yeah.
OMAR: Yes.
DS: So you woke up in the morning. From the beginning what happened?
OMAR: Got up. Done myself.
DS: Yeah
DS: Yeah.
OMAR: And then afterwards I didn't feel like eating that much
DS: Alright.
OMAR: And after [that] I just left isn't it?
DS: No, no, no, no, no, no. there's a lot before that …

Omar then mentioned that some guys arrived with some news.

DS: What guys? Who are these?
OMAR: I don't know, don't know.
DS: Have you ever seen them before?
OMAR: I won't tell you because you know when the person closes the door straight away, you can't tell can you …

Omar provided no description of the visitors and then he and Hassan left the property.

DS: What time did you leave?
OMAR: I left about, I'm not sure.
DS: Alright, no worries. So you left with him?
OMAR: I left with him and afterwards …
DS: In his car or walking?
OMAR: Yeah it's in his car.

Ds: Right.
OMAR: Then afterwards I was sleeping, I ...
DS: No, no, no, no, no, no. No. Don't jump forward because I'm trying to pin
          movements down with a view to catch these other people.

Shortly after this Omar explained that he got out of the car to get some drinks.

DS: Right.
OMAR: I got some drinks then I came back, then I fell asleep. And after that I don't
          know, when I woke up I don't know if, I don't know if it's me or it's the
          radio he was talking to someone. I don't know if he picked someone up
          or he didn't pick someone up.
DS: Look.
OMAR: Yeah.
DS: Yasin.
OMAR: I'm telling you.
DS: [In a raised voice] No you're not. You're not telling me the truth now.
          Alright. You're in the car, you go and get some drinks and then you're
          saying that you fell asleep and that it might have been the radio or he
          might have been talking to someone. Yasin we are trying to catch people
          that are intent on killing as many people as they can.

And a few sentences later, also in a raised voice:

DS: Don't tell me that you fell asleep in the car and that you don't know what
          happened. You're in the car, you go and get some drinks. You come back
          to the car. Where were you going, what happened then?
OMAR: I was going to Stockwell.

Such clarity did not persist for long.

DS: Right hold on, hold on. So he's driven, has he driven to Stockwell tube?
OMAR: Yes he's driven to Stockwell tube.
DS: Right and whereabouts did he park up?
OMAR: It's some, some corner way, some alleyway, some flat or some ... you know
          like, you know like them, I don't know them flats what they're called.
          Third, fourth floor something. And he just put my bag there ...

So, at the conclusion of two interviews, after 91 minutes of dialogue, little detail
had emerged. The officers were working well as a team and were content to ask a range
of open and direct questions to try to focus Omar's responses, but without success.
At times they challenged Omar's evasiveness and reticence, including interrupting
him to emphasize their point, and on occasions their raised voices revealed their
frustration and annoyance. Hardly the gladiatorial conflict portrayed by sections of
the media.

After a break of 20 minutes, the third interview commenced at 12.31 and finished
at 1.17 p.m., and there is a noticeable change in tactics by the officers after the opening
legal preliminaries. For 10 minutes one officer reminded Omar of his position and

the context – more than 50 people had been killed only two weeks earlier. He did not let Omar interrupt him, he reminded him of the evidence against him and he made a number of pleas for Omar to help the investigation. The range of tactics is interesting: appealing for help and the use of maximization – accusing him of attempting to engage in mass killing and reminding him that 'if convicted you will go to prison, for a substantial length of time'. This was followed by reassurance and an emphasis on when and how the courts might look favourably on anything he told the police. In the adversarial legal system this negotiation strategy might be considered legitimate by some, but others may consider it an inducement. What follows is an abridged version of the 10-minute section:

DC: I am not saying this to you in a threatening manner at all; I'm just explaining things [so] that you fully understand the circumstances. We're asking you these questions urgently, 'cos we're desperate to save peoples lives. We got three (3) other suicide bombers on the loose out there that we need to get, because its our job to save people lives and stop other people dying and to save their lives, ok

OMAR: Yeah

DC: We're desperate to help people, that's why this is so [with emphasis] important, you are the most important man in this police station, in this interview room, alright. You've a lot of responsibility on your shoulders. Now the evidence against you …

OMAR: … mmm …

DC: I suspect may eventually end up being substantial, at the moment we are in very early days of this investigation, ok. But there are various options that may happen to you. One of them is that you might be released because there's no evidence to suggest that you've done anything. That doesn't seems to be the case at the moment because we've already got you at Warren Street with an explosive device on your back.

OMAR: I don't have any explosive device

DC: [Reminds Omar of the evidence and continues] You have to realise what we're talking here is attempted mass murder, all the people in that tube would've been killed, we're talking about you attempting to kill several people. Now, some of the tube trains on the previous attack up to twenty (20) people plus died. We're talking about attempted mass murder here. Now, what may happen, and again I'm just putting you in the picture, it's not a threat, I'm just putting you in the picture, it's that it may eventually be the case, that you go to court …

OMAR: Yeah.

DC: … and all the evidence will be put before a court ok. And it may be that you will be charge[d] with offences relating to you attempting to kill a number of people. In my experience that if you are convicted, if you are convicted you will go to prison, for a substantial length of time. [The officer explains that they have not believed Omar up to now and continues] However, I've understand the position that you're in, ok. I want to make you fully aware that there are facilities and there is a system set up where you can provide us with information …

OMAR:	… mmm …
DC:	… you can tell us exactly what happened, you can tell us who the people are, and tell us more than what you're telling us now, and you can tell us the absolute truth, and stated cases in the past have said at court, but ultimately this would be the, up to the court system, the judicial system. Do you understand what I mean by that?
OMAR:	Yeah, yeah.
DC:	Ultimately, it would be up to them. However, the stated cases in the past have said, that if you're convicted and think about the evidence that is mounting against you, you would receive a substantial reduction in you sentence.
OMAR:	That's why I'm, that's why …
DC:	[Interrupting Omar he continues] It's very easy to keep saying that, I believe you no more. I think you, you do know more and I think that you're probably, a bit concerned, and you're bit frightened … [and he then reassures Omar that his solicitor will support all that he has said and culminates with] The courts will look upon anything you say very favourably, ok. You've got to start thinking about you now, 'cos eventually these other people will be arrested and I, and I hope and pray they are not found once they've killed themselves and or other people, I really do.

The other officer then reminded Omar of his position and started to minimize his involvement before making reference to a religious perspective and appealing to his self-worth and self-esteem:

DS:	Yassin what we are saying is that you are in it up to here, alright. The way that you can make it better for yourself is for us to be able to tell the court, the excerpts [he accepts] that went on, but the fact to the matter is that nobody was killed, because of what he did, 'cos it didn't work. But what he has done is he's helped the police catch the other people that are out there, that the whole country are worried that they are out there, planning and doing, to do another one. And this time it might work, yeah. So, the court will think, ok then this guy did try and do it but he didn't, as it happened it didn't work, he didn't kill anyone, he didn't murder anyone, but fair play to his credit he did at least give the police information that led them to arrest these other people, and all the people involved in it.
OMAR:	Yeah
DS:	Yeah
OMAR:	Yeah
DS:	Now, I know as you do that in your rucksack was a device, lets call it device, was a bomb. I know, I'm fairly sure that there were wires coming from that device that you had to touch together to set it off. I know, or I'm convinced that you touched those wires, it went bang, but it didn't go a big bang. The consequences of that are, you're still here. My God Allah has decided … That this wasn't the time for you to die. So, maybe he's saying to you this is your chance to be a man of worth for the rest of man, and helped [help] find these other people, to stop them doing what you tried to do last week. For that [a]side, you understand what we're saying about the court?

OMAR: Yes, I know, I understand

The culmination of this alternative approach was for the DS to ask about the plan:

DS: Four (4) of you went out and about the same time, there were four (4) pops,
       they never went off. What was the plan?
OMAR: I don't know about any plan.
DS: [In a raised voice] Don't, don't say that Yassin, you didn't know about any
       plan.

To the chagrin of the officers, Omar returned to his obfuscating responses and he continued when further subjects such as detonation wires in his rucksack were covered, which led the DS to exclaim, ' ... right this is rubbish and I'm not here for that'.

What followed was a series of questions surrounding a review of videotape evidence of a number of suspects, including Omar, entering the Oval underground station within seconds of one another. The officers pointed to this joint approach as evidence of planning and a conspiracy to bomb the underground system but Omar remained vague and non-committal in all his answers.

DS: Right ok then, do you think it might've been you just going through there at
       twelve twenty-three, sixteen (12.23.16)
OMAR: I don't know, I'm not sure

Throughout this video sequence the officers failed to obtain any positive information, and at one point Omar said, 'You will be, it will be used against me.' This was not the first time that Omar indicated that he was concerned about what would be used against him. This is an interesting point, as this interview started with a change of tactics specifically aimed at addressing this point – but had there been a new strategy authorized by the SIO or had the officers used the intervening period between interviews 2 and 3 to realign their tactics without reference to others?

If their intention was to outline that the court would look favourably on him if he assisted the police, did they go far enough with this tactic to reassure him? We can return to this discussion in due course as the third interview culminated with a considerable amount of footage of the Underground stations and included some where panic-stricken passengers could be seen leaving the Underground alongside the terrorist suspects. Indeed, as the officers showed a moving image of Hassan (the owner of the flat), Omar continued to prevaricate – 'let me just see that picture ... '; ' ... because the picture looks different isn't it'; 'I'm not sure, ... ' – and this section culminated with:

OMAR: From what I understand, I heard, didn't the police not surround him or
       something?
DC: Don't worry about ...
DS: That's why we trying to catch him now
OMAR: But why did the police ...
DS: [A very irritated DS] It doesn't matter why, he got away, and he was going to
       kill people, the same as yourself.

A lengthy silence followed. The officer had voiced his frustration at yet another diversionary attempt by Omar to avoid questions on the identity of others by asking general questions about police activity. The third interview finished with the officers still inquiring about the identity and addresses of other suspects.

The fourth interview took place from 1.35 to 2.20 p.m., a total of 45 minutes, and it started some 17 minutes after the finish of the previous tape. Early on, we hear Omar declaring:

> OMAR: John earlier, I would've said, 'No I want my lawyer'. But since he said to me this people, they are Muslim people involved, Christian, this, this, that and I've lived here and you know people are, even in here people have showed me kindness, so I don't want to be hard hearted, so I'm trying to help as much as possible, and that's, that's what I want to do, 'Cos I think I don't have, I don't have, if I had something to hide then I would, but I don't have. I want to help you, so that's why I'm corporating all the way ...

Unfortunately, Omar returned to his obfuscating and opaque responses in relation to a range of subjects, including additional suspects and addresses and peroxide containers at his flat but no details are forthcoming. The final three-minute interview took place in the presence of a solicitor but no new information was obtained.

Discussion

Returning to the review of CT police interviewing styles (see Table 3.1), we saw that 'use of evidence', which covered the production of exhibits, photographs and other materials, was the most popular tactic identified, but it tended to occur in a rather sterile and perfunctory atmosphere. The absence of a probing and challenging questioning regime in comparison with other criminal cases was unexpected, and it may be mitigated to some degree by the fact that a number of arrests in terrorist cases are made to preserve life and maintain public safety, with suspects often arrested before there is time to gather sufficient evidence against them, and this has consequences for the interviewing officers who have little or no credible evidence to put to them. But this could not account for all the cases reviewed, and officers were often content to receive partial information from the suspects – partial names and addresses, and non-specific locations – and these were not followed up with a second phase of questioning.

Further examination showed that there was little or no variation introduced by the officers. There were no checks and no intrusive questions were asked – no subtle references to test the depth and veracity of the information. The interview process was often a support mechanism for the officers and a stress-free episode for the detainee. I found little evidence of any exposition of the many tactics and strategies advocated within the relevant police and psychological literature (Gudjonsson, 2003;

Pearse, 2009). This was somewhat unexpected, as persons detained and interviewed by the police for criminal or terrorist offences are, according to Home Office literature, likely to be subject to a regime of particularly probing questions. For example, in the codes of practice that accompany the Police and Criminal Evidence Act (PACE) 1984 (Home Office, 2014), both Code C (which deals with criminal cases) and section H (which deals with terrorist cases) state with regard to the question of fitness to be interviewed:

> In assessing whether the detainee should be interviewed, the following must be considered:

> (c) How the nature of the interview, which could include particularly probing questions, might affect the detainee. (Code C, Annex G, p. 72; Code H, Annex G, p. 60)

The absence of challenges again highlights the issue first raised by the author in the mid-1990s (Pearse & Gudjonsson, 1996) and endorsed more recently by other authorities in this field (Shaw, 2012). The timing of this study of terrorist cases may be relevant as, unlike the earlier research, it took place sometime after the national police training package in investigative interviewing (PEACE) had been delivered to all police officers, but the skills necessary to engage and challenge and to probe responses had not featured as part of that training.

The absence of any form of intrusive questioning was responsible for my summary that, in this CT study, interviews with terrorist suspects could best be described as 'Polite, non-threatening and often non-productive' (Pearse, 2006, p. 12). This view was endorsed by Lord Carlile who noted that 'in terms of interview product there is little or none' (Carlile, 2005, p. 38). As a result of the findings of this research, the author designed and delivered to serving officers throughout the UK a specialist counter-terrorism interviewing training course that addressed many of the issues identified.

In the hypothetical ticking bomb scenario (see Table 3.2) we do see an increase in suggested tactics and a whole range are listed that include the use of challenges and coercive and manipulative methods in a case where the officers have been told that the terrorist has actually planted a bomb in a public place, although given the methodological considerations perhaps the best measure of this scenario lies in a comparison with the genuine ticking bomb interview with Omar.

In terms of the officers' performance the author detected a number of different stages to the interview. In the first instance, the sergeant asks the majority of the questions and does so in a fast and forthright manner. His colleague interjects with exhibit details and seeks some clarification while allowing the sergeant to engage in a range of challenging tactics and leading and closed questions. Later on the constable makes an appeal to Omar in the light of the evidence against him, and introduces an opportunity for sentence reduction if Omar will assist the police; but, as we shall discuss, this is very disjointed and lacks clarity. The officers are not impressed with the elusive and evasive nature of the answers they are getting. This leads to raised voices from one of the officers, and his annoyance can be detected. At times both officers ask questions one after the other before Omar can respond, and they have a tendency to use closed alternative questions, for example, 'Where on the floor on the sofa?'; 'In his car or walking?'; or 'Is he 20 is he 30?'

This represents a brief critical appraisal but overall this was not an oppressive interview, especially in light of the context and climate of the occasion. The officers wanted specific and detailed information from Omar in relation to the location and identity of other bombers and bomb-making equipment, and this was not forthcoming. There are a number of legal issues that could be addressed, such as the nature of the cautions given and the focus by the officers on general aspects of the offence, but, to gain a deeper insight into this interaction, it is important to examine the replies given by Omar and the extent to which the officers picked up the emerging themes. Quite early on Omar said:

> I don't mind saying anything to you but what it is is I don't want to say anything which is gonna make things worse for me. Because if I'm, if I giving you … '

Unfortunately the officer interrupted and pressed him for more information about the other bombers. On other occasions Omar made reference to this same point – will answering the questions make matters worse for him and will what he says be used against him? In the third interview, one of the officers actually starts the interview with an appeal to Omar to think about how the courts will respond if he provides accurate information – but the dialogue is vague, lengthy and non-specific; it is wrapped up in tactics designed to maximize his anxiety and it only hints at what a court might or could do. For example:

> I am not saying this to you in a threatening manner at all …

> … what we're talking here is attempted mass murder, all the people in that tube would've been killed, we're talking about you attempting to kill several people. Now, some of the tube trains on the previous attack up to twenty (20) people plus died. We're talking about attempted mass murder here. Now, what may happen, and again I'm just putting you in the picture, it's not a threat …

The notion of 'threat' was aligned with references designed to reinforce the serious nature of the case. Yet this was an incredibly important stage: here was a failed suicide bomber asking for information about the implications for him if he revealed the whereabouts of the other bombers – in basic negotiation or bargaining parlance, what was in it for him? Eventually the officer mentioned 'stated cases', 'court system' and finally, after almost 10 minutes, 'you would receive a substantial reduction in you sentence'. Why did it take so long to make a straightforward offer? From the moment Omar became a wanted man, up to the point of arrest and thereafter on his trip to the police station and while detained prior to interview, the subject of negotiation, compromise, offering something in exchange for a concession was very likely to be at the forefront of his thoughts. It is accepted that, in a very small minority of failed suicide bomber cases, the bombers' religious and ideological belief system is so strong that they will not even speak to the authority figures, but the experience in the Middle East and elsewhere is that the vast majority of them will enter into a dialogue.

We do not know in this case if there was a strategic direction from the SIO or if the officers took it on themselves to broach the subject of sentence reduction in the manner they did. What is clear is that it was left unresolved and that a crucial bargaining opportunity was missed. We will see in Chapter 4 by Max Hill, QC, that it is perfectly acceptable for the SIO to grant limited immunity by instructing the interviewing officers that, as he puts it, 'tell us where the bomb is, and we wont use your answer against you'.

The officers' hesitant approach suggests that they were concerned about being seen to offer an inducement, or was it perhaps a systemic issue, something frowned on by the prosecution system in the UK? It is a well-used prosecution tactic in other jurisdictions but appears to be rarely exploited in the UK. In the United States the prosecuting attorney is an integral part of the investigation process and, from a very early stage, is ready to negotiate with the individual concerning immunity from prosecution or sentence reduction in what is known as a 'proffer agreement'. It is a frequently used provision that has become very well established in the criminal process to the extent that many such deals are instigated at the behest of defence counsel. It is ingrained in the psyche of the investigators and represents a major part of the investigation and prosecution process (US Attorney P. J. Fitzgerald, pers. comm., 2005).

In the UK offers of immunity are covered by section 71 of the Serious Organised Crime and Police Act 2005 which became law in April 2006 but the best estimate to date is that the number of written notices can be measured in single figures. In truth, both procedures require a written notice and agreement between the parties and are therefore intrinsically lengthy, but the principle of such arrangements has been fully accepted within the US legal framework and less so by their UK counterparts.

In public safety cases in the UK, however, there is no need for conferences between legal counsel and written agreements, as guidelines have been in place since 1981 (Crown Prosecution Service, 2012) that allow interviewing officers to make a clear and unambiguous offer, and this has been reinforced by the recent Court of Appeal judgment outlined in Chapter 4 by Max Hill, QC. What we can say is that, on those occasions when the subject was raised by Omar, the officers may not have heard his request but they failed to address the issue and, when they did introduce it, it was lost in a plethora of assorted tactics that served to confuse rather than provide clarity. Opportunities were lost to collaborate, negotiate or compromise in the most crucial of police interviews, the ticking bomb scenario.

Is this reluctance to get straight to the point by the officers the result of a lack of awareness or of training? Currently, the management of and preparedness for ticking bomb scenarios is not addressed in the national police training course and the opportunity to collaborate and compromise with a suspect in the unique setting of an urgent public safety interview needs to be addressed. It would appear to the author that the C in PEACE needs to be more extensively researched and fully explored because it is at this juncture that the real issues and soul of this very social interaction – challenge, collaboration and compromise – are to be found.

The introduction of PEACE as a training vehicle has succeeded in refocusing the direction of all police interviews away from a confession-based approach towards a more ethical information-gathering style. The PEACE concept has been introduced in a number of other countries, but in purely Darwinian terms it is imperative that the underlying philosophy and practice continue to evolve and adapt to an ever-changing environment. Supporting infrastructure has been introduced for management and administrative purposes but there has been little adaptation or variation of the model itself. (One recent exception appears to be the Garda Síochána Interview Model, as outlined in Chapter 6 by Geraldine Noone.)

Conclusion

The finding from the CT research which identified the lack of intrusive and probing questioning on the part of police officers interviewing terrorist suspects, their inability to respond to a changing environment and their remaining content to accept answers without reservation or without challenge is of some concern. The first national CT interviewing course was designed and delivered by the author to address these and other culture-related issues and to provide the interviewing officers with the knowledge, skills and confidence to be flexible and spontaneous and, where necessary, to engage in 'particularly probing questions'.

In public safety cases the concept of compromise, collaboration and negotiation needs to become a recognized tactic and an accepted part of the investigation and prosecution process. It was not mentioned by the CT officers in their survey, but the author would argue that, had the interviewing officers in the Omar case been aware of the strength of the legal support that would have allowed them to offer immunity, the proposition could have been made at a very early stage and in simple and straightforward terms – 'tell us where the bomb is and we wont use your answer against you' – and it is likely such a forthright declaration would have shifted the dynamics of the exchange. In future ticking bomb or life-at-risk scenarios, interviewing officers under the proper direction of their SIO need to be fully aware of this legitimate bargaining tactic.

References

Bimmerle, G. (1993). 'Truth' drugs in interrogation. Center for the Study of Intelligence, Central Intelligence Agency. Retrieved 28 May 2014 from https://www.cia.gov/library/center-for-the-study-of-intelligence/kent-csi/vol5no2/html/v05i2a09p_0001.htm

Carlile, A. (2005). *Report on the operation in 2004 of the Terrorism Act 2000*. London: Stationery Office. Retrieved 21 May 2014 from http://www.schedule7.org.uk/wp-content/uploads/2014/01/2004_Carl.pdf

Clarke, C., & Milne, R. (2001). *National evaluation of the PEACE investigative interviewing course*. Police Research Award Scheme Report No. PRAS/149. Institute of Criminal Justice Studies, University of Portsmouth.

Crown Prosecution Service. (2012). *Queen's evidence: Immunities, undertakings and agreements under the Serious Organised Crime and Police Act 2005*. Retrieved 21 May 2014 from http://www.cps.gov.uk/legal/p_to_r/queen_s_evidence_-_immunities _undertakings_and_agreements_under_the_serious_organised_crime_and_police _act_2005/index.html

Griffiths, A., & Milne, R. (2006). Will it all end in tiers? Police interviews with suspects in Britain. In T. Williamson (Ed.), *Investigative interviewing: Rights, research, regulation* (pp. 167–189). Cullompton, UK: Willan.

Gudjonsson, G. H. (2003). *The psychology of interrogations and confessions: A handbook*. Chichester, UK: Wiley.

Gudjonsson, G. H., & Pearse, J. (2011). Suspect interviews and false confessions. *Current Directions in Psychological Science, 20*(1), 33–37.

Hawkins, N. (2012). Interviewing: The prosecution perspective. *Investigator, 2*, 31–33. Retrieved 21 May 2014 from http://www.the-investigator.co.uk/files/The_Investigator _-_Issue_2_2012.pdf

Home Office. (2014). *Police and Criminal Evidence Act, 1984 Codes of Practice* (rev. ed.). London: HMSO. Retrieved 25 July 2014 from https://www.gov.uk/government /collections/police-and-criminal-evidence-act-1984-pace-current-versions

Pearse, J. J. (1997). *Police interviewing: An examination of some of the psychological, interrogative and background factors that are associated with a suspect's confession*. Doctoral thesis, University of London.

Pearse, J., & Gudjonsson, G. H. (1996). Police interviewing techniques at two South London police stations. *Psychology, Crime and Law, 3*, 63–74.

Pearse, J., & Gudjonsson, G. H. (1999). Measuring influential police interviewing tactics: A factor analytical approach. *Legal and Criminological Psychology, 4*, 221–238.

Pearse, J. (2006). *The effectiveness of police interviews with terrorist suspects*. Restricted report. London: Metropolitan Police Service.

Pearse, J. (2009). The investigation of terrorist offences in the United Kingdom: The context and climate for interviewing officers. In R. Bull, T. Valentine, & T. Williamson (Eds.), *Handbook of psychology of investigative interviewing* (pp. 69–90). Chichester, UK: Wiley-Blackwell.

Pearse, J. (2011). Interrogation tactics and terrorist suspects: A categorisation process. In A. Silke (Ed.), *The psychology of counter-terrorism* (pp. 135–151). London: Routledge.

Shaw, G. (2012). Challenging task. *Investigator, 2*, 56–61. Retrieved 21 May 2014 from http://www.the-investigator.co.uk/files/The_Investigator_-_Issue_2_2012.pdf

Williamson, T. M. (1993). From interrogation to investigative interviewing: Strategic trends in the police questioning. *Journal of Community and Applied Social Psychology, 3*, 89–99.

Williamson, T. M. (1994). Reflections on current police practice. In D. Morgan and G. Stephenson (Eds.), *Suspicion and silence: The rights of silence in criminal investigations* (pp. 107–116). London: Blackstone.

Williamson, T. M. (2006). Towards greater professionalism: Minimizing miscarriages of justice. In T. Williamson (Ed.), *Investigative interviewing: Rights, research, regulation* (pp. 147–166). Cullompton, UK: Willan.

Legal Case

R v. Ibrahim and others [2008] 2 Cr App R 23

4

Urgent Interviews and the Concept of Oppression in Terrorist Cases

Max Hill, QC

The law in this country has long recognized the right of suspects to communicate with a lawyer, and thereby not to be held incommunicado. For the past three decades, this right has been enshrined in section 58 of the Police and Criminal Evidence Act 1984 (PACE). The suspect's cherished ability to 'make a phone call' to a solicitor from a police station is rarely subject to interference. There are, however, exceptions and this chapter will examine such cases in the context of terrorist investigations.

Although not unique to terrorist cases, the use of urgent interviews (otherwise known as public safety interviews) is a singular feature of police investigations into suspected terrorist offences in the United Kingdom. The events of 21 July 2005, when five failed suicide bombers ran loose in London, provide an opportunity to examine in some detail the imperatives of the police investigation in this hazardous 'ticking bomb scenario', where time is of the essence and public safety paramount.

This chapter is intended to introduce and analyse the concept of urgent interviews, and to consider the subsequent use of such interviews in later court proceedings. Recent challenges to the admissibility of urgent interviews by the defence will be considered, as will the potential for excluding such interviews.

Authorizing Urgent Interviews and Delaying Access to Legal Advice

Public safety: The background to authorization

Public safety considerations apply to terrorism cases with greater frequency than any other area of criminal investigation. Where the grounds for an urgent interview are made out, which is the exclusive responsibility of the senior investigating officer (SIO), the situation is serious indeed.

Investigating Terrorism: Current Political, Legal and Psychological Issues, First Edition. Edited by John Pearse.
© 2015 John Wiley & Sons, Ltd. Published 2015 by John Wiley & Sons, Ltd.

Consider the atmosphere in London in the days immediately following the carnage of 7 July 2005 (7/7), when 52 innocent commuters lost their lives, and the near calamity 14 days later (21/7), when four (out of five) bombers detonated powerful improvised explosive devices on public transport and came within a heartbeat of repeating 7/7, thwarted only by technical failure between initiation of the detonators and the main charge. Consider the words, recorded in a written statement produced at trial, of the SIO in that case (Detective Superintendent Doug McKenna) as he reviewed the state of affairs after 21/7 but before all the bombers had been found:

> My overriding priority was public safety ... The net effect ... was that the need to identify and locate all those involved in the events of 21/7 was the overriding priority of the investigation. There existed a very real fear that another attack could be mounted, either by those who had carried out the attacks on 21/7, or others ... I directed that (a further) interview be conducted to comprehensively exhaust the potential of obtaining information, which could lead to averting the potential harm to the public. (Transcript of officer's evidence)

Moreover, consider the words of the Court of Appeal in giving judgment in April 2008, dismissing the appeals of the four men convicted of conspiring to murder commuters on 21 July:

> Without minimising the personal impact on those who were using the transport system at the time when the bombs were detonated, it is sufficient for present purposes to note that all five men made their escapes. They were then at large for some days. It is virtually impossible to imagine the pressure and concerns which must have been felt by the police investigating teams. Two weeks earlier four bombs had been successfully detonated with the dreadful consequences with which we are familiar, and they were now faced with four more bombs, again in the transport system, which had been detonated, but failed to explode. The bombers involved on 7th July had perished, but the perpetrators of the second intended atrocity were at large, free to repeat their murderous plans, and to do so more effectively. They had to be found and detained, and the immediate objective of the investigation, including interviews of those arrested in connection with these incidents, was directed to public safety. (*R v. Ibrahim and others* [2008] 2 Cr App R 23 at para. 5)

The burden placed on investigating officers is surely difficult to overstate: on the one hand, the need to protect and preserve the ordinary rights of a detained suspect, and, on the other, the need for information which might directly impact on the safety of the general public, in the hunt for bombs and bombers. As the Court of Appeal put it, 'they had to be found'.

The legislative framework

The statutory framework for the conduct of urgent interviews with detained persons (hereafter suspects) is to be found in the Police and Criminal Evidence Act 1984 (PACE) and the Terrorism Act 2000 (TACT).

Section 58 of PACE entitles a suspect to legal advice through consultation with a solicitor on request; this entitlement can be delayed only on the authorization of a senior officer on reasonable grounds. This is the basic regime applicable to all suspects not held under the terrorism legislation and, by design, the decision to delay access should be taken only in a limited number of circumstances. It should be remembered that PACE, which came into force in January 1986, was designed to modernize the investigation of crime and to legislate for the detention and treatment of suspects. Prior to PACE, access to a solicitor could best be described as haphazard. Thus, after much public consultation, the right to legal advice was enshrined in primary legislation and crucially, under section 59, a national duty solicitor scheme was established in order that suspects could have such advice and that it was free.

For those who are detained on suspicion of terrorist offences, the entitlement to legal advice is encapsulated in Schedule 8 to TACT. As with the ordinary provisions of PACE, a senior officer (superintendent or above) may authorize delay to such entitlement in circumstances set out in the legislation and articulated in a series of accompanying codes of practice. Code H to PACE, for example, is concerned with the detention, treatment and questioning of suspects related to terrorism in police custody by police officers. Code H is heavily influenced by the general provisions of Code C, which relates to suspects detained for non-terrorist offences, but provides further powers and guidance to senior officers as to the circumstances in which legal advice may be delayed in terrorist cases, including where urgent interviews are conducted with the suspect during that delay.

Schedule 8 to TACT, at Part I, paragraph 8(4), allows for a delay in access to legal advice where a senior officer has reasonable grounds for believing that one of the following consequences will result:

(a) interference with or harm to evidence of a serious arrestable offence,
(b) interference with or physical injury to any person,
(c) the alerting of persons who are suspected of having committed a serious offence but who have not been arrested for it,
(d) the hindering of the recovery of property obtained as a result of a serious offence or in respect of which a forfeiture order could be made under section 23,
(e) interference with the gathering of information about the commission, preparation or instigation of acts of terrorism,
(f) the alerting of a person and [sic] thereby making it more difficult to prevent an act of terrorism,
(g) the alerting of a person and [sic] thereby making it more difficult to secure a person's apprehension, prosecution or conviction in connection with the commission, preparation or instigation of an act of terrorism. (Terrorism Act, 2000[1])

PACE Code H came into force on 25 July 2006. It applies only to suspects detained under section 41 and Schedule 8 to TACT, that is, suspects arrested where there are reasonable grounds for suspecting that they are 'terrorists' within the meaning of section 40 of TACT, and provides guidance as to when 'the exercise of the right of access to legal advice may be delayed exceptionally only as in Annex B' (Code

H, para. 6.4). Annex B provides for an officer of superintendent rank or above to sanction such delay where that officer has reasonable grounds for believing that the exercise of the right to legal advice will have one of the consequences set out in Schedule 8 (see above).

According to Code H, paragraph 6, the delay may be only for as long as necessary, and in any event not beyond 48 hours from the time of arrest. In all cases a suspect must be allowed to consult a solicitor for a reasonable time prior to any court hearing (Code H, Annex B, para. 7).

Urgent interviews in practice

By applying all of the above, senior officers engaged in terrorist investigations have the power to order urgent interviews with suspects. The result is that officers can be tasked at very short notice to conduct one or more interviews with a suspect who has requested access to a solicitor but who has not been afforded access to any independent legal advice before or during the urgent interviews. The statutory regime requires that investigating officers or SIOs can authorize such interviews only with reasonable grounds. It is not a requirement that those officers tasked to conduct the urgent interviews play any part in the authorization process, nor that they have undertaken the process of formulating reasonable grounds for so acting. Authorization is the duty and sole responsibility of the SIO. Execution of the task, in other words conduct of the duly authorized interviews, is the duty of the officers so tasked. It follows that best practice dictates the need for clarity and transparency whenever there is an authorization. SIOs, who may be remote from the police station in which the suspect is held and therefore without access to the detention record of the suspect (custody record), need to ensure that rigorous attention is given to record-keeping, which must include effective communication with the nominated officer at the station responsible for the welfare and detention of the suspect (custody officer).

Using urgent interviews in evidence: The legal background

The issue of delaying access to legal advice, and the question of whether a court or jury should be permitted to hear evidence of an interview conducted while access to legal advice has been delayed, have both been considered on many occasions by the courts. This is not a 'terrorism only' arena.

Before reviewing some of the legal cases, both domestic and international, a few words are necessary about the 'adverse inference' regime. Generally speaking, suspects are cautioned on arrest, and again at the time of interview, to the effect that anything they say may be used against them in subsequent proceedings. Moreover, silence at interview may be the subject of an adverse inference whereby a later jury is invited to consider why the suspect did not mention when questioned any fact or matter on which he or she later relies at trial. So silence in interview can be used to bolster other evidence tending to demonstrate guilt. (See also Chapter 5 by Peter Carter on this point.)

However, where interviews are conducted without access to legal advice, the general situation ceases to apply, and the suspect cannot be criticized for silence. It is an important safeguard, but of little help to the suspect who does talk during interview and who may find that compromising answers are then used in evidence. In *R v. Samuel* (1988) QB 615 the Court of Appeal was asked to consider a case in which legal advice had been delayed pursuant to section 58 of PACE; in the course of his judgment Hodgson J referred to the right to obtain legal advice as 'perhaps the most important right given … to a person detained by the police'.

The attaching of great importance to the right to legal advice has been echoed by the European Court of Human Rights (ECHR) in a number of cases involving suspects arrested under the terrorism legislation of Northern Ireland. The jurisprudence of the ECHR bears on the courts and legal framework of the United Kingdom, and as such it is worth considering a few cases very briefly, by way of background to the system to which terrorist cases in the UK are now subject.

In *Murray v. United Kingdom* (1996) 22 EHRR 29 at paragraph 63 the ECHR said this:

> National laws may attach consequences to the attitude of an accused at the initial stages of police interrogation which are decisive for the prospects of the defence in any subsequent criminal proceedings. In such circumstances Article 6 (the right to a fair trial) will normally require that the accused be allowed to benefit from the assistance of a lawyer already at the initial stages of police interrogation. However, this right, which is not explicitly set out in the Convention, may be subject to restrictions for good cause. The question, in each case, is whether the restriction, in the light of the entirety of the proceedings, has deprived the accused of a fair hearing.

Murray was arrested in January 1990 under the prevention of terrorism legislation then in force in Northern Ireland. He requested to consult a solicitor but was denied legal advice for 48 hours (in accordance with the applicable legislation), during which time he was interviewed under caution, being informed that adverse inferences could be drawn from a failure to answer questions. He remained silent throughout those interviews. He was later permitted to consult a solicitor, although that solicitor was not present during subsequent interviews, and thereafter he indicated that he had been advised not to answer questions. At his trial the judge drew adverse inferences against Murray for his failure to answer questions. The ECHR found no breach of Article 6(1) of the Convention in the drawing of adverse inferences per se, but did find that 'Having regard to the very strong inferences which the trial judge drew … the decision to deny [Murray] access to a solicitor unfairly prejudiced the rights of the defence and rendered the proceedings against him unfair'.

In *Magee v. United Kingdom* application no. 28135/95 (Judgment 6/9/2000), the applicant had similarly been denied access to legal advice, having been arrested pursuant to anti-terrorism legislation, but Magee confessed during the period when legal advice was delayed, and the prosecution case at his trial rested largely on these admissions. Although the trial court did not draw adverse inferences from Magee's silence prior to his confession, the ECHR nonetheless found that his Article 6 rights had been breached. Although in this particular case the court found that Magee had been held in 'psychologically coercive' conditions and in an atmosphere 'designed to sap his will and make him confess to his interrogators', it nonetheless stated the following at paragraph 45:

> It is true that the domestic court found in the facts that the applicant had not been ill-treated and that the confession which was obtained from the applicant had been voluntary. The Court does not dispute that finding. At the same time, it has to be noted that the applicant was deprived of legal assistance for over forty-eight hours and the incriminating statements which he made at the end of the first twenty-four hours of his detention became the central platform of the prosecution's case against him and the basis for his conviction.

Averill v. United Kingdom application no. 36408/97 (Judgment 6/9/2000), decided on the same day as *Magee*, again concerned a suspect arrested under anti-terrorism provisions in Northern Ireland (albeit that, by the time his case was heard at the ECHR, the applicant Averill had escaped prison and was unlawfully at large). Averill remained silent throughout 37 interviews carried out over five days; his access to legal advice was delayed for the first 24 hours. At trial the case against him was based on forensic evidence; he gave evidence and called alibi witnesses. The judge drew a 'very strong adverse inference' against the applicant in respect of his silence during interview. The Court found no violation of Convention rights per se in the delaying of access to legal advice, but it did find such a violation as the result of the adverse inference later drawn against Averill at his trial, in respect of a time when he had been denied access to a lawyer.

In summary then, the jurisprudence of the ECHR by the turn of this century seems clear: delaying of access to legal advice may be carried out in accordance with a suspect's rights, but these will be violated if adverse inferences are permitted from the suspect's silence in interview at a time prior to the receipt of legal advice. The decision in *Magee* also allows for the possibility that a suspect who makes admissions at a time when he has been denied access to legal advice may later be able to argue successfully that such admissions should not be admitted as evidence at his trial, particularly where they are central to the case against him, although it must be noted that the harsh conditions in which Magee was held and questioned seem to have had a significant bearing on the findings of the ECHR.

Before leaving this topic, however, there is a further and more recent strand of case law, European and domestic, which requires careful scrutiny. The ECHR in *Salduz v. Turkey* (2009) 49 EHRR 19 held that denial of access to a lawyer, even when justified through compelling reasons, must not unduly prejudice the defendant's Article 6 rights. This decision was approved and maintained in *Gafgen v. Germany* (2011) 52 EHRR 1. The UK Supreme Court considered *Salduz* in the context of the Criminal

Procedure (Scotland) Act 1995 in *Cadder v. HM Advocate* (2010) UKSC 43. Lord Hope, in a speech with which all other members of the court agreed, held that the effect of *Salduz* in Scotland was that

> section 14 of the 1995 Act should be read and given effect so as to preclude the admission in evidence of any incriminating answers obtained by the police from a detainee who was subjected to questioning without access to legal advice. As a general rule, such evidence was inadmissible.

The potential consequences of *Cadder* have been considered in cases which have reached the UKSC since, namely *Ambrose v. Harris (Procurator Fiscal Oban)*; *Her Majesty's Advocate v. G* [2011] 1 WLR 2435, SC; *Her Majesty's Advocate v. M*; and *Her Majesty's Advocate v. P* [2011] 1 WLR 2497, SC. These cases were decided in October 2011, and reached different conclusions as to whether evidence obtained in response to police questioning without access to legal advice was compatible with the Article 6 fair trial guarantee, according to the individual circumstances of each case. The UKSC therefore found no absolute rule that questioning an accused without access to a lawyer violates defendants' rights. They also determined that the rule in *Cadder* does not necessarily apply to exclude answers to questions put to suspects during searches of premises.

These are recent cases. It still remains to be seen whether the principle enunciated in *Salduz* and applied to Scottish cases by *Cadder* will be applied in England and Wales. The statutory basis for restricting the right of access to legal advice is different. It may be argued that the principles are the same. We shall have to wait and see whether, and when, these arguments are deployed in a PACE or TACT terrorism case.

Adverse Inferences in Practice Code H

In light of the case law, Code H recognizes that because urgent interviews are conducted only in exceptional circumstances, namely where public safety considerations apply and where those considerations are such as to justify denial of the normal right of access to a solicitor, the ramifications of such interviews must differ from the general regime applicable to non-urgent interviews.

Specifically, Annex C to Code H (mirroring the non-terrorist suspects: Code C, Annex B at C15) provides: 'When a suspect detained at a police station is interviewed during any period for which access to legal advice has been delayed … the court or a jury may not draw any adverse inferences from their silence.' The general regime under sections 34, 36 and 37 of the Youth Justice and Criminal Evidence Act 1999 (adverse inferences) falls away, because the suspect is interviewed without access to a solicitor. It follows that, where a suspect is subject to urgent interview and where he or she exercises the right to silence when questioned, no subsequent use can be made of such silence.

Old-Style Caution

It follows also that the so-called old-style caution, which makes no reference to adverse inferences, applies to urgent interviews: 'You do not have to say anything, but anything you do say may be given in evidence', and interviewing officers should take care to administer the correct caution. This means that a suspect who chooses to answer questions during urgent interviews already knows that those answers may be given in evidence. Whereas silence during urgent interviews cannot permit adverse inferences, answers which are less than truthful *can* be used against the suspect.

It seems to me that the draughtsmen of the relevant legislation clearly contemplated that urgent interviews might be introduced in evidence at any later trial which the suspect may face. If this were not so, one might ask why bother with any caution at the outset of such interviews? If the purpose of these interviews is nothing more than gathering information to protect the public interest, no formal caution would be necessary.

Public Policy Considerations

The view expressed above is not universally accepted. For a recent example, we can consider the conclusion reached by Mr Justice Fulford in ruling on the admissibility of urgent interviews conducted with three of the 21/7 bombers convicted at Woolwich Crown Court in July 2007 (at para. 169 of the Ruling given 27 February 2007):

> It was suggested in argument that safety interviews should never be introduced in evidence before the jury for reasons of public policy. The argument presented is that if it became known that cooperation by a suspect to save death, injury or serious damage to property could lead to the introduction of his statements – made for that purpose – into the trial, that would operate as a material disincentive to future suspects to assist in this way ... For my part, it is for the police alone in these circumstances to decide whether or not to offer a suspect an undertaking that anything they say will not be used in evidence. If they wish to offer that high level of protection to the interviewee, that is their choice. Here they cautioned each of the three defendants that anything they said may be given in evidence and there are no public policy reasons for preventing the prosecution from giving this evidence to the jury. (*R v. Ibrahim and others* [2008] EWCA Crim 880 at para. 35)

Fulford J's words have now been scrutinized by the Court of Appeal, before whom all of the 21/7 bombers appealed their convictions and their sentences (life imprisonment with a minimum recommendation of 40 years in each case). In giving their judgment, in which all of the appeals against conviction and sentence were dismissed, the court said this:

The circumstances in which it is directed by a senior police officer that safety interviews should take place are operational, in short, how best, in a situation of immediate urgency, to secure public safety. The pursuit of this objective with a suspect who is invited to provide the police with relevant information may produce crucial evidence incriminating him in the offence for which he has been detained or indeed other offences. The admission of the safety interviews or their fruits, in evidence at a subsequent trial is subject to the ordinary principles governing a fair trial, and the over-arching provisions in section 78 of The Police and Criminal Evidence Act 1984 (PACE). Much would turn on the nature of the warning or caution, if any, given by the police to the suspect. Thus, for example, if the suspect were to be assured in terms that any information provided by him would not be used against him, that would provide a powerful argument against the admission of incriminating evidence obtained in consequence. Much, too, may turn on whether the interviews produce evidence directly relevant to the charge which led to the suspect's original detention, or whether the first connection that the prosecution may establish against him with any offence arises directly from his full co-operation with them during the course of the safety interview. As ever, these will be fact specific decisions, to be made in the overall circumstances of each individual case. What however is clear is that the legislative structure does not preclude the use of the evidence obtained in safety interviews and, given the existing safeguards available to a defendant and the obligation on the trial judge to make the judgment necessary to enable him to exercise his discretion under section 78 of PACE, it would be wholly inappropriate for this court to impose the kind of self-denying ordinance which the (appellants') submission based on public policy grounds would require. ([2008] 2 Cr App R 23 at para. 36)

As well as providing clarity on the law, this judgment, and the ruling by Mr Justice Fulford which it upheld, leaves open the possibility that senior investigating officers may authorize urgent interviews where the suspect is specifically told that his answers will *not* be used in later evidence. This remains a case-specific decision for the relevant officer to make. Whatever the legal regime, in future an officer facing immediate threat to life through a bomb plot or a hostage scenario could decide that seeking answers to questions designed to preserve public safety so overrides the ability to record and preserve a suspect's answers for future use in court that a deal should be struck: 'tell us where the bomb is, and we wont use your answer against you.'

For present purposes, however, those involved in the prosecution can and should approach urgent interviews on the basis that they are both lawful and admissible: lawful when authorized in the correct manner by an SIO who operates within the confines of the statutory regime; and admissible provided that the manner in which the interview is conducted does not offend sections 76 or 78 of PACE. As mentioned in the judgment, section 78 concerns the question of fairness; specifically, it provides a discretion for the court to exclude evidence which would otherwise be admissible against a defendant on the basis that it would be unfair to adduce it and, under section 76, there is *always* a need to ensure that interviews are properly conducted and do not become oppressive.

Oppression

By section 76(2) of the Police and Criminal Evidence Act 1984:

> If, in any proceedings where the prosecution proposes to give in evidence a confession made by an accused person, it is represented to the court that the confession was or may have been obtained – (a) by oppression of the person who made it … the court shall not allow the confession to be given in evidence against him except in so far as the prosecution proves to the court beyond reasonable doubt that the confession (notwithstanding that it may be true) was not obtained as aforesaid.

Oppression, as defined by section 76 of PACE and the authorities that interpret that section, carries no additional meaning merely because the interview in question is urgent and/or is conducted without the presence of a solicitor. Therefore, officers should conduct urgent interviews in the same fashion as they would non-urgent interviews, and subject to the same requirements of form and content which their experience of section 76 and the authorities provides. There is nothing to fear merely by reason of the special circumstances which apply when public safety considerations make the interview urgent.

Relevant case law

The cases on the interpretation and meaning of 'oppression' are well known. In *R v. Fulling* 85 Cr App R 136, the then Lord Chief Justice held that the word 'oppression' in section 76(2)(a) of PACE should be given its ordinary dictionary meaning – that is, the exercise of authority or power in a burdensome, harsh or wrongful manner; unjust or cruel treatment of subjects, inferiors, or the imposition of unreasonable or unjust burdens – and that such oppression would be likely to entail some impropriety on the part of the interrogator.

In *R v. Heaton* (1993) Crim LR 593, the (next) Lord Chief Justice considered a (non-urgent) interview with a suspect who was described by a doctor as 'not exceptionally bright', 'possibly of a dull normal intelligence' and 'very suggestible'. Heaton was convicted of the manslaughter of his baby son, who had been shaken to death. In interview he admitted holding the child in the air and shaking him until his head was flopping. As to the manner in which the interview (with solicitor present) was conducted, the court noted that voices were slightly raised but there was no shouting and no oppressive hostility; the pace of the interview was slow and the appellant was given time to consider his replies. Some questions were repeated several times but not inappropriately. The interview was not found to be oppressive.

For a more recent consideration of section 76 of PACE, see the House of Lords judgments in *R v. Mushtaq* [2005] 2 Cr App R 32 HL. The appellant was charged with conspiracy to defraud and with possessing material designed or adapted for the making of a false instrument. In the course of the trial the prosecution sought to lead evidence of a statement that amounted to a confession made to the police officers who interviewed him. The appellant applied to exclude that evidence under section 76(2) on the ground that it had been obtained as a result of oppression by the officers. In this case, the oppression alleged was to the effect that the officers had offered inducements to the defendant, by threatening to refuse bail and to exaggerate his involvement in the crime if he failed to cooperate. Following a *voir dire* (an examination of the issues in the absence of the jury), during which the officers denied any impropriety, the judge held that the evidence was admissible. The same allegation of oppression was made before the jury but the appellant gave no evidence in support of it. In summing up, the judge directed the jury that if they were sure that the confession was true they could rely on it even if it had been, or might have been, made as a result of oppression or other improper circumstances. The appellant was convicted. He appealed against the conviction on the ground that the judge's direction was incompatible with his right against self-incrimination guaranteed by Article 6 of the Convention for the Protection of Human Rights and Fundamental Freedoms. The Court of Appeal dismissed the appeal. The appellant appealed to the House of Lords (the UK Supreme Court, as it is today), who held that the purpose of section 76(2) of the 1984 Act was to exclude confession evidence unless the prosecution could establish that it was obtained fairly and in reliable circumstances, that is, without oppression. To permit the jury to rely on a confession which it considered was, or might have been, obtained by oppression or improper means was inconsistent with that purpose. Accordingly, section 76(2) required that the jury be directed that, if they considered that the confession had been, or might have been, obtained by oppression or in consequence of anything said or done that was likely to render it unreliable, they should disregard it. Notwithstanding this reasoning, the appeal was in fact dismissed on the basis that the appellant had not given any evidence to support the allegation of oppression, and therefore, the House of Lords concluded, there was no evidence of oppression for the jury to consider.

Before leaving the authorities on oppression, it is worth remembering the words of Lord Carswell in his opinion in *Mushtaq*:

> I am content to use the definition propounded by Lord MacDermott in an address to the Bentham Club in 1968 and adopted by the Court of Appeal in R. v. Prager (1972) 56 Cr App R 151 at 161, [1972] 1 W.L.R. 260 at 266: '… questioning which by its nature, duration or other attendant circumstances (including the fact of custody) excites hopes (such as the hope of release) or fears, or so affects the mind of the subject that his will crumbles and he speaks when otherwise he would have stayed silent'. (*R v. Mushtaq* [2005] 2 Cr App R 32 HL)

No interviewing officer, whether conducting urgent or non-urgent interviews, can afford to forget the requirements of section 76 of PACE. However, this does not mean that urgent interviews need be conducted in fear of automatic exclusion by the courts if later attempts are made to introduce them at trial. In the 21/7 case, urgent interviews conducted over several hours, during which interviewing officers made repeated and blunt requests for information necessary to ensure public safety, were held to be admissible. The suspected bomber had been arrested at 5.20 a.m. in Birmingham, several days after the failed bomb plot, and was taken to London and seen by a doctor who certified that he was fit for detention and interview. The urgent safety interviews commenced at 10.25 a.m. and lasted until 4.21 p.m., in all a total of three hours and four minutes of actual interview.

Officers repeatedly asked the suspect to account not only for his own movements on and since 21/7, but for any information as to the location of the other bombers. During the interviews fresh information was coming in from an ongoing police search of the north London flat in which it was believed the bomb mixture had been made. This was a dynamic situation, with officers pressing for any information on what had happened to the other bombers. It transpired that two of them were holed up in another flat, in which the bombs had been assembled on the morning of 21/7 itself. Over the next 24 hours, the second flat was found, a stand-off took place between the bombers and armed officers, and the bombers were brought out of the premises which were found to contain makeshift weapons ready to repel intruders.

Conclusion

It is only to be expected that those who act for defendants charged with serious terrorist offences will continue to challenge the legal regime which governs the conduct of urgent interviews in any case where the prosecution seek to use the content of those interviews against defendants at trial. Defence lawyers would hardly be doing their duty if they did not ensure that every proper challenge to the prosecution case was mounted and pursued with vigour. Indeed, as we have seen, appeals against conviction lodged by the 21/7 bombers were dismissed in due course, but not before the Court of Appeal made this observation:

> Those suspected of terrorist offences, if rightly suspected, are likely to be able to provide assistance to investigating officers performing their responsibilities for public safety. An interview process which, so far as possible, enables the police to protect the public is a necessary imperative. These interviews are variously described as 'safety interviews', or 'urgent' or 'emergency interviews'. The suspect is interviewed for information which may help the police to protect life and prevent serious damage to property to be obtained. The question whether the results of such interviews should then be used as evidence against the suspects, impinging as it sometimes may on the principles governing protection against self-incrimination, is delicate. ([2008] 2 Cr App R 23 at para. 33)

Given all of the above, five concluding suggestions emerge:

1   Law and practice provide for urgent interviews. When authorized by SIOs, such interviews must be conducted immediately and diligently with public safety in mind.

2   A failure by a suspect to answer questions put during an urgent interview cannot give rise to adverse inferences at trial (hence the need to remember that the old-style caution should be administered); however, anything said by a suspect – whether amounting to admissions or lies – may be admissible at trial.

3   Admissibility will always be measured by the wide discretion afforded to judges under section 78 of PACE, by which the overall fairness of the proceedings is protected. Rather than placing a defined limitation on the admissibility of safety interviews, the section 78 discretion was described as one of 'the existing safeguards available to a defendant' (see para. 36 of the Court of Appeal judgment in the 21/7 case, [2008] 2 Cr App R 23).

4   While section 76 of PACE considerations are ever present, it is worth noting that in 21/7, where safety interviews of some defendants continued over a six-hour period during which very little access was afforded to solicitors, the unsuccessful appeals against conviction were directed towards the legal framework of the SIO's authorization, *not* towards the manner or length of the interviews themselves.

5   The conclusion of Mr Justice Fulford, upheld on appeal, stands: 'I do not consider that there has been a material infringement of the right on the part of any of these accused to exercise his defence rights ... Moreover, there is nothing unfair in admitting this evidence ... Without hesitation, it is my decision that these interviews in their entirety are admissible, having applied the particular wording of section 78 PACE and having weighed the requirements of Article 6 ECHR' (*R v. Ibrahim and others* [2008] 2 Cr App R 23 at para. 57 and at para. 168 of the original Fulford ruling on safety interviews above).

Note

1   At http://www.legislation.gov.uk/ukpga/2000/11/schedule/8 (retrieved 22 May 2014).

Legal Cases

[2008] 2 Cr App R 23
Ambrose v. Harris (Procurator Fiscal Oban)
Averill v. United Kingdom ECHR application no. 36408/97 (Judgment 6/9/2000)
Cadder v. HM Advocate (2010) UKSC 43
Gafgen v. Germany (2011) 52 EHRR 1
Her Majesty's Advocate v. G [2011] 1 WLR 2435, SC
Her Majesty's Advocate v. M
Her Majesty's Advocate v. P [2011] 1 WLR 2497, SC
Magee v. United Kingdom ECHR application no. 28135/95 (Judgment 6/9/2000)
Murray v. United Kingdom (1996) 22 EHRR 29
R v. Fulling 85 Cr App R 136

R v. Heaton (1993) Crim LR 593
R v. Ibrahim and others [2008] EWCA Crim 880
R v. Mushtaq [2005] 2 Cr App R 32 HL
R. v. Prager (1972) 56 Cr App R 151
R v. Samuel (1988) QB 615
Salduz v. Turkey (2009) 49 EHRR 19

5

Defence Counsel in Terrorism Trials

Peter Carter, QC

This chapter provides an insight into the role of defence counsel in terrorism trials. It also covers (to a lesser degree) the role of defence solicitors. In passing, it touches on the human rights issues that are likely to arise in trials of this type. Terrorism trials produce particular evidential and practical problems for those representing defendants that are probably unforeseen by anyone who has not actually engaged in the process. Safety or urgent interviews play an inevitable part in terrorism investigations and the diverse nature of the suspects leads to risks that their rights are thereby compromised. I shall cover some of the questions that safety interviews provoke and which have so far had limited attention. The relationship between safety interviews and adverse inferences is particularly acute – and at what risk to the rule of law?

Role of Defence Counsel

Defence counsel acts as an advocate, not a mouthpiece. His or her job is not to secure an acquittal – it is to 'endeavour to protect his client from conviction except by a competent tribunal and upon legally admissible evidence sufficient to support a conviction for the offence charged'.[1] According to the Bar Standards Board *Handbook* (2014), defending and prosecuting counsel share the same fundamental duties and standards. Our primary duty is to the court, that is, the administration of justice, not the particular judge who is trying the case. If the judge is wrong, rude or unfair, it is our duty to say so – whether we are prosecuting or defending. We have no choice in the cases we defend or prosecute, in what is known as the 'cab rank rule'. The Code of Conduct requires us to accept instructions in any case that falls within our professional competence and which does not conflict with an existing

Investigating Terrorism: Current Political, Legal and Psychological Issues, First Edition. Edited by John Pearse.
© 2015 John Wiley & Sons, Ltd. Published 2015 by John Wiley & Sons, Ltd.

professional commitment. As counsel are instructed in terrorism cases long before the trial date is fixed, there is no choice in the matter if he or she is competent, that is, sufficiently experienced to take on the case. We cannot refuse to act if we don't like the case or the defendant. That does not mean that we act with any less professional commitment to the interests of our client.

We must be courteous to the judge, even when pointing out that he or she is wrong. We must be independent and exercise our skills and judgment accordingly. This means that prosecuting counsel will not agree to indict a particular offence because someone in the government or Crown Prosecution Service (CPS) thinks it will attract good publicity or because the police tell him or her that the defendant needs locking up. It means that defence counsel should not ask questions that he or she thinks unnecessary, irrelevant or offensive just because the client wishes it.

We don't appease the judge in order to enhance our own careers. The conduct of the military defence lawyers in Guantanamo Bay illustrates the high professional standards of independence that are expected. That conduct contrasts with that of the lawyers in the Department of Defense and the White House whose responsibility for the torture at Guantanamo and Abu Ghraib has been documented (Sands, 2008).

Defence counsel should not conduct the case in a particular way solely in order to gain favour with the solicitor or client. Courts are not the place for political speeches. As the Court of Appeal explained in *R v. Hobson* [1998] 1 Cr App R 31:

> Counsel's job, in the proper performance of his or her duties to the client and to the court, is to exercise judgment and discretion as to the way in which the client's case can best be presented, and to give such advice, if necessary, in forceful terms, as in his or her view, the circumstances required. Because a client wishes a particular question to be asked, point to be made or witness to be called, it does not follow that the question must be asked, the point made or the witness called. (See also *R v. Ulcay* [2007] EWCA 2379; *R v. B* [2005] EWCA 805, [2006] Crim LR 54.)

Independence of our advocates and judges is an essential feature of the democratic process. It is no coincidence that when tyrants want to impose absolute rule they sack senior judges and imprison lawyers, for example, as in Zimbabwe or under Pervez Musharraf in Pakistan. In Colombia, lawyers and judges are the targets of drug barons. The United Kingdom, like a limited number of countries, has an independent legal profession and judiciary. The effect of that independence has been noticeable in the United States (the Guantanamo cases, among both civilian and military lawyers, *Rasul v. Bush*, 2004) and in Israel (the prohibition on torture, *Israel v. The State*, HCJ 5100/94, 26 May 1999). Alarmingly, it required our own House of Lords to tell the Home Secretary and Attorney General that English law does not tolerate torture. In that case, Lord Bingham described himself as 'startled, even a little dismayed' that counsel for the Secretary of State could argue that evidence obtained by torture was admissible (*A v. Home Secretary* [2005] UKHL 71 at para. [51]). One of the best examples of counsel combining courtesy with resolute independence is Sir Sydney Kentridge in his cross-examination of one of the officers involved in the Biko

Inquest in apartheid South Africa. The witness wished to be questioned in Afrikaans. Sir Sydney insisted, politely, on the evidence being given in English, as the constitution permitted, and because it was a language his clients understood (Bizos, 2000, pp. 52–53).

We must be courteous to witnesses – which is not the same as failing to test their evidence. Some witnesses are bullies and need to be exposed. On the other hand, if counsel browbeats a vulnerable witness, we have exceeded our duty and juries rightly hate it.

We act in accordance with the evidence. We do not create evidence. We may put an interpretation on facts that suits our case, but we do not suggest what witnesses should say and we do not tell our clients what would be a good defence.

How should a police officer or witness react to cross-examination? Most will probably have come across at least one case in which counsel has behaved in a manner that failed to live up to these standards – or at least appeared to do so. When you come across a lawyer strongly arguing a case *you* believe to be wrong, it can be very irritating. The role of the witness is as witness, to provide information to be used in court – the witness who becomes an advocate has lost integrity as a witness and has no place as an advocate. In the same way, an advocate who takes on the role of witness ends up being useless at both. Juries rarely get it badly wrong. In serious cases at least, the public should be able to rely on a strong and independent judge to keep things on track. For example, in *R v. B* [2005] the Court of Appeal approved a guillotine imposed by the trial judge on unnecessary cross-examination by defence counsel.[2]

The most significant difference between the duties of prosecuting and defence counsel is that prosecuting counsel has a duty to put all relevant material before the court (subject to public interest immunity, which I shall deal with later). This inevitably includes evidence that tends to undermine the prosecution case. Defence counsel has no comparable duty to provide evidence inconsistent with the client's case, but neither can counsel mislead the court. Counsel cannot, for example, put forward as genuine a document that the client has instructed him or her is false. Neither can defence counsel suppress evidence. If a defendant tells him or her something that harms his or her defence, and asks, 'What should I say if I'm asked about that?' the advice must be, 'Tell the truth'. That basic difference in approach to the duty of disclosure is diminished but by no means abolished by the increasing obligation on the defence to identify the defence case and respond to requests for written admissions.

Legitimate Defence Tactics when Representing Someone Charged with Terrorism

In an adversarial system such as ours, defence lawyers must be diligent and persistent in order to ensure that the types of miscarriages that have plagued our criminal justice system in the past are made as unlikely as is humanly possible. It is important to distinguish between those tactics that are legitimate and those that are not. Where a lawyer descends to illegitimate tactics during interview, then the entire investigation and trial process might be undermined, the investigation because an important piece of evidence might be missed as a result of the officer being distracted, and the trial process in the event that the lawyer instructed at trial is not the same as the one who acted during interview, and is able properly to challenge what happened during interview on the basis of the previous lawyer's incompetence or worse.

At the pre-charge investigation stage, the principal aim of defence lawyers is to discover as much about the prosecution case as possible without disclosing anything about what the accused is saying, or possibly not saying. The lawyer will try and assess whether there really is any evidence as opposed to suspicion. It is the lawyer's job to ensure that the client is not kept in custody unless there is lawful justification. What may sometimes appear to be intrusive questions about the investigation will be aimed at identifying any weakness in the 'reasonable' grounds for suspicion. After all, why should we assume the investigators have got it right? The Police and Criminal Evidence Act 1984 (known as PACE) Code H6 Notes for Guidance state:

> The solicitor's *only* role in the police station is to protect and advance the legal rights of their client. On occasions this may require the solicitor to give advice which has the effect of the client avoiding giving evidence which strengthens a prosecution case. The solicitor may intervene in order to seek clarification, challenge an improper question to their client or the manner in which it is put, advise their client not to reply to particular questions, or if they wish to give their client further legal advice. (Code H para. 6C; emphasis added[3])

That *only* is a big task. If done properly, it ensures that the client's interests are protected and any subsequent prosecution will be free from distracting issues about procedural fairness and propriety. It is very much in the investigators' interests to ensure that the solicitor's job is done properly and without undue interference.

One question the defence lawyer should ask is: Which offence is being investigated? There are so many offences now within the ambit of 'terrorism' that the lawyer will need to know what level of terrorist offence is suspected. This can affect the outcome of applications for warrants of further detention. An offence that involves piecing together a myriad of evidence of a very serious offence, some from computers seized at various addresses, is a very different type of investigation from one where a person has been videoed inciting violence, has been heard by an undercover officer encouraging young people to travel to a terrorist training camp, or was arrested in possession of documents showing his or her connection with terrorist training.

How long is the client to be detained before a decision is made about charging? When and how often is he or she to be interviewed? What disclosure will be made pre-interview? Will the lawyer have sufficient opportunity to consider it with the client? The lawyer is inevitably forced into a reactive role, but will wish to be proactive – or at least seem to be so in order to keep the investigators and the custody officer under pressure to make a decision about charging or releasing, or to justify continued detention. The Privy Council has decided that under the common law a police officer is entitled to detain a suspect for a reasonable time in order to determine whether the incident is serious (*Ramsingh v. Trinidad & Tobago* [2012] UKPC 16).

Investigators have to make decisions about how much information to disclose before each interview. As a prosecutor, I am in favour of drip-feeding information to see the effect it has. Needless to say, as a defence lawyer I would want to know as much as possible. In particular, I would want to know whether the client should give an explanation in interview or risk a later adverse inference at trial by remaining silent. Will silence provide the prosecution with added ammunition against the client, or will it mean that there is insufficient evidence to charge?

Increasingly, counsel are instructed to attend police stations to advise clients and to make submissions on applications for further detention. Defence lawyers are aware that when a client answers questions in the early part of an investigation, and then makes no answers when the questions get too close to the heart of the allegation, it looks far worse than if the client were to remain silent throughout.

If the suspect has been denied access to a lawyer under PACE Code H, Annex B, the lawyer will want to test whether that decision was appropriate. On what grounds was it made? How much information was given to the client? Was he or she interviewed? What was said in the interview? The lawyer will expect – and I think is entitled to know – what was said in any interview both by the questioner and by his or her client at a time when legal access was denied. It is not sufficient to assume that the client will be able to inform him or her of this. The interviewing officers will inevitably refer to the decision of the senior investigating officer (SIO), but that does not absolve the interviewing officers from responsibility for dealing fairly with the suspect, and questioning the SIO's decision if necessary. And yes, I do mean that.

For investigators, choosing the moment to make the disclosure that would trigger a special caution is a matter of fine judgment. Such cautions can be introduced so as to require a suspect to account for his or her presence at a certain location or his or her possession of certain items. Failure to do so adequately can be brought up at any subsequent trial and the judge and jury may make an adverse inference accordingly (see sections 34, 36 and 37 of the Youth Justice and Criminal Evidence Act 1999[4]). If sprung on the suspect and the lawyer, it will look like a trick. Part of the investigator's skill is to identify those suspects who have information to share and who may therefore be diverted from the prosecution process. In such cases, a proper professional relationship with the defence lawyer will be of great assistance.

Why Certain Lawyers Are Instructed and Potential Conflict of Interest

It is obvious that a limited number of firms of solicitors currently appear in the majority of terrorist trials. The reasons are various – some of these solicitors have been practising in more mundane areas of law in a location where their clients are predominantly Muslims; some have experience of conducting terrorist trials going back to the IRA cases; and some are established criminal firms which happen to have become involved in this type of work. Some Muslim clients prefer to be represented by someone of a particular gender. Client choice based on gender or ethnicity has limited effect. This must be so. A client should not be able at the outset to set his or her own agenda; that would be inconsistent with the principles of our criminal justice system by demanding the right to a lawyer of a particular race, gender or religion. They cannot object to the race, gender or religion of the trial judge or of the jurors. If such a proposition were suggested, I confidently expect it would be firmly squashed.

There is a suspicion that some lawyers acting for clients accused of terrorist offences sympathize too closely with those of their clients who hold extreme views. In some cases there is a suspicion of a political element in the way the case is conducted – an element that should not feature in any case. There is, of course, the risk of mistaking an excellent and successful defence lawyer for someone who sympathizes with the extremist views of his or her client. But there is no harm in adopting a sceptical approach. Whenever I am instructed by a firm for the first time in a serious case, I have to be alert for any sign that my solicitor has not given professional and independent advice, or that I am expected to compromise my independence. Sometimes bad advice is given in good faith, for example to remain silent in interview, when a more experienced lawyer might have advised answering the questions.

Once or twice, when prosecuting, I have thought that it was not in the interests of one of the defendants to be represented by the same solicitor as another defendant. It looked too much as if the reason was that the co-defendant wanted to make sure that the second defendant stuck to the script and did not implicate the main defendant. Inevitably that situation can arise during the investigation. A subtle interview can be frustrated if the solicitor representing that client is then representing another suspect and tells him everything that was said in the previous interview.

Dealing with Obstructive, Incompetent or Inexperienced Legal Representatives

In exceptional circumstances – and it must be exceptional – PACE Code H paragraphs 6.10–17 and Annex B justify excluding legal representatives. This is particularly applicable to non-qualified representatives of solicitors' firms. It is a drastic step to prevent a nominated legal representative from acting for a suspect. But in appropriate circumstances it is justified. Examples of conduct justifying the lawyer's exclusion are given in Code H, Notes for Guidance, paragraph 6C, as (a) answering the questions or (b) preparing a written response. I do not think that can possibly be regarded as exhaustive. Where a lawyer is acting for more than one client and there is reason to believe (perhaps as a result of credible intelligence that cannot see the light of day in court) that the lawyer is acting as an agent of one client in order to coach another, then the police should be robust in preventing such attempts to frustrate the investigation. Where the legal representative is obviously inexperienced, that person is unlikely to be able to give appropriate advice. This not only hampers the immediate investigation, but it may lead to the prosecution being denied the use of adverse inferences from silence in interview. It can also harm the suspect's interests: a detailed explanation may result in no charges being brought; answering questions may be in the client's best interests if it is to be one of the many terrorism cases in which there is a guilty plea. Although the circumstances in which a legal representative can be excluded are restricted, investigators are entitled to consider whether the suspect's interests are being harmed by an inexperienced legal representative. In *Bernard v. Trinidad & Tobago* [2007] UKPC 34 the Privy Council decided that a defendant convicted of murder could not receive a fair trial when he had been represented by counsel with three months' experience. Although that is an extreme case, the principle can apply to representation at a police station in terrorism investigations.

Where there are multiple suspects, the ideal is for interviews to be conducted simultaneously, with briefing breaks. If a lawyer acting or seeking to act for more than one client objects, then officers could insist that an alternative lawyer is instructed (from either the same firm or another), or – in cases of real urgency – that the interview continues in the lawyer's absence if he or she is not willing to relinquish representation of that client. This must occur only in extreme cases. But, where necessary, police should not be afraid to consider it. It might avoid a greater problem later when the conflict of interest becomes apparent, and is provided for in section 13 of the Notes for Guidance for PACE Code H. It is a very serious matter for the prosecution to interfere in a suspect's choice of lawyer, or appear to be doing so. The right in Article 6 of the European Convention on Human Rights (ECHR) to 'legal assistance of his own choosing' sounds definitive (6(3)(c)).[5] In reality, suspects and defendants do not have unfettered choice. It depends on who is available as well as whether the person selected has the necessary expertise.

Access to legal advice can become a problem when several suspects have been arrested and are all in custody at the same police station. There may be insufficient interview rooms to allow the lawyers to see their respective clients as soon as they arrive at the police station. A lawyer representing more than one defendant will mean that legal advice has to be staggered. Delay caused in these circumstances can be used later at trial as a means of attacking the integrity of the investigation, perhaps suggesting that the police have deliberately delayed access or kept suspects waiting as a ploy.

Police should not be distracted by such considerations. Provided they are doing their job in accordance with PACE and the codes, and have proper regard for the welfare of the prisoners, they can be confident that the courts will support them. The fact that defence lawyers make a fuss does not mean that they are correct.

Urgent Interviews (Public Safety Interviews)

The decision to conduct an urgent or public safety interview will inevitably be subject to scrutiny (1) when the lawyer arrives and (2) at trial.[6] A safety interview is justified only when it is urgent. Urgency is the keyword. Any delay in conducting such an interview is likely to result in the argument that it could not have been such an emergency as to justify delaying access to a lawyer. On the other hand, conducting an interview prematurely may mean that the evidence is garbled or incomplete, and a proposition is put to the suspect that turns out to be wrong. Information based on intelligence is particularly problematic. Conducting a safety interview on a false factual basis might cause any evidence obtained in later interviews (including adverse inferences from silence) to be lost as a result of an argument on admissibility.

In safety interviews, silence cannot give rise to an adverse inference (see Criminal Justice and Public Order Act 1994, sections 34(2a), 36(4a) and 37(3a)[7]). It should not in any event be the purpose of such an interview to achieve some subsequent forensic gain from the accused's silence. What is wanted is information for the immediate protection of the public. Straying unnecessarily into territory about the suspect's involvement in the offence will risk an application to exclude evidence from that and all subsequent interviews.

A controversial issue is whether answers given in safety interviews are admissible in evidence. No doubt if they support the defence case the defence will put them in evidence even if the prosecution do not. But what if the answers include admissions, or lies? In the *R v. Ibrahim and others* case (21 July 2005 attempted bombings), as Max Hill describes (see Chapter 4), Fulford J ruled that answers in safety interviews were admissible against the defendants. His ruling involved an intricate distinction between the admissibility of lying denials of involvement as against the prohibition on adverse inferences from failing to mention a fact relied on at trial. The Court of Appeal has approved that ruling. I consider that the fundamental protection provided by access to legal advice is undermined by that decision. It therefore conflicts with the European Court of Human Rights' (ECtHR) decisions that a fair trial requires an accused to have access to legal advice at all important stages of the procedure when evidence might be obtained against him or her (see *Murray v. UK* (1996) 22 EHRR 29 and *Condron v. UK* (2001) 31 EHRR 1). On 22 May 2012 the ECtHR ruled that their appeal was admissible on the question whether putting the safety interviews before the jury rendered the trial unfair in contravention of Article 6. All other grounds were declared inadmissible. The hearing of that appeal of the three applicants – Ibrahim, Mohammed and Omar – remains pending. The court ruled that the appeals be consolidated. It is possible that the court will find a violation of Article 6, but the Court of Appeal can refuse to overturn the convictions (should the case be brought back before them) on the grounds that the unfairness did not in this case lead to unsafe verdicts because the remaining evidence was overwhelming. It is even possible that the ECtHR will declare that their judgment – that there was a violation – is a sufficient remedy for the violation and will not require the UK to reconsider the safety of the convictions.[8]

The Court of Appeal in *R v. Ibrahim and others* supported the idea that in appropriate circumstances the interviewing officers can give an undertaking that the answers will not be used in evidence. The Court laid down no guidelines. The decision has to be an operational one. It will obviously be made by the officer who has authorized that the safety interview take place. But that does not preclude the interviewing officers from expressing their own views about the likely efficacy of such a strategy, nor does it exempt them from their independent responsibility to ensure that the codes are honoured and that a suspect is not deprived of access to a lawyer inappropriately. I consider that the subsequent decision of the Supreme Court in *R v. Cadder* [2010] UKSC 43 supports that interpretation of the law. However, there are some lawyers who argue that *Cadder* is not determinative of the issue (see the article in [2012] *Crim LR* 357 – 368). I argued before Fulford J in the 21 July case that use by the prosecution of answers given in safety interviews would undermine the value of the process. Some suspects in those circumstances will be sophisticated terrorists, the very people with access to the information needed to protect the public. If they think that anything they say will be used against them, they are less likely to provide that information. If the suspect does not fall into that category, then it is unlikely that the terrorist organizers will have given him or her the kind of information that safety interviews are designed to reveal.

This then poses the dilemma: What use can be made of answers given in response to an undertaking that the answers will not be used in evidence? Obviously, they cannot be used by the prosecution, but what about a co-defendant? The interview could be admissible for them, unless the interview fell foul of the provisions of section 76A of PACE which deals with the concept of oppression that I shall discuss later.

Another issue with safety interviews is the wording of the caution. It is in my view inadequate if the answers are later to be admitted in evidence. The prescribed caution is:

> You do not have to say anything, but anything you say may be given in evidence. (PACE Code H, Annex C, at para. 2[9])

Where the prohibition on drawing adverse inferences arises after an interview has been given using the now conventional caution, then the difference must be explained in ordinary language. The Notes for Guidance suggest:

> The caution you were previously given no longer applies. That is because after that caution you asked to speak to a solicitor but have not yet been allowed an opportunity to speak to a solicitor.
>
> That means that from now on, adverse inferences cannot be drawn at court and your defence will not be harmed because you choose to say nothing. Please listen carefully to the caution I am about to give you because it will apply from now on. You will see that it does not say anything about your defence being harmed. (Code H, Annex C, Notes for Guidance, para. C1[10])

Why should this explanation be given only after there has been some change? It does mean that after any arrest (when the conventional caution will have been given) any safety interview should be preceded by such an explanation.

Any answers given during a safety interview will be open to challenge where the appropriate caution is not given. Even if it is given, there is the argument that admissibility should not be determined by the wording of the caution; rather the wording of the caution should be designed to reflect the proper legal status of the interview. In the absence of a lawyer, how is a person under arrest (and therefore suffering some anxiety) supposed to understand the legal net in which he or she is caught?

Additional problems arise when the suspect's first language is not English. Any apparent problem with comprehending will be raised at court as an argument against admissibility – not just of the safety interviews but of subsequent interviews which, it will be said, are tainted by the failings of the caution. What is the status and role of an interpreter in safety interviews? If it is an independent person, then the delay in securing the interpreter's attendance undermines the urgency. If such a person is to be present at the interview, how do you guarantee confidentiality? If the interpreter can attend, why not a lawyer? A better option might be to have police officers who speak the detainee's language attached to the Counter Terrorism Command. That produces obvious practical problems of predicting (without stereotyping) likely suspects by language. Were such an officer to act as interpreter, it must be made clear to the interviewee that the interpreter is part of the police team, otherwise arguments about entrapment would arise. A police officer cannot act as interpreter when access is given to a lawyer at which time the discussion will be covered by legal professional privilege. When communications are subject to legal professional privilege, that privilege binds the interpreter as well as the lawyer.

Safety interviews have a legitimate and obvious place in investigations. It would be a failure of our criminal justice system if a desire (by judges or prosecutors) to obtain an evidential advantage were to frustrate their legitimate purpose. I suggest that, whatever the wording of the caution suggested in PACE, the police need to make sure that the suspect actually understands in simple language the purpose and effect of the interview. Words like 'adverse inference' require detailed explanation by judges to juries; it is unrealistic to assume a suspect will readily comprehend the finer points of the term.

An indication of the flaws in this small but important area of law is that the prohibition on drawing adverse inferences from silence during a safety interview is absolute. That applies even if the defendant adduces the content of the safety interviews. Any failure to mention significant facts cannot be put in the balance against him or her to counter a defendant's evidence that he or she has been consistent about his or her defence.

Length of Detention and Interviews

To obtain admissions or even silence in the face of accusations in order that they can then be used against the suspect is a waste of time if the interview is ruled inadmissible because the suspect was under undue pressure. The effect of the pressure of detention on suspects inevitably varies according to the individual. It is not predictable. Answers given by a person in interview that appear to support the investigators' information, or provide details of the involvement of the interviewee or others in terrorist activity, but which turn out to be untrue are as damaging to an investigation as they are to the person who makes the false admission.

The fiascos of Guantanamo and of detention without trial of foreign nationals under Part 4 of the Anti-Terrorism Crime and Security Act 2001[11] have shown the futility of using protracted detention in the fight against terrorism. Interviewing throughout 28 days of detention will, in most cases, result in a credible allegation by the defence of oppression. The value of anything obtained from the suspect at the end of such a process is questionable and effectively rendered void by the House of Lords in *A v. Secretary of State for the Home Dept* [2004] UKHL 56 who decided that the device of declaring the derogation from Article 5 of the ECHR (the right to security and liberty) was unlawful and ineffective.

However, terrorist investigations often take months to complete. In the 2007 *Barot* [2007] EWCA Crim 1119 case (where he planned simultaneous attacks in London and the United States), arrests had been made in August 2004. Evidence continued to be served until March 2007. By the time the case came to trial in May 2007 (when all but one pleaded guilty) some encrypted computer files remained inaccessible. This time-scale demonstrates that in the most serious cases there is no period of pre-charge detention that could possibly be regarded as reasonable and would still enable the investigation to be substantially complete. Fraud investigators generally have the luxury of investigating bank accounts and computer material over many months while the suspects are on police bail. For obvious reasons, that is not realistic in terrorism cases. The former Attorney General has now agreed with the proposals made by Liberty that the existing 28-day period is more than adequate to prefer holding charges so that the investigation can then continue post-charge. The judge would also regularly review progress in the case and ensure that interviews are not conducted for too long or too frequently or on repetitive topics. I expect an objection to this would be that the judiciary do not wish to become investigating judges. Section 22 of the Counter-Terrorism Act 2008 (in force from 10 July 2012) now provides for post-charge interviews of defendants charged with offences of or related to terrorism.

Because of the imperative of time limits laid down in the terrorism legislation and PACE Code H, even with the extended time allowed for terrorism cases, interviews will be conducted at a time when the material seized is still being examined and while the premises themselves are still subject to minute forensic search. This presents a dilemma. Defence lawyers in interview will demand maximum disclosure of what the investigation has so far revealed. Yet the police may not be in possession of the latest information. If the police make assumptions, the defence lawyers both then and at trial will assume that those assumptions were based on hard evidence and seek to explore disclosure of unused material on that basis. It will be awkward to say that the proposition put in interview was not based on any evidence. It might diminish the value of the entire interview. It might lead to an accusation that the defendant was deliberately misled and so induced either to say or not to say something.

Protracting interviews so that the results of examination can be available creates a separate problem. A lawyer advising a suspect in interview may say that his or her client intends to answer no questions, and so there is no point interviewing him or her, and that he or she should be either charged or released. There is value to the prosecution in continuing to ask pertinent questions, and in particular those that can lead to adverse inferences. Defence lawyers will seek to undermine the foundation for such inferences – by challenging the legitimacy of the continued interview, for example, saying that it was a ploy to gain time and justify further extension; or by arguing that the pre-interview disclosure was inadequate or misleading, or that the defendant had insufficient time to consult because of pressure from the investigators to conduct an interview, or that the defendant was by then too tired, or frightened of the implications of what was alleged against him or her to be able to give a fair account of him- or herself in interview.

On some occasions defendants change their lawyers between interview and trial. That happened in the fertilizer case, *R v. Omar Khyam and others* [2008] EWCA Crim 1612. That is partly the result of word in the prisons – defendants awaiting trial usually think they know more about the trial process than the lawyers advising them and may apply to be represented by a solicitor recommended by one of their fellow prisoners. Sometimes they are wise to do so. When they do, the new lawyer may feel free to challenge the interviews by claiming the advice given to the defendant was defective. It must be dispiriting when this happens if the lawyer advising in interview was inadequate, but the police thought there was nothing they could do about it. So, failure to act can come back to haunt the police.

The Risk of Oppression

I want to develop a theme from section 76(8) of PACE.[12] 'In this section "oppression" includes torture, inhuman or degrading treatment, and the use or threat of violence (whether or not amounting to torture).' This is a similar test to that in Article 3 of the ECHR: 'No one shall be subjected to torture or to inhuman or degrading treatment or punishment.' The Convention not only prohibits such treatment, but places an obligation on the state (by Article 1) to protect those within its power (not confined to its citizens) and to investigate and prosecute any instances of such conduct. This obligation to investigate and prosecute is reinforced by the UN Convention against Torture and Other Cruel, Inhuman or Degrading Treatment or Punishment (1987), to which the UK is a party. This is an obligation the international community takes seriously.[13] You cannot simply say that, because the mistreatment occurred elsewhere and was not committed by you or other officers, you can ignore it. This is relevant to police work because they will sometimes be dealing with suspects who arrive from detention overseas in places where torture is used. The prosecution cannot use any material that has been obtained as a result of torture and, where someone has been or may have been the victim of torture, the police must be scrupulous in ensuring that the detainee is not suffering from its effects (e.g., post-traumatic stress disorder, or PTSD) and that he or she understands what methods the investigating police will use. I shall return to this topic later. In some cases, a psychologist should be invited to assess the suspect before any interview takes place.

The test of torture or inhuman or degrading treatment is a demanding one in ECHR law. However, an interview will be oppressive if the officers browbeat the suspect by shouting at him or her. This will be particularly so if the suspect is vulnerable or suggestible. In the Cardiff Three case, *Paris, Abdullahi and Miller* (1993) 97 Cr App R 99, the defendant (Miller) had been interviewed over several days. Lord Taylor, Chief Justice, said:

> We have read the transcripts of the tapes and have heard a number of them played in open court. It became clear that the two pairs of officers employed different methods. Greenwood and Seaford were tough and confrontational. Evans and Murray were milder in manner, aiming to gain the appellant's confidence and persuade him to accept their version of the facts. We are bound to say that on hearing tape 7, each member of this Court was horrified. Miller was bullied and hectored. The officers, particularly Detective Constable Greenwood, were not questioning him so much as shouting at him what they wanted him to say. Short of physical violence, it is hard to conceive of a more hostile and intimidating approach by officers to a suspect. It is impossible to convey on the printed page the pace, force and menace of the officer's delivery, but a short passage may give something of the flavour …
>
> In our view, although we do not know what instructions he had, the solicitor appears to have been gravely at fault for sitting passively through this travesty of an interview. We are told he was called to give evidence at the first trial but not the second, and he agreed in evidence, having heard the tapes played, that he ought to have intervened. (*Paris, Abdullahi and Miller* (1993) 97 Cr App R 99 at 104)

Judith Ward (1993) was not a case of oppression, but is an example of how a vulnerable person can make compelling confessions that are not true:

> It is rare, but not unknown, for a person who is not subjected to any improper pressure or an inducement to confess to crimes he or she has not committed. It is even more rare for somebody, in such circumstances, to confess to crimes as grave as those for which Miss Ward stood trial. Nevertheless our criminal courts, and all those who owe a duty to do what is necessary to ensure that the courts arrive at proper verdicts, must take account of the possibility that confessions, though not the result of any impropriety, may be untrue. For this reason amongst others it is essential that those who are responsible for a prosecution and for the provision of evidence upon which the prosecution is based should comply with their basic duty to seek to ensure a trial which is fair both to the prosecution, representing the Crown, and to the accused. In failing to disclose evidence in the various respects we have described, one or more members of the West Yorkshire Police, the scientists who gave evidence for the prosecution at the trial and some of those members of the staff of the D.P.P. and counsel who advised them, to whom we have earlier referred, failed to carry out this basic duty. We greatly regret that as a result a grave miscarriage of justice has occurred. (*Judith Ward* (1993) 96 Cr App R 1 at 67)

Since PACE, instances of oppression (and even allegations of oppression) have become extremely rare. An allegation was made on behalf of Ibrahim in the 21 July case that the police had improperly denied him access to a lawyer so that he would be under pressure during interview. That allegation was rejected.

What about Confessions Relied on for a Co-accused?

Section 76A of PACE contains largely similar provisions to section 76, but with some significant differences. It is a provision that has so far been little used, but is likely to feature more prominently, especially now that it can be combined with the hearsay provisions of the Criminal Justice Act 2003[14] to make admissible on behalf of defendant B what defendant A said to the police or to anyone else. A confession made by one accused and not admissible for the prosecution, or not relied on by the prosecution, can, under this provision, be used in evidence on behalf of a co-accused, unless it has been obtained by oppression or by anything said or done that is likely to make it unreliable. The burden of proving that it was *not* obtained by oppression and so on is on the defendant who is seeking to rely on it. The standard of proof is the balance of probabilities (subsection (2)) and not the criminal standard required if the prosecution seek to admit it.

Section 76A creates a risk of causing prejudice to a defendant who is deprived of using exculpatory material because of oppressive conduct to the co-accused who made the confession. The answer is one for trial counsel and the judge to decide. It may in extreme cases result in dropping the case against the defendant who is prejudiced.

Between Charge and Trial

During this period the case will take shape. Defence lawyers will seek to obtain from the court a finite time-scale for service of prosecution evidence and a guillotine on service after that date. That rarely succeeds. They will need to be alert to the possibility of post-charge interviews under Section 22 of the Counter-Terrorism Act 2008. They will also seek to gain access to whatever unused material the prosecution has. Lawyers who do not prosecute often believe that the prosecution has access to unlimited resources and infinite amounts of material.

An essential task of investigators is to identify all the material that has been generated by the investigation and has come into their possession, as well as other information in the hands of third parties of which they are aware. It is a time-consuming and, I expect, a tedious job. It is essential if an otherwise well-conducted investigation does not unravel years later with the quashing of the conviction(s) because of some inadequacy in the disclosure of relevant material. It is important to identify with precision what was found where – in some instances to the exact part of a desk or table, and in relation to what other material. I have known defendants evade awkward cross-examination because prosecuting counsel was unable to establish that a particular document was under the nose of the defendant moments before his arrest.

For some years defence lawyers would engage in efforts to force the prosecution to a position where they could not disclose some material and would have to discontinue the prosecution. The current disclosure regime makes that extremely unlikely.

Judges apply the protocol as laid down by the Court of Appeal, 'Disclosure: A Protocol for the Control and Management of Unused Material in the Crown Court':

> 2   The House of Lords stated in *R v. H and C* [2004] 2 AC 134, at 147: 'Fairness
>   ordinarily requires that any material held by the prosecution which weakens its
>   case or strengthens that of the defendant, if not relied on as part of its formal case
>   against the defendant, should be disclosed to the defence. Bitter experience has
>   shown that miscarriages of justice may occur where such material is withheld
>   from disclosure. The golden rule is that full disclosure of such material should be
>   made.'
> 3   However, it is also essential that the trial process is not overburdened or diverted
>   by erroneous and inappropriate disclosure of unused prosecution material, or by
>   misconceived applications in relation to such material.
> ...
> 63 The public rightly expects that the delays and failures which have been present
>   in some cases in the past where there has been scant adherence to sound dis-
>   closure principles will be eradicated by observation of this Protocol. The new
>   regime under the Criminal Justice Act and the Criminal Procedure Rules gives
>   judges the power to change the culture in which such cases are tried. It is now the
>   duty of every judge actively to manage disclosure issues in every case. The judge
>   must seize the initiative and drive the case along towards an efficient, effective
>   and timely resolution, having regard to the overriding objective of the Criminal
>   Procedure Rules (Part 1). In this way the interests of justice will be better served
>   and public confidence in the criminal justice system will be increased.[15]

Of course, this protocol ignores the problem of intercept evidence, as it must. The government's failure to allow intercept evidence, in some form, to be given in evidence remains a potential source of injustice and danger to the public.

Before they obtain full disclosure, the defence must set out their case in writing and answer requests for admissions on apparently non-contentious facts. This is where a problem frequently arises, as I shall explain when I describe the problems faced by defence lawyers. In summary, defendants in terrorist trials often do not trust the prosecution or the courts, or even their own lawyers. The system set out in the protocol requires cooperation from the defendant. To achieve that, the defendant must trust the process. Some never will and the trial system must offer them a fair trial without their active participation.

A useful development in the disclosure exercise is the occasional appointment of *special counsel* to assist the court. This was approved by the House of Lords in *R v. H and C* (above and see paragraph 2 of the Disclosure Protocol on this page) and has been used on a few occasions. It works well, and is to be contrasted with the unsatisfactory role of the special advocate in the Special Immigration Appeals Commission (SIAC) identified by the House of Lords in *Secretary of State for Home Dept v. MB* [2007]. In that case, Baroness Hale warned of the need to be vigilant against claims to unnecessary secrecy: 'There is ample evidence from elsewhere of a tendency to over-claim the need for secrecy in terrorism cases' (see also Turner & Schulhofer, 2005).

Special counsel have access to the 'closed' material and provide a means of enabling the interests of the defence to be presented to the trial judge who must decide what material of potential value to the defence should be disclosed, and in what form. In *R v. Bourgass,* also known as the ricin case (2006), I was able to say in open court that I considered that the disclosure made, and the form in which it was made, satisfied the court's duties of ensuring a fair trial. That did not stop counsel for Bourgass arguing that the disclosure was unsatisfactory. His argument got nowhere. In the fertilizer case of *Khyam and others* [2008] substantial time was spent on a series of applications for disclosure. Had special counsel been appointed, all the issues would have been dealt with as a single exercise and, I believe, a large amount of time would have been saved, together with the inevitable suspicion of defence counsel (and presumably their clients) that something was being kept from them. The Court of Appeal did not criticize the trial judge for not appointing special counsel, and referred to the comment made by the House of Lords in *R v. H and C* that special counsel should be appointed only in exceptional cases. But that is not the same as saying that it would not have contributed to the greater efficiency of the trial. Terrorism trials can be difficult for all involved. Most fit the description 'exceptional'. Adopting procedures that take the potential sense of injustice away must serve the public interest by preventing unnecessary interruptions to the trial and by removing defendants' resentment and unwillingness to comply with court orders that defendants make appropriate admissions and defence disclosure.

Trial

When defending at trial I am looking to undermine the prosecution case where possible. Those possibilities arise in the following ways:

- lack of integrity in continuity of exhibits;
- reliance on unproved hearsay in questions in interview;
- mismatches between what is put in interview and the evidence;
- evidence of sloppiness in making notes or records;
- witness statements made by civilian witnesses that show signs of being drafted by a police officer, especially if it is the same officer who witnessed a number of disputed statements or where the statement differs significantly from the taped witness interview;
- the manner in which interviews are conducted;
- hostages to fortune, for example, expressions of opinion by witnesses of fact;
- expert evidence – has the expert had all the relevant material including (where available) the defence case statement or interview, or has he or she only considered the prosecution version?
- hyperbole in the way the prosecution case is presented, either by counsel or by the investigators.

If the police have done their job competently and fairly, I will not want to ask any questions with which they will disagree. If they have not, then I will try and exploit their failure to reach the high standard expected. When the police are in the witness box, in the eyes of the jury they represent the state. If my case requires me to challenge their evidence on a basis that they do not accept, then my advice is that they should not accept it. Be courteous but firm. I shall, if possible, get the police to agree with me. If I can't I shall challenge their accuracy. Only where I can justify it will I challenge their honesty.

Problems in Defending

This section attempts to improve understanding, not gain sympathy. Why should the defendant trust me when I turn up to see him or her in conference for the first time? Sometimes it takes several visits to see the defendant in custody before a real professional relationship develops. Until that happens, it is difficult to discuss the case and take instructions. It is impossible during that period to give the kind of realistic, sometimes robust, advice that professionalism requires. As mentioned above, defendants in terrorist cases sometimes prefer the advice of their fellow prisoners to that of their counsel.

The first problem is *adverse publicity*. How do you secure a fair trial, that is, a trial by an impartial jury? The same problem occurs in any notorious case, and it is something that must be overcome. The courts are understandably not sympathetic to these points. Serious cases must be tried. Defendants feel that the odds are against them before the trial starts. Telling them that the evidence is far more important than the publicity, or that nothing will sound as prejudicial as prosecuting counsel's opening to the jury, has limited effect; for example, see *R v. Abu Hamza* [2006] EWCA Crim 2918.

The need to provide a *defence statement* to the court and the prosecution is a real problem. Defendants do not understand why they should contribute to their own prosecution, nor why they should tell their own counsel any details of their case. Trying to persuade them that it is in their best interests to serve a defence statement, and that, in order to do so, they need to give full instructions can take months. This problem has been increased by section 60 of the Criminal Justice and Immigration Act 2008, which came into force from 3 November 2008 (SI 2008 No. 2712 (C. 118)), requiring defendants to identify the facts on which they intend to rely. In most cases, that is a sensible and desirable change. But, in terrorism cases, defendants fear that any defence they provide will give the prosecution the opportunity to find evidence to disprove it. They are right. That is part of the function of a defence statement, to avoid the prosecution being taken by surprise on an issue they could disprove if given adequate notice. Defence counsel find themselves badgered by judges and prosecutors to comply with the law on defence disclosure. We are prevented by the rules of legal professional privilege from explaining the problems we are facing in the particular case. As a result, however much we try to persuade the clients to participate in what we hope is a fair trial, it is understandable why they think that cooperation with the court is of limited value. It becomes difficult to comply with the protocols for disclosure and management of long and complex terrorism cases. And then, just when we are beginning to get to grips with the issues, the prosecution serve voluminous additional evidence to which we are expected to respond in an unrealistic time. Defendants feel harassed and then are unwilling to cooperate, even with a process that is designed to ensure a fair trial.

The next problem is *confidentiality*. Terrorist suspects at HM Prison Belmarsh believe that conversations with their lawyers are bugged. There is reason to think that our clients' concerns are not simply paranoid. It is difficult taking instructions on masses of material – much of it in digital format – when clients refuses to discuss details for fear of being overheard. If we ask them to put it in writing, there is the risk that their cell will be searched and the documents seized or at least examined. That happens regularly. They are belatedly given computers to prepare their cases. These are periodically seized and the contents deleted. These are special computers provided by the prison so that prisoners have no means of access to any illicit material or to the Internet. It all adds to the sense of harassment and mistrust. If we cannot do anything about it, why should they trust us to achieve a fair hearing in court? Material that *is* provided to the client must be left with the prison staff. It often takes over a week for it to reach the client. We do not know what is happening during that period.

If the prosecution are correct, and these are dangerous people, then of course we need to know that special steps are being taken to avoid their plotting violence while in custody, or being acquitted on some false basis. The pleas of guilty to very serious offences entered by a substantial number of defendants in terrorist cases demonstrate that the intelligence and evidence are often accurate in important respects. However, for those contesting their guilt, we, their lawyers, are left with the sense that the presumption of innocence has a limited role, that legal professional privilege is not protected.

Dealing with defendants who are foreign nationals and for whom English is not their first language presents further difficulties. There is no formal standard for interpreters, although an association of court interpreters now exists (see PACE Code H, paragraph 13.1). The quality of interpreters varies alarmingly. Unless a member of the defence legal team understands the language, there is no means of checking that the interpreter is translating correctly. The problem usually becomes apparent only when it is too late to correct it in the course of the trial.

Some terrorist defendants who are foreign nationals have suffered trauma in their own country; they may have been subjected to torture or members of their family may have been killed. They are not very receptive to assurances that officials in the UK will secure a fair trial for them. Despite these problems, it is the duty of defence counsel to promote the overriding principles of the Criminal Procedure Rules, namely:

1.1 The overriding objective

(1) The overriding objective of this new code is that criminal cases be dealt with justly.

(2) Dealing with a criminal case justly includes –

    (a)   acquitting the innocent and convicting the guilty;

    (b)   dealing with the prosecution and the defence fairly;

    (c)   recognising the rights of a defendant, particularly those under Article 6 of the European Convention on Human Rights;

    (d)   respecting the interests of witnesses, victims and jurors and keeping them informed of the progress of the case;

    (e)   dealing with the case efficiently and expeditiously.[16]

These standards apply to all involved in the criminal justice system. How well we do it determines how successfully we apply the rule of law. The rule of law, properly understood in its context of fair and open justice, is an essential feature of a democratic society.

Notes

1   'Written standards for the conduct of professional work', para. 11.1, retrieved 22 May 2014 from https://www.barstandardsboard.org.uk/regulatory-requirements/the-old-code-of-conduct/written-standards-for-the-conduct-of-professional-work/

2   See also the Fraud & Complex Trial Protocol in Archbold (1994, appendix N, para. 6(v)(a)).

3   Police and Criminal Evidence Act 1984 (PACE), Code H, retrieved 22 May 2014 from https://www.gov.uk/government/uploads/system/uploads/attachment_data/file/306664/2013_PACE_Code_H.pdf

4   Youth Justice and Criminal Evidence Act 1999, retrieved 22 May 2014 from http://www.legislation.gov.uk/ukpga/1999/23/contents

5   European Convention on Human Rights, retrieved 22 May 2014 from http://www.echr.coe.int/Documents/Convention_ENG.pdf

6   See Chapter 3 by John Pearse and Chapter 4 by Max Hill, QC, on this subject.

7   Criminal Justice and Public Order Act 1994, retrieved 22 May 2014 from http://www.legislation.gov.uk/ukpga/1994/33/contents

8   It is even possible that the ECtHR will declare that their judgment – that there was a violation – is a sufficient remedy for the violation and will not require the UK to reconsider the safety of the convictions.

9   Police and Criminal Evidence Act 1984 (PACE) Codes of Practice, retrieved 22 May 2014 from https://www.gov.uk/police-and-criminal-evidence-act-1984-pace-codes-of-practice

10   See n. 9.

11   Anti-Terrorism, Crime and Security Act 2001, retrieved 22 May 2014 from http://www.legislation.gov.uk/ukpga/2001/24/contents

12   Max Hill, QC, discusses this in Chapter 4.

13   For example, see General Comment No. 31 by UN Human Rights Committee, 26 May 2004, UN Doc. CCPR/C/21/Rev.1/Add.13, retrieved 22 May 2014 from http://daccess-dds-ny.un.org/doc/UNDOC/GEN/G04/419/56/PDF/G0441956.pdf?OpenElement

14   Criminal Justice Act 2003, retrieved 22 May 2014 from http://www.legislation.gov.uk/ukpga/2003/44/contents

15 'Disclosure: A protocol for the control and management of unused material in the Crown Court', retrieved 22 May 2013 from http://www.judiciary.gov.uk/wp-content/uploads /JCO/Documents/Protocols/crown_courts_disclosure.pdf

16 The Criminal Procedure Rules, retrieved 22 May 2014 from http://www.justice.gov.uk /courts/procedure-rules/criminal/docs/2012/crim-proc-rules-part-01.pdf

References

Archbold, J. F. (1994). *Criminal pleading, evidence and practice*. London: Sweet & Maxwell.

Bar Standards Board. (2014, January). Handbook. Retrieved 29 May 2014 from https://www.barstandardsboard.org.uk/media/1553795/bsb_handbook_jan_2014.pdf

Bizos, G. (2000). *No one to blame: In pursuit of justice in South Africa: Personal account of inquests into some deaths in detention under apartheid*. Cape Town: David Philip.

Sands, P. (2008). *Torture team*. London: Allen Lane.

Turner, S., & Schulhofer, S. J. (2005). *The secrecy problem in terrorism trials*. New York: Brennan Center for Justice at NYU School of Law.

Legal Cases

[2012] Crim LR 357–368

A v. Home Secretary [2005] UKHL 71

A v. Secretary of State for the Home Dept [2004] UKHL 56

Bernard v. Trinidad & Tobago [2007] UKPC 34

Condron v. UK (2001) 31 EHRR 1

Israel v. The State, HCJ 5100/94, 26 May 1999, Public Committee against Torture

Judith Ward (1993) 96 Cr App R 1

Murray v. UK (1996) 22 EHRR 29

Paris, Abdullahi and Miller (1993) 97 Cr App R 99

Ramsingh v. Trinidad and Tobago [2012] UKPC 16

R v. Abu Hamza [2006] EWCA Crim 2918

R v. Barot [2007] EWCA Crim 1119

R v. Bourgass [2006] EWCA Crim 3397

R v. Cadder [2010] UKSC 43

R v. H and C [2004] 2 AC 134

R v. Hobson [1998] 1 Cr App R 31

R v. Ibrahim and others [2008] EWCA Crim 880 at [33]–[36] and [55]–[57]. The references to the ECtHR appeals are 50541/08, 50571/08 and 50573/08.

R v. Omar Khyam and others [2008] EWCA Crim 1612

R v. Ulcay [2007] EWCA 2379

Rasul v. Bush (2004) 542 US 466

R v. B [2005] EWCA 805, [2006] Crim LR 54

Secretary of State for Home Dept v. MB [2007] UKHL 46, 31 October 2007

6

An Garda Síochána Model of Investigative Interviewing of Witnesses and Suspects

Geraldine Noone

The social, political and cultural landscape of Ireland has changed utterly over the past four decades, and policing has had to adapt and evolve dramatically in response to these changes. Much of the focus was on the pressing problem of the repercussions from the violent conflict in Northern Ireland and the rapid escalation in heroin use and trade in the urban centres. Police resources were concentrated on crime prevention and security solutions.

In this changing environment one of the core investigative tools, investigative interviewing, and approaches to it changed little. No research on investigative interviewing had been commissioned or conducted by An Garda Síochána (AGS).[1] Indeed, until recently, little research conducted on investigative interviewing internationally has been recognized or applied to the Irish policing context. The reasons for this are complex and may include factors such as a perception among policy-makers that the current system of learning their trade in the operational sphere from more experienced interviewers was serving the force well. Another factor may be an element of resistance to the idea that academics have anything to offer practitioners.

In 2007 this situation changed when the Garda Commissioner approved a new model of investigative interviewing: the Garda Síochána Interviewing Model (GSIM). Basic training to support this model commenced in 2009 for all interviewers and, more recently, advanced training has been delivered to specialist interviewers who are involved in serious and complex investigations. The model and training have been well received and, while there has been no opportunity to conduct a review to date, there is anecdotal evidence of improved interviewer performance, especially at the advanced level, as a result of interviewers using the model. GSIM has also been well received by a multidisciplinary steering committee established by the Department of Justice and Equality to oversee matters relating to interviewing of persons detained at Garda stations.

Investigating Terrorism: Current Political, Legal and Psychological Issues, First Edition. Edited by John Pearse.
© 2015 John Wiley & Sons, Ltd. Published 2015 by John Wiley & Sons, Ltd.

This chapter, which provides the first detailed description of the background and development of the model, its conceptual framework and its key components, will introduce the new model, describe the components and outline the rationale for them and the training involved in each phase. The context in which investigative interviewing takes place in Ireland will also be described, together with the background to this initiative and a brief literature review relating to investigative interviewing models used by other police forces, before concluding with some observations about challenges for the future.

Legacy of the Conflict in Northern Ireland

From the start of the Troubles in Northern Ireland in 1969 until the Good Friday Agreement in 1999 and the subsequent decommissioning of weapons by the Irish Republican Army (IRA), much of the resources of the state were concentrated on security and on the fallout from the Troubles, south of the border. Many of those involved in terrorist activity in Northern Ireland were living south of the border or on the run there and engaging in criminal activity to fund their activities.[2] It is accepted that 'terrorist' is a subjective term which can be used to encompass a wide range of people, including freedom fighters, insurgents, revolutionaries, subversives, and dissidents. This situation influenced all aspects of life in Ireland and it helped shape the criminal justice system, and in particular the AGS approach to crime investigation and investigative interviewing. Members of the IRA refused to recognize the courts and presented as interview-resistant, engaging in counter-interrogation tactics.

The first tranche of legislation in Ireland governing the arrest and detention of suspects – the Offences Against the State Act 1939 (amended in 1996) – was largely used to deal with these individuals. This legislation authorizes special courts (three judges, no jury) and powers of stop, search, seizure, arrest, detention (72 hours) and *interrogation*. This may be one of the reasons why this legislation is still being used in response to non-terrorist-related crime. Much of the case law and practices that have emerged from this time were in reaction to legal challenges relating to the detention and interrogation of suspects by Gardaí using this legislation. For example, case law reinforcing the Judges' Rules (*People [Attorney General] v. Cummins*, 1972) (guidelines for police officers involved in the investigation of crime drawn up by judges in 1912 and reinforced over the years by legal precedent) and defining voluntariness of confession and inducement/oppressive questioning emanate from this time. It could be argued that the genesis of the *challenge* phase of an interview was also laid down during this time, albeit interrogation is what was being referred to.

a Section 30 detention is not intended to be a 'genteel' encounter. It is clear that the very word interrogation means more than some form of gentle questioning and, providing there are no threats or inducements or oppressive circumstance, then the Gardaí will always be entitled to persist with their questioning of a suspect. (*People [DPP] v. McCann* [1988] 4 IR 397, Court of Criminal Appeal, quoting from Supreme Court in *People [DPP] v. Shaw* [1982] IR1)

When asked about their right to challenge or engage in robust interaction during interviews, Gardaí will always refer to this 'genteel encounter' quote. However, it is their interpretation of 'genteel' that has sometimes proved problematic, because of lack of guidelines about its nature and severity.

Ireland is currently experiencing a deep economic recession following the boom years of the 'Celtic Tiger'. The last recession in the 1990s saw an escalation in drug trafficking and drug-related activity which waned in the 2000s (NCC, 2001). The 1990s were a very traumatic decade for crime in Ireland, with increased organized crime gang activity which saw turf wars for the profits from drug trafficking that resulted in the creation of criminal empires and gang lords. This activity culminated in June 1996 with the murders of journalist Veronica Guerin by an organized crime gang and of Detective Garda Gerry McCabe by a dissident IRA gang during a robbery. There were 40 other murders that year, the highest figure since the foundation of the state in 1921, and more recently there were 42 murders in 2011 (CSO, 2012). At this time there was a public perception that a new super-criminal had emerged against whom new measures were needed (Vaughan, 2004). The government's reaction to this perception resulted in new legal powers and resources for AGS, including the establishment of the Criminal Assets Bureau (CAB) and the Criminal Justice (Drug Trafficking) Act 1996 and amendment to the Offences Against the State Act 1939. The result of this was that many of the leading criminals were prosecuted and convicted and others moved their activities abroad. These initiatives resulted in a decrease in criminal activity in Ireland until the mid-2000s, when new and more sophisticated gangs established a foothold in the urban centres. This criminal activity was at its height in 2007 when there were 77 murders recorded in Ireland (CSO, 2012). A large percentage of these took place in Limerick City, which suffered severely because of gangland crime. Many of these criminals stood trial in the Special Criminal Courts established under the Offences Against the State Act 1939 (as amended 1996) because their activities, including intimidation of witnesses and potential jury members, were seen as a threat to the state.

'Burglary, Kidnapping, Smuggling, Fuel Fraud: Ireland's Rising Crimes' (2011) is how a national newspaper, the *Irish Times*, described the type of crime that is currently prominent in Ireland. Kidnapping refers to 'tiger kidnapping', a crime involving the taking hostage of financial institution employees and their family members until the institution hands over a sum demanded by the kidnappers. These crimes are carried out by highly organized gangs that often include up to 12 criminals who are involved in the intimidation of their own members, potential witnesses, jury members and Gardaí. The organizers of these crimes will rarely have 'hands-on' involvement in them. When the hands-on people are arrested, and they regularly are, they invariably rely on their right to silence throughout interview. Some of these gang members are former or dissident terrorists and they are very forensically aware, leaving very few, if any, clues behind. They are also well versed in counter-interrogation techniques.

It is within this context that investigative interviewing evolved in Ireland. Informal intelligence-driven interviews were at the heart of crime investigation. In these situations interviewers educe information from individuals who, for various reasons (fear, intimidation, reluctance to be perceived as an informer by their community), are not willing to go on record. While this information is invaluable for opening up other lines of enquiry, saving lives or preventing further atrocities, it is not possible to use it in criminal prosecutions. However, successful prosecutions in court are one of the primary goals of AGS and the challenge was, and still remains, how to turn sensitive information or intelligence into evidence that is admissible in court. This is why, notwithstanding the importance of intelligence to an investigation, formal interviews with witnesses and suspects will always be the key element of any investigation. One of the many reasons this is so is because only the interview can provide insight into 'intent, thoughts and feelings' (Gudjonsson, 1992, p. 7), which are necessary proofs for most prosecutions; these descriptions and stories are also more persuasive to a jury than documents, charts and similar forms of evidence.

There is, and always has been, external pressure on the police to preserve the security of the state, solve crime and bring offenders to justice. This pressure is magnified when the crime under investigation captures the public's imagination, impacts on the public's perception of safety and security and/or receives a high level of media attention. In circumstances such as these, it can be argued that external pressure transfers to the intimate environment of the suspect interview room. For example, in the trial of an individual charged with involvement in the Omagh bombing, two interviewers were accused by the trial judge, Mr Justice Barr, of falsifying the interview notes (Walsh, 2009, sec. 31.15). In the trial of a suspect in the murder of journalist Veronica Guerin (*People [DPP] v. Ward*, 1998), a suspect's confession was rendered inadmissible by the judges of the Special Criminal Court because it followed a threat by interviewing Gardaí to bring the suspect's girlfriend and elderly parents to the station (Healy, 2004, sec. 10.33). Indeed, some of this emphasis on confessions comes from the judiciary itself: 'the law regards a confession statement as one of the strongest elements of a prosecution case' (Morris, 2008, Vol. 1, sec. 1.47). In the context of an interview with a suspect who is interview-resistant, the goal is to strike a balance between engagement that is meaningful and challenge that is ethical and productive, while respecting the suspect's autonomy and right to silence.

With this in mind, AGS introduced in 2009 a model for interviewing witnesses and suspects, and, although this was the first time the organization had taken a formal approach to this subject, the actual drivers for change were two separate tribunals of inquiry into the activities of certain Gardaí: the Birmingham Inquiry and the Morris Tribunal.

Influence of Public Inquiries

The Birmingham Inquiry and the Morris Tribunal were the most recent forums to bring the practices of AGS under the spotlight and they reflected public disquiet about police practice. Both of these were government-appointed inquiries which raised concerns about the activities of certain Gardaí and fears of miscarriages of justice.

Birmingham Inquiry: Dean Lyons

In March 1997 two women, Mary Callinan and Sylvia Sheils, were murdered in their home at Grangegorman, Dublin. In July 1997 a 22-year-old man, Dean Lyons, became the first suspect in the investigation. He had previous convictions for burglary and he had been telling people, including prison officers while on remand for unrelated charges, that he had been involved in the killings. He was arrested, detained and questioned in relation to the deaths and he confessed to killing both women. He was charged with murder and remanded in custody awaiting trial. In August 1997 another man, arrested on suspicion of killing two other people, confessed to the murders of the two women in Grangegorman, although he recanted this confession soon afterwards. Dean Lyons spent nine months on remand. His confessions were examined by Professor Gisli Gudjonsson, an international expert in false confessions who had been commissioned by the defence (and the lead author of Chapter 7 in this volume). Having assessed Mr Lyons, Gudjonsson found that he was suggestible and susceptible to leading questions put to him by the interviewing Gardaí. He concluded that Lyons's two murder confessions were unreliable because of his psychological vulnerabilities at the time of his detention and questioning, and identified fundamental flaws in the way he had been questioned. The Director of Public Prosecutions (DPP) withdrew the charges against him. Lyons died of a heroin overdose in 2000; nobody has yet been tried for the Grangegorman killings.

In February 2006 a commission of investigation, in accordance with the provisions of section 32 of the Commission of Investigation Act 2004 (No. 23 of 2004), with sole member Mr George Birmingham, Senior Counsel, was established. Its remit was to enquire into the following specific matters:

1   the circumstances surrounding the making of a confession by Dean Lyons (deceased) about the deaths of Ms Mary Callinan and Ms Sylvia Sheils in March 1997 in Grangegorman Dublin 7,
2   the adequacy of the Garda assessment of the reliability of Mr Lyons' confession both before and after he was charged with murder, and
3   the adequacy of information provided by the Garda Síochána on the morning of 27 July 1997 to the Director of Public Prosecutions and in particular whether any additional information should have been provided at that time. (Birmingham, 2006, p. 12)

The commission concluded that Dean Lyons was not abused or ill-treated during his detention. It also concluded that his admissions were not produced by oppression or coercive conduct on the part of the Gardaí, nor were they produced as a result of anything in the nature of a bribe or inducement. There was no deliberate attempt to frame Dean Lyons (Birmingham, 2006). However, the commission also concluded, on the basis of Professor Gudjonsson's report, that Lyons was able to provide accurate details of the murders, which it is now accepted he did not commit, as a result of the manner in which he was interviewed by Gardaí, that is, he was probably fed with crime details between interviews.

The Morris Tribunal and recommendations

On 24 April 2002 a 'Tribunal of Inquiry was set up Pursuant to the Tribunal of Inquiry (Evidence) Acts 1921–2002 into the activities of certain Gardaí in the Donegal Division' (police division in the north-west of the Republic of Ireland). Known as the Morris Tribunal, it was set up under the chairmanship of Mr Justice Fredrick R. Morris. Its terms of references included:

> Conducting an investigation in relation to the death of Mr Richie Barron, Raphoe, Co Donegal on the 14th October 1996. In particular, the arrest and treatment of persons in custody in connection with the investigation, the progress, management and effectiveness of the Garda Investigation with particular reference to management of informants. (Morris, 2008, sec. 1.14, p. 8)

The Morris Tribunal sat for seven years and produced 10 reports. Among the conclusions arrived at were the following:

- The investigation into the death of Mr Richie Barron was conducted in a most negligent manner.
- False evidence was manipulated by members of the investigation team.
- Proper investigation methods were not employed.
- Statements were not properly taken from witnesses.
- Rumours were taken as truth.
- Officers were driven by an extreme form of tunnel vision.
- Innocent people were arrested.
- False confession was procured from Mr Frank McBrearty Jnr.
- The confession procured from Mr Frank McBrearty Jnr was the product of complete and systematic failure of policing at many levels from senior officers to the members conducting interviews with witnesses and suspects.

The tribunal heard evidence from national and international experts in investigative interviewing: Professor Gisli Gudjonsson, King's College, London; Detective Chief Inspector Shaw, Northumbrian Constabulary; Inspector Donal John Adam, Royal Canadian Mounted Police; Ms Mary Schollum, Consultant; Chief Superintendent John O'Mahony, AGS; and Chief Superintendent Kevin Ludlow, AGS. After hearing their evidence, the tribunal observed that 'every step should be taken to ensure false confessions are not procured. Whatever training, procedures and interview techniques that are necessary to minimize risk of this occurrence in future should be examined and adopted' (Morris, 2008, p. 1179).

The tribunal recommendations included the following:

- the PEACE model or a close equivalent be implemented by AGS;
- leadership of a high quality be provided by senior officers of AGS to ensure the model is implemented and accepted by all levels of the organization;
- specialist training be implemented;
- refresher courses be periodically provided;
- workplace assessments take place;
- a national coordinator for investigative interviewing be appointed with oversight and responsibility of the strategy to be implemented, full responsibility and authority to ensure that proper training is carried out, and to ensure that implementation of the strategy is fully accepted and executed by Gardaí at all ranks;
- a national committee comprising representatives from AGS, Director of Public Prosecutions Office, Attorney General's office, the Bar Council and the Council for Civil Liberties be formed, with responsibility for formulating and recommending policy relating to investigative interviewing;
- the legal caution be reviewed to eliminate the need for interviewers to take a written memorandum of interview. (Morris, 2008, pp. 1241–1244)

In seeking to encourage the adoption of a structured, consistent approach to investigative interviewing in Ireland, the Honourable Mr Justice Fredrick R. Morris, chair of the Morris Tribunal, encouraged AGS to adopt a consistent, structured approach to interviewing equivalent to PEACE, which he described as simply 'A vehicle by which challenge may be fairly mounted' (Morris, 2008, p. 1231). He was responding to concerns raised by senior Garda officers that the adoption of the PEACE model by AGS would erode the organization's effective use of challenge in investigative interviews. He accepted that the AGS did not have to adapt PEACE to the 'exclusion of reasonable adaptations thought necessary by AGS' (p. 1232).

The issues highlighted by the inquiries mentioned above, and the recommendations of the Morris Tribunal, in particular, led to AGS developing and adopting a new model of investigative interviewing, An Garda Síochána Interviewing Model (GSIM). AGS were keen to ensure that appropriate challenge was embedded in the model and the model created the outright opportunity to challenge within the context of appropriate subject-specific considerations. Before looking at this model in more detail, we shall look at the experience in other countries that informed the development of this model.

Investigative Interviewing in Other Jurisdictions

United Kingdom: PEACE model of interviewing

In January 1986 the legislation to make mandatory the electronic recording of suspect interviews, the Police and Criminal Evidence Act (PACE) 1984 (Home Office, 1985), was introduced in the United Kingdom following a number of cases of miscarriages of justice. By 1992 police stations across the UK were equipped to audio-record all suspect interviews, and subsequent research revealed just how limited the interviewing practice was. For example, Baldwin (1992) identified the interviewing skills as inadequate; Moston, Stephenson, and Williamson (1992) concluded that they were characterized by accusatorial interrogation styles and assumptions of guilt; Gudjonsson (1992, 2003) and Bull and Cherryman (1996) concluded that there were corrupt practices by police and poor interviewing techniques. Following these research findings, the PEACE[3] model of investigative interviewing was introduced in the UK in 1993, whose principles were to 'provide a framework to encourage an ethical and open-minded approach to investigative interviewing' (Shaw, 1996, quoted in Shawyer, Milne, & Bull, 2009). Post-PEACE research results were generally positive, although limited communication skills and lack of competence when challenging suspects' account were identified (Clarke & Milne, 2001). Shaw (2012) found weakness in the model with regard to challenging uncooperative suspects, while Pearse and Gudjonsson (1996) detected the absence of challenges in their study and recommended that the C should also represent 'challenge'. Later Gudjonsson and Pearse (2011) noted that the model had failed to evolve since its inception. Reservations were also expressed by Assistant Commissioner O'Mahony in his testimony to the Morris Tribunal where he described the tendency of interviewers using the model to adopt a formulaic style of interviewing which failed to 'accommodate sufficiently strong challenge' (quoted in Morris, 2008, pp. 1227–1228). These are some of the reasons that PEACE in its current form was not considered a suitable option for Ireland.

United States: The Reid Technique

The most widely known and published interviewing model in the US investigative community is the Reid Technique of interviewing and interrogation. This technique combines factual analysis, behavioural analysis and interrogation, and its focus is to induce a confession from a guilty suspect. This technique has been criticized because of its emphasis on persuasion, psychological manipulation, deception detection and certainty of guilt which can be contributory factors to false confessions (Gudjonsson, 2003; Gudjonsson & Pearse, 2011; Kassin & Gudjonsson, 2004; Kassin et al., 2010). Electronic recording of all suspect interviews is not compulsory or widespread in the United States, and this makes it difficult to conduct an accurate analysis of the effectiveness of the Reid Technique (Gudjonsson, 2012). Because of these criticisms and because elements of it are incompatible with the rules of evidence and legal precedent in this jurisdiction, the Reid Technique could not be considered as an option for adoption by AGS.

Norway, Sweden and Denmark

Because electronic recording of police interviews is not compulsory or widespread in these three Nordic countries, the process is not open, accountable or transparent.

This makes it difficult to conduct an accurate assessment of the system. However, in 2002 Norway introduced the KREATIV[4] model of investigative interviewing.

The European Committee for the Prevention of Torture and Inhuman or Degrading Treatment or Punishment (CPT) visited Norway, Sweden and Denmark, where it carried out research and made recommendations in relation to investigative interviewing. The latter included a recommendation that Norway should 'draw up a more detailed code of practice on police interrogations' (Fahsing & Rachlew, 2009, p. 41). CPT made no direct criticisms about the conduct of suspect interviews in Denmark but they did highlight issues concerning delays in administering suspects. They made no criticism of suspect interviews in Sweden but they did recommend that the electronic recording of suspect interviews should take place.

KREATIV was the Norwegian police force's response to these recommendations and it is influenced by PEACE. The existing interview training was reviewed in Sweden in 2004 but the Swedish police did not adopt a structured model of interviewing like PEACE or KREATIV. In 2005 the Danish Police College introduced a five-day interview training programme for detectives based on KREATIV, but with separate approaches for interviewing witnesses and for interviewing suspects. A review has not yet been carried out to measure the effectiveness of these changes, and indeed that would be difficult considering there is still no widespread electronic recording of suspect interviews in Norway, Sweden or Denmark (for a comprehensive review, see Fahsing & Rachlew, 2009).

New Zealand

In 2005 the PEACE model of investigative interviewing was introduced in New Zealand but, having examined the UK experience, the New Zealand authorities took steps to ensure that the issues identified above would not be replicated in their jurisdiction. They established a unit, staffed by experts in investigative interviewing, that serves as a one-stop shop in relation to all aspects of interviewing including ownership, training, supervision, monitoring and advising. They also created awareness among the managerial ranks by conducting information seminars and training workshops in the divisions (Grantham, 2010).

Garda Síochána Interviewing Model

In May 2007 the Garda Commissioner approved the establishment of a working group to examine issues pertaining to investigative interviewing under the title 'Investigation of Crime – Interviewing of Witnesses and Suspects – Manual of Guidance'. Its remit was to draft a manual of guidance for the interviewing of witnesses and suspects based on national and international best practice and research. As a result of this work, AGS developed and adopted the GSIM. This model emphasizes the importance of seeking an account of knowledge from all interviewees and represents a shift from a confession-seeking approach with suspects to an information-gathering approach. It consists of three key elements: the generic phases; an interview subject-specific approach; and a competency framework for interviewers. It takes an interview subject-specific approach, taking account of the interviewee's level of cooperation and intellectual and psychological capacity rather than the traditional approach to victim, witness or suspect where the main focus is on their role in and attitude towards the criminal justice process. I will now provide an insight into the generic phases of the model and the rationale for them and then outline the interview subject-specific component of the model, before describing the interviewer competency framework.

Overview of GSIM

An overview of the model and its component parts is provided in Figure 6.1. This model for investigative interviewing in AGS provides a framework for interviewing all categories of persons of interest during criminal investigation, regardless of their status as victim, witness or suspect, or of their approach to the investigation. An important distinction between the GSIM and other approaches to investigative interviewing is that it places an emphasis on the specific considerations of the individual being interviewed rather than taking a generic approach to victim, witness and suspect interviews. It provides a professional approach to interviewing and constitutes an effective methodology for investigative interviewing which is ethical throughout.

Generic phases

Planning and preparation
This is the first and most important phase of the interview process (see Figure 6.2), and the first and most important step in this phase is identifying the objectives

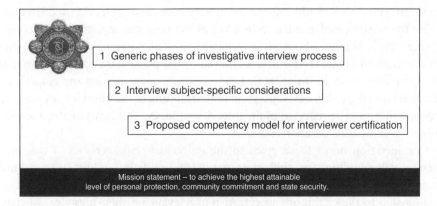

Figure 6.1 An overview of the GSIM

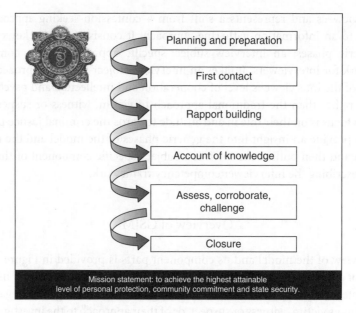

Figure 6.2 The generic phases of the interview process

for the interview. What is it for? What is to be achieved by this interview? These objectives will inform the strategy. Without them, the interview will, at best, lack focus. At worst, it will deteriorate into a repetitive, possibly coercive engagement. A well-thought-out set of objectives that have been agreed with the senior investigating officer (SIO) and all other interested parties will also help to measure the success of the interview, for example: Were the objectives achieved? What is left to achieve? How can this be achieved, and why were they not achieved? This is necessary for all interviews, whether of victim, witness or suspect.

Planning and preparing is not just about gaining an in-depth knowledge of the file and its legal requirements. At the very least, any interview conducted as part of an investigation should add value to the investigation, and preserving and strengthening the existing evidence has to be a key objective of any investigative interview. Preparation is as much about *who* as *what, why, when, how* and *where*. Developing an approach to the interview that is tailored to the particular individual is one of the key pillars of GSIM. In order that they are truly open-minded and empathetic, the interviewers need to develop a good understanding of the interviewee's perspective and this must be reflected in the interview strategy. This is where the interview subject-specific considerations come in.

Consideration needs to be given to the individual characteristics of the interviewee: vulnerabilities (psychological, mental, intimidation, addictions); cultural issues; sexual orientation; previous experience of the criminal justice system; relationship to the victim or suspect. Also of relevance is their lifestyle, associates and any issues that might act as a block to rapport building or fuel resistance. It is argued that interviewees' decision-making is driven by their perception of what is happening (Gudjonsson, 2003), which is relevant to both witnesses and suspects. A thorough background check of the interviewee during the plan and preparation phase will help reveal issues that may influence their attitude towards the interview process. An interviewee's perception of what is happening will not always be obvious to the interviewers. However, using this model with a conscientious application of its emphasis on subject-specific considerations, no manipulation or unfair practice should occur that may distort the interviewee's perceptions of what is happening. The generic phases are designed to provide opportunities for explanations, rapport building, appropriate questioning and presentation of evidence that are both appropriate for the individual concerned and ethical throughout.

The success of a suspect interview cannot be measured by whether or not a confession is achieved. Confessions are generally welcomed, but they are not always necessary. The pressure to achieve them can be counter-productive and they may be pursued to the detriment of gathering information that is of evidential value. While confession is not the primary focus of an interview with a suspect, consideration needs to be given to factors that may inhibit a suspect's decision to confess or to engage with the process. For this reason, wherever possible, planning should include issues such as the pre-arrest strategies. For example, 'hard' arrests and dawn raids can heighten physiological arousal and squander good first contact opportunities and interview time. A well-planned, flexible approach that takes account of an individual's needs rather than a one-size-fits-all approach will help alleviate this problem.

Planning and preparation involves developing an interview strategy for the strategic use of evidence and eliminating conceivable manoeuvres relevant to the specific case. For example, in an investigation of a tiger kidnapping involving several suspects, the overall aims of the interviews would be to solidify the associations and sightings between the key players and to ensure the specific objectives of the individual interviews eliminate possible defences before the evidence is presented.

All too often details of the investigation are disclosed to a witness or victim and focused or leading questions are asked before an account of their own knowledge has been elicited. This may have the effect of contaminating the witness's memory of the event, or causing them to fail to disclose information that they had but were not directly asked about. In the case of a suspect, the evidence is often presented prematurely during interview and all that is then needed from the suspect is an explanation *that is reasonable in the circumstances* or an alibi, and this is sometimes achieved through payment, threats or coercion rendering inference provisions and existing evidence weak or useless.

Experience indicates that a suspect will often be ambivalent as to whether or not to engage, at what level, with whom, at what stage; whether or not to confess, to partially confess, and so on. It is important that the interviewer recognizes this ambivalence and manages it appropriately. Autonomy is also an issue that plays out in the interrogation setting because of the influence of the power myth on some interviewers where they engage in overt displays of power as a result of their anxiety that their control over the suspect is weak or compromised (Heydon, 2004) and the actual and perceived constraints on the suspect's autonomy. This is a very powerful dynamic in the interview room.

The interview plan will involve developing a thorough knowledge of the interviewee in order to identify their potential approach to the interview process. Any possible resistance should be identified and strategies developed for managing the interviewee in order to maximize the level and accuracy of the information elicited from the interview.

First contact

This phase includes introductions, explanations about rights, ground rules, procedures, outlining the matter under investigation and the interviewee's role in it, the time frame involved and the route map. One of the functions of this phase is to remove uncertainty for the interviewee and to allow the interviewer to get a baseline for the interviewee's abilities, level of understanding and attitude. It also takes account of pre-interview issues that might impact on the interview: circumstances of arrest and detention; timing of arrest; interviewee's previous experience of the criminal justice system; and external factors such as partners, spouses, employers and co-accused. It is also the phase where the foundation stones for rapport that were developed in the plan and preparation phase are built on.

Rapport

Research indicates that rapport is essential to investigative interviewing (Fisher & Geiselman, 1992; Holmberg & Christiansen, 2002; Shepherd, 1991). For this reason it is a stand-alone phase of the GSIM as well as an underlying principle. It is also intended to be a thread running through the entire process. This thread is based on the *ethical parameters* described by Ridgeway (2000), where rapport is inherent in a balanced humanitarian interaction. It is characterized by empathy and active listening and its purpose is multifold: to encourage compliance, reduce resistance, gain an insight into the interviewee's characteristics, abilities, background and possible motives or opportunities for committing the crime; and to facilitate the eliciting of an account. It is intended as a natural stepping stone into the account of knowledge phase.

Identifying and reflecting the emotional needs of the interviewee will save a lot of time and unnecessary conflict. Identifying these needs starts at the plan and preparation phase, and training at level 3 (advanced level) develops skills in recognizing and managing emotions. Consideration also needs to be given to the risks and rewards for the suspect of cooperating or resisting engagement. Rapport building is about creating a non-judgemental, non-coercive atmosphere conducive to disclosure.

Account of knowledge

This phase is based on the *report everything or free narrative* principles of the cognitive interview (Fisher & Geiselman, 1992) and is designed to elicit an account from the interviewee in his or her own words at his or her own pace. Control of the flow of information is transferred to the interviewee and the interviewer's job is to encourage and guide the interviewee through the account with active listening, skilled questioning and adherence to a plan. A practice has developed whereby some interviewers engage in a formulaic question-and-answer approach. This approach does not add value to the investigation. Merely asking questions of a witness does not allow a free narrative account of the event. Rather, it allows the interviewer to control the pace and direction of the interaction, which limits the quantity and accuracy of the information disclosed. When interviewing a suspect, the purpose of this question-and-answer style seems to be merely 'putting' evidence to the suspect. 'There is no rule of law that a person suspected of a crime must have put to him, or her, the material upon which AGS suspect their involvement in the crime. Nor is it necessary to produce the statements of witnesses or accomplices which implicate the prisoner.' It can, however, 'be desirable for a person facing an accusation of complicity in a crime to be given the opportunity to proffer an explanation for apparently incriminating circumstances' (Morris, 2008, p. 51). Putting evidence or statements to a suspect should be done only as part of an interview plan which determines what will be used and when, keeping in mind that it should be used strategically.

Assess, corroborate, challenge
The purpose of this phase is to evaluate the account given, clarify any ambiguities, corroborate it from existing evidence and challenge any aspect of the account where necessary. Given the importance of witness evidence in a trial, it is imperative that their account be assessed, corroborated and challenged as far as possible. The planning phase will have given the interviewer a thorough knowledge of the matter under investigation and any other available evidence. The account offered should be compared to the known facts of the case and the human factors relating to memory and perception. Eyewitness testimony should be assessed using the guidelines encompassed under the mnemonic ADVOKATE: amount of time under observation, distance, visibility, obstructions, known or seen before, any reason to remember, time lapsed, errors or material discrepancies. These steps help make an assessment of the completeness or accuracy of the account. Interviewers should be mindful that a witness's credibility can be challenged during a trial under the following criteria: previous inconsistent statements, bias on the part of the witness, previous convictions of the witness, veracity of the witness, physical or mental disability of the witness (Healy, 2004). The potential for these problems should be explored during this phase. If there are ambiguities, inconsistencies or evasiveness, they may be removed with further probing, which may render challenge unnecessary. Issues should be followed up systematically and an individual topic should be exhausted before moving on to the next. Topic hopping and interruptions allow skimming, and it will not be easy on a subsequent review of interview notes to determine if the interviewee was deliberately evasive or simply did not get the opportunity to elaborate on his or her account. This was the problem in a recent investigation where the victim subsequently became a suspect and was to be arrested on suspicion of withholding information. In preparation for his arrest, examination of his previous interviews

was unhelpful because the interviewers had not been thorough enough in probing each topic.

Challenge should be characterized by persistence and patience, active listening and a deep understanding of the case file. It must be based on evidence that has been validated, verified and categorized according to its strength. It is a problem-solving phase, not a cross-examination or an 'I put it to you' approach. Interviewers should be mindful that a suspect has the right to remain silent. They are not obliged to answer any questions. Suspects are entitled to a 'basic constitutional right to fair procedure while in custody' (Judges of the Special Criminal Court in *People (DPP) v. Ward*, 1998). These constitutional rights impose the principle of fairness and dictate that a statement must be voluntary and free from oppression, inducement, threat or promise in order for it to be admissible in a court of law. Oppression has been described as including physical or psychological pressure (*People [DPP] v. Shaw*, 1982).

When conducting an investigation, Gardaí are not obliged to accept the first answer given to their enquiry, so challenge can be robust where appropriate but it must not be carried out in a manner designed to oppress, intimidate or humiliate. It is permissible to challenge the suspect on the honesty and completeness of his or her account, and this may be done in a frank, forthright manner, within the context of a rapport-based interaction. Behaviour that has been deemed oppressive in the past includes physical violence; showing bloody post-mortem photographs; using degrading language like 'murdering bastard' or 'Satan'; yelling; belittling protestations of innocence with foul dismissal (Morris, 2008, ch. 1).

The planning and preparation phase should determine the level, focus and appropriateness of the challenge and the appropriateness of challenge can be determined by interview subject-specific considerations. For example, consideration needs to be given to factors such as the interviewee's age, ability, life experience, previous arrest history and connection to the crime or offenders. Issues relating to appropriateness of challenge include the voluntariness of the information disclosed and oppressive questioning. These are governed by the Criminal Justice (Treatment of Persons in Custody in Garda Stations) Regulations Act 1997 and the Judges' Rules (*People [Attorney General] v. Cummins*, 1972). However, the court will apply a *subjective test* over and above these provisions which takes into account the specific circumstances at the precise time the disclosure was made:

> What may be oppressive as regards a child, an invalid, or an old man or someone inexperienced in the ways of this world may turn out not to be oppressive when one finds that the accused person is of a tough character and an experienced man of the world. (*People [DPP] v. Pringle, Court of Criminal Appeal*, quoted in Healy, 2004, p. 297)

Closure

This phase has both a legal and a psychological function. It comprises a review of the account which may lead to new information and the need to revert to a mini account phase; an outline of what happens next; referral to other agencies (if appropriate); dealing with any questions or issues raised by the interviewee; and an appreciation of the interviewee's time and efforts. Again, this phase will be very subject-specific, as some interviewees will need more reassurance and explanation than others. Where sensitivities have been raised by the interview, the interviewee may need to be referred to another agency or released into the custody of a friend or family. In a suspect interview, where the suspect relies on his or her right to remain silent, the closure phase will involve a summary of the evidence. The purpose of this phase is to satisfy legal requirements, consolidate an account given, leave the interviewee in a positive frame of mind and leave the door open for future contact. One problem for interviewers is that they do not know how much interviewees know about the event. Interviewees may have information they did not disclose for various reasons, for example, because of the way they were questioned; failure to recall; not considering it important or relevant; fear; or hostility. Interviewers will not necessarily be aware at the end of the interview that they have failed to gather this information, and a good closure leaves open the possibility that it might be offered in the future. It is the closing of the relationship which began at the *first contact* phase. Each interview with a detained suspect should have a closure phase where topics covered are summarized and the scene is set for subsequent interviews. This is particularly important if there is going to be a new interview team.

Interview Subject-Specific Considerations

The approach adopted by the GSIM to the different categories of interview subjects distinguishes between interviewees on the basis of their style of interaction rather than their status as a victim, witness or suspect. The categories of subjects to be considered are:

1   cooperative injured party
2   uncooperative injured party
3   cooperative witness
4   uncooperative witness
5   vulnerable witness
6   cooperative suspect
7   uncooperative suspect
8   interview-resistant suspect
9   vulnerable suspect.

These categories can be seen in terms of four broad distinct interview subject types, with reference to the numbered list above:

- cooperative interview subject (1, 3, 6);
- uncooperative interview subject (2, 4, 7);
- interview-resistant subject (8);
- vulnerable interview subject (5, 9).

Cooperative interview subject

Most witnesses fall into this category (which includes categories 1, 3 and 6 above) in light of the fact that a witness cannot be compelled to make a statement. Research shows that the standard of witness interviews is significantly lower than the standard of suspect interviews (Clarke & Milne, 2001). This is not surprising, considering that suspect interviews are likely to be recorded and subject to scrutiny and also considering that police officers place greater emphasis on suspect interviews than on witness interviews (Stockdale, 1993/2005; Strongman, 1994). This occurs despite the fact that the initial interviews with key witnesses, including victims, determine the appropriate direction of the investigation and a timely and successful conclusion. Yet, a cursory glance at any investigation file or Book of Evidence (documents served on the defendant on behalf of the DPP in Ireland, prior to trial) shows that key witnesses will sometimes have been interviewed up to 10 or 11 times, indicating that little planning or preparation went into the initial interviews. The approach of interviewers should be guided by a style of interaction characterized by patience and support for the interview subject. Control over the interview should largely be afforded to the interviewee. Training is provided in skills such as planning, active listening, eliciting a free narrative account, systematic probing of topics, memory enhancing techniques such as context reinstatement, changing of perspective, sensory recall and the use of the ADVOKATE principle.

Uncooperative interview subject

Uncooperative interview subjects (incorporating categories 2, 4 and 7) are individuals who engage in the interview process at some level but who display, or are expected to display, reticence in offering information about the substantive issue under investigation. This behaviour may range from avoiding the interview, evasiveness, deceit, to refusal to answer particular questions. Interviews should be guided by a predetermined interview strategy which will help develop an understanding of the individual and consider their motivation for lack of cooperation, for example, rational choice, fear of penalty, face-saving, protecting themselves or others. Training at level 3 competency is designed to enhance the interviewer's ability to develop an understanding of the interviewee's perspective and to be flexible in his or her approach to the interview. Training is provided in skills such as planning, rapport building, confirmation bias, tunnel vision, appropriate questioning, appropriate challenge, strategic use of evidence techniques, vulnerability, fear and intimidation, suggestibility, safeguards against false confessions, active listening, eliciting a free narrative account, systematic probing of topics, memory enhancing techniques and oppressive questioning.

Interview-resistant subject

Interview-resistant subjects (category 8) are individuals who engage in counter-interrogation strategies. Such strategies may range from an individual's self-tailored and pre-planned approach (e.g., career criminal) to actual detailed instructions and indoctrination as part of an organized group (e.g., organized crime syndicate, terrorist organization). There tends to be a preconceived assumption among some interviewers that particular interviewees will resist and thus it becomes a self-fulfilling prophecy on their part. In other cases, the resistance can be addressed and removed with a level of understanding and planning. Interviews with resistant subjects should be guided by the interview plan which will determine the most appropriate first contact and rapport-building strategy. It will also determine the appropriate strategy for disclosure of evidence. Training skills are provided in planning, appropriate first contact, rapport building, motivation, theme development (not to be confused with theme development in the Reid Technique; theme development in the GSIM is not about minimization but rather is a conduit through which interviewers display an understanding of the interviewee's perspective), presentation of the evidence, factors that may fuel resistance and skills that act against educing further resistance.

Vulnerable interview subject

Vulnerable interview subjects (categories 5 and 9) may be so categorized on the basis of, but not limited to, the following characteristics: age, intellectual disability, mental health, addiction, psychological vulnerability and intimidation. In some cases, the vulnerability may be evident or known prior to interview. In these circumstances the appropriate special measures can be applied, for example, having an appropriate adult or support present, or using a specialist interviewer. Training to develop skills in the following topics is provided: interview planning, identifying and managing vulnerabilities, appropriate ethical and legal measures, managing appropriate adults, suggestibility, eliciting free narrative, questioning and appropriate challenge. Interviewers trained at level 3 will have knowledge and skills in identifying and managing interviewees who fall into this category. In some cases an individual may not be identified as vulnerable until such time as they have undergone a psychological test post-interview. However, if the interview was conducted within the parameters of the model, particularly with regard to their free narrative account prior to any questioning or challenge, the integrity of their testimony will be ensured. Only appropriately trained interviewers, who are aware of the reality and the dynamics of suggestibility and false confessions, should be deployed to interview vulnerable subjects.

Proposed Competency Model for Interviewer Certification

This tiered approach to interviewer competency and training reflects the importance of achieving basic skill and experience at the lower levels before advancing to develop knowledge and skills for the more serious or complex situations (Figure 6.3). The skills necessary for conducting an investigative interview have been undervalued

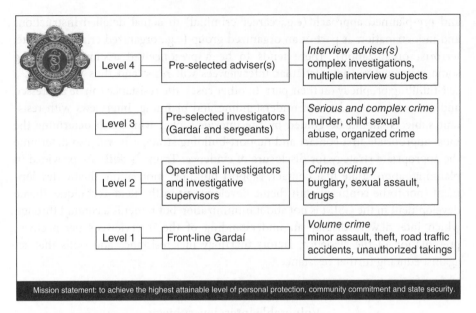

Figure 6.3   Competency framework for interviewer certification

and underestimated in the past. Advanced training at levels 3 and 4 is long and intensive. Knowledge is developed through lectures, discussions and case studies. Skills are developed and knowledge applied using real interview scenarios, simulations and role play. Feedback is provided by experienced trainers who are also trained interview advisers and operational interviewers. If trainees are found not to have developed to the degree of competency necessary at this level, they are not certified to interview in serious and complex investigations.

Conclusion

Since the foundation of the state in 1921, AGS has had to evolve rapidly to be effective in its response to political, social and economic changes. One of the biggest challenges the organization faced was the threat posed to the security of the state by the violent conflict in Northern Ireland. Many other states are now experiencing a similar challenge because of the new threats posed by the onset of international terrorist campaigns. Until recently, one of the areas least well served by the organization was the area of investigative interviewing, but this changed in 2007 when the GSIM was developed for investigative interviewing. This chapter has, for the first time, introduced this model to a wider audience.

The emphasis in the GSIM is on rapport-led interviewing, with effective use of challenge, based on available evidence. The generic phases are designed to provide a structured framework for investigative interviewing that is ethical, flexible and accountable. They are based on empirical research and international best practice.

It takes an interview subject-specific approach, taking account of the interviewee's level of cooperation and intellectual and psychological capacity rather than the traditional approach to victims, witnesses and suspects. The main focus of this traditional approach is their role in and attitude towards the criminal justice process.

The interviewer competencies are designed to ensure that only appropriately trained interviewers are deployed for the specific circumstance. Interviewers trained to level 3 competency will have the advanced knowledge and skills to deal with all subject-specific categories.

The subject-specific considerations ensure that the genetic phases are appropriate and flexible in dealing with the challenges presented by individuals rather than employing a one-size-fits-all approach. This approach of adapting the interview style to the behaviour and vulnerabilities of the interviewee (i.e., to the *who*), whether a witness or a suspect, is one of the unique features of the model. It provides a greater flexibility than the generic PEACE model.

While the GSIM is still in its infancy, it is already considered by some commentators as 'more dynamic and flexible than PEACE in terms of challenging uncooperative interviewees' (Gudjonsson, 2012, p. 117), who also notes: 'Unfortunately, the PEACE model technique does not appear to have evolved sufficiently since its introduction in the UK in the early 1990s and it needs to become more innovative with regard to challenging the denials of uncooperative suspects' (p. 118). With regard to suspect interviews, the model goes some way towards addressing what Gudjonsson and Pearse (2011) consider to be the main police interview challenge for the future: 'to develop transparent and accountable interview techniques that maximize the number of non-coerced true confessions while minimizing the rate of false confessions' (p. 36).

The GSIM has a number of advantages over other approaches: it has been designed and guided by the experience of other forces; it places equal emphasis on interviews with witnesses and victims as with suspects; and it accommodates potential vulnerabilities within these categories. Training and a framework are provided for interviewers to engage with each category based on the individual considerations relevant to the interviewee rather than their status in the investigation. One integral component of the model, *challenge*, is already supported by case law and legal precedent. The model now provides guidance and a framework for an ethical subject-specific challenge. It is informed by scientific research, and training in the use of this model will continue to reflect best practice and scientific knowledge into the future. It is also flexible enough to accommodate any changes in practice that might evolve in the future. For example, in Ireland there are currently no legal provisions for the presence of a legal adviser during an interview with a suspect. Any changes in this situation can be accommodated quite easily. The interview plan will inform the briefing of the legal advisers. There are already moves afoot to remove the legal requirement to record the suspect interview in writing. Again, the model can accommodate this change without the need for any revision.

The challenge for GSIM is to remain dynamic and flexible and to evolve sufficiently into the future. In order for this to happen, certain issues need to be considered by the organization. For example, managerial support is imperative if the cultural shift necessary for such a change in approach and practice is to take place. Time needs to be set aside for planning, as Dixon noted: 'There is no point in inserting … that preparation is vital for a good interview if officers' workloads are not managed so that time to prepare is available' (2006, p. 337). There needs to be a re-evaluation of and consensus on what constitutes a good interview and, consequently, a good interviewer. Workplace assessments need to be conducted to ensure that knowledge and skills developed at training are transferred to the workplace. Research shows that skills dissipate within weeks of training and become redundant within six to eight weeks without monitoring and feedback from supervisors (Clarke & Milne, 2001; Powell, 2005). That witness interviews are increasingly likely to be electronically recorded, and that suspect interviews are always electronically recorded, make these very much achievable.

Acknowledgements

The author wishes to acknowledge the contribution of the Garda Commissioner and the Working Group on Investigative Interviewing under the chairmanship of Chief Superintendent Kevin Ludlow.

Notes

1   An Garda Síochána (Guardians of the Peace) is the national police force of Ireland and members of the force are usually referred to as Gardaí (plural) or Garda (singular).
2   'Terrorist' is used in this context according to the *Oxford English Dictionary* definition of 'a person who uses terrorism (extreme fear) in pursuit of political aims'.
3   PEACE being a mnemonic for planning and preparation; engagement and explanation; account and clarification; closure; and evaluation.
4   In translation, KREATIV encompasses the rule of law, ethics and empathy, active awareness, trust through openness, information and a valid scientific foundation.

References

Baldwin, J. (1992). *Video-taping police interviews with suspects: An evaluation*. Police Research Series Paper No 1. London: Home Office.

Birmingham, G. (2006). *Report of the Commission of Investigation (Dean Lyons Case)*. Retrieved 4 June 2014 from http://www.justice.ie/en/JELR/DeanLyonsRpt.pdf/Files /DeanLyonsRpt.pdf

Bull, R., & Cherryman, J. (1996). Investigative interviewing. In F. Leishman, B. Loveday, and S. P. Savage (Eds.), *Core issues in policing*. London: Longman.

Burglary, kidnapping, smuggling, fuel fraud: Ireland's rising crimes. (2011, 4 July). *Irish Times*. Retrieved 25 May 2014 from http://www.highbeam.com/doc/1P2-29059035.html

Central Statistics Office (CSO). (2012). Homicide offences. Retrieved 28 June 2012 from http://www.cso.ie/Quicktables/GetQuickTables.aspx?FileName=cja01c1.asp& TableName=Homicide+Offences&StatisticalProduct=DB_CJ

Clarke, C., & Milne, R. (2001). *National Evaluation of the PEACE investigative interviewing course.* Police Research Award Scheme. London: Home Office.

Dixon, D. (2006). Regulating police interrogation. In T. Williamson (Ed.), *Investigative interviewing: Research, rights and regulation* (pp. 167–189). Cullompton, UK: Willan.

Fahsing, I. A., & Rachlew, A. (2009). Investigative interviewing in the Nordic region. In T. Williamson, B. Milne, & S. Savage (Eds.), *International developments in investigative interviewing* (pp. 39–65). Cullompton, UK: Willan.

Fisher, R. P., & Geiselman, R. E. (1992). *Memory enhancing techniques for investigative interviewing: The cognitive interview.* Springfield, IL: Thomas.

Grantham, R. (2010). Investigative interviewing, PEACE, ECI and conversation management are recognised internationally as best practice but how do you convert experienced practitioners to investigative interviewing? In *Proceedings of the 3rd annual conference of the International Investigative Interviewing Research Group. Evaluation and effectiveness of investigative interviewing: A multi-disciplinary approach* (pp. 29–30). Norwegian Police University College, Stavern, 22–24 June 2010.

Gudjonsson, G. H. (1992). *The psychology of interrogations, confessions and testimony.* Chichester, UK: Wiley.

Gudjonsson, G. H. (2003). *The psychology of interrogations and confessions: A handbook.* Chichester, UK: Wiley.

Gudjonsson, G. H. (2012). False confessions and correcting injustices. *New England Law Review, 46*, 689–709.

Gudjonsson, G. H. & Pearse, J. (2011). Suspect interviews and false confessions. *Current Directions in Psychological Science, 20*, 33–37.

Healy, J. (2004). *Irish laws of evidence.* Dublin: Thomson, Round Hall.

Heydon, G. (2004). *The language of police interviewing: A critical analysis.* Basingstoke, UK: Palgrave Macmillan.

Holmberg, U., & Christianson, S. A. (2002). Murderers' and sex offenders' experience of police interviews and their inclinations to admit and deny crimes. *Behavioural Science and the Law, 20*(1–2), 31–45.

Home Office. (1985). *Police and Criminal Evidence Act, 1984.* London: HMSO.

Judges Rules. (1912). Narrated in *People [Attorney General] v. Cummins* [1972] IR 312 (SC).

Kassin, S. M., Drizin, S. A., Grisso, T., Gudjonsson, G. H., Leo, R. A., & Redlich, A. P. (2010). Police-induced confessions: Risk factors and recommendations. *Law and Human Behaviour, 34*, 3–38.

Kassin, S. M., & Gudjonsson, G. H. (2004). The psychology of confessions: A review of the literature and issues. *Psychological Science in the Public Interest, 5*, 33–67.

Morris, F. (2008). *Report of the Tribunal of Inquiry set up pursuant to the Tribunal of Inquiry (Evidence) Acts 1921–2002 into the activities of certain Gardaí in the Donegal Division (The Morris Tribunal)* (Vols. 1–3). Dublin: Government Publications Office.

Moston, S., Stephenson, G. M., & Williamson, T. M. (1992). The effects of case characteristics on suspect behaviour during police questioning. *British Journal of Criminology, 32*, 23–40.

National Crime Council of Ireland (NCC). (2001). Crime statistics. Retrieved 4 June 2014 from http://www.crimecouncil.gov.ie/statistics_cri_crime_table3.html

Pearse, J., & Gudjonsson, G. H. (1996). Police interviewing techniques at two south London police stations. *Psychology, Crime, and Law, 3*, 63–74.

Powell, M. B. (2005). Improving the reliability of child witness testimony in court: The importance of focusing on questioning techniques. *Current Issues in Criminal Justice, 17(1)*, 137–143.

Ridgeway, B. J. (2000). The hermeneutical aspects of rapport. *Dissertation Abstracts International: Section A: Humanities Social Sciences, 60*(7-A), 2527.

Shaw, G. (1996, 16 February). Investigative interviewing: Supervision. *Police Review*, pp. 20–21.

Shaw, G. (2012). Challenging task. *Investigator Magazine, 2*, 56–61. Retrieved 4 June 2014 from http://www.the-investigator.co.uk/files/The_Investigator_-_Issue_2_2012.pdf

Shawyer, A., Milne, B., & Bull, R. (2009). Investigative interviewing in UK. In T. Williamson, B. Milne, & S. Savage (Eds.), *International developments in investigative interviewing* (pp. 24–38). Cullompton, UK: Willan.

Shepherd, E. (1991). Ethical interviewing. *Policing, 7*(1), 42–60.

Stockdale, J. E. (1993/2005). Management and supervision of police interviews. Police Research Group. Repr. in M. Schollum (Ed.), *Investigative interviewing: The literature*. Wellington, New Zealand: Office of the Commissioner of Police.

Strongman, K. T. (1994). *Interview training in the New Zealand police*. Wellington: New Zealand Police.

Vaughan, B. (2004). Accounting for the diversity of policing in Ireland. *Irish Journal of Sociology, 13*(1), 49–70.

Walsh, Dermot P. J. (2009). *Human rights and policing in Ireland: Law policy and practice*. Dublin: Clarus.

Legal Cases

People [Attorney General] v. Cummins [1972] IR 312, SC

People [DPP] v. McCann [1988] 4 IR 397

People [DPP] v. Pringle [1981] 2 Frewen 57, CCA

People [DPP] v. Shaw [1982] IR 1

People [DPP] v. Ward [1998], Special Criminal Court, 27 November 1998; CCA, 22 March 2002

7

Risk Assessment of Terrorist Offenders
A Challenge Too Far?

Gisli H. Gudjonsson, Adrian West and Amy McKee

A *Sunday Times* article highlighted the duplicitous behaviour of some terrorist prisoners: 'Lie, say you have reformed, be set free and strike again' (Gadher, 2012). This lies at the heart of the need for the risk assessment of terrorist prisoners and highlights the public concerns that, even while serving their sentences in prison, terrorists are 'spreading their message of hate' (p. 1) and inciting violence. In response to the *Sunday Times* article, a spokeswoman for the Ministry of Justice is reported to have said that 'The National Offender Management Service ("NOMS") recognizes the risks posed by extremist offenders and those who seek to radicalize others and takes their responsibilities to effectively manage these risks seriously' (p. 13). This response from the Ministry of Justice highlights the two key elements involved in a general or a generic, as well as terrorist, risk assessment: first, the vulnerabilities and risk factors associated with becoming involved with terrorist activities in the first place; and, secondly, the risk assessment and management of convicted terrorists during their detention and after completion of their sentence. This chapter focuses principally on the latter, but will also address the literature regarding the former.

There are well-established and validated risk assessment procedures and tools available for violent recidivism, which are routinely used in correctional and forensic institutional settings (Gudjonsson & Young, 2007; Skeem & Monahan, 2011; Yang, Wong, & Coid, 2010). Unfortunately, this does not hold true for the risk assessment of offenders whose crimes are principally motivated by extreme political, religious or ideological views (Pressman, 2009). Indeed, there is an absence of empirical research in this area of risk assessment, there are no empirically validated measures available for an actuarial risk assessment, and the field is dominated by a lack of consensus among professionals (Dernevik, Beck, Grann, Hogue, & McGuire, 2009a, 2009b; Gudjonsson, 2009).

Investigating Terrorism: Current Political, Legal and Psychological Issues, First Edition. Edited by John Pearse.
© 2015 John Wiley & Sons, Ltd. Published 2015 by John Wiley & Sons, Ltd.

The lack of consensus among the psychology profession is perhaps best illustrated by the outcome of a working party set up by the British Psychological Society (BPS) in 2008 to develop a *Position Paper: The Psychological Risk Assessment of Those Convicted for Terrorist Related Offences* in order to assist psychologists working in this area. After a draft 'Position Paper' was produced and sent out for consultation in 2010, it was abandoned after it emerged that there was no consensus among those consulted and insufficient evidence available to produce an informed position paper that could be supported by the British Psychological Society.

In this chapter the authors review: (1) the general issues about risk assessment (i.e., the general context within which terrorist risk assessment falls); (2) the key conceptual issues relating to terrorist risk assessment (e.g., who is being assessed, for what purpose, and in what context?); (3) identifying the key issues and risk factors relevant to an evaluation; (4) professional and ethical issues relating to terrorist risk assessment, including the methods available and their limitations; and (5) practical and delivery issues.

Generic Risk Assessment and Management

Kraemer et al. (1997) define risk assessment as 'The process of using risk factors to estimate the likelihood (i.e., probability) of an outcome occurring in a population' (p. 340). In relation to terrorism risk assessment, Monahan (2012) adopts the following definition of terrorism: 'The calculated use of unlawful violence or threat of unlawful violence to inculcate fear, intended to coerce or to intimidate governments or societies in the pursuit of goals that are generally political, religious, or ideological.' There are many other definitions of terrorism and related terms such as 'radicalization', 'radicals', 'extremists' and 'extremist violence', which Pressman (2009) discusses in detail.[1] He argues that 'terrorism' is a dynamic term: it has many forms and involves many types of individuals and groups; it is premeditated, motivated by ideology and grievances rather than personal vengeance, and is intended to cause fear as well as acts of violence.

The above definitions focus only on the first component of a risk assessment. As stated at the beginning of the chapter, the objective of violent risk assessment is broader than merely estimating the risk of violence. It should also provide guidance about how the risk can be managed or mitigated by appropriate intervention (Pressman, 2009; Webster, Douglas, Eaves, & Hart, 1997). For example, the Historical Clinical Risk Management-20 (HCR-20) has a 'companion guide' which provides practitioners with advice about how to devise risk management strategies prompted by the HCR-20 violence risk factors, for example, helping offenders to develop realistic plans for discharge; 'building stable environments' and effective support in the community; avoiding adverse peer groups and their influences; motivating offenders to comply with remediation efforts.

With regard to the management and intervention of extremist (terrorist) prisoners, Silke (2011) argues that, while prisons potentially provide an opportunity for combating terrorism (for example, by the use of de-radicalization programmes), there is an increased international recognition that it also provides an opportunity for terrorists to recruit and radicalize new members and to support existing members within and outside the prison (e.g., via the Internet). Without better understanding of this radicalization process within prisons, Silke (2011) argues, de-radicalization programmes are unlikely to be successful and may even be counter-productive (e.g., result in the early release of potentially high-risk convicted terrorist offenders). Concerns have been raised that 'Hardened militants cannot be rehabilitated and need to be made to cease their activities, through the courts or in other ways' (Burke, 2007, p. 312).

Skeem and Monahan (2011) make the point that treatment and management recommendations and strategies, following the basic risk assessment, are useless unless they are 'translated into an individual supervision and treatment plan (rather than simply filed away) and systematically targeted with appropriate services (rather than ignored in resource allocation)' (p. 41). Furthermore, they argue that 'even well-validated instruments offer little direct validity data for the treatment-relevant variables they include' (p. 42) and that 'This is a crucial issue to address in future research if tools continue to be sold on the promise of informing risk reduction' (p. 41).

Skeem and Monahan (2011) argue that the current risk assessment process 'exists on a *continuum of rule-based structure*, with completely unstructured (clinical) assessment occupying one pole of the continuum, complete (actuarial) assessment occupying the other pole, and several forms of partially structured assessment lying between the two' (p. 39; emphasis original). They conceptualize this risk assessment process as having four key components:

1   identifying empirically valid risk factors;
2   finding a method for measuring the risk factors;
3   employing a procedure for combining the scores on the risk factors;
4   providing an estimate of violence risk.

According to this conceptualized framework, the purely (unstructured) clinical approach does not meet criteria for inclusion in any of the four structured components. Within this structured approach 'The clinician selects, measures, and combines risk factors and produces an estimate of violence risk solely according to his or her clinical experience and judgment' (Skeem & Monahan, 2011, p. 39). The reliance on a standard list of risk factors meets the first component (identifying factors); the Historical Clinical Risk Management-20 (HCR-20; Webster et al., 1997) fulfils two of the components (identifying factors and measuring risk factors); the Classification of Violence Risk (COVR; Monahan et al., 2001) and the Level of Service Inventory (LSI; Andrews, Bonta, & Wormith, 2004) meet the first three components (identifying factors, measuring risk factors and combining risk factors); and only the Violence Risk Approach Guide (VRAG; Quinsey, Harris, Rise, & Cormier, 2006) meets all four components (identifying factors, measuring risk factors, combining risk factors and producing a final risk estimate).

Of the five approaches reviewed by Skeem and Monahan, the unstructured clinical approach has the poorest empirical support due to relative lack of sensitivity (i.e., the proportion of high-risk persons correctly identified) and specificity (the proportion of no or low-risk persons correctly identified) (Lidz, Mulvey, & Gardner, 1993), whereas the structured risk assessment measures 'are well validated for the groups to which an individual belongs' (Skeem & Monahan, 2011, p. 41).

There are other measures available for assessing the risk of violence, which are not included by Skeem and Monahan in their review, including the Psychopathy Checklist – Revised (PCL-R; Hare, 2003), the General Statistical Information for Recidivism (GSIR; Bonta, Harman, Hann, & Cormier, 1996), the Violence Risk Scale (VRS; Wong & Gordon, 2001), the Offender Group Reconviction Scale (OGRS; Copas & Marshall, 1998), and the Matrix 2000 for Violence (RM2000V) and Sexual Violence (RM2000V) (Thornton, 2007).

Meta-analyses

Recently, three important meta-analysis reviews have been conducted on the efficacy of commonly used violence risk assessment measures (Campbell, French, & Gendreau, 2009; Fazel, Singh, Doll, & Grann, 2012; Yang et al., 2010). Campbell et al. (2009) found in their review of 88 studies that there was little variation in the mean effect sizes of common actuarial and/or structured risk assessment measures, such as the HCR-20, the LSI/LSI-R, the PCL/PCL-R/PCL: SV, the VRAG and the GSIR scale, for predicting institutional violence, whereas instruments including dynamic risk, as well as static factors, were superior in predicting violent recidivism compared to those focusing on static factors only (e.g., VRAG).

Yang et al. (2010) conducted a similar meta-analysis, but attempted to overcome some of the conceptual and methodological limitations of previous studies by using multilevel regression analysis. They compared the predictive efficacy of nine commonly used risk assessment measures in predicting violent recidivism from 28 studies, including the HCR-20, the LSI-R, the PCL-R and the VRAG, and found that all nine measures and their subscales predicted violence at about the same moderate level of predictive efficacy with the exception of PCL-R Factor 1, which predicted violence only at chance level among men. Yang et al. concluded: 'After almost five decades of developing risk prediction tools, the evidence increasingly suggests that the ceiling of predictive efficacy may have been reached with the available technology' (2010, p. 759). They recommended that 'Efforts should be directed towards investigating situational contingencies that precipitate violence' and that 'More studies of violence prediction should be undertaken with female participants as the pattern of prediction results for women appeared significantly different, in many instances, from those of men' (p. 761).

Fazel et al. (2012) conducted a systematic review and meta-analysis of the use of nine commonly used risk assessment instruments to predict violence, sexual and general offending in 73 samples involving 24,827 people from 13 countries.

The review showed that instruments designed to predict violent offending performed better than those aimed at predicting sexual or general offending. The authors concluded that:

> Although risk assessment tools are widely used in clinical and criminal justice settings, their predictive accuracy varies depending on how they are used. They seem to identify low risk individuals with high levels of accuracy, but their use as sole determinants of detention, sentencing, and release is not supported by the current evidence. Further research is needed to examine their contribution to treatment and management. (Fazel et al., 2012, p. 1)

In spite of the development of a number of sophisticated actuarial risk assessment measures for predicting general violence, the views of the international psychology profession are polarized when it comes to applying group data to evaluating risks regarding an individual case (Skeem & Monahan, 2011). For example, Hart, Michie, and Cooke (2007) argue that the margins of error regarding the prediction of violence in an individual case are 'virtually meaningless' (p. 263) and 'it is clear that predictions of future offending cannot be achieved, with any degree of confidence, in the individual case' (p. 259). Hanson and Howard (2010) contest this position, and Skeem and Monahan (2011) argue that 'group data theoretically can be, and in many areas empirically are, highly informative when making decisions about individual cases' (p. 40), citing the work of Grove and Meehl (1996).

The Pathway into Terrorism

Burke (2007) makes the point that 'Modern Islamic terrorists are made, not born' (p. 306), which also applies to other types of terrorist, and argues that the pathway into terrorism involves a three-stage progression:

1   There is the perception, belief or feeling that something is not right or unjust and needs to be corrected (i.e., perceived legitimate grievances).
2   The belief that the perceived problem (grievances), whether cosmic or personal, cannot be resolved without action that goes beyond society's political and legal framework (i.e., lack of faith in a political and legal system, feelings of disempowerment).
3   The acceptance of an ideology (i.e., a process of radicalization) that allows anger and perceived grievances to be translated into the symbolic realm, hope of resolution, feelings of commitment to the cause, suspension of normal moral barriers to violence and justification for terrorist acts.

While it is important to play close attention to the actions of the offender in their commission of terrorist acts, this often needs to be considered within the broader context of a network of relationships with other 'terrorists' (Merari, 2005, 2010; Post, 2007).

Suicide Terrorists

Merari (2010) has recently completed a study that involved identifying the character-istics of suicide terrorists (defined as those who intentionally kill themselves in order to kill others for political or ideological ends). He has collected data on almost 3,000 suicide bombers worldwide between 1974 and 2008. Of those the majority (95%) were male, although marked differences between the various terrorist groups were noted (e.g., groups motivated by Islamic religious ideology almost exclusively use males, whereas groups motivated by national or ethnic sentiments more often use women); they were generally young (mean age = 20.9 years) and similar in age to other terrorists, mainly single, tended to be educated (this information is limited to mainly Palestinian and British terrorists and the 9/11 hijackers), and most apparently held a radical Islamic belief or were raised in a Muslim society.

In addition to Merari's review of the cases on his database, he conducted two small but informative studies, one focusing on interviewing the families of 34 Palestinian suicide bombers, and the other on a small study of 15 Palestinian 'would-be suicides' (i.e., who were apprehended before completing their mission) and 12 controls (i.e., non-suicide terrorists with similar demographic background).

As far as the characteristics of the 34 deceased suicide bombers are concerned, all were male, the mean age was 22.6 years, 91.2 per cent were single and 79.4 per cent had, prior to their suicide mission, been actively involved in political militancy. The most striking feature of the description of the personality of the deceased (53.6% of the sample) was that they were introverted, inhibited and loners. This finding is important, because it appears to corroborate the findings from the direct psychologi-cal assessment of the participants of the would-be suicides in the separate controlled study. The majority (60.0%) of the would-be suicide participants, according to the findings from a clinical interview and psychological testing, were diagnosed as being 'dependent-avoidant' in their personality, in contrast to 16.7 per cent of the controls. Both dependent and avoidant personality traits fall into Cluster C in the *DSM-IV*, which has been found to be associated with an elevated level of compliance with a medium effect size as measured by the Gudjonsson Compliance Scale (Gudjonsson & Main, 2008). The would-be suicide participants were also found to be significantly more likely than the controls to have depressive and suicidal tendencies.

Merari concludes that a comprehensive understanding of suicide bombers needs to consider three interrelated components: (1) the social or community environment (i.e., the political context); (2) organizational dimensions, such as group processes, involvement and influences; and (3) the characteristics and vulnerabilities of the individual.

Conceptual Issues

Monahan (2012) has recently written the most comprehensive, insightful and authoritative paper available on the individual risk assessment of terrorist offenders.

This timely paper addresses the most salient conceptual and methodological challenges that need to be made if the risk assessment of terrorism is to match the progress that has been made in the assessment of other types of violence. Monahan makes the point that since the September 11, 2001, attack in the USA, research and writings have focused principally on Islamic (or jihadi) terrorism, which he thinks has important implications for the type of risk factors considered important in terrorism.

Monahan asks whether the focus in the risk assessment should be on 'terrorism in general' (i.e., all terrorist activities are seen as having similar punitive risk factors) or on 'a specific type of terrorism' (e.g., is there a need to consider the type of terrorist organization, type of terrorist activity and the specific role played?). The type of terrorist activity is certainly likely to be important. For example, important psychological differences have been found between suicide bombers, including would-be suicide bombers, and other terrorists (Merari, 2010). 'Lone wolf' terrorists are more often found in the United States than in the other countries; their rates of psychological disturbance and social difficulties are found to be relatively high, and many apparently rely on beliefs and ideologies of validation generated and transmitted by extremist movements (Kroner, Mills, & Reddon, 2005).

The role played in the terrorist organization is also undoubtedly important. For example, distributing leaflets and terrorist material and fund-raising in order to support violent attack are psychologically different from direct terrorist activity (i.e., physically killing people). However, progression may be important here. For example, Merari (2010) found that, among Palestinian suicide bombers, 'prior to their last deadly mission, 27 of the 34 suicides (79.4%) were involved in various intifada activities against Israeli forces' (p. 90).

There are many types of terrorist organizations with different ideologies (e.g., Irish Republican Army, Taliban, al-Qaeda, Tamil Tigers, Chechen rebels, animal rights activists and extreme right political organizations), which may function differently in terms of the radicalization process, recruitment and group pressure.[2] For example, while 95 per cent of suicide bombers are male, a disproportionate number of female suicide bombers have been reported for members of the Turkish PKK (Partiya Karkere Kurdistan, or Kurdistan Workers Party), the Chechen rebels, and Tamil Tigers (Merari, 2010). Merari argues that the evidence shows that suicide bombers motivated by Islamic religious ideology are almost exclusively represented by males, whereas those motivated by national or ethnic sentiments more commonly also use females.

Monahan cites the work of Gartenstein-Ross and Grossman (2009) to indicate that 'home-grown' terrorists of the jihadi type in the United States and the United Kingdom come from less privileged socio-economic and poorer educational backgrounds and have fewer occupational prospects than is typically observed of the 'global terrorist movement as a whole' (p. 17). Therefore, whether the jihadi terrorist is home-grown or foreign suggests different risk factors. This highlights the complexity of the risk assessment of terrorists.

According to Monahan, the key factors that are known to predict common violence – criminal history, an irresponsible lifestyle, psychopathy or criminal attitudes and substance use (see Gudjonsson & Young, 2011; Kroner et al., 2005) do not appear to generalize to terrorist violence (e.g., Post, 2007; Silke, 1998). However, violent attitudes, including the acceptance of violence as legitimate means in conflict resolution, are important predictors of violent behaviour (see Gudjonsson, Sigurdsson, Sigfusdottir, & Young, 2012) and may be an important driving force on the path to violent action (Pressman, 2009).

Major mental illness (i.e., schizophrenia) is found in about 10 per cent of cases in homicides (Taylor & Gunn, 1999), but appears rarer in cases of known terrorists (Merari, 2010; Monahan, 2012). The exception may be lone wolf terrorists (Kroner et al., 2005) and those attacking public figures (James et al., 2007, 2010).

Monahan raises the issue about whether terrorism should be viewed as 'an event' or as 'a process' that unfolds over time. A process model is probably more meaningful. For example, Horgan (2008) argues that the involvement in terrorism is a complex psychosocial process that consists of three distinct phases: (1) becoming involved, (2) being actively involved (i.e., engaging in terrorist activity), and (3) disengaging (which may not necessarily result in subsequent de-radicalization).[3] As far as risk assessments of prisoners are concerned, all three steps need to be considered, but how to achieve a sustained disengagement from the previous terrorist activities is also likely to be a key management issue, that is, how to manage or mitigate the risk of continued terrorist activity – the more hardened, involved and dedicated the terrorist activist the less likely it is that rehabilitation will work (see Burke, 2007). It is also important to distinguish between the risk factors associated with the personality of 'leaders' (e.g., self-righteousness, narcissism, high level of self-confidence, dominance) and 'followers', the latter being likely to be of a more compliant temperament than the former.[4]

Terrorist Risk Assessment Tools

As far as risk assessment tools are concerned, Monahan (2012) argues that, without a clear understanding from the onset about

> whether we are attempting to assess the risk of terrorism in the aggregate, or of specific types of terrorism – or of specific phases in the process of becoming or of remaining a terrorist, or of specific roles in terrorist activities – we are unlikely to produce a coherent body of empirical data on the risk of assessment of terrorism. (p. 18)

This will determine whether or not broad or narrow outcome measures are required for evaluating risk.

Roberts and Horgan (2008) suggest that the framework of the HCR-20 could be used to structure the terrorist risk assessment. However, since the HCR-20 was developed to assess risk of violence among mentally disordered offenders (i.e., those with mental illness or personality disorder), its application to extremist offenders is likely to be of limited value because of the apparently relative absence of mental disorder among this population (Monahan, 2012).

Pressman (2009) argues that, out of existing structured professional judgement tools, the HCR-20 and the *Professional Manual for Structured Assessment of Violence Risk in Youth* (SAVRY; Borum, Bartel, & Forth, 2006) are the two most relevant tools for assessing the risk of terrorist violence. The SAVRY is based on a similar framework to the HCR-20 and is designed to be used with 12- to 18-year-olds. In contrast, the HCR-20 is designed to be used with adult males and females who have mental health problems and personality disorder and with prisoners – 'with general psychiatric, forensic psychiatric, and correctional populations in mind' (Douglas, Webster, Hart, Eaves, & Ogloff, 2002, p. 5). There appears to be a general consensus that conceptually psychopaths and violent extremists share few common characteristics. Therefore, the PCL-R is probably not suited for the terrorism risk assessment (Monahan, 2012; Pressman, 2009), but in cases where psychopathy does coexist it should be considered as an additional (incremental) risk factor. The recent work of Merari (2010) suggests that some Palestinian (non-suicide) terrorists are highly impulsive and emotionally unstable and that 25 per cent of them possess psychopathic tendencies.[5] Therefore, more research is needed in this area before firm conclusions can be drawn that personality disorder and psychopathic traits are not prevalent among terrorists.

Pressman (2009) argues that most of the knowledge about risk factors related to terrorism comes from retrospective case studies or individuals or radical groups. What appears to be the case from the available evidence is that there is little overlap between the risk factors found to be relevant in predicting general criminal violence and those considered relevant to ideologically motivated violence. Pressman lists the following as being the major predictors of violent extremisms:

- attitudes justifying violence;
- the dehumanization of the identified targets;
- the rejection of peaceful and democratic means of resolving injustices and historical grievances.

According to this framework, the likelihood of terrorist violence is increased when individuals have already taken steps to engage in violent action (e.g., non-state-sponsored military training) and are involved in social networks supporting terrorist violence.

Pressman has incorporated the major risk factors of terrorist violence into a structured risk assessment tool, labelled Violent Extremism Risk Assessment (VERA). The VERA was designed to be used for individuals who have a history of extremist violence or have been convicted of such offences, and was initially intended to be used as a conceptual research tool in order to generate debate and discussion. In view of the fact that the HCR-20 was specifically developed for persons with mental illness and/or personality disorder, Pressman argues that the HCR-20 may therefore be of little value in evaluating the future risk of violent extremists, particularly when major differences exist in terms of motivation and background factors. She suggests four key differences: (1) the HCR-20 being heavily weighted on mental illness factors, which are uncommonly found among terrorists; (2) that terrorists, unlike other offenders, often do not have a previous criminal history; (3) that terrorists have not consistently been found to have experienced problems with education, employment and/or childhood maladjustment; and (4) that terrorists are not generally observed to be impulsive and aggressive prior to their terrorist offence. In general, they seem to be normally functioning individuals.[6]

Pressman estimates that 15 (75%) of the HCR-20 had little or no direct relationship with the risk factors identified for violent extremists. The five relevant items were: unresponsiveness to treatment (C5), plans lack feasibility (R1), exposure to de-stabilizers (R2), lack of personal support (R3), and non-compliance with remediation attempts (R4).

According to Monahan (2012), the current VERA (Version 2; Pressman & Flockton, 2010) consists of 31 items, which are grouped into five categories:[7]

1   beliefs and attitudes;
2   context and intent;
3   history and capability;
4   commitment and motivation;
5   protective factors. (Pressman & Flockton, 2010)

Monahan (2012) notes that the salient terrorist risk factors identified by Pressman and Flockton (2010) overlap with those suggested by Horgan (2008) and McCauley and Moskalenko (2011). Reviewing the different conceptual headings from previous research, Monahan identifies four central categories of terrorism risk factors, which incorporate the essential components of previous categorization and could be used to broadly guide terrorist risk assessment:

1   ideologies (e.g., ideological beliefs, ideas and commitment being the potential driving force for terrorist action);
2   affiliations (e.g., association with other people who hold similar ideologies and commit terrorist acts);
3   grievances (e.g., personal and group grievances acting as a driving force for anger and terrorist violence);
4   moral emotions (e.g., feelings of one's own group's 'sacred values' being violated, feelings of disgust, feeling morally obliged to engage in violence).

An important neglected emotion regarding terrorist risk assessment is the absence, or temporary suspension, of empathy regarding the intended targets of violence. Baron-Cohen (2011) discusses the important role of empathy in reducing terrorist-related activities and concludes that 'each drop of empathy waters the flowers of peace … and the only way forward will be through empathy' (pp. 126–127).

All four categories of terrorism risk factors identified by Monahan are potentially influenced by cultural factors. There is evidence that culture predicts affective responses (Markus & Kitayama, 1994). Recent experimental evidence shows that the reverse is also true. Ashton-James, Maddux, Galinsky, and Chartrand (2009) found that affect can also determine the expression of culture and suggest that the 'reciprocal forces between affect and culture create the current self: Who one is – one's behaviours, cognitions, and self-construals – at any given point in time depends on the fundamental interplay between affect and culture' (p. 345). However, there is no evidence that intimate understanding of the terrorist's culture is necessary to conducting a risk assessment. Of greater importance is the understanding of the four central categories of terrorism risk factors listed above, which can be helpfully interpreted within Beck's (1999) cognitive basis of anger, hostility and violence, which principally links both common and terrorist violence to such processes as dichotomous (black/white) thinking, cognitive distortions and the activation of a hostile mind-set. The activation of a hostile mind-set emphasizes the importance of combination of dysfunctional cognitions and heated emotions in terrorist violence.

Beck (1999) views the collective self-images of the extremist groups 'as righteous and committed to a noble cause' (p. 137). Their violent actions

> can be traced to the convergence of several interpersonal and psychological processes; the contagion of highly charged antagonistic ideas, the stereotyping and ultimately the framing of the opposition as the Enemy, and the lifting of inhibitions against murder. Indeed, the pre-emption of traditional notions of the value of human life by a higher, sacred cause that sanctions terrorist activities removes the psychological block to committing violent acts, including murder. (Beck, 1999, p. 157)

Monahan (2012) argues that it is unlikely that any risk assessment tool involving the assessment of terrorist risk can be prospectively validated because terrorist violence is too infrequent for a sufficiently large sample to be validated, in contrast to general violence, and because of other logistic problems (e.g., releasing many high-risk individuals as determined by an assessment tool). He concludes that a more realistic method of validation would involve relying on the 'known group' method of validation, whereby expected risk factors from known terrorists are compared with those of a matched group of non-terrorists. This would require the necessary infrastructure to provide access to the relevant groups of terrorists and non-terrorists and their cooperation.

Further Current Tool Developments

The National Offender Management Service, whose staff engage in casework and risk assessment of offenders convicted under terrorist legislation, has recently been engaged in the development of risk assessment and risk management tools for extremist (terrorist) prisoners (Lloyd & Dean, 2012). The risk assessment tool is referred to as Extremism Risk Guidance (ERG-22+) and consists of items rated on a three-point scale ('No evidence', 'Some evidence', 'Strong evidence'). The ERG-22+ has, as its name suggests, 22 risk factors associated with terrorist offending behaviour.[8] The emphasis within the ERG is on a case formulation approach as a conceptual framework for conducting assessments consistent with a structured professional judgement methodology.

The two management tools that have been developed concurrently are the Motivation and Engagement Intervention (MEI) and the Health Identity Intervention (HII). According to Lloyd and Dean (2012), the MEI and the HII have been piloted on 20 offenders from a variety of extremist backgrounds, and 'Emerging findings are positive and recommendations will address not only the content of the programmes but also matters concerning their commissioning, facilitation and support' (p. 35). Alongside the ERG-22+, Extremism Risk Screening (ERS) emerged, which has been designed as a screening assessment tool to consider intelligence on suspected terrorist offenders around three key domains: engagement, intent and capability.[9] Each of the domains has a variety of indicators encapsulated within it that information assessors may use as guidance in assessing whether an individual can be considered to be at risk of engaging in acts of terrorism.

Engagement

This domain considers whether there is any evidence of engagement or involvement with a group, cause or ideology. The important aspect of this domain is to evaluate whether an individual has aligned themselves with a person or an organization known to be supportive of violence or other illegal activity in order to further its aims. Often an individual becomes engaged with a cause because it meets a personal need, such as creating a sense of belonging, providing money, status or a sense of power and control.

Intent

For an individual merely to identify themselves as sharing the interests of an extremist group is not in itself sufficient for agencies to begin to consider intervention. There needs to be some evidence that an individual is willing to progress their chosen cause through violent or illegal means (i.e., there is a commitment and attitude that justifies violence). As such, information is required about what individual actions the person is taking in terms of expressing their beliefs. There needs to be an ability to overcome inhibitions against violence towards others and, as such, an individual's previous criminal history is also of relevance here.

This domain considers what might best be described as disinhibiting factors – attitudes, beliefs or circumstances which reduce someone's inhibitions to offend, for example, empathy, morality and feelings of shame. Cognitive distortions should also be examined. For example, is the individual able to justify and rationalize their beliefs by selective abstraction of information that confirms their thinking while ignoring that which conflicts with their beliefs?

Capability

In early versions of the ERS, it was considered that if somebody did not appear to rate highly on the dimensions of engagement and intent then the assessment of capability was unnecessary. However, as with all risk assessments, the assessment of somebody's risk is a dynamic process. Assessors should consider all domains in the initial assessment such that effective management plans are in place and can be activated or modified should there be further intelligence to indicate that more robust management is required.

Capability should also be assessed to determine how quickly an individual may be able to put any plans into action. For example, someone who has the capability as a result of training or experience in making explosives may need more time to put violent plans into action, whereas someone who has a generic capability to be violent may need very little time to move to an 'action' phase. While it was originally intended for the assessment of prison intelligence, the ERS can potentially be employed in wider criminal justice settings and is a useful organizational framework for assessing suspected terrorist offenders.

However, these tools, like the VERA, need to be used with caution in view of the absence of any empirical validation of their efficacy. Both measures appear to be conceptually and theoretically meaningful and do incorporate Monahan's (2012) proposed four central categories of terrorism risk factors (ideologies, affiliations, grievances and moral emotions).

Professional Issues

1   A central ethic of competent clinical practice is that it should be based on current knowledge of the behavioural science evidence base. Professional registration with the Health & Care Professions Council (HCPC) is the standard requirement for psychologists working in the National Health Service or the prison service. Importantly, HCPC registration involves adherence to the responsibilities set out in the Standards of Conduct, Performance and Ethics. Both the HCPC and the BPS (through its Code of Ethics and Conduct) address the issue of professional competence. The HCPC requires that health professionals ensure that their professional knowledge, skills and performance are of a high quality, up to date and relevant to their field of practice. This means that they should only practise in those fields in which they have appropriate education, training and experience. The HCPC also instructs that health professionals practise within the limits of their knowledge, skills and experience. Similarly, the BPS requires that psychologists seek consultation and supervision when appropriate.

2   Post (2007) makes the point that 'All too many terrorist experts have never laid eyes upon a terrorist, much less spoken with one' (p. 8). This raises serious professional concerns. Horgan (2011) has recently drawn attention to the need for professionals to overcome the challenges involved in interviewing terrorists, including methodologically sound collection of interview data and improved communication and transparency among researchers.

3   When conducting a risk assessment, it is important that the interviewer utilizes all relevant sources of information (e.g., self-report, collateral information, observational data and relevant psychometric test results[10]). Careful preparation for this task is essential. The interviewer should optimize the likelihood of more frank disclosures if they can demonstrate a detailed knowledge of the terrorist's history and current circumstances.

4   West and Greenall (2011) emphasize the importance of reviewing collateral sources in order to understand the motivations and actions of the offender in the index offence. In their view, over-reliance on the self-report of the offender jeopardizes the accuracy of assessments, and they provide an innovative index offence assessment guidance methodology as a useful adjunct to a standard clinical evaluation.

5   Although terrorist incidents remain extremely low-frequency events, our perceptions of the risk of such events occurring are influenced by the ease with which instances of an event can be recalled (Monahan, 2012). Accordingly, those attempting to assess those convicted of terrorism offences should be mindful of how the current national and international threat environments can combine with our deeply rooted fears of such events to influence our best efforts at an objective and dispassionate assessment.

6   The knowledge about terrorism and related threat and risk assessment is growing, but it is likely that assessors are still relying to varying degrees on naive implicit models of how terrorists act. There are still no standardized and validated risk assessment tools available for conducting terrorist risk assessment and great controversy within the psychology/psychiatry profession about how such assessment should be completed. Therefore the need to seek and use peer review articles, authoritative books and other forms of advice is of importance in this area of work. In many instances appropriate supervision is desirable, if not essential.

7   The clinical risk assessment and management task is more straightforward if a client has a previous record for the behaviour that is causing concern. For example, if the assessment task is to understand an individual's violent behaviour, then previous violence can be examined in order to provide indications as to what future risk scenarios might be encountered. However, when assessment is conducted on individuals about whom there is no prior offending and where there is a very limited evidence base for conducting the risk assessment, the task becomes more problematic. For offences considered under UK terrorism legislation there are limited literature and tools to assess risk. We are still in the developmental stages, with extremism related to violent offending being less well researched

than other forms of violence. In view of this, terrorism risk assessors need to make the limitations of their methodology clear in the report.

Clinical Experience

Commonalities observed in our clinical experiences of convicted terrorists are typically that they have been socially isolated from a young age, been bullied at school and lack family support. This seems to create an enduring sense of not belonging anywhere. This continues into adulthood, with individuals being unable to find themselves a fulfilling role in society and feeling mostly on the sidelines. With some of the cases we encountered, there was an ongoing conflict between wanting to fit in and be accepted, while at the same time not valuing those whom they do encounter who are part of mainstream society. For example, one of the younger interviewees we encountered appeared to feel a marked sense of being different from others. He did not feel any connection with other people and was acutely anguished about this. He particularly felt this lack of connectedness in his interactions with women, although he made repeated efforts to form relationships, none of which were successful.

We have also encountered a number of individuals who, as well as having schizoid-type traits (i.e., lack of interest in social relationships, a solitary lifestyle, emotional coldness), also presented with marked narcissistic traits (i.e., inflated feelings of self-worth, excessive need for admiration, strong self-entitlement), which appeared to compensate for underlying feelings of worthlessness. This narcissism combined with the schizoid traits outlined above results in individuals who derive little from social relationships and, indeed, often perceive others to present a threat. This alienation from society, together with a sense of entitlement, can result in a toxic mix whereby violent action against the perceived mainstream is seen as justified.

Some of the sample have been interested in, and have identified with, infamous and notorious school shooters, notably Eric Harris and Dylan Klebold (Columbine). This appears regularly in the diary writings of younger people. There is also often interest in various notorious male murderers. One individual identified with serial killers and was envious of their notoriety. He made numerous references to wanting to be infamous. This young man saw himself as a homicidal outsider. This is not so much linked to a terrorist ideology but to a pervasive sense of an alienated position in society. However, this individual had already demonstrated a readiness to research religious and extreme political groups. Therefore, unless some pro-social intervention occurred, he remained at risk of trying to find a group that supported his attitudes and beliefs and of acting violently to secure his membership and gain the much longed for notoriety. This suggests that vulnerable individuals may seek out groups, including terrorist organizations, that may fulfil their personal needs. The opposite may also occur. Vulnerable people may be targeted by organizations and indoctrinated into their ideologies and violent militancy.

In approaching these socially isolated individuals, interviewers adopt an interviewing style that attempts to understand why these young men feel so cut off from society, why they believe it necessary to respond to this isolation in a retaliatory manner, and to provide them with the necessary help to overcome their psychological problems and their dysfunctional way of coping with them. As such we recommend a counselling style (as opposed to a more assertive interrogatory style), based on motivational interview approaches (Miller & Rollnick, 2002), which will optimize the conditions in which potential offenders are more likely to talk about their thoughts and actions.

Multidisciplinary Working: Police, Probation and Security Services

Working in conjunction with other agencies allows access to further information that can inform the risk assessment. One of the first ports of call is to access full criminal records and data on the Police National Computer (PNC). These provide details of the index offence as well as insight into the development of an individual's criminal career with particular reference to their juvenile history. This information can facilitate an early judgement as to whether the person's current involvement with extremism is on a continuum of antisocial criminality or is potentially an attempt at the redemption of criminality and may be led by a rediscovery of faith. For example, within a person's offending history, examination of the frequency and severity of early offending and the number of custodial disposals would be of interest.

When assessing a person already convicted of a terrorist-related offence, the main aspects of the offence topic areas should include the level of planning, involvement in the planning, involvement in surveillance of targets, behavioural try-outs and other aspects of intelligence gathering. There is a need to identify the main ideological influences, media (i.e., Internet sites accessed), individuals that they have associated with and their ideologues. This helps to provide a provisional determination about their justificatory arguments and rationales.

As with many forensic assessments, understanding the context of a person's offending behaviour is paramount. Other agencies may be able to assist in identifying whether there were any earlier incidents seen as exemplar action or to enable the identification of symbolic targets.

Conclusions

In contrast to the more generic risk assessment of violence, the risk assessment of terrorist prisoners is still in its infancy. In spite of this, our knowledge of the potential risk factors and the development of a conceptual framework and innovative assessment tools have grown considerably since 2008. In response to the urgent need to develop formal tools, the introduction of the Canadian Violent Extremism Risk Assessment (VERA 2) and the United Kingdom NOMS' Extremism Risk Guidance (ERG-22), even if they have not yet been empirically validated, provides innovative conceptual frameworks for the identification and measurement of potential relevant risk factors, which incorporate Monahan's (2012) four central categories of terrorism risk factors. This development represents a major progression in an area that is apparently so complicated and problematic that one of the world's foremost experts on risk assessment, Professor John Monahan, believes that it is highly unlikely that the scientific community will ever be in a position to validate any actuarial risk assessment tools in this area prospectively. In spite of the absence of the relevant infrastructure for rigorous scientific validation, there is a need to rely on currently available existing methodologies, which should be continually guided and modified by the advancement of our future knowledge and research base. Perhaps this is an area where a real challenge can drive scientific thinking further than is currently imaginable.

Notes

1 Pressman uses the terms 'violent extremists' and 'violent extremism' to describe 'violent terrorists' and 'violent terrorism', respectively.

2 Post (2007) identifies three key types of terrorist organizations: nationalist-separatist terrorism (e.g., Palestinian terrorists of Fatah, the IRA), social revolutionary terrorism (e.g., Italian Red Brigades, Revolutionary Armed Forces of Colombia) and religious extremist terrorism (e.g., Hezbollah, Hamas, al-Qaeda).

3 Horgan's (2005) book on the psychology of terrorism is also important for those involved in terrorist risk assessment.

4 See the work of Post (2003, 2007). According to Post (2007), 'The role of the leader is crucial in drawing together alienated, frustrated individuals into a coherent organization. The leader provides a "sense-making" unifying message that conveys a religious, political or ideological justification to their disparate followers' (p. 8). Merari's (2010) work on suicide bombers is relevant here in view of their elevated level of compliance.

5 This study is based on a small sample from one group of terrorists and the findings therefore need to be treated with caution.

6 As discussed before, there is an absence of research in this area and the work of Merari (2010), from small group samples, suggests that general terrorists, in contrast to suicide bombers, are often highly impulsive, emotionally unstable and more likely to possess psychopathic tendencies. Neither group had any participants who were psychotic or had a previous history of hospitalization in a mental institution.

7 Dr Elaine Pressman and her colleague John Flockton presented their work on the VERA 2 at the Division of Forensic Psychology Annual Conference in Cardiff on 28 June 2012, and explained that the VERA 1 had been refined following consultative work with and feedback from experts in the field of terrorist risk assessment. The VERA 2 is currently being used in Australia and Indonesia for the risk assessment of convicted terrorists (this work is being conducted by John Flockton), but only as an additional (structured) information-gathering tool. According to Dr Pressman, there are currently no data available on the psychometric properties and validity of the VERA 2.

8 Unlike the VERA 2, the ERG-22+ does not only focus on direct violent terrorist offending. It includes being in possession of terrorist material that supports terrorist violence and radicalization, which is a part of the current UK terrorist legislation. This broadens

the scope of the risk assessment from that used in the USA and Australia, where the focus is more specifically on direct violent terrorist offending.

9 The focus is on identifying risk factors and relevant criminogenic needs, if appropriate, that may assist with the management and intervention of future risk, using a 'risk–need–responsivity' (RNR) framework (see Andrews & Bonta, 2010). The psychometric properties of the ERG-22+ remain unknown.

10 We have sometimes found the MCMI-III helpful for diagnostic purposes. Normative data is available on prisoners (Gudjonsson, Wells, & Young, 2011) and secure unit patients (Gudjonsson & Main, 2008).

References

Andrews, D. A., & Bonta, J. (2010). *The psychology of criminal conduct* (5th ed.). Albany, NY: Lexis Nexis/Anderson.

Andrews, D., Bonta, J., & Wormith, J. (2004). *Manual for the level of service/case management inventory (LS/CMI)*. Toronto: Multi-Health Systems.

Ashton-James, C. E., Maddux, W. W., Galinsky, A. D., & Chartrand, T. L. (2009). Who I am depends on how I feel: The role of affect in expression of culture. *Psychological Science, 20*, 340–346.

Baron-Cohen, S. (2011). *Zero degrees of empathy: A new theory of human cruelty.* London: Allen Lane.

Beck, A. (1999). *Prisoners of hate: The cognitive basis of anger, hostility and violence.* New York: Harper.

Bonta, J., Harman, W. G., Hann, R. G., & Cormier, R. B. (1996). The prediction of recidivism among federally sentenced offenders: A revalidation of the SIR scale. *Canadian Journal of Criminology, 38*, 61–79.

Borum, R., Bartel, R. A., & Forth, A. (2006). *SAVRY: Professional manual for Structured Assessment of Violence Risk in Youth.* Lutz, FL: Psychological Assessment Resources.

Burke, J. (2007). *Al-Qaeda: The true story of radical Islam* (3rd ed.). London: Penguin.

Campbell, M., French, S., & Gendreau, P. (2009). The prediction of violence in adult offenders: A meta-analytic comparison of instruments and methods of assessment. *Criminal Justice and Behavior, 36*, 567–590.

Copas, J., & Marshall, P. (1998). The Offender Group Reconviction Scale: The statistical reconviction score for use by probation officers. *Journal of the Royal Statistical Society, 47*, 159–171.

Dernevik, M., Beck, A., Grann, M., Hogue, T., & McGuire, J. (2009a). The use of psychiatric and psychological evidence in the assessment of terrorist offenders. *Journal of Forensic Psychiatry & Psychology, 20*, 508–515. doi:10.1080/13501760902771217

Dernevik, M., Beck, A., Grann, M., Hogue, T., & McGuire, J. (2009b). A response to Dr. Gudjonsson's commentary. *Journal of Forensic Psychiatry & Psychology, 20*, 520–522. doi:10.1080/13501760902771258

Douglas, K. S., Webster, C. D., Hart, S. D., Eaves, D., & Ogloff, J. R. P. (2002). *HCR-20: Violence risk management companion guide.* Vancouver: Mental Health Law and Policy Institute, Simon Fraser University.

Fazel, S., Singh, J. P., Doll, H., & Grann, M. (2012). Use of risk assessment instruments to predict violence and antisocial behaviour in 73 samples involving 24 827 people: Systematic review and meta-analysis. *British Medical Journal, 345*, e4692 doi:10.1136/bmj.e4692

Gadher, D. (2012, 19 January). Lie, say you have reformed, be set free and strike again. *Sunday Times*, pp. *1*, 12–13.

Gartenstein-Ross, D., & Grossman, L. (2009). *Homegrown terrorists in the U.S. and U.K.: An empirical examination of the radicalization process.* Foundation for Defense of Democracies, Center for Terrorism Research. Retrieved 26 May 2014 from http://www.defenddemocracy.org/media-hit/review-homegrown-terrorists-in-the-us-and-the-uk/

Grove, W. M., & Meehl, P. E. (1996). Comparative efficiency of informal (subjective, impressionistic) and formal (mechanical, algorithmic) prediction procedures: The clinical–statistical controversy. *Psychology, Public Policy, and Law, 2*, 293–323.

Gudjonsson, G. (2009). The assessment of terrorist offenders: A commentary on the Dernevik et al. article and suggestions for future directions. *Journal of Forensic Psychiatry & Psychology, 20*, 516–519. doi:10.1080/13501760902771233

Gudjonsson, G. H., & Main, N. (2008). How are personality disorders related to compliance? *Journal of Forensic Psychiatry & Psychology, 19*, 180–190.

Gudjonsson, G., Sigurdsson, J. F., Sigfusdottir, I. D., & Young, S. (2012). A national epidemiological study of offending and its relationship with ADHD symptoms and associated risk factors. *Journal of Attention Disorders, 18*(1), 3–13. doi:10.1177/1087054710385068

Gudjonsson, G. H., Wells, J., & Young, S. (2011). Motivation for offending among prisoners and the relationship with Axis I and Axis II disorders and ADHD symptoms. *Personality and Individual Differences, 50*, 64–68.

Gudjonsson, G. H., Wells, J., & Young, S. (2012). Personality disorders and clinical syndromes in ADHD prisoners. *Journal of Attention Disorders, 16*, 304–313. doi:10.1177/1087054710385068

Gudjonsson, G. H., & Young, S. (2007). The role and scope of forensic clinical psychology in secure unit provisions: A proposed service model for psychological therapies. *Journal of Forensic Psychiatry & Psychology, 18*, 534–556.

Gudjonsson, G. H., & Young, S. (2011). Predictors of offending and critical incidents among prisoners. *European Psychiatric Review, 4*, 15–17.

Hanson, R. K., & Howard, P. (2010). Individual confidence intervals do not inform decision-makers about the accuracy of risk assessment evaluations. *Law and Human Behavior, 34*, 275–281.

Hare, R. D. (2003). *The Hare Psychopathy Checklist – Revised* (2nd ed.). Toronto: Multi-Health Systems.

Hart, S. D., Michie, C., & Cooke, D. J. (2007). Precision of actuarial risk assessment instruments: Evaluating the 'margins of error' of group versus individual predictions of violence. *British Journal of Psychiatry, 190*, 60–65.

Horgan, J. (2005). *The psychology of terrorism.* London: Routledge.

Horgan, J. (2008). From profiles to pathways and roots to routes: Perspectives from psychology on radicalization into terrorism. *Annals of the American Association of Political and Social Sciences, 618*, 80–94. doi:10.1177/0002716208317539

Horgan, J. (2011). Interviewing the terrorists: Reflections on fieldwork and implications for psychological research. *Behavioral Sciences of Terrorism and Political Aggression, 4*, 195–211. Retrieved 26 May 2014 from http://www.tandfonline.com/doi/abs/10.1080/19434472.2011.594620#preview

James, D., Meloy, J., Mullen, P., Pathe, M., Farnham, R., Preston, L., & Darnley, B. (2010). Abnormal attentions toward the British royal family: Factors associated with approach and escalation. *Journal of the American Academy of Psychiatry and the Law, 38*, 329–340.

James, D., Mullen, P., Meloy, J., Pathe, M., Farnham, F., Preston, L., & Darnley, B. (2007). The role of mental disorder in attacks on European politicians 1990–2004. *Acta Psychiatrica Scandinavica, 116*, 334–344. doi:10.1111/j.1600-0447.2007.01077.x

Kraemer, H., Kazdin, A., Offord, D., Kessler, R., Jensen, P., & Kupfer, D. (1997). Coming to terms with the terms of risk. *Archives of General Psychiatry, 54*, 337–343.

Kroner, D., Mills, J., & Reddon, J. (2005). A coffee can, factor analysis, and prediction of antisocial behavior: The structure of criminal risk. *International Journal of Law and Psychiatry, 28*, 360–374. doi:10.1016/j.ijlp.2004.01.011

Lidz, C., Mulvey, E., & Gardner, W. (1993). The accuracy of predictions of violence to others. *Journal of the American Medical Association, 269*, 1007–1011. doi:10.1001/jama.269.8.1007

Lloyd, M., & Dean, C. (2012). Intervening with extremist offenders. *Forensic Update, 105*, 35–38.

Markus, H. R., & Kitayama, S. (1994). The cultural construction of self and emotion: Implications and social behavior. In S. Kitayama & H. R. Marcus (Eds.), *Emotion and culture: Empirical studies of mutual influence* (pp. 89–130). Washington, DC: American Psychological Association.

McCauley, C., & Moskalenko, S. (2011). *Friction: How radicalization happens to them and us.* New York: Oxford University Press.

Merari, A. (2005). Social, organizational and psychological factors in suicide terrorism. In T. Bjorgo (Ed.), *Root causes of terrorism: Myths, reality and ways forward* (pp. 70–89). London: Routledge. doi:10.4324/9780203337653_chapter_6

Merari, A. (2010). *Driven to death: Psychological and social aspects of suicide terrorism.* New York: Oxford University Press.

Miller, W. R., & Rollnick, S. (2002). Motivational interviewing (2nd ed.). New York: Guilford.

Monahan, J. (2012). The individual risk assessment of terrorism. *Psychology, Public Policy, and Law, 18*, 167–205. doi:10.1037/a0025792

Monahan, J., Steadman, H., Silver, E., Appelbaum, P., Robbins, P., Mulvey, E., et al. (2001). *Rethinking risk assessment: The MacArthur Study of Mental Disorder and Violence.* New York: Oxford University Press.

Post, J. M. (Ed.) (2003). *The psychological assessment of political leaders.* Ann Arbor: University of Michigan Press.

Post, J. M. (2007). *The mind of the terrorist: The psychology of terrorism from the IRA to al Qaeda.* New York: Palgrave Macmillan.

Pressman, D. E. (2009). *Risk assessment decisions for violent political extremism.* 2009-02. Ottawa. Retrieved 5 June 2014 from http://www.publicsafety.gc.ca/cnt/rsrcs/pblctns/2009-02-rdv/2009-02-rdv-eng.pdf

Pressman, D. E., & Flockton, J. (2010). *Risk assessment decisions for violent political extremism version 2: The manual.* Unpublished paper.

Quinsey, V. L., Harris, G. T., Rice, M. E., & Cormier, C. A. (2006). *Violent offenders: Appraising and managing risk* (2nd ed.). Washington, DC: American Psychological Association.

Roberts, K., & Horgan, J. (2008). Risk assessment and the terrorist. *Perspectives on Terrorism, 2*, 3–9.

Silke, A. (1998). Cheshire-cat logic: The recurring theme of terrorist abnormality in psychological research. *Psychology, Crime & Law, 4*, 51–69. doi:10.1080/10683169808401747

Silke, A. (2011). Terrorists and extremists in prison: Psychological issues in management and reform. In A. Silke (Ed.), *The psychology of counter-terrorism* (pp. 123–134). London: Routledge.

Skeem, J., & Monahan, J. (2011). Current directions in violence risk assessment. *Current Directions in Psychological Science, 20,* 38–42. doi:10.1177/0963721410397271

Taylor, P. J., & Gunn, J. (1999). Homicides by people with mental illness: Myth and reality. *British Journal of Psychiatry, 174,* 9–14.

Thornton, D. (2007). *Scoring guide for the risk matrix 2000.9/SVC.* Retrieved 26 May 2014 from http://www.birmingham.ac.uk/Documents/college-les/psych/RM2000scoringins tructions.pdf

Webster, C., Douglas, K., Eaves, D., & Hart, S. (1997). *HCR-20: Assessing risk for violence (version 2).* Vancouver: Simon Fraser University.

West, A. G., & Greenall, P. V. (2011). Incorporating index offence analysis into forensic clinical assessment. *Legal and Criminological Psychology, 16,* 144–159.

Wong, S., & Gordon, A. (2001). The Violence Risk Scale. *Bulletin of the International Society for Research on Aggression, 23,* 16–20.

Yang, M., Wong, S., & Coid, J. (2010). The efficacy of violence prediction: A meta-analytic comparison of nine risk assessment tools. *Psychological Bulletin, 36,* 740–767. doi:10.1037/a0020473

8

Hostage Negotiation and Communication Skills in a Terrorist Environment

Simon Wells

We are on the way, what are we going to say?

On 21 July 2005 reports reached police that a series of attempts had been made to detonate bombs on the London transport system. The events took place only two weeks after four suicide bombers had made such attacks on London and killed 52 people. The initial reports indicated that the devices had not gone off but one of the attackers was trapped on an underground train. A call was received by the negotiator team at New Scotland Yard who were requested to attend the scene, make contact with the attacker and negotiate him off the train peacefully. As the team prepared to respond, a comment was made by one member, 'We are on the way, what are we going to say?'

This chapter outlines what negotiators now consider essential in preparing for this type of scenario and more widely in negotiating with 'terrorists'. The observations made have been tested in theatre, for example, in dealing with the kidnapping of Ken Bigley in Iraq by al-Qaeda in 2004.

The Metropolitan Police Service (MPS) has trained hostage and crisis negotiators (HNs) following a series of incidents in the 1970s in the UK and overseas, including a prison siege in New York, a terrorist siege in Balcombe Street, London, and the holding of hostages on trains and at a school in Holland (Strentz, 2006). In 1974, in partnership with the New York Police Department and the Federal Bureau of Investigation, the MPS designed a course for senior police officers to train them to become hostage and crisis negotiators. HNs are called to assist an incident commander in dealing with three broad categories of incident:

- barricades (with or without a hostage);
- suicide intervention;
- hostage taking (hijacking and kidnap).

Investigating Terrorism: Current Political, Legal and Psychological Issues, First Edition. Edited by John Pearse.
© 2015 John Wiley & Sons, Ltd. Published 2015 by John Wiley & Sons, Ltd.

At the early stage of an incident, the HN will listen to the incident commander, who is usually a senior police officer, in order to understand what that incident commander is trying to achieve. In nearly all cases, this is a peaceful resolution to the incident, without the loss of life. For example, if a person believed to be suicidal is barricaded in a house, the incident commander will want them to come out voluntarily without having to risk the use of police officers to force entry and physically remove them from the barricade. Therefore the role of the HN is to engage the person in crisis in conversation and persuade them to come out. They will not make any decisions about the overall aim but will rather continue engaging in conversation, gaining information which can help the incident commander to better understand what is happening. Therefore the role of a HN during most incidents is to:

- attempt to bring the crisis to a peaceful resolution, without the loss of life;
- buy time, in order to allow plans to be developed and resources to be deployed;
- gain information to help the incident commander to understand as much as possible about the incident and the individual(s) involved.

The majority of incidents HNs deal with in the UK are suicide interventions, followed by domestic barricades and then crimes gone wrong. The latter can range from long-term armed sieges, such as the 15-day Hackney siege in December 2002–January 2003 (Cowan, 2005), to shorter incidents, like a burglary where a criminal has been discovered committing a crime, has no means of escape and refuses to leave the location.

In the UK all HNs are police officers, all are volunteers and, according to Johnston (2010), all should have the following strengths:

- be excellent communicators and have the ability to listen;
- be able to accept that at times they will be placed under enormous stress;
- be able to work as part of a team;
- be ready to follow instructions and accept that it is not about winning but about saving lives;
- resilience, patience, an even temper, professional knowledge, self-assurance, empathy and passion.

Another important attribute is flexibility (Johnson, 2010; Vecchi, Van Hasselt, & Romano, 2005). HNs have to accept that one week they could be on a high-rise building trying to persuade a suicidal person not to jump, and the following week they may be in Afghanistan trying to communicate with the Taliban in order to assist the British government in dealing with the kidnapping of a British national. It is important to understand what the role, responsibilities and attributes of a HN are, and that many of the skills used on the high-rise building are the same as those needed to deal with terrorist groups anywhere in the world.

There have been many instances of police having to communicate with people who have been labelled 'terrorists'. The interpretation of the 'terrorist' label can be the key to understanding the type of negotiation approach adopted. On many occasions subsequent political or social changes have resulted in the group or individual losing the label, and therefore, even at the time of the incident, adopting a non-judgemental approach is vital. An example of a change in label is in relation to Martin McGuinness who was labelled a terrorist when he was a member of the Provisional Irish Republican Army (PIRA) but is now a politician and member of the Northern Ireland Assembly, and recently ran for the presidency of Ireland. This chapter will interpret the term 'terrorist' in the prevailing context at the time of the incident. To understand the suggested approach, it is important to know that how a person is labelled may help in the process of communicating with them, and that HNs should not be influenced by labels but should understand them and attempt to remain detached from them.

The chapter will discuss how stereotypes of terrorists can be misleading, and how the context of incidents can help a negotiator to understand why ordinary people act in extraordinary ways. It will also consider how a negotiator makes a first impression and can use their knowledge and the information available to them to consider the 'thin slices' of language, gestures and behaviour being displayed by the terrorists (Ambady, Bernieri, & Richeson, 2000). The chapter will then discuss listening and communication skills and how we influence people. As the chapter progresses, practical examples will be given of the skills described.

The three types of terrorist incidents that will be used to develop an understanding of how HNs negotiate with terrorists are:

- hijacking
- kidnapping
- siege/barricades.

Hijacking

An explanation of a hijacking is given by Theaxton (2006). In 1985 a pro-Palestine group from the Abu Nidal Organization (ANO) hijacked a Pan Am flight, scheduled to fly from Karachi to London, and, while on the ground in Pakistan, held the passengers and some crew hostage. From the terrorists' perspective, there were numerous unforeseen complications; for example, some of the flight crew escaped and some of the cabin crew were Indian rather than the expected US nationals. This caused confusion and difficulties in communication for all sides. Multiple communicators were used by the Pakistani authorities; it is argued that this did not contribute to the objective of saving lives (Theaxton, 2006). This chapter will highlight the role of the HN in creating a single line of communication to reduce confusion and enhance communication.

Kidnapping

In 2004 Ken Bigley, together with two US citizens, was taken hostage in Iraq by an al-Qaeda-inspired group which made extreme threats and demands. Tragically all three hostages were murdered. Communications between the hostage takers and the authorities were initially carried out through the media and then via an intermediary. During the protracted period of communication Bigley managed to escape; unfortunately he was recaptured and then murdered. The ability to communicate with a group perceived by some to be incapable of negotiating was shown to be possible. The ability to communicate, engage in a dialogue and interact with the terrorists helped to reduce the kidnappers' demands and made it possible for Bigley to escape. Aspects of this kidnapping will be discussed in this chapter.

Siege/barricade

In 1980 a group of terrorists demanding autonomy for Khuzestan Province in Iran took control of the Iranian Embassy in London. They made contact with the authorities and submitted their demands. The communications and negotiations took place over six days during which certain demands were met and concessions given; for example, hostages were released and public statements broadcast on behalf of the group (Johnson & West, 1983). In the latter stages it became apparent that the siege was not going to end in a negotiated settlement and an armed intervention was undertaken by the military to end the siege which was broadcast to the world. The negotiations showed the benefit of buying time and gaining intelligence. By buying time the military were able to rehearse their intervention on the basis of up-to-date information and intelligence gained by the HN during the siege, and from other sources (e.g., covert intelligence from cameras and microphones).

While each incident faced by an HN is unique, there are general principles of communication and negotiation which apply in all cases. These will be discussed and linked to real-life incidents to show how the skills are relevant to saving lives even in the most extreme circumstances.

Planning and Preparation: Creating the Right Environment

We begin by assessing planning and preparation, creating an approach based on what we know, what has happened so far and what our objectives are. Our assessment will include the following considerations:

- What planning and preparation does an HN need to consider and undertake?
- Given some of the myths about people involved in terrorism, are stereotypes helpful?
- What is the context? Is the situation planned or unplanned?
- At the first encounter, what first impressions do the group and the HN give each other?
- What information is available from thin slices of behaviour or language?
- How do we use listening and observation skills to help us to understand the incident and its meaning for the group or person?
- How do we influence the group or person?

Planning and preparation are crucial for negotiators prior to any incident. There have been many examples of terrorist encounters with negotiators over the years (Brandt & Sandler, 2009; Dolnik, 2011; Johnson & West, 1983; Theaxton, 2006), and it is imperative that anyone involved in negotiation, who might encounter a terrorist siege or incident, study and learn from past events to better understand some of the reasons why these incidents occur, the nature and type of behaviour displayed by 'terrorists' and the outcomes of past events.

It is commonly agreed that there is no single terrorist personality (Horgan, 2003, 2008; Silke, 2003; Wilson, 2003). Crenshaw (1990) suggests that

> We can analyse terrorism at the level of the individual practitioner or the collective actor, the terrorist group. In turn both actors, individual and group, must be seen in relation to society as a whole. Similarly terrorism alters the behaviour of individuals, collective actors such as the terrorist organisation or the government, and societies. The integration of these levels of analysis is a significant problem for research on terrorism. (p. 249)

In teaching negotiators to better understand the integration of people and terrorist groups, it is worth considering the strategic perspective of the group, the attitude of the community they 'represent' towards the strategic perspective, and the number and type of willing volunteers. Where these three factors come together in a particular configuration, the likelihood of terrorist events, particularly suicide attacks, is increased (Pape, 2005).

Stereotypes

Giving negotiators the opportunity to examine their own personality, behaviour and pathway to being a negotiator is a key part of preparation. In many ways, people who undertake terrorist activity are ordinary people involved in an extraordinary activity. People who subscribe to al-Qaeda's ideology are not demographically similar, that is, in terms of age, gender, occupation, social class, personality or education (Horgan, 2003; Taylor & Horgan, 2006). There is no evidence of a particular single pathway to being involved in terrorism (Horgan, 2003, 2008). Those who subscribe to terrorism may not be demographically different from any HN asked to negotiate with them. Hence, an introspective approach on the part of the HN, by examining their own motivations and character, can help them in preparing to engage with terrorists.

Some of the recent findings about those involved in terrorist activity have been crucial: while they may not have similar personalities or follow similar pathways, they do have similar vulnerabilities (Horgan, 2008; Travis, 2008). These vulnerabilities can give us an important insight into why messages aimed at converting a person to terrorism have a particular resonance, and may begin to answer the question why some are willing to act, and in some cases die, for a cause. The relevant vulnerabilities considered include the following:

- *Travel.* The person visits a country or location where they are made aware of injustice and corruption or witness suffering, and are made to feel that they can make a difference, and/or that groups are suffering because of a particular label or identity (e.g., religious, racial or other cultural aspect).
- *Migration.* The person or group migrates to escape persecution and/or find a better life and discovers that the host is not accommodating and again persecutes them because of their identity or label (Horgan, 2003).
- *Lack of achievement.* The person or group perceives that they are not achieving because of an identity or label being attached to them, or by which they identify themselves (e.g., Catholics in Northern Ireland, Muslims in Britain) (Horgan, 2008).
- *Involvement in crime.* When the person or group attempts to re-enter the mainstream community after having gone against its social norms, they are rejected. They are more likely to be accepted and 'forgiven' by extremist groups or by others who are similarly outside the norms of society (Travis, 2008).
- *Ideological or religious naivety.* Faced with a new or novel problem, many look to their past experience to make decisions. Naivety about a religion or ideology may result in a person relying for support to make decisions on limited past experience or what others may suggest (Wiktorowicz, 2004).

In terms of preparation, it is crucial that negotiators are helped to understand that those whom they may face are not people driven to terrorism by a personality disorder or mental illness. Taylor and Quayle (1994) quoted a terrorist leader from Northern Ireland, who declared that 'there are very few, what do you call them … Psychopaths … they'd stand out like a sore thumb and everyone would know them' (p. 107). Those involved with al-Qaeda or any other terrorist groups are just as likely to have a personality disorder or mental health issue as anyone in the general population (Horgan, 2003). It is relatively easy to demonstrate to HNs that if they were terrorist leaders they would not want to recruit someone with a personality disorder or who was mentally ill onto their team.

To sum up the issues surrounding the profiling of terrorists, the House of Commons Report into the 7 July 2005 bombings (7/7) bombings stated:

> What we know of previous extremists in the UK shows that there is not a consistent profile to help identify who may be vulnerable to radicalisation. Of the 4 individuals here, 3 were second generation British citizens whose parents were of Pakistani origin and one whose parents were of Jamaican origin; Kamel Bourgass, convicted of the Ricin plot, was an Algerian failed asylum seeker; Richard Reid, the failed shoe bomber, had an English mother and Jamaican father. Others of interest have been white converts. Some have been well-educated, some less so. Some genuinely poor, some less so. Some apparently well integrated in the UK, others not. Most single, but some family men with children. Some previously law-abiding, others with a history of petty crime. In a few cases there is evidence of abuse or other trauma in early life, but in others their upbringing has been stable and loving. (House of Commons Report, 2006, p. 31)

Understanding how people are affected by 'push' and 'pull' factors helps to explain that they get involved in terrorism for a variety of reasons. Push factors are internal feelings, opinions, vulnerabilities or beliefs; pull factors are external messages or events. The terrorists have to have a push factor (for example, lack of achievement) and a pull factor (such as believing a message), to accept that the two are connected and to be able to see that their actions are in line with the message. HNs have to consider pull factors, for example, that the terrorists believe in the message.

The al-Qaeda message is simple: 'You are a Muslim, Muslims are under attack and it is your duty to defend Muslims with violence' (Bin Laden, 2005). If the recipient of the message has vulnerabilities and believes that those vulnerabilities are a result of being Muslim, the message is more likely to resonate. If they believe that undertaking violent actions on behalf of al-Qaeda is in line with the message and will make a difference, they are more likely to act (Pape, 2005). Yet there are many people who are Muslim, who believe they are under attack, yet do not get involved in terrorist activities. Perhaps this is because they have an attractive alternative, or the message or messenger does not resonate with them to draw them to al-Qaeda. This is a key issue when HNs prepare for a terrorist incident. Having assessed why someone might be involved in terrorism, what part of the message may have resonated with them and what potential attractive alternatives exist, the HN is armed with the necessary information to influence the person and thereby deal with the incident by negotiation and not by force.

How does having a better understanding of why people get involved in terrorist incidents prepare the negotiator for the incident? First, it shows that the stereotype of the terrorist as crazy is misleading and unhelpful. Secondly, the creating of a context of listening and understanding, without being judgemental, may be the best way forward. Listening may enable the HN to identify the vulnerabilities that lead someone to be attracted to a group (push factors), how the message from the group or leader persuaded the person to be involved (pull factors) and what keeps them engaged. This may yield opportunities to use their skills to influence and to identify and use attractive alternatives. For example, during the kidnapping of Ken Bigley, the family issued statements to the effect that if Zarqawi released Bigley (the group holding him was led by a Palestinian Jordanian, Abu Musab al-Zarqawi), it would be seen as humane by the population of Iraq.

Some may state, rightly, that certain people or groups cannot be negotiated with, either through policy (Parham, 2007) or behaviour (e.g., the 9/11 hijackers). This chapter suggests that, as long as the HN can communicate and use the skills discussed here, they and their skills will be relevant and useful in most situations.

Context: Planned or Unplanned

The context in which the incident takes place is also a key issue for an HN and the incident commander. The first consideration should be whether the incident confronting the HN is planned or unplanned. Planned means that the person or group holding the hostages or setting up the incident, for example Bigley's kidnapping, planned it. Bigley was taken and held and demands were made. The group holding him knew that at some stage they were likely to be communicating with an HN. Similarly the Iranian embassy siege/barricade was an event where the hostage takers knew that an HN would make contact (Johnson & West, 1983; Wilson, 2003).

An unplanned incident relates to a context where the group or person does not expect to be communicating with an HN. This can occur when a plan goes wrong or police intervene unexpectedly. The planned 21 July 2005 (21/7) attacks in London, where the would-be bombers' devices did not go off, are a good example. Some time after the planned attacks, two members of the group were located in a residential location and a siege took place that was unplanned. After the 2004 al-Qaeda attack in Madrid, part of the group were located and an unplanned siege occurred during which all the group and one police officer at the location died (Silber, 2012).

Some incidents have both planned and unplanned aspects, for example the Mumbai attacks of November 2008, during which terrorists attacked over a number of days. They set off bombs, undertook random shootings against various high-profile locations (railway stations, restaurants, etc.) and held hostages while making demands. In the end 164 people were killed with over 308 injured. The group responsible was identified as a Pakistan-based Islamist group (Jenkins, 2009). Some of the events were planned (e.g., the taking of hostages in a Jewish centre), but some of the terrorists being trapped in the Taj Hotel and unable to continue the attack was unplanned (Jenkins, 2009).

In a planned event, the context is likely to have been determined by the terrorist. In an unplanned event, for example post-21/7 or the Madrid siege, the incident and the HN tend to set the context. Context can also include the situation and circumstances relevant to the group or leader. In the case of Bigley's kidnapping, Zarqawi, the leader of the terrorist group, was a Palestinian operating in Iraq. In order to obtain and maintain support from the Iraqi population, he considered that being seen to operate on their behalf would lead to more support from them. Zarqawi made demands for the release of Iraqi women from prison, thus linking his action to an important issue for the local population.

Does the context (whether it is planned or unplanned) impact on how the HN approaches the incident? It should not make the initial approach any different. However, the response from the terrorists may be different depending on the context. All negotiations tend to begin with a straightforward HN introduction, which includes:

- who they are;
- why they are speaking to the terrorists; and
- a summary of the events that have occurred.

Thus a first impression is created.

First Impressions and Thin Slicing

During a briefing prior to the commencement of any negotiation, the HN needs to judge the extent of planning involved and to start the process of establishing the incident commander's first request, which in nearly all cases is to make contact with the terrorists. The first few minutes of most incidents are likely to be chaotic and to lack clear focus. The first impression is therefore extremely important, as it can either alleviate the chaos or compound it. In the early stages there will be information given away by the terrorists and the HN. This process of information giveaway is known as 'thin slicing' (Ambady, Bernieri, & Richeson 2000; Ambady & Rosenthal, 1993), where both parties either consciously or unconsciously make decisions about a situation by considering the other's words, behaviour and gestures (Ambady, Hallahan, & Rosenthal, 1995).

The HN needs to consider what impact they wish to have. Do they wish to display authority or a willingness to listen, or can the two be integrated? If a first impression has been made, how accurate are we in our judgement of the type of person we are negotiating with? People are accurate in terms of predicting certain aspects of a person they are dealing with within the first five minutes of an encounter (Ambady et al., 2000; Ambady, LaPlante, Nguyen, Rosenthal, Chaumeton, & Levinson, 2002; Borkenau, Mauer, Riemann, Spinath, & Angleitner, 2004). As each party in a negotiation will, either consciously or unconsciously, be making quick decisions about the other, it is crucial to consider the type of first impression we make. One of the most influential impression management techniques has been shown to be credibility through expertise, knowledge and goodwill (Curhan & Pentland, 2007). Any opening interaction should contain aspects of those three areas. An example may be:

> 'Hello, my name is Simon, I am with the police. Is everyone OK in there? I am here to listen to you.'

This may be followed by a summary of what has taken place so far, in particular before the negotiators arrived. Depending on how it is delivered in terms of accent, tone of voice and fluidity, this opening statement covers the three aspects of credibility:

- knowledge: 'I am with the police';
- expertise: 'I am here to listen to you';
- goodwill: 'Is everyone OK in there?'

First impressions can be crucial in reducing chaos and creating an environment in which to communicate. If London faced a Mumbai-style attack, the information available would come from multiple sources and in all likelihood be confusing and contradictory. One of the early decisions of the police and government (HMG) would be to reassure the public and to begin to create a favourable first impression. This message would be aimed at the public and perhaps the terrorists. The role of the HN would be to be aware of these messages and to ensure that, when they are requested to assist the incident commander or HMG, their opening lines and first impression reinforce them (Neville-Jones, 2010). An example of this occurred during the kidnapping of Ken Bigley. The HMG message, at first, was that HMG does not negotiate with terrorists. On the HN's arrival in Iraq the messaging added that 'HMG was willing to listen and had people in Baghdad willing to do so'. It was a credible message which led to a response, albeit through the media, from the group holding Bigley: 'We repeat our demand of Iraqi women being released from Iraqi prisons.'

Two-way communication assists in understanding points of view, concerns and opinions (Hargie, 2006). When an environment has been created or a statement made which should elicit a response, the ability to listen to the response is crucial.

Listening Skills

Having made contact and given a first impression, the HN needs to listen to the response. When lives are at risk, it is crucial to a negotiation to understand why a person or group may want to kill. To begin to understand why, the HN needs to collect information. This can come from observation, intelligence gathering and listening to the terrorist(s). Negotiators in the United Kingdom use the model of active listening (Giebels & Noelanders, 2004; Hargie, 2006; Kelley, 1950; Rogers, 1951, 1959; Taylor & Donald, 2003) as a means of listening and understanding. This can be broken down into three components:

- focused listening;
- responsive listening;
- communication encouragers.

Focused listening

Focused listening refers to those aspects of the conversation or negotiation where the HN has to put themselves in the best place to hear what the person is saying. This includes creating an environment where the words spoken and the non-verbal communications are communicated and heard. Preparation would include what the HN knows about the speaker, the context they are in and what interactions may be possible. How can the negotiator avoid confirmation bias (for example, the stereotype that terrorists are all 'crazy')? (Klayman, 1995). What information is already available? How have other HNs reacted in similar situations? Is there anything out of their control that is likely to impact on the terrorist's cognition and behaviour, for example a media message from a government or police officer?

Responsive listening

This is a communication skill whereby an HN focuses on what the speaker is saying and allows the speaker to say what they want to say, without being interrupted or forced to change what they are saying as a result of the HN's behaviour. The skills include the use of:

- *Minimal encouragement* (Rogers, 1951), whereby the HN makes a sound or uses a phrase (e.g., 'OK', 'Go on'). Using this tactic, the listener takes their turn in the conversation and expects the speaker to carry on giving their account.
- *Echoing/mirroring language*, also known as mimicry (Lakin & Chartrand, 2003), where the last word or phrase is repeated. This works in two ways: it shows that the listener has listened to the entire sentence, but the questioning intonation (raised voice at the end) can make the mirror or echo sound like a question, which requires clarification.
- *Energy word or phrase*: while giving an account, a speaker may display passion or give extra inflection to a word or phrase; the technique is to repeat that phase or word.

PERSON IN CRISIS:	I was determined to do well at school.
HN:	Determined.
PERSON IN CRISIS:	Yes I went to school with my brother, and I wanted to impress my parents.
HN:	Impress.
PERSON IN CRISIS:	Yes they always favoured my brother.

The aim is to listen and to identify the passion, energy and commitment in the language or statements being made. At times the HN may wish to know an answer to a specific question, but the terrorist may not wish to discuss this; by continuing to stick to the terrorist's line of communication, the HN can better understand the agenda the terrorist has, and can come back to the specific question later. If, in the above scenario, an explicit question had been asked, for example 'What school did you go to?', this would have deflected the person in crisis from the narrative they wished to impart and the agenda would have switched unhelpfully from the person in crisis to the HN.

Communication encouragers

When the terrorist pauses at any point of a narrative, the HN can repeat back what has been said. There are two means of repeating back: summary and paraphrase. A summary tends to be a longer version of the speaker's narrative and to contain words and phrases used by them (linking back to mimicry), whereas a paraphrase would be a shortened version, and would use the HN's interpretation of the narrative given. For example, this is the speaker's narrative:

> 'I got onto the train at Lancaster station yesterday; it was full as the previous train was cancelled. I had to stand next to a man who was talking on his mobile loudly the whole way to London. Even though the ticket cost a fortune, I had to stand, listening to the man, oh and the buffet ran out of hot water so no tea.'

A summary would be something like this:

> 'So, as I have understood it, you got the train from Lancaster station yesterday; the train was full, as the previous train was cancelled, so you had to stand. Next to you was a man who spoke on the phone the whole journey. It wasn't only that the buffet ran out of water, so there was no tea.'

Whereas a paraphrase might sound like this:

> 'You used the train yesterday. It was full, you had to stand, had no tea and had to put up with someone on the phone for the whole journey.'

In negotiation situations, emphasis is placed on the importance of using these methods. A summary can show good listening skills if the person using them is accurate. A minor mistake is likely to be corrected; however, a major error can lead to the speaker believing that the narrative they have given has not been listened to. In the above scenario, if the summary were to say Manchester instead of Lancaster, then the speaker is going to have doubts about whether the listener is interested in their story.

Using a paraphrase can also lead to misunderstandings. HNs need to be careful not to sound patronizing. This tends to occur when the paraphrase is short and misses the passion or emotion within the account, for example:

> 'You caught the train yesterday and had a bad journey.'

While this may account for the story, it does not show why the speaker had a bad journey. The description of the speaker having to stand, having to listen to another person's conversation and the buffet car having no water, so no refreshments were available, indicates that the speaker was dwelling on these issues. By not showing that you have fully understood the emotions behind the story, by paraphrasing them back to the speaker in this way, the listener may sound as though they were not interested.

Another skill used by HNs, particularly faced with a crisis situation such as a suicide intervention, is to use summaries to clarify points. When listening to a long emotional narrative, even the best listeners can struggle to hear or understand what the speaker means from the words used. Therefore, adding clarifications during the summary can demonstrate genuine interest and make the speaker add detail or correct misunderstandings. This is called *emotional labelling*. It is a simple method of recognizing a person's emotion, which has been found to lessen confrontation (Logan, 2012). This technique relies on the listener observing the speaker's emotions and then commenting on them. Emotion can be displayed through how the person speaks, their intonation, the words they use, their body language (face, eyes, etc.) and their reaction to stimuli (Tonks, Williams, Frampton, Yates, & Slater, 2007).

One of the first objectives in any negotiation is to reduce tension and begin building rapport based on a two-way conversation. During a conversation, if a person in crisis feels that they are being judged, it may result in less rapport between both parties. The HN should engage in non-judgemental behaviour, including using emotional labelling. This is an example of a judgemental approach:

PERSON IN CRISIS: (Standing up and shouting from a roof top) Just get back and
                      leave me alone.
HN: I can't go back because you are angry.
PERSON IN CRISIS: (Shouts) Just get back.

This is an example of a non-judgemental approach, using emotional labelling:

PERSON IN CRISIS: (Standing up and shouting from a roof top) Just get back and
                      leave me alone.
HN: I can't go back, as its sounds as if you are angry.
PERSON IN CRISIS: I am not angry, I just want to be left alone.

A non-judgemental approach has gained more information about a person's needs and emotion. It may also mean that the HN is more liked than someone who, according to the person in crisis, is judging them. A positive correlation has been shown between liking and whether a person is more likely to be persuaded or influenced (Cialdini, 2007).

Terrorist incidents can be confusing, and many people have suggested that any communication is pointless. However, by listening to the demands, the HN may get a better understanding of the motivation behind the attacks. While engaged in two-way dialogue, the HN is able to buy time for the incident commander and perhaps gain intelligence and, most significantly, begin to understand the reasons for the incident.

The kidnapping of Ken Bigley provides an example of communication encouragement. Ken Bigley was a British national living and working in Iraq following the invasion in 2003. In 2004 Bigley was living with two US nationals in an area of Baghdad where there was no protection by Western forces or forces loyal to the Iraqi interim government. In the early morning of 16 September 2004 the three were kidnapped in what appeared to be a planned abduction. When first reports reached the two governments a statement was released stating that the governments were aware of reports of a kidnap and were looking into them. HNs were deployed to Iraq, and on 18 September the group released a video. This video showed the three men blind-folded and a man with a gun standing behind them. The group's statement demanded the release of women prisoners from custody otherwise the first hostage would be killed within 48 hours. Both the US and UK governments released a statement that they did not negotiate with terrorists and demanding the men's release. Forty-eight hours later the first hostage was beheaded. A statement was read prior to the murder, repeating the group's demand for the release of the women prisoners, and conclud-ing with another deadline of 24 hours before the next hostage would be killed. At this stage, HNs were in Iraq and able to influence the statement issued by govern-ment. This time the UK statement was in line with HMG policy – that they did not negotiate with terrorists but were willing to listen. Unfortunately, 24 hours later the second US citizen was murdered, leaving Bigley as the remaining hostage.

The initial objective of the HN and incident commanders was to move beyond the demands (the release of Iraqi women prisoners) to the underlying needs, testing whether they were linked to self-esteem, status and affiliation (Arkowitz, Westra, & Miller, 2008). The group holding Bigley was led by Abu Musab al-Zarqawi, and it was believed that they were holding him in Fallujah, which had been at the centre of violence and insurgency against US forces. Shortly before the kidnap, four US security guards had been abducted, murdered and then dragged through the streets before being hung from a bridge over a river that runs through Fallujah. In terms of affiliation, the need to be connected to others was hypothesized as being crucial for Zarqawi. In order to be able to operate and survive in the area, Zarqawi needed the support of the local population, and by making the demands he may have wanted to show them that he was acting in their interests rather than his own. The use of the 'willing to listen' message was aimed at drawing Zarqawi into a dialogue.

The listening skills were initially employed through the media. During the second week, it became apparent that the terrorist group were listening. Prime Minister Tony Blair had appeared on the morning television news to state that he had sent people to Iraq who were willing to listen. This was followed a few hours later by a video of Ken Bigley stating that Blair was a liar and there were no people willing to listen. The next HMG message repeated the 'willing to listen' message and acknowledged that the group wanted the women prisoners released, mimicking or echoing the language used by the group: 'We do not negotiate with terrorists. However, we are willing to listen and have people in Baghdad ready to do so. We understand the group want women released from Iraqi prisons' (Straw, 2004). The following week Zarqawi sent an intermediary to engage with HMG.

Influence skills

In any form of contact between HNs and 'terrorists' there will, hopefully, come a point where there is the possibility of influencing the group's intentions or behaviour.

It is unlikely that the group will change their attitude; however, short-term compliance may be achievable. This is important because, if we are attempting to persuade, the principles of persuasion (Cialdini, 2007; Perloff, 2003) are crucial. What principles have been shown to affect how influential a message is? According to Cialdini (2007), there are six principles of persuasion:

1 liking
2 authority
3 reciprocity
4 commitment/consistency
5 social validation/proof
6 scarcity.

Liking
People prefer to say 'yes' or find it more difficult to say 'no' to individuals whom they like (Perloff, 2003). Several factors may enhance a person's liking for another. This can include:

- *physical attractiveness*: we automatically assign traits such as talent, kindness, honesty and intelligence to good-looking individuals (Cialdini, 2007);
- *similarity*: even something as simple as similarity of clothing can have a positive impact on the likelihood of compliance (Embwiller, Deaux, & Willits, 1971);
- *compliments*: making positive comments about a person can result in our liking the other person more, even if we know that flattery can be false (Drachman, deCarufel, & Inkso, 1978).

In 2003 Mark Henderson, a British citizen, was visiting the Sierra Nevada region of Colombia. Together with other tourists, he was kidnapped by a left-wing group, the ELN (National Liberation Army). Over the 100 days of his captivity, a negotiation took place between the group and a priest whom they knew and trusted and who acted as an intermediary between HMG and the kidnappers. The main aspect of the priest's background that they liked was his personal knowledge and experience of the region the ELN were seeking to represent. This perceived similarity between the group and the priest and liking resulted in their listening and perhaps in their eventual release of Henderson (Moss, 2011).

Identifying a person whom a group will trust based on liking is an issue for HNs. In many areas of the world, similarity between an HN intermediary and the group can be the key to dialogue and influence.

Authority
Cross-culturally there is strong pressure to comply with, or at least pay attention to, the requests or demands from authority (Perloff, 2003). Milgram (1974) states that people are more likely to obey authority when or if they:

- take the word of an expert rather than think for themselves or use short cuts;
- are socialized to obey, having been brought up by parents/guardians to obey authority, for example, teachers and doctors;
- perceive that a person has soft authority (the qualities of a person) – credibility (defined as trustworthiness, knowledge and goodwill) and expertise;
- conform by resorting to external representations in the form of symbols (uniform, title).

HNs need to display authority, as this can buy time and in certain circumstances save lives. At the conclusion of the Iranian Embassy siege in 1980, as the SAS were preparing to storm the building, the HN made contact with the leader of the terrorists. They discussed the delivery of a coach and the logistics of how the group would leave the embassy. As this conversation continued, there were loud explosions, which led to the terrorist stating that he was putting the phone down. The HN stated that there were no noises and everything was 'OK'. At this point, the HN bought time and allowed the police officer being held hostage the chance to detain the terrorist (T. Lock, pers. comm., 2012).

Another positive example of authority was the kidnapping in 2007 of British Embassy staff and others in Ethiopia close to the border with Eritrea. Ethiopia and Eritrea have been in conflict for many years and both sides use insurgent groups to act on their behalf (Doward, Loomes, & Burke, 2007). The kidnapping took place in the Afar region of Ethiopia, a remote desert region which is the scene of hostilities between the Ethiopian government and insurgents, where the insurgent groups seek to represent the Afar people but are allegedly backed by the Eritrean government.

The British Embassy staff and their guides had been visiting the area controlled by the Afar when an attack took place on Ethiopian government tax collectors, during which the group were kidnapped. It was suspected that the hostage takers had moved the group over the border into Eritrea, that they were an Afar group and potentially controlled by the Eritrean government. The HN and HMG strategy was to reach out to senior members of the Eritrean government and request that they use their influence, through their authority, to obtain the hostages' release. Initially the terrorists allowed the hostages medical support, and two days later they released them. While, for political reasons, the Eritrean government could not confirm that it was their influence that had led to the release (Doward et al., 2007), there is little doubt the authority it had over the group had a significant impact (Press Association, 2007).

Reciprocity
Reciprocity is defined as 'reciprocal state or relationship; mutual action, dependence. Further as mutual exchange or mutual reduction of tariffs' (Ferguson & Corr, 2012). Reciprocity, the need to return favours, is seen to be cross-culturally important (Gouldner, 1960). If one person gives something to another, even if the giver is not especially likeable, the recipient often will feel an uncomfortable sense of imbalance and indebtedness if they cannot reciprocate. The impetus for reciprocity is powerful,

since it applies even to uninvited gestures and can spur unequal exchange (Cialdini, 2007; Gouldner, 1960).

Reciprocity can impact on people for the following reasons:

- It creates a sense of obligation
  - even if the receiver does not like the giver;
  - even if the gift/favour was uninvited.
- It is cross-cultural.
- It includes concessions counting as a gift, and the return gift is often larger than the original gift/favour.

During one life-at-risk negotiation, a HN gave a packet of biscuits to a person threatening suicide in a deliberate attempt at engagement. Not only did that succeed, in that the subject thanked him and said that he appreciated what had happened, but these were the first words he had spoken in 12 hours. The gift of the biscuits was not reciprocated, but it still made the recipient feel obliged to respond. Reciprocity can also act on participants in a conversation. Some feel obliged to listen to an account of events if they have been given the opportunity to relay events first.

A simple example of reciprocity occurred in 2006 when an insurgency group kidnapped seven UN peacekeepers in the Democratic Republic of Congo. After a period of negotiation, during which two soldiers were released, the final five were released when the leader of the kidnap group was supplied with fuel for a vehicle and clothing to appear at an election rally. The reciprocal arrangement was that the UN would supply the fuel and clothing, thus enabling the leader to lay down his arms and be involved in the democratic process, in line with UN policy, while he released the hostages (Agence France-Presse, 2006).

Commitment/consistency

People want to be seen as consistent in their words, beliefs, attitudes and deeds. This is especially strong if they have openly committed themselves to a position. Most people will stick to these positions because, if they do not, they perceive that others would see them as being unsure of themselves or untrustworthy (Moriarty, 1975).

Commitment/consistency acts by creating a:

- powerful drive to be consistent: once we have made a choice, we experience the pressure to behave in a way that is consistent with it;
- momentum of compliance, which leads to acceptance of suggestions, produces agreement and allows the person in agreement to recognize that the ideas are more acceptable (Cialdini, 2007).

Consistency can also be linked to decisions: people want to be seen to be consistent with their opinions, on the basis that most people cannot hold on to an opinion they do not believe in, and therefore if they act consistently their opinion must be true (Cialdini & Goldstein, 2004).

This aspect of consistency has led to an influence and persuasion technique called 'foot in the door' (Cialdini, 2007), where an agreement made by the listener is shown to be linked to a further agreement and so on. The listener needs to make an active agreement, not just comply. If the request can be viewed as a social norm (a socially positive behaviour, e.g., helping a worthwhile cause), then being asked to perform a small task will connect the first socially acceptable favour with the second larger socially acceptable favour. If a person sees the larger request in a negative way, they can recall their behaviour in the first act and desire to act in a consistent way; therefore, they may overcome any uncomfortable feelings or doubts about acting in an opposite way and act in a manner consistent with their first 'helpful' behaviour (Perloff, 2003). In terms of negotiation, this is a very important aspect of influence. For example, if a hostage taker treats an injured hostage, it becomes more difficult for them to hurt the hostage later in any siege. Perloff (2003) describes this as being inconsistent with past behaviour and therefore difficult to overcome.

Since 2005 there have been kidnappings and other types of insurgency activity in the area known as the Niger Delta in Nigeria. Because of its significant oil reserves, international oil companies have been operating in the area for a number of years. As a result, there has been an increase in pollution and allegations that the profits from this activity have benefited members of the Nigerian government rather than the local population (Oriola, 2012). The main group behind the insurgency in this area is called the Movement for the Emancipation of the Niger Delta (MEND) (Department of Foreign Affairs and Trade, 2009; Oriola, 2012). From 2006 to 2008, there were numerous kidnappings of Western oil workers in the region.

The demands of MEND over this period were strikingly similar. They called for a fairer distribution of the wealth created by the oil industry, the prevention of pollution and the development of the region's infrastructure. The UK government's publicly stated position in relation to the demands was one of listening, and reasserting its stated policy towards the area, of reducing pollution, developing roads, schools and infrastructure and a fairer distribution of wealth (Foreign & Commonwealth Office, 2012). In order to be seen as consistent and to show their commitment to their stated position, MEND released the hostages once the United Kingdom restated its policies, which were in line with their demands.

Social validation/proof

According to Cialdini (2007), 'We will use the actions of others to decide on proper behaviour for ourselves, especially when we view those others as similar to ourselves', and 'the greater the number of people who find any idea correct, the more the idea will be correct' (p. 116). Social proof occurs when a person looks to others in order to determine how to think and behave (Weinstein, 1993). To quote Cialdini (2007) again: 'one means we use to determine what is correct is to find out what other people think is correct' (p. 116). People are social animals and live in social groups, and feel a need to remain in the group and to adhere to its social norms. Social proof can be especially influential under two conditions:

- *Uncertainty*: When a person is unsure of their surroundings and the situation is ambiguous, they may be more inclined to pay attention to the actions of others and to accept those actions as correct (Cialdini & Goldstein, 2004).
- *Similarity*: People are more inclined to follow the lead of others whom they see as similar to themselves; this is described as subscribing to social norms (Perloff, 2003).

The letters, media appeals and leaflets used during the kidnapping of Ken Bigley were aimed at social proof, emphasizing the role of the family by stating that Bigley was a family man and that his mother and sons needed him. Zarqawi also used this method by demanding the release of women and making videos that highlighted the humiliation of women detained in Iraqi prisons. If there were a Mumbai-style attack in London, then one aspect of the communication strategy would be to emphasize that the group need to consider when their actions become ones that harm their cause and the community they claim they represent (Pape, 2005).

In 2004 Margaret Hassan, who had lived in Iraq for many years and was married to an Iraqi, was kidnapped by terrorists in Baghdad. She was working for the charity CARE International, which assisted the most vulnerable in Iraq. The group that had kidnapped her demanded the withdrawal of British troops from Iraq. While there is dispute as to what occurred during the kidnapping (Barton, 2006), one of the HMG strategies was to emphasize her background to try to influence the group to release her. This strategy enlisted the support of the people whom she had assisted, in particular, women and those with disabilities. Unfortunately, Margaret was murdered. The justification publicly given by the hostage takers was that CARE International had supplied water to the airport run by the Iraqi interim government. While it will never be known whether this was the real motivation for the murder or what impact HMG's appeals had, both sides used social proof for influence. The kidnappers' view was that it was not in the Iraqi population's interest to have a functioning airport controlled by the Iraqi interim government, while HMG held that it was unjustified to take Margaret hostage because she helped the most vulnerable Iraqis.

Scarcity

People typically perceive things that are rare or difficult to obtain as being more valuable than those that are plentiful and easily obtained. They also respond to losses (e.g., the loss of freedoms) by desiring the lost item more than before. Scarcity of a desirable item may invoke a feeling of yearning and the thought that 'I must have that'. Studies looking at potential loss (Gonzales, Aronson, & Costanzo, 1998; Meyerwitz & Chaiken, 1987) have shown that highlighting what a person may lose has a positive impact on how much they are likely to take a particular action. Scarcity works because:

- opportunities seem more valuable when they are less available;
- people are motivated more by potential loss than potential gain;
- a sudden drop from abundance to scarcity is a powerful motivator;
- there is a strong emotional reaction to the thought of losing something.

To build up pressure and to use scarcity, many groups will set time-scales or deadlines for their demands to be met. For example, Zarqawi set a 48-hour, then a 24-hour, deadline for the release of women prisoners. This was probably aimed at putting additional pressure on decision-makers to act.

Conclusion

This chapter proposes that the skills and approaches HNs use can have an impact on terrorist negotiation, in particular, approaching each incident in a non-judgemental way, taking time to consider and reflect on why an ordinary individual may have chosen to engage in an extraordinary activity. The HN needs to create and make an influential first impression, then listen to and observe the response, before beginning to expose the terrorist's underlying motivations for the action. As this progresses, the HN should utilize their listening skills before attempting to influence the group.

Case studies have shown that, as a result of HNs employing these skills, some incidents have been resolved without the loss of life. With further research into terrorism, terrorists and communication skills used in antagonistic situations, further progress will be made. In the meantime many people are being and will be held hostage in terrible situations; some face mistreatment and perhaps even murder. It is imperative that HNs and others involved in this field continue to respond to and to strive to understand this complex issue.

References

Agence France-Presse. (2006). DR Congo militia frees Nepalese peacekeepers. Retrieved 26 May 2014 from http://reliefweb.int/report/democratic-republic-congo/dr-congo-militia-frees-nepalese-un-peacekeepers

Ambady, N., Bernieri, F. J., & Richeson, J. A. (2000). Toward a histology of social behavior: Judgmental accuracy from thin slices of the behavioral stream. In M. P. Zanna (Ed.), *Advances in Experimental Social Psychology* (Vol. *32*, pp. 201–272). San Diego: Academic Press.

Ambady, N., Hallahan, M., & Rosenthal, R. (1995). On judging and being judged accurately in zero-acquaintance situations. *Journal of Personality and Social Psychology, 69,* 518–529.

Ambady, N., LaPlante, D., Nguyen, T., Rosenthal, R., Chaumeton, N., & Levinson, W. (2002). Surgeons' tone of voice: A clue to malpractice history. *Surgery, 132*(1), 5–9.

Ambady, N., & Rosenthal, R. (1993). Half a minute: Predicting teacher evaluations from thin slices of behaviour and physical attractiveness. *Journal of Personality and Social Psychology, 64,* 431–441.

Arkowitz, H., Westra, H., & Miller, W. (2008). *Motivational interviewing in the treatment of psychological problems*. New York: Guilford.

Barton, F. (2006). The betrayal of Margaret Hassan. Retrieved 26 May 2014 from http://www.dailymail.co.uk/news/article-389368/Betrayal-Margaret-Hassan.html

Bin Laden, O. (2005). *Messages to the world: The statements of Osama Bin Laden* (B. Lawrence, Ed.). London: Verso.

Borkenau, P., Mauer, N., Riemann, R., Spinath, F. M., & Angleitner, A. (2004). Thin slices of behaviour as cues of personality and intelligence. *Journal of Personality and Social Psychology, 86*, 599–614.

Brandt, P., & Sandler, T. (2009). Hostage taking: Understanding terrorist event dynamics. *Journal of Policy Making, 31*(5), 758–778.

Cialdini, R. (2007). *The psychology of persuasion*. New York: Collins.

Cialdini, R., & Goldstein, N. J. (2004). Social influence: Compliance and conformity. *Annual Review of Psychology, 55*, 591–621.

Cowan, R. (2005). Inquest finds gunman in 15-day siege shot himself. Retrieved 26 May 2014 from http://www.theguardian.com/uk/2005/jan/18/ukcrime.rosiecowan

Crenshaw, M. (1990). Questions to be answered, research to be done, knowledge to be applied. In W. Reich (Ed.), *Origins of terrorism: Psychologies, ideologies, theologies, states of mind* (pp. 247–260). New York: Cambridge University Press.

Curhan, J., & Pentland, A. (2007). Thin slices of negotiation: Predicting outcomes from conversational dynamic within the first 5 minutes. *Journal of Applied Psychology, 92*(3), 802–811.

Department of Foreign Affairs and Trade. (2009). Nigeria. Australian Government. Retrieved 5 June 2014 from http://www.smarttraveller.gov.au/zw-cgi/view/Advice/Nigeria

Dolnik, A. (2011). Negotiating hostage crises with new terrorists. *Studies in Conflict and Terrorism, 34*(4), 267–294.

Doward, J., Loomes, N., & Burke, J. (2007). Kidnap Britons sighted in Eritrea. Retrieved 26 May 2014 from http://www.theguardian.com/world/2007/mar/04/travelnews.ethiopia?INTCMP=ILCNETTXT3487

Drachman, D., deCarufel, A., & Inkso, C. (1978). The extra credit effect in interpersonal attraction. *Journal of Experimental Social Psychology, 14*, 458–467.

Embwiller, T., Deaux, K., & Willits, J. (1971). Similarity, sex and requests for small favours. *Journal of Applied Social Psychology, 1*, 284–291.

Ferguson, E., & Corr, P. (2012). Blood, sex, personality, power, and altruism: Factors influencing the validity of strong reciprocity. *Behavioral and Brain Sciences, 35*, 25–26.

Foreign & Commonwealth Office. (2012). *The Foreign Office's human rights work in 2011*. Retrieved 26 May 2014 from https://www.gov.uk/government/publications/the-foreign-offices-human-rights-work-in-2011

Giebels, E., & Noelanders, S. (2004). *Crisis negotiations: A multiparty perspective*. Veenendaal, The Netherlands: Universal.

Gonzales, M., Aronson, E., & Costanzo, M. (1998). Increasing the effectiveness of energy auditors: A field experiment. *Journal of Applied Social Psychology, 18*, 1046–1066.

Gouldner, A. W. (1960). The norm of reciprocity: A preliminary statement. *American Sociological Review, 25*(2), 161–178.

Hargie, O. (Ed.) (2006). *Handbook of communications skills*. London: Routledge.

Horgan, J. (2003). *The search for the terrorist personality*. In A. Silke (Ed.), *Terrorists, victims and society: Psychological perspectives on terrorism and its consequences* (pp. 3–27). Chichester, UK: Wiley.

Horgan, J. (2008). From profiles to pathways and roots to routes: Perspectives from psychology on radicalization into terrorism. *ANNALS: American Association of Political and Social Sciences, 618,* 80–94.

House of Commons Report. (2006). *Report of the official account of the bombings in London on 7th July 2005.* Retrieved 26 May 2014 from http://www.fas.org/irp/world/uk/7-july-report.pdf

Jenkins, B. M. (2009, 28 January). Terrorists can think strategically: Lessons learnt from the Mumbai attack. Testimony presented before the Senate Homeland Security and Government Affairs Committee. Retrieved 26 May 2014 from http://www.rand.org/content/dam/rand/pubs/testimonies/2009/RAND_CT316.pdf

Johnson, H., & West, I. (1983). The Iranian embassy siege. *Medico-Legal Journal, 51*(4), 202–216.

Johnston, D. (2010). A history of hostage negotiation. Retrieved 26 May 2014 from http://www.londonarbitrators.org/downloadable-documents

Kelley, H. (1950). The warm–cold variable in first impressions of persons. *Journal of Personality, 18*(4), 431–439.

Klayman, J. (1995). Varieties of confirmation bias. *Psychology of Learning and Motivation, 32,* 385–418.

Lakin, J., & Chartrand, T. L. (2003). Using nonconscious behavioral mimicry to create affiliation and rapport. *Psychological Science, 14,* 334–339.

Logan, C. (2012). Risk assessment: Specialist interviewing skills for forensic practitioners. In C. Logan & L. Johnstone (Eds.), *Managing clinical risk: A guide to effective practice* (pp. 259–293). London: Routledge.

Meyerwitz, B., & Chaiken, S. (1987). The effect of message framing on breast self-examination attitudes, intentions and behaviour. *Journal of Personality and Social Psychology, 52*(3), 500–510.

Milgram, S. (1974). *Obedience to authority.* New York: Pinter & Martin.

Moriarty, T. (1975). Crime, commitment, and the responsive bystander. *Journal of Personality and Social Psychology, 31,* 370–376.

Moss, S. (2011). Kidnap revisited: How I met my former captor. Retrieved 26 May 2014 from http://www.theguardian.com/world/2011/jan/26/my-kidnapper-colombia-hostage-mark-henderson

Neville-Jones, P. (2010). British police in training for Mumbai-style attack. Retrieved 5 June 2014 from http://www.telegraph.co.uk/news/uknews/terrorism-in-the-uk/8383097/Baroness-Neville-Jones-British-police-in-training-for-Mumbai-style-attack.html

Oriola, T. (2012). The Delta creeks, women's engagement and Nigeria's oil insurgency. *British Journal of Criminology, 52*(3), 534–555.

Pape, R. (2005). *Dying to win: The strategic logic of suicide.* New York: Random House.

Parham, P. (2007). UK Statement at the International Peace Institute: UK policy to hostage taking. Retrieved 26 May 2014 from http://webarchive.nationalarchives.gov.uk/20130217073211/http://ukun.fco.gov.uk/en/news/?view=News&id=22835387

Perloff, R. (2003). *The dynamics of persuasion: Communications and attitudes in the 21st century* (2nd ed.). New York: Erlbaum.

Press Association. (2007, 14 March). Ethiopia blames Eritrea for kidnappings. Retrieved 26 May 2014 from http://www.theguardian.com/world/2007/mar/14/ethiopia

Rogers, C. R. (1951). *Client-centred therapy: Its current practice, implications and theory.* London: Constable.

Rogers, C. R. (1959). A theory of personality and interpersonal relationships as developed in the client-centered framework. In S. Koch (Ed.), *Psychology: A study of a science.* Vol. 3: Formulations of the person and the social context (pp. 184–256). New York: McGraw-Hill.

Silber, M. (2012). *The al Qaeda factor: Plots against the West.* Philadelphia: University of Pennsylvania Press.

Silke, A. (2003). *Becoming a terrorist.* In A. Silke (Ed.), *Terrorists, victims and society: Psychological perspectives on terrorism and its consequences* (pp. 29–53). Chichester, UK: Wiley.

Straw, J. (2004). Jack Straw's full statement about Ken Bigley. Retrieved 26 May 2014 from http://news.sky.com/story/300243/jack-straws-full-statement-about-ken-bigley

Strentz, T. (2006). *Psychological aspects of crisis negotiation.* Boca Raton, FL: Taylor & Francis.

Taylor, M., & Horgan, J. (2006). A conceptual framework for addressing psychological process in the development of the terrorist. *Terrorism and Political Violence, 18*(4), 585–601.

Taylor, M., & Quayle, E. (1994). *The terrorist.* London: Brassey's.

Taylor, P., & Donald, I. (2003). Foundations and evidence for an interaction based approach to conflict negotiation. *International Journal of Conflict Management, 3–4,* 213–232.

Theaxton, M. (2006). *What happened to the hippy man?* Oxford: Alden.

Tonks, J., Williams, W., Frampton, I., Yates, P., & Slater, A. (2007). Assessing emotion recognition in 9–15 year olds: Preliminary analysis of abilities in reading emotion from faces, voices and eyes. *Brain Injury, 21*(6), 623–629.

Travis, A. (2008). MI5 report challenges views on terrorism in Britain. Retrieved 26 May 2014 from http://www.theguardian.com/uk/2008/aug/20/uksecurity.terrorism1

Vecchi, G., Van Hasselt, V., & Romano, S. (2005). Crisis (hostage) negotiation: Current strategies and issues in high-risk conflict resolution. *Aggression and Violent Behaviour, 10*(5), 553–551.

Weinstein, N. (1993). Testing for competing theories of health protective behaviour. *Health Psychology, 12,* 324–333.

Wiktorowicz, Q. (2004). *On radical Islam rising: Muslim extremism in the West.* Lanham, MD: Rowman & Littlefield.

Wilson, M. (2003). *The psychology of hostage taking.* In A. Silke (Ed.), *Terrorists, victims and society: Psychological perspectives on terrorism and its consequences* (pp. 55–76). Chichester, UK: Wiley.

Part III
Individual and Group Perspectives

9

Understanding Suicide Terrorism
Insights from Psychology, Lessons from History

Andrew Silke

If in January 2000 you had told someone that in the coming decade the United Kingdom would fall victim to a sustained campaign of suicide bombings carried out by Islamist extremists, most of whom were born and raised in England (and many of whom had actually been raised as Christians), it is unlikely anyone would have believed you. The UK was no stranger to terrorism at this time. Memories of IRA terrorism were fresh. The most lethal bombing of the whole period of the Troubles occurred in 1998, while the 1990s had witnessed a series of massive truck bombings on mainland Britain. Terrorism was a familiar creature. But suicide attacks? Surely not.

Yet, here we are in the midst of a sustained campaign of suicide attacks. Attacks and attempted attacks are now taking place on an annual basis. Thankfully, the terrorist failures far outnumber the successes, but the successes cause enough damage and death to give serious pause for thought. The IRA never killed as many in one attack as four inexperienced bombers managed on 7 July 2005. That we have not had repeated slaughters in the UK is only the result of intensive investigation and pure luck. That luck cannot hold forever and the plots keep coming.

How then does one understand this new threat, a threat which at first glance seems alien to anything that has preceded it on these shores? How do we understand this new enemy? In the past 40 years, at least 80 different terrorist groups in 52 separate countries have used suicide tactics. Suicide attacks have killed nearly 35,000 people, maimed over 80,000 more and inflicted economic damage now conservatively estimated to be well over £100 billion (and far higher by some estimates) (Hafez, 2007; Pape, 2005; Silke, 2003). Suicide terrorism has struck across the globe; attacks have been carried out in both North and South America, in the Middle East, in Europe, in Africa and in Asia. More than any other terrorist tactic, suicide assaults are the ones

---

Investigating Terrorism: Current Political, Legal and Psychological Issues, First Edition. Edited by John Pearse.
© 2015 John Wiley & Sons, Ltd. Published 2015 by John Wiley & Sons, Ltd.

most likely to result in fatalities among the terrorist's targets, and they are also the assaults that are most difficult for authorities to defend against. Quite simply, suicide attacks are the most potent tactic in the modern terrorist's arsenal.

In order to prevent and combat suicide terrorism, one first needs a clear understanding of suicide terrorists. However, such an understanding is often badly lacking in the West. Myth and innuendo dominate much of the wider perception of who suicide terrorists are, what drives them, how terrorist groups view and organize these tactics and what might be done to prevent and deter such extremists. Informed and balanced writing on suicide terrorism is rare, drowned out in a deluge of material which paints the bombers as deranged fanatics who are brainwashed and duped into acts of incomprehensible violence (see also Chapter 10, by Robert Lambert).

On 7 July 2005 the first Islamist suicide bombings in Europe were carried out in the UK. Four suicide bombers (three of whom were British-born) detonated bombs in London during the morning rush hour. Fifty-two people were killed by the bombers and more than 700 were maimed and injured. Exactly two weeks later, on 21 July, more extremists attempted to carry out a second wave of suicide attacks on London's transport system, but this time the devices failed to detonate and no one was killed. Further attempts to carry out suicide attacks in the UK followed.

The fact that a growing number of 'home-grown' terrorists were willing to carry out suicide attacks represented a disturbing (and, to many, a deeply surprising) development and left the authorities and others struggling to understand the radicalization process which can produce such extremists within the relatively stable and prosperous states of Western Europe. It is somehow easier to understand suicide bombers emerging from communities mired in very violent conflicts in deprived parts of the world. That an extreme environment can produce extreme acts is understandable. But the question of how individuals born, raised and living in the stable and comparatively prosperous world of the West can turn to suicide terrorism is much more difficult to answer. The role that the environment plays is less apparently obvious. The door seems open to interpretations based on internal psychology, on mental illness and abnormal personalities. In truth, environment is still the key factor but it takes more effort to realize this (Silke, 2008).

One of the most powerful myths about modern suicide terrorism is that it is at essence a product of Islam. The argument that suicide terrorism is a uniquely Islamic phenomenon quickly dissolves from even a cursory examination of history. While there is malaise in that great religion which has witnessed the rise of al-Qaeda and similar groups such as the Islamic State (IS) in Syria and Iraq, one does not need to draw on the Quran alone to justify suicide attacks. Indeed, the first recorded suicide attack that history provides us with is not from an Islamic warrior but rather from a Jewish judge. The Old Testament of the Bible provides a detailed account of the death of the Jewish judge (ruler) and hero Samson. Captured by his enemies, the Philistines, tortured and mutilated, Samson was taken to their main hall to be tortured in public yet again:

And Samson said unto the lad that held him by the hand, Suffer me that I may feel
the pillars whereupon the house standeth, that I may lean upon them. Now the house
was full of men and women; and all the lords of the Philistines were there; and there
were upon the roof about three thousand men and women, that beheld while Samson
made sport. And Samson called unto the LORD, and said, O Lord GOD, remember me,
I pray thee, and strengthen me, I pray thee, only this once, O God, that I may be at once
avenged of the Philistines for my two eyes. And Samson took hold of the two middle
pillars upon which the house stood, and on which it was borne up, of the one with
his right hand, and of the other with his left. And Samson said, Let me die with the
Philistines. And he bowed himself with all his might; and the house fell upon the lords,
and upon all the people that were therein. So the dead which he slew at his death were
more than they which he slew in his life. (Judges 16: 26–30)

Thus, according to the Bible, in this one act of destruction, Samson killed as many
people (men, women and children if the word 'lad' is an indication) as the 9/11
hijackers killed in 2001. What is telling, however, is that the Bible does not condemn
Samson's actions. On the contrary, Samson's suicide is presented as an act of redemption as well as of vengeance, which is interesting given the general Judaeo-Christian
proscription of suicide. While the Bible in other places does prohibit killing and suicide, it is quite clear in this passage that Samson's actions were condoned. He asked
God for strength and this was granted. Thus, for a Christian or Jew who questions
whether suicide killing can be sanctioned by their religion, the story of Samson provides explicit evidence that it can (even when women and children are among the
victims). Clearly, it is not just Islam which can provide mixed messages on this issue.

Close examination of most major cultures will throw up examples like Samson.
Heroes who sacrifice themselves for a cause are a recurring motif in most societies
(Silke, 2006). Individuals and groups who resist in the face of hopeless odds and
certain death are heralded as icons of courage and honour. There is widespread pride
in their defiance. Consider, for example, the 300 Spartans who refused to surrender
to a Persian army perhaps 250,000 strong at the battle of Thermopylae in 480 BC.
Nearly 2,500 years later, we continue to write books and make films of this battle and
in every case it is the Spartans who are portrayed as the heroes.

Suicide terrorists are in many respects the modern inheritors of this legacy. They
and their supporters certainly see their actions as heroic, courageous and noble
(Silke, 2004). One of the obstacles to understanding suicide killing is that, if you
do not sympathize with the cause, it is difficult to see the perpetrator as anything
but an evil psychopath or, at best, as a vulnerable person who has been cynically
manipulated and brainwashed. However, if one has some sympathy with the cause,
then such explanations begin to ring hollow.

For example, if you had had the opportunity to kill Adolf Hitler in 1943 (and thus
end not only the military conflict but also the genocide of the Holocaust), while
sacrificing your own life in the attempt, would you have done it? What would you

think of someone who did agree to do this? Would you think of such a suicide bomber as a hero who sacrificed themselves for clearly just and sufficient reasons? Or would you see them as a brainwashed fanatic who has been coerced or 'radicalized' into killing themselves this way?

On 20 March 1943, Rudolph-Christoph von Gersdoff faced just this dilemma. A German army officer who was a veteran of the Eastern Front, he was scheduled to escort Hitler and other leading Nazis through a museum exhibition of captured Soviet weaponry in Berlin. Only a few days before the exhibition tour, Gersdoff was summoned to a meeting with a senior officer involved in plotting against Hitler. When Gersdoff appeared at the meeting:

> Tresckow spoke 'with the utmost gravity' about the situation and the 'absolute neces-
> sity' of saving Germany from destruction. Then he abruptly broached the question of
> whether Gersdoff would undertake an assassination attempt in which he would prob-
> ably be blown up himself. Gersdoff reflected briefly and agreed. (Fest, 1996, p. 195)

Hitler visited the exhibition in the company of Göring, Himmler, Donitz and Kei-tel. When Gersdoff saw Hitler approaching, he ignited the fuse to the bomb hidden under his clothes, and then kept close to the Führer as he walked among the exhibits. However, the rushed nature of the operation – involving, as it did, only a few days' planning and preparation – had not given the plotters enough time to acquire a short fuse to detonate the explosives. Instead, Gersdoff had to use a 10-minute fuse. He attempted to delay Hitler's progress by explaining the significance of the different exhibits, but the latter showed little interest and rushed through the halls. To every-one's surprise, after only two minutes the Führer left the building through a side door. Appalled, Gersdoff could only rush to the nearest toilets, where he ripped out the fuse to the bomb.

So what do we make of Gersdoff? Was he misguided, evil or a hero? Your immedi-ate reaction will probably depend a great deal on how you view his cause. If you think that killing Hitler was justified under the circumstances, then Gersdoff's actions will seem more reasonable and acceptable, and his willingness to sacrifice himself in the attempt a reflection of enormous personal courage.

Suicide terrorists today believe that they are fighting as great an evil as the one Hitler embodied for Gersdoff. They regard suicide actions as sometimes necessary and justified. Certainly these are themes that occur repeatedly in the video testi-monies recorded by many suicide terrorists before their missions. For example, the first confirmed British suicide bombing occurred in 2003 when two British nation-als carried out a suicide attack in Tel Aviv on behalf of Hamas. In a video testimony released by Hamas after the attack, the two bombers spoke to the camera in a more informal and free-flowing manner than was usually the case.[1] This was especially so with Asif Mohammed Hanif, the younger of the two men, who did most of the talking. Together they addressed a number of key themes:

1   They provided clear acknowledgement that they were about to carry out a mar-
    tyrdom operation: 'Fellow Muslims, we left Britain to look for martyrdom.'

2   They justified the attack on the basis of Israeli provocations: '[Jews] are raping
    our women, killing our children'; 'We will take revenge and we will get the Jews
    and the Crusaders out of the land of Islam.'

3   They encouraged viewers to support the attacks and even become bombers them-
    selves: 'You Muslims are sitting in your houses, watching whatever is happening
    here to your Muslim brothers in Palestine. We want to be martyrs for Allah and
    we want you to be martyrs for Allah as well ... OK, even if you're not going to
    fight with us, please at least look into the facts ... '

The video tackles questions such as whether the bombers were coerced, tricked or
brainwashed into carrying out the attack. The bombers emphasize that they know it
is a suicide mission, ruling out the possibility that they were tricked or duped; that
they have volunteered or actively sought out the mission, undermining the idea that
they had been coerced or pressured; and they also highlight their own intelligence,
education and skills to undermine the view that they were somehow brainwashed
into carrying out the attack: 'Allah has not created us stupid, he has given us intellect
in order to use it.'

These themes occur again and again in other video testimonies, including those
compiled by British suicide bombers. It is worth quoting the video of Mohammad
Sidique Khan, the leader of the July 7 suicide bombers, in detail here:

> I'm going to keep this short and to the point because it's all been said before by far
> more eloquent people than me. And our words have no impact upon you, therefore
> I'm going to talk to you in a language that you understand. Our words are dead until
> we give them life with our blood.
>
> I'm sure by now the media's painted a suitable picture of me, this predictable propa-
> ganda machine will naturally try to put a spin on things to suit the government and to
> scare the masses into conforming to their power and wealth-obsessed agendas.
>
> I and thousands like me are forsaking everything for what we believe. Our driving
> motivation doesn't come from tangible commodities that this world has to offer. Our
> religion is Islam – obedience to the one true God, Allah, and following the footsteps
> of the final prophet and messenger Muhammad ... This is how our ethical stances are
> dictated.
>
> Your democratically elected governments continuously perpetuate atrocities against
> my people all over the world. And your support of them makes you directly responsible,
> just as I am directly responsible for protecting and avenging my Muslim brothers and
> sisters.
>
> Until we feel security, you will be our targets. And until you stop the bombing,
> gassing, imprisonment and torture of my people we will not stop this fight. We are
> at war and I am a soldier. Now you too will taste the reality of this situation. ('London
> bomber', 2005)

Videos made of and by suicide terrorists provide some remarkable insight into these
actors. Like the video testimonies, these are clearly intended to give a particular
picture of the perpetrators and their cause. Certain issues and motivations will

be focused on and emphasized while others will be glossed over or else ignored entirely. Nevertheless, while they may be subjective in nature, these videos provide an unusual but useful insight into the psychology of the perpetrators and the groups they belong to.

For example, in one film seen by the author which describes a series of suicide bombings in Iraq, all of the bombers separately call on the viewer to join their cause and carry out jihadi attacks. These calls are followed by footage showing the bombers' successful attacks. The calls follow a very similar theme which is well illustrated in the quote below, taken from a speech one suicide bomber made to the camera just before he drove off on his mission:

> We call our brothers – by the will of Allah – to join us and to not delay in doing so. Everyone who watches this video should know that – by Allah – there is nothing between us and the Firdaws[2] except the pressing of a button. We ask Allah to grant us acceptance, success and correct aim, as well as to grant you the ability to join us.

These personal calls from each of the bombers are then backed up by a narrated call at the end of the video which emphasizes the similarities between the viewer and the bombers and again calls on the viewer to follow their example:

> [These] are real events that have occurred and are continuing to occur in [Iraq] and the heroes [suicide bombers] featured in this production are people just like us. They had lives just like our lives, homes like our homes. They had sons and daughters, fathers and mothers. Some of them had universities that they were looking forward to graduating from with the highest of degrees, and some of them had businesses that they were preoccupied with expanding. However, they all refused humiliation and disgrace, weakness and degradation. They were pained by the weakness of the Islamic nation and the pouncing of other nations upon it … They were pained by the situation of the youth of Islam, and what they are in of misguidance and loss; the youth of Islam who used to pulverise the Kings of the East and the Caesars of the West; today find themselves lost between the pop stars of the East and the immorality of the West. So they decided to make Hijrah[3] for the sake of Allah and in order to give victory to this Upright Religion.

Despite the indiscriminate and extreme violence of many terrorist attacks, the vast majority of research on terrorists has concluded that they are not mentally or psychologically abnormal (Horgan, 2005). On the contrary, many studies have found that terrorists are actually psychologically much healthier and far more stable than other violent criminals. For example, Wilfred Rasch's (1979) work on German terrorists produced some very important early insights. Working as a psychiatrist, Rasch examined a number of terrorists who had been captured by the West German authorities. Included in his sample were a number of infamous individuals such as Andreas Baader, Gudrun Ensslin and Ulrike Meinhof who were the leaders of the Red Army Faction.

Despite the fact that another psychologist had previously claimed that Baader was a sociopath (Cooper, 1977), Rasch concluded, after detailed and close contact with the captured terrorists, that 'nothing was found which could justify their classification as psychotics, neurotics, fanatics or psychopaths' (1979, p. 80). Even though Baader and the others would shortly afterwards commit suicide in prison, Rasch could not even diagnose these individuals as 'paranoid'. He examined a further 40 suspected terrorists and again could not find any evidence of psychological abnormality.

The differences between Rasch's findings and those of Cooper are worth looking at more closely. Rasch came to his conclusions only after extensive personal contact with the captured terrorists. Cooper, on the other hand, never actually met them; rather, he came to his conclusions entirely through second-hand sources such as magazine stories and books. This is a common trend in research on terrorists. Those researchers and 'experts' who suggest that terrorists are psychologically abnormal tend to be the ones who have had the least contact with actual terrorists. In stark contrast, those researchers who have met with terrorists find that suggestions that they are somehow abnormal simply do not stand up to close scrutiny. Direct research on terrorists from Spain, Northern Ireland, Israel and elsewhere has confirmed this finding: most terrorists simply are *not* crazy. While there are rare instances of individuals with personality or psychological abnormalities being involved in terrorism, such individuals are the exception rather than the rule. Where they do occur they tend to be figures on the fringe of the movement rather than key members. For the vast majority of terrorists, whatever their reasons for becoming involved in terrorism, it is not because they are psychologically deviant or abnormal. Somewhat surprisingly, psychologists have gradually been forced to accept that the most notable characteristic of terrorists is their normality.

This unexpected finding even applies to suicide terrorists, where again most perpetrators appear to have a relatively unremarkable psychology (Silke, 2003). No suicide terrorist personality has been identified. They are a surprisingly varied group of actors and it would be astonishing if they all fit comfortably into one profile or category.

Why do these people become involved in suicide terrorism? At one level, it is important to recognize that they do not describe the act as 'suicide', nor do they see it in those terms. Rather, they see it in terms of sacrificing themselves for a worthy and justified cause. Psychologically this represents an important difference. Consider, for example, the following comments from Sheikh Yusuf al-Qaradawi:

> Those who oppose martyrdom operations and claim that they are suicide are making a great mistake. The goals of the one who carries out a martyrdom operation and of the one who commits suicide are completely different … The suicide kills himself for himself, because he failed in business, love, an examination, or the like. He was too weak to cope with the situation and chose to flee life for death. In contrast, the one who carries out a martyrdom operation does not think of himself. He sacrifices himself for the sake of a higher goal, for which all sacrifices become meaningless. (quoted in Aaron, 2008, p. 89)

These comments referring to jihadi martyrs mirror very closely comments made in relation to Japanese kamikaze pilots during the Second World War. For example,

176 *Andrew Silke*

consider the comments Lt General Torashiro Kawabe made to US interrogators after the war:

> We believed that our spiritual convictions and moral strength could balance your material and scientific advantages. We did not consider our attacks to be 'suicide'. The pilot did not start out on his mission with the intention of committing suicide. He looked upon himself as a human bomb which would destroy a certain part of the fleet … [and] died happy in the conviction that his death was a step towards the final victory. (quoted in O'Neill, 1999, pp. 130–131)

Thus we should not automatically expect the patterns common in 'ordinary' suicides to be replicated in suicide terrorists. Certainly, the evidence suggests that the terrorists do not seem to follow those patterns.

One key element is recognizing that the decision to carry out a suicide attack ('martyrdom operation') has not been made quickly or abruptly. Instead, the journey to that stage is best seen as a gradual process. Becoming a terrorist is, in the first instance, an issue of socialization. This is certainly the case with jihadi extremism, where individuals tend not to join the jihad as isolated individuals. Rather, it is within small groups that they gradually become radicalized. This is a trend identified by both Sageman (2004) and Bakker (2007) who reviewed the life histories of hundreds of jihadi terrorists.

In his analysis of 242 jihadis, Bakker (2007) found that these individuals tended to become involved in terrorism through networks of friends or relatives and that generally there were no formal ties with global Salafi networks. In short, the individuals were not becoming radicalized as a result of the efforts of an al-Qaeda recruiter, but rather the process was occurring independently. Within this group context, they gradually adopt the beliefs and faith of their more extreme members in a psychological process known as *risky shift*. As both Sageman and Bakker found, this new Salafi faith led to their becoming more isolated from their childhood friends and family, and to an ever-increasing dependence on and loyalty to the group. With an increasing focus on this small group, their religious faith became more important and more intense. The polarization experienced within the group, combined with an increased sense of group identity and commitment, helped to radicalize individuals and facilitate their entry into the jihad in a way that was approved by their new social peers.

Any given society will possess some minorities and other disaffected groups who rightly or wrongly perceive that the world is treating them harshly. In some cases, there are genuine and very substantial causes for grievance. Individuals who belong to or identify with such disaffected groups share in a sense of injustice and persecution. It is from such pools that individual terrorists emerge. The move from disaffected to violent extremist is usually facilitated by a catalyst event. Normally, this is an act of extreme physical violence committed by the police or security forces or other rival group against the individual, family, friends or simply someone they can identify with. The shooting of a father and his 12-year-old son by Israeli soldiers in September 2000 at Netzarim acted as such a catalyst event for Palestinians. Captured on television, the shooting of the two as they cowered behind a water barrel contributed to a dramatic resurgence in terrorist violence in the region. The sense of belonging to a beleaguered group, combined with the experience of an act (or acts) of extreme violence against either oneself or significant others, is the impetus for some to engage in terrorism (also discussed in Chapter 11 by Karl Roberts).

It is important to emphasize that one does not need to experience events first-hand to be affected by them. Vicarious exposure through television or the Internet can have the same impact. In the past, many IRA members who came from the Irish Republic reported that it was what they had seen on television that motivated them to join the group. They had no relatives or friends living in Northern Ireland – and most had never even been to the province – but media coverage of violence there played a critical role in convincing them to join. Similarly, today most jihadi recruits have never been to Iraq, Afghanistan, Syria or Israel. They have no direct connections with those countries, no friends or family living there. However, they do have a sense of connection with the conflict, and the media coverage of the conflict – combined with very graphic coverage in jihadi videos – acts as an important catalyst in the radicalization process.

Ultimately, most suicide bombers are volunteers and already possess an intention or willingness to take part in suicide attacks. With rare exceptions, the groups do not coerce them into it. Suicide bombers tend to be volunteers who have chosen the option of a suicide action even where other avenues for violence remained open to them. Indeed, leaders of terrorist groups are often instructed to turn away youths who wish to take part in suicide attacks. As one senior member of Islamic Jihad put it, 'Some of the youths insist they want to lead a suicide operation ... My orders are to persuade them not to go, to test them. If they still insist they are chosen' (Kushner, 1996, p. 332).

Conclusions

The Chinese general Sun Tzu warned thousands of years ago, 'If you know neither the enemy nor yourself, you will succumb in every battle.' History and psychology give us some powerful tools for understanding suicide terrorism. History quickly teaches us that this tactic is not the reserve of any one religion, and there are many examples from the past of individuals with very different motivations who were willing to sacrifice their lives in an effort to kill others. Thus it is a mistake to see modern suicide terrorism as inherently an 'Islamic problem'. Similarly, history also teaches us that perspective is important. If we sympathize with the perpetrator's cause (such as an attempt to kill Hitler), we tend to explain the perpetrator's decisions and motivations in very different (and usually much more positive) ways. If we disagree with the aims, then explanations begin to cluster around issues such as the brainwashing, indoctrination, grooming and radicalization of vulnerable personalities. The truth almost certainly lies somewhere in between.

The lesson from psychology is that there is no obvious suicide terrorist personality. This seems to match with much of what history shows, that individuals reach the point of carrying out a suicide attack through a long process, a process which generally has more to do with ordinary social psychology than with clinical or abnormal psychology. Used effectively, these insights can be tremendously helpful in stripping away many of the myths and assumptions which surround debates on suicide terrorism, and leave us with a much more realistic assessment of the perpetrators – who they are, how they see themselves and what forces motivate and drive them. As Sun Tzu would have recognized, a more realistic understanding is a vital first step in developing more effective approaches for both countering and preventing the threat.

Notes

1   The descriptions and quotations that follow derive from videos viewed by the author, both on the Internet and from security organizations.
2   Firdaws (فردوس) is the highest level of heaven in Islamic tradition. This is where the prophets, the martyrs and the most truthful and pious people dwell.
3   The Hijrah refers to the Prophet Muhammad's migration from Mecca to Medina in 622 CE. The word *hijrah* means to leave a place to seek sanctuary or freedom from persecution or freedom of religion or any other purpose. *Hijrah* can also mean to leave a bad way of life for a good or more righteous way.

References

Aaron, D. (2008). *In their own words: Voices of jihad*. Santa Monica, CA: Rand.

Bakker, E. (2007). *Jihadi terrorists in Europe, their characteristics and the circumstances in which they joined the jihad: An exploratory study*. The Hague: Clingendael Institute.

Cooper, H. H. A. (1977). What is a terrorist: A psychological perspective. *Legal Medical Quarterly, 1*, 16–32.

Fest, J. (1996). *Plotting Hitler's death: German resistance to Hitler 1933–1945*. London: Weidenfeld & Nicolson.

Hafez, M. (2007). *Suicide bombers in Iraq: The strategy and ideology of martyrdom*. Washington, DC: United States Institute of Peace.

Horgan, J. (2005). *The psychology of terrorism*. London: Routledge.

Kushner, H. (1996). Suicide bombers: Business as usual. *Studies in Conflict and Terrorism, 19*, 329–338.

London bomber: Text in full. (2005, 1 September). Retrieved 29 May 2014 from http://news.bbc.co.uk/1/hi/uk/4206800.stm

O'Neill, R. (1999). *Suicide squads*. London: Salamander.

Pape, R. (2005). *Dying to win: The strategic logic of suicide terrorism*. New York: Random House.

Rasch, W. (1979). Psychological dimensions of political terrorism in the Federal Republic of Germany. *International Journal of Law and Psychiatry, 2*, 79–85.

Sageman, M. (2004). *Understanding terrorist networks*. Philadelphia: University of Pennsylvania Press.

Silke, A. (2003). The psychology of suicidal terrorism. In A. Silke (Ed.), *Terrorists, victims and society: Psychological perspectives on terrorism and its consequences* (pp. 93–108). Chichester, UK: Wiley.

Silke, A. (2004). Courage in dark places: Reflections on terrorist psychology. *Social Research, 71*(1), 177–198.

Silke, A. (2006). The role of suicide in politics, conflict and terrorism. *Terrorism and Political Violence, 18*(1), 35–46.

Silke, A. (2008). Holy warriors: Exploring the psychological processes of jihadi radicalisation. *European Journal of Criminology, 5*(1), 99–123.

10

Taking Anders Breivik Seriously as a Political Terrorist

Robert Lambert

Terrorist or Madman?

This chapter is concerned to probe the motivation, methodology and state of mind of Anders Breivik, a resident of Oslo, who on 22 July 2011 carried out the worst acts of criminal violence seen in Norway during the lifetimes of the majority of his fellow citizens. The chapter was written prior to Breivik's trial, save for this paragraph, a postscript and some footnotes which were written at the end of the trial in June 2012 and updated after the court's verdict was delivered in August 2012. Significantly, and unusually, the trial was not primarily concerned to prove Breivik's role in the attacks, which he freely admitted, but rather to establish his legal responsibility: was Breivik sane? For his part, Breivik was adamant to demonstrate to the court that he was acting rationally in pursuit of a clear and urgent political agenda. In summary he argued in court that, as youth members of the governing Labour Party, his victims on Utøya Island were complicit in a failed policy of multiculturalism which threatened the established fabric of Norwegian society which he sought to defend. In contrast, he regretted the deaths of his 'innocent' victims in Oslo city centre who were instead, he inferred, necessary collateral damage in the same defensive war. In the event, the court decided that Breivik was legally responsible for his actions. Nevertheless, reporting on the case was far more concerned with Breivik's personal life than with his role as a far right political terrorist.

Breivik went to great lengths to explain his motivation and strategy during an unusually long period of terrorist preparation and planning in which he wrote a detailed account of his political beliefs and his rationale for adopting a terrorist strategy (Berwick, 2011). Of course, it would be naive to take his written account at face value, still more to regard it as an accurate reflection of all that he was doing and

Investigating Terrorism: Current Political, Legal and Psychological Issues, First Edition. Edited by John Pearse.
© 2015 John Wiley & Sons, Ltd. Published 2015 by John Wiley & Sons, Ltd.

thinking during the years leading up to his violent acts. It does, however, provide a valuable starting point for what is a necessarily tentative approach to his motivation, strategy, tactics and state of mind. Clearly, in the fullness of time, access to the court transcript, the police investigation of the case and the full medical reports on Breivik will shed far more light on these questions than a distant preliminary academic analysis of this kind can hope to achieve. Indeed, by the time this chapter is published, far more will be known and understood about Breivik's motivation, state of mind and tactical planning than is available now. However, it is hoped that this provisional analysis will place Breivik's case in a wider context of political terrorism in general, and extremist nationalist political violence in particular.

Using Alex Schmid's established typology as a guide (Schmid, 1983, 2004, 2011), the chapter argues that Breivik should be taken seriously as a political actor carrying out an act of political terrorism – a particular kind of political violence. It consists of a preliminary attempt to reconcile two competing commentaries: on the one hand, Breivik as a violent extremist nationalist pursuing an anti-Muslim agenda; on the other hand, Breivik as an insane gunman, who should be denied the political role he claims. While preferring the former to the latter, the chapter finds merit in both perspectives and looks towards the scholarly work of specialist academics to present a contextual if provisional analysis of Breivik's case. In doing so it attempts to reduce the tension between the two opposing viewpoints – the political and the pathological. The case for Breivik's insanity revolves around a medical assessment carried out by court-appointed psychiatrists ('1996: Massacre', 2011).[1] From this perspective, Breivik, suffering from paranoid schizophrenia, acted compulsively based on 'a delusional thought universe'. In support, Breivik is cited alluding to himself as a future regent of Norway pending a takeover by a Templar-like organization where he would be 'Regent', with duties including the construction of reservations for native Norwegians in which they would conduct 'breeding projects' ('Anders Behring Breivik may avoid jail', 2011). Significantly, 'Templar' or 'Knights Templar' refers to a military order in the Middle Ages that fought in the Crusades against Muslims and later the term developed Freemasonry connotations (Barber, 1994). Breivik, who wears Masonic regalia in a propaganda photograph, is familiar with both usages and shares this interest with other extremist nationalists, for example Paul Ray, a founding member of the English Defence League (EDL), who has featured in police investigations into Breivik's attack (Taylor, 2011). The case for Breivik's insanity is vigorously championed by an influential strand of commentary that preceded an authoritative medical assessment about Breivik's abnormal mental condition, and seeks to deny him a role as a political terrorist (e.g., Leader, 2011).

The case for Breivik as a political terrorist acting in pursuance of an 'anti-Muslim', 'extremist nationalist' (Lambert, 2013) or far right agenda, known by Breivik and many of those taking part in it as the 'counter-jihad' movement (Ali et al., 2011), is made in a separate strand of commentary exemplified by Tad Tietze, a psychiatrist and left-wing commentator in Australia (Tietze, 2011a, 2011b; see also Myhre, 2011; Ottersen, 2011). Tietze objects to the 'medicalising or psychologising [of] fascist violence' which, he argues, fails to acknowledge 'how social contexts and practices shape the boundaries of what [violence] people are willing to engage in' (Tietze, 2011b, p. 1479).

To discern validity in both opposing commentaries is to follow a middle path suggested, if not explicitly argued, by Simon Baron-Cohen, professor of developmental psychopathology at the University of Cambridge. Breivik, Baron-Cohen suggests, necessarily possesses a 'psychopath's lack of affective empathy' while recognizing that Breivik's use of violence is the product of a 'carefully planned political project' (Baron-Cohen, 2011). To follow this path is therefore to grant equal significance to both the individual pathology of a terrorist actor such as Breivik and the wider political context in which he operates. It is also to maintain a strong focus on what Breivik actually did and on his articulate rationale for doing so. Of course, any approach to understanding Breivik's motivation, method and state of mind is necessarily provisional, not least pending full details of Breivik's medical examinations. In addition, as part of a contextual approach, Breivik's case is compared with other terrorist cases, including Ted Kaczynski's case, known as the Unabomber's nail bombing campaign in the United States (Kaczynski, 1995, 2010); al-Qaeda's 9/11 attacks in the United States (Wright, 2006); and cases of violent extremist nationalism in the United Kingdom and Germany (Gable & Jackson, 2011; Lambert 2013; Wagner, 2011). The chapter concludes by considering Breivik's potential influence in extremist nationalist circles in the future.

22 July 2011

To recall, on 22 July 2011 Anders Breivik, disguised in a police uniform, exploded a car bomb close to government offices in the Norwegian capital, Oslo, killing eight people. Although the bomb did not kill Jens Stoltenberg, the Norwegian prime minister, or any senior politicians, there was every likelihood that it could have done and may well have been intended to do so.[2] In any event, Breivik was adopting a familiar terrorist tactic at this point and was almost certainly committing an act of political violence. Had he been arrested at or near the scene of the bombing, or if for any other reason he had been restrained or incapacitated at this point, it seems likely that the question of his role as a terrorist actor and the question of his sanity would not have become as newsworthy and controversial as they did ('Norway commission', 2011). Instead it is the nature of his next act of calculated violence that led to significant professional and popular interest in his motivation and his mental state. Following a carefully researched and meticulously planned operation, Breivik immediately left the scene of the bombing and drove to the island of Utøya, where a summer youth camp of Norway's governing Labour Party was being held.

Before addressing Breivik's extraordinary violence on Utøya island, it is worth noting that his willingness to plan and his ability to carry out two consecutive acts of terrorism entirely on his own places him in a unique category in the history of political violence. The overwhelming majority of terrorist actors do not employ the tactic of conducting two consecutive and markedly different acts of political violence in quick succession. By doing so Breivik showed a high level of original and innovative strategic and tactical thinking that no doubt contributed to an initial failure by police to connect the two incidents – quite likely a tactical benefit that Breivik planned to achieve. Of course, Breivik had the advantage of operating in an environment where counter-terrorist operational capacity had never been tested by a serious terrorist incident of any kind, never mind to the extent that he intended it would be on this calm public holiday Friday in the middle of summer. However, even if he had implemented his innovative terrorist plan in a city like London (the city he adopts when signing his political manifesto), which has developed well-rehearsed counter-terrorist responses through hard-won experience, it seems reasonable to suggest that experienced counter-terrorist practitioners would not have expected to deal with a lone wolf bomb attack followed by a lone wolf mass shooting at another location of the kind Breivik planned and carried out. This is not to overstate Breivik's tactical skill but it would be wrong to ignore the methodological aspects of his plan when seeking to understand how, as well as why, he acted as he did. Moreover, by approaching motivation and methodology together, there will be a better chance of unpacking the long planning process involved in the case. Much of that work will be for the future; for now it serves to highlight the extent to which Breivik demonstrated tactical skills of exactly the kind that were needed for the exceptional task he had set himself.

Once landed on Utøya, Breivik, displaying shocking ruthlessness, proceeded to calmly shoot dead 69 people – mostly teenagers – and seriously injure many others. In doing so he departed from the conventional repertoire of terrorist tactics adopted in the West and allowed himself to be portrayed as an apolitical 'spree killer'[3] instead. As a direct result, Breivik is one of only a handful of modern terrorists to have become a household name in Europe. If there are a few households where his name does not trigger immediate recognition, then reference to his photograph almost certainly will. Numerous pictures of Breivik in the media – a tall, fit, blond, blue-eyed, composed and purposeful-looking 32-year-old Norwegian – have made him instantly recognizable, not least because his seeming respectability and normality confound the nature of his violent and brutal actions. It seems highly likely – although purely speculative – that a photograph of Breivik wearing a dark blue military-style wetsuit, peering purposely into the sights of an assault rifle, has become the most well-known media image of 2011 (e.g., 'Norway shootings', 2011). To this extent he might be said to have exceeded the primary goal of terrorists, namely to achieve publicity or propaganda for a political cause (Schmid, 1983, 2004, 2011). It was probably to this end that Breivik chose to include this particular photograph in a propaganda video which he posted on YouTube shortly before he carried out his act of terrorism ('Norway shootings', 2011).

Breivik as a Political Terrorist

To be sure, *2083 – A European Declaration of Independence*, Breivik's 1,500-page political manifesto (Berwick, 2011), provides clear evidence of his appreciation and deployment of a fundamental connection between an act of terrorism and the political cause it seeks to promote. He appears to understand that urgent terrorist action is an effective propaganda tool in a wider political struggle. It is a key ingredient in understanding the motivation of all terrorist actors, not just those who espouse an extremist nationalist agenda. Notwithstanding a plethora of competing accounts about the defining characteristics of terrorism, it is always instructive to reflect on the seminal work of Alex Schmid to appreciate the importance of political communication in this context. Terrorism, he suggests, is a form of communication that 'cannot be understood only in terms of violence' (Schmid, 2004). Rather, for Schmid, 'it has to be understood primarily in terms of propaganda' so as to penetrate the terrorist's strategic purpose (p. 205).

However, taken in its entirety, *2083* also suggests how Breivik's determination to ensure publicity for his act of terror may have backfired and unintentionally served to reduce public interest in the political cause he intended to promote. This is to suggest that, by choosing to be innovative in his terrorist method and adapting the tactic of a spree killer to his own terrorist purpose, he failed to calculate how this form of innovation might diminish his role as a serious political actor in the eyes of his audience – or at least his wider audience. He may also have overlooked the extent to which both his fastidious and idiosyncratic approach to political exposition and his ruthless approach to political violence may have alienated potential followers. For example, very few extremist nationalists who are prepared to engage in political violence for the same cause as Breivik would be likely to countenance his method of stalking and his use of dum-dum bullets, which had the intended effect of inflicting massive disfigurement on his victims, whether they were killed or seriously injured. When planning this aspect of the attack, he appears to have lost sight of the fact that by forsaking random victims as in a conventional terrorist bomb attack, like the one he had committed hours earlier, he was now seen to be hunting and killing individuals in a manner that suggested gratuitous cruelty above and beyond his polit-ical cause. This suggests a lack of empathy with his intended target audience among extremist nationalists, as well as with his wider public audience and with the victims he targeted to murder.

Breivik circulated *2083* to a long list of online contacts immediately before the attacks on 22 July. In it he claimed his actions were his contribution to a campaign to defend Europe from a Muslim invasion, which was being enabled by what he called 'cultural Marxists' in Norway's Labour Party and the European Union. While the extent of his personal contact with the email recipients of *2083* is necessarily unclear, what is known publicly at this stage is sufficient to suggest that he had long-term knowledge of, and a high level of familiarity with, the arguments of like-minded activists who shared some or all of his concerns about the growth of Muslim com-munities in Europe and the (perceived) fault of governments in allowing it. Notwith-standing such clear political motivation, two court-appointed psychiatrists, Torgeir Husby and Synne Soerheim, reported on 29 November 2011 that Breivik had 'devel-oped the mental disorder of paranoid schizophrenia' and was therefore assessed to be insane at the time of the attacks and consequently, on this medical view, unfit to be tried for murder ('Anders Behring Breivik may avoid jail', 2011). Immediately, the 'Norwegian public, politicians and experts alike' were reported to be 'expressing surprise at the diagnosis of insanity'. According to one newspaper report, Breivik was said to have 'found the verdict insulting and that although he had feared it, he had not expected this outcome'.[4] The media gave 'minute descriptions of how Breivik spent years planning his attacks' and it followed that his 'ability to do so makes it difficult for many people to accept that he cannot be held to account for them' (Anda, 2011).

Tad Tietze, a psychiatrist himself, argues that 'it's not that psychiatrists intentionally find mental disorder where there is none, but that they are always looking to the possibility of providing a treatment for an illness as a humane and rational option' (Tietze, 2011c). It follows, on his account:

> they will ... have a natural bias towards diagnosing in order to treat; that is, to do something rather than nothing. Such a trend has probably been exacerbated in an era where politics itself has been downgraded in favour of the notion of people as self-interested individual actors in a free market. The very idea of ideology has become unfashionable and so a Breivik becomes harder to comprehend, and therefore is more easily packaged as being mentally ill. Even if Breivik did show signs that he had slipped into a state that could sensibly be considered 'psychotic', his actions cannot be divorced from the social context and political networks from which he emerged.

Like many other terrorist strategists, Breivik intends that his terrorist acts will indeed serve as a precursor to a civil war. In his case, a civil war in which Europe's present political elite are eventually defeated and replaced by nationalist governments that tackle the threat Islam is perceived to pose to Europe's safety and well-being (Berwick, 2011). While it has not been possible to read the full psychiatric reports on Breivik, it seems reasonable to assume that the delusional tendencies attributed to him do not extend to a belief that he shares this negative view of Islam with thousands of others in Europe and the United States, including many influential commentators. Rather, his delusion appears more likely to centre on his ambitious perception of his own leadership role in a coherent 'counter-jihad' movement.

Breivik and Kaczynski

To place Breivik within Schmid's inherently political typology is to risk a certain objection from scholars who argue that lone wolf terrorists should be considered separately, outside of a political framework. Thus, for Franco Ferracuti, a criminologist, 'there is no such thing as an isolated terrorist – that's a mental case' (quoted in Hunsicker, 2006, p. 23). This approach seems unreasonably dismissive while at the same time helping to explain the support it provides to accounts that seek to diminish Breivik's connection to an extremist nationalist milieu. To a certain extent, the risk of political marginalization is always likely to be greater for a lone wolf operator like Breivik. In the circumstances it is interesting to note comparisons between Breivik and Ted Kaczynski, known as the Unabomber, the most infamous lone wolf terrorist in US history. Breivik's *2083* manifesto is one of the most detailed written rationalizations for terrorist action since *Industrial Society and Its Future*, written by Kaczynski (1995, 2010). While it would be perfectly tenable to suggest that both Kaczynski and Breivik suffer from a delusion of connectivity to the real world, the fact remains that both men have written persuasive rationalizations for political violence. That both men have been assessed (by at least some court-appointed psychiatrists) to be insane might diminish their potential influence in the wider population. However, by examining Kaczynski's case, it becomes clear that Breivik's coherent call to political terrorism has future potential to inspire and galvanize supporters in the small extremist nationalist milieu it is primarily aimed at.

To summarize, in 1971 Kaczynski moved to a remote cabin in Lincoln, Montana, where he lived as a recluse. He claims to have started a postal bombing campaign after watching the wilderness around his home being destroyed by development. From 1978 to 1995, Kaczynski posted 16 bombs to targets including universities and airlines, killing three people and injuring 23. In 1995 he sent a letter to the *New York Times* and promised to 'desist from terrorism' if the newspaper published his manifesto. Immediately after publication of his manifesto in the *New York Times*, Kaczynski began to be taken seriously as a political activist, an exemplar of an emerging type: the 'eco-terrorist' (Eagan, 1996). Like Breivik, Kaczynski argues that his bombings were extreme but necessary actions so as to attract media attention to an urgent political campaign. Urgent, for Kaczynski, so as to halt the erosion of human freedom necessitated, he argued, by modern technologies. Also like Breivik, Kaczynski wrote at far greater length and in far greater detail than many potential followers and allies might aspire to themselves. When reading it himself, Breivik is likely to have been aware that Kaczynski's wide-ranging manifesto had been revised and republished and was the subject of critical attention two decades after it was written (Kaczynski, 2010). It had not been forgotten: to the contrary, Kaczynski's voluminous prison writing was now the subject of a university collection and his former log cabin home and the items he used to make bombs were in a museum. While Breivik obviously lacks Kaczynski's formal erudition, it would be wrong to deny the comparison on that basis alone. Breivik might be said to be in tune with extremist nationalist 'counter-jihad' politics in the same way that Kaczynski tapped into radical environmentalist politics. For some inarticulate extremist nationalists Breivik might appear as authoritative and knowledgeable as Kaczynski does to some radical environmentalists (Zerzan, 2002).

Interestingly, although Kaczynski was not explicitly motivated to commit terrorist acts because of extremist nationalist politics, his analysis overlaps in places with Breivik's. Breivik's manifesto contains several unreferenced passages from Kaczynski's work (Hough, 2011). Throughout Kaczynski's text the theme of an embattled native population being beaten into submission by a left-leaning government that is not serving its own people holds his various strands of argument together. Like

Breivik, he is concerned to represent the 'white majority' who are, Kaczynski argues, being neglected by the left in favour of 'black people': 'For example, if one believes that affirmative action is good for black people, does it make sense to demand affirmative action in hostile or dogmatic terms?' (Kaczynski, 2010, p. 3).

Breivik appears to have been drawn to Kaczynski's case because of a shared frustration at government failure to recognize and tackle an urgent problem and a willingness to take direct terrorist action in an effort to attract media attention for his cause and to influence government policy. In this respect Breivik is not unlike another US lone wolf terrorist, Timothy McVeigh, who carried out the most devastating terrorist attack in the United States prior to 9/11. In 1995 McVeigh's Oklahoma City bomb attack killed 168 people, injured 680 more, destroyed or damaged 324 buildings within a 16-block radius, destroyed 86 cars, left a further 258 buildings engulfed in hazardous shards of shattered glass, and caused at least $652 million worth of damage. Given Breivik's assiduous attention to Kaczynski's published work, he is likely to have read the Unabomber's account of meeting McVeigh in prison and Kaczynski's largely favourable account of the Oklahoma City bomber. In turn, McVeigh expressed admiration for Kaczynski after the same prison meeting (Michel & Herbeck, 2001, pp. 398–402). If Breivik noted Kaczynski's mild criticism of McVeigh for paying insufficient attention to the 'innocence' of his random victims, he may well have taken the view that his own act of terrorism, like Kaczynski's, involved a majority of carefully targeted victims and a smaller number of 'innocent' victims.

At the very least, it can safely be said that Breivik's meticulous planning for his own attack included reference to Kaczynski's case, also an individual terrorist, who outwitted the FBI for over a decade. Notwithstanding the obvious differences in their chosen terrorist tactics, it is striking that both men demonstrated high-calibre strategic and tactical skills when concealing their preparatory terrorist acts from potential police detection. Kaczynski opted for a long-term low-level bombing campaign that took years to capture the kind of public attention he aspired to. For over a decade he consistently succeeded in planning to avoid detection and arrest. When he was finally arrested it came after he had he succeeded in publishing his political manifesto. Breivik was equally concerned that his political manifesto should be published to make plain his motivation. While clearly Breivik did not have to conceal himself against an active police investigation in the way that Kaczynski did, he still succeeded in concealing his plans during a long preparatory process. Terrorist skill sets of this calibre are in short supply and highly valued by terrorist organizations (Kenney, 2007, 2008; Lambert 2011). It is therefore sufficiently clear that, whatever their psychotic delusions might amount to in medical terms, they did not in any sense diminish the capacities the two men needed to succeed as terrorists.

Unlike Kaczynski, Breivik showed no squeamishness about witnessing the deaths of his victims. Indeed, the careful planning he undertook appears to have included an anticipation that he would need psychological strategies or coping mechanisms to be able to complete his task. Certainly, Geir Lippestad, his lawyer, was able to confirm that 'his client had taken drugs before going on the rampage [so as] "to be strong, efficient and awake"'. The fact that Breivik said he was 'sorry that he had to do this but it was necessary because he [was] in a war' (Rayner, 2011) demonstrates close parallels with many familiar experiences in terrorism and modern warfare. Throughout the same interview, Lippestad provides compelling unwitting testimony in support of Breivik's claim to have been acting in pursuit of a carefully crafted terrorist campaign. Indeed, Lippestad's immediate impression of his client's insanity was premised on an understanding that for his client to hold and execute such a plan was prima facie evidence of madness. '[Breivik's] in a war', Lippestad reported, 'and he says that the rest of the world, particularly the Western world don't understand his point of view, but in 60 years time we all will understand it' ('Norwegian gunman', 2011).

Eventually Lippestad concludes that Breivik is insane because he 'is not like any one of us'. In fact, experience suggests that Breivik is 'unlike us' because he has resorted to terrorist violence for exactly the same kind of reasons that terrorists in all kinds of movements have always done over the last hundred years or more (Lambert, 2011). Breivik's manifesto is consistent with the sentiments and methods of Europe's burgeoning violent extremist nationalist milieu. This is the same milieu that appeared to sustain his morale during a long process of strategic and tactical terrorist planning. Although such unusual behaviour from a defence lawyer towards a client might be explained by the extreme nature of Breivik's brutality, it seems unlikely that Lippestad would have uttered such views to a press conference had his client been inspired by al-Qaeda and not extremist nationalist politics.[5] On the other hand, it did unconsciously follow the conduct of Kaczynski's lawyers (Greenberg, 1999).

Like Breivik, Kaczynski was subjected to a psychiatric examination and found to be a paranoid schizophrenic and therefore insane, although, unlike Breivik, he was immediately deemed competent to stand trial. The question of competency to stand trial relates to legal and procedural differences between the United States and Norway and not between the medical assessments. Like Breivik, Kaczynski was adamant that his lawyers should scrupulously explain the political motivation for his actions. Instead, driven by an imperative to avoid Kaczynski being sentenced to the death penalty his lawyers sought to consolidate the medical assessment of their client's insanity, exactly against his instructions.

Psychotherapist Gary Greenberg corresponded with Kaczynski in prison and became sceptical of the medical diagnosis of paranoid schizophrenia, in part because, in his words, 'the mental health industry will reduce the political to the personal every time' (Greenberg, 1999). Greenberg (1999, p. 7) takes issue with Dr David Foster, a psychiatrist who interviewed Kaczynski five times. Foster claims that Kaczynski had 'paranoia about psychiatrists' that reflected his 'system-based failure to cooperate fully with psychiatric evaluation'. Greenberg also notes that Kaczynski's own lawyers conspired against him by insisting on his insanity. Nevertheless, Greenberg notes, 'in the public eye, Kaczynski had only been a political figure for a blink' (1999, p. 14). Of course, Greenberg was commenting before Kaczynski's serious reputation and his credibility had been partially restored – especially in radical environmentalist circles (Zerzan, 2002). Tietze (2011a) argues that the same psychiatric process has achieved the same 'de-politicising' purpose in Breivik's case. That may be true in mainstream circles but among Breivik's target audience – the one he aims to inspire and galvanize – it may well prove to be counter-productive. It is also to reckon without the concerns expressed by Breivik's victims, especially the families left bereaved.

Debating Breivik's Motivation: Commentators, Academics and Activists

In the immediate aftermath of the attacks Simon Jenkins provided an emphatic account insisting that Breivik was neither engaged in terrorism nor sane (Jenkins, 2011). Breivik, on Jenkins's account, is 'so insane he can see nothing wrong in shooting dead 68 young people in cold blood' and is 'so exceptional as to be of interest to criminology and brain science, but not to politics'. Furthermore, Jenkins insists, Breivik is 'plainly very sick', 'merely deranged', expressing 'some vague hatred of society' that 'tells us nothing about terrorism' and has instead committed 'a terrible but random act of insanity'. Terrorism, for Jenkins, is 'a specific and rational political form: the use of violence to achieve a multiplier of fear through a civilian population to a particular end'. Jenkins pays no regard to Breivik's clear explanation for his target selection which fits an established rationale for terrorism. In response, Torbjørn Ottersen objects that Jenkins ignores 'not only the specificity of the terrorist's stated purpose, but also his rhetorical and ideological connections'. Specifically, Ottersen notes:

> Christian Tybring-Jedde, leader of the Oslo Progress party and a member of the Norwegian parliament, wrote last year that the Labour party had 'stabbed Norwegian culture in the back'. This narrative ... is a key argument advanced by the right in Norway and, along with intimations that the Norwegian Labour party has a secretive network of operatives within the civil service ready to undermine any rightwing government, is advanced with worrying regularity. (Ottersen, 2011)

Professor David Wilson, a leading criminologist specializing in serial killers and spree killers, but with no background in terrorism studies, was asked by the *Daily Mail*, a right-wing UK daily newspaper, to explain Breivik's motivation. He was able to so without once addressing Breivik's political motivation, dealing instead with him as a spree killer. 'Tellingly,' Wilson claims, 'unlike so many spree killers, including Britain's own Derrick Bird[6] in Cumbria, England, and Thomas Hamilton[7] in Dunblane, Scotland [Breivik] did not shoot himself, but instead allowed the police to take him into custody' (Wilson, 2011). Cambridge psychologist Kevin Dutton also specializes in the study of spree killers and takes Wilson's analysis a stage further by arguing that 'what happened on Utoya Island wasn't about immigration, or so-called Eurabia, or the Eurocrats' plot against the people'. 'In fact,' he suggests, 'it wasn't really about ideology or religion at all. That's just the window dressing. It was all about *him*. Breivik. And his deep-seated feelings of inadequacy in relation to the opposite sex' (Dutton, 2011; emphasis original).

Baron-Cohen offers a middle path between the seemingly polar opposite perspectives of those endorsing Breivik's insanity and those promoting his political role. He does so by highlighting parallels between Breivik and Adolf Hitler:

> At 8.30 pm on 8 November 1923, Hitler (then aged 34) burst into the largest beer hall in Munich, fired a shot into the ceiling and jumped on a chair, yelling: 'The national revolution has broken out!' Breivik also thought he was starting a revolution. When arrested, Hitler wanted to use the trial to make political speeches, just as Breivik hoped to do. Sent to prison for five years, Hitler wrote Mein Kampf, a long ideological justification for his racist actions that also has many parallels with Breivik's manifesto. Hitler's diatribe against the 'Jewification' of Europe parallels Breivik's diatribe against the 'Islamification' of Europe. Both were men convinced by the rightness of their beliefs; both were willing to sacrifice people to achieve their ends. (Baron-Cohen, 2011)

Not only does Baron-Cohen capture the sense in which Breivik shares Hitler's ruthless disregard for the sanctity of the lives of a community regarded as a threat to national identity, but he also highlights the risk of ignoring the extremist politics that Hitler then and Breivik now represent. As Tietze reminds us, 'during most of the 1920s the Nazis were considered to be a marginal annoyance by the political mainstream'. 'At the time of the failed Beer Hall Putsch in 1923' (described above by Baron-Cohen), Tietze recalls, the Nazis 'could garner only 3% of the vote, and even less in 1928'. Given that in Breivik's Europe far right parties enjoy far greater leverage than their Nazi predecessors, it is salutary to reflect on the fact that by 1930 the German economic crisis 'triggered by the Wall Street Crash had torn German society asunder, shattering the livelihoods of millions of people' (Tietze, 2011a) and allowing Hitler the foothold for power he had long sought as an outsider. When, after the Holocaust, Hitler's Nazi henchmen were put on trial in Nuremburg, attempts to theorize Nazism as 'a form of psychopathology' were only exposed and laid to rest under the watchful eye of philosopher Hannah Arendt who instead alerted the world to the 'banality of evil' (Arendt, 2005; Tietze, 2011a).

It has only been in recent years that academic research has finally laid to rest the persistent and popular notion that terrorists are predisposed to insanity or psychiatric or psychological abnormality. Whatever the cause terrorists pursue, and – in those cases where they survive the terrorist attacks they carry out – whenever they are examined by medical experts, their sanity and normality are invariably established. Even Nazi war criminals were eventually shown to be psychologically healthy and normal and indistinguishable from a sample of average American civilians (Silke, 2004). In this regard, Silke has done more than most to explain that psychological abnormality or anomaly is rarely a trait in terrorists. Instead, rigorous examinations conducted over three decades point to the fact that terrorists are perfectly rational and approach their chosen tasks in much the same way as soldiers. In Breivik's case the risk is that this research will be side-stepped on the basis that it does not apply to lone wolves – as already noted in relation to Ferracuti's assessment.

Frazer Egerton reasonably notes that, while the argument against the psychological abnormality of terrorists has been won conclusively at the intellectual level, it remains impervious to defeat both within and outside this specialist field of study (Egerton, 2011). By way of example, he cites the experienced terrorism studies scholar Walter Laqueur who claims that 'madness, especially paranoia, plays a role in contemporary terrorism'. 'Not all paranoiacs are terrorists', Laqueur suggests, 'but all terrorists believe in conspiracies by the powerful, hostile forces and suffer from some form of delusion and persecution mania ... madness plays an important role, even if many are reluctant to acknowledge it' (Egerton, 2011, p. 23; Laqueur, 2001). Egerton is unconvinced, preferring Silke's description of an academic 'propensity to claim that psychological abnormality lies at the root of an individual becoming a terrorist as "Cheshire Cat logic"' (Egerton, 2011, p. 24). Cheshire Cat logic refers to the cat in Lewis Carroll's *Alice in Wonderland* who believed that there were only mad people in Wonderland, and so to be in Wonderland was to be mad. For Egerton this 'determination of many to see psychological problems as a root cause is reminiscent of a famous study by the psychologist David Rosenham where a population with regular mental health were admitted to psychiatric hospitals', where staff 'were unaware that such an experiment was being conducted'. Citing Rosenham, Egerton notes how 'these hospital employees routinely and consistently interpreted the actions of the new "patients" as attributable to psychological abnormality purely on the basis of their presence in the hospital' (Egerton, 2011, p. 25; Rosenham, 1973).

While it is clearly appropriate to place Breivik in a separate category of lone wolf terrorism, it would be wrong to dismiss the sense in which Breivik identifies with a nascent terrorist movement that operates on behalf of extremist nationalism or the far right in Europe. Indeed, it is clear from Breivik's manifesto that he regards his terrorist actions on 22 July 2011 as being a necessary part of a galvanizing process aimed at strengthening and emboldening the movement.

Utøya Island and the World Trade Center

It will be useful to consider Breivik's methodology, something he talks about in vague strategic terms in *2083* but about which he is silent in terms of the tactics he employed on 22 July. In doing so, it may be illuminating to consider the media impact of Breivik's attacks – a prime purpose of terrorism. Very few terrorist attacks achieve sustained political and media attention. Instead, most terrorist attacks hit the headlines briefly and very soon afterwards the identities of perpetrators and victims are forgotten by all except those who have been directly affected or who have a direct professional or academic interest in the event. Breivik is therefore immediately noteworthy for having conceived and executed a terrorist attack that has received sustained political and media attention (e.g., 'Anders Behring Breivik', 2011). In this respect his planning and execution of the attacks on Utøya shares the same rare distinction as the al-Qaeda terrorist attack on the World Trade Center in New York (Wright, 2006) a decade earlier. Strictly speaking, of course, both attacks were part of coordinated terrorist actions which included other targets: for Breivik, a bomb attack on a government building in Oslo; for al-Qaeda, an aeroplane 'bomb' hitting the

Pentagon and one other that was prevented from reaching its target. However, it is Breivik's cold-blooded slaughter of young Labour Party activists on Utøya Island and al-Qaeda's airborne assault on the twin towers of the World Trade Center that have galvanized and ensured sustained political and media attention.

Notwithstanding meticulous planning, neither Breivik nor al-Qaeda's 9/11 strategists could have calculated exactly the extent to which one of their targets – respectively, the Labour Party Youth Rally on Utøya and Ground Zero (the site of the destroyed World Trade Center) – would come to eclipse the others in the political, media and public consciousness. Instead, Breivik might reasonably have anticipated that his more conventional terrorist attack on a government building would have achieved equal or even greater media interest than it did. Indeed, had the Norwegian prime minister been present in his office at the time of the attack and been killed, then of course both media and political interest would have been greater in that leg of a carefully scripted two-part operation. Still less would Breivik have been able to plan and calculate in advance that the death toll on Utøya island would far exceed the numbers killed by his bomb in Oslo.

Similarly, at the planning stage, the al-Qaeda conspirators who executed 9/11 might have supposed that airborne attacks on the Pentagon and (potentially) the White House (National Commission, 2004) would have attracted equal media attention to attacks on the World Trade Center. Again, as in Breivik's case, the potential killing of a leading politician, in this case the US president, however remote, will always occur and appeal to strategists planning terrorist attacks of this kind. Such are the indeterminate elements of terrorist attacks that strategists and tactical planners must leave to chance. Suffice to say that what Breivik and al-Qaeda's 9/11 strategists had in common was an ability to plan and execute terrorist attacks that were guaranteed to achieve massive and sustained political and media attention, even if they were never able to determine the exact nature and development of that attention.

Interestingly, in both cases there was an initial period when the media captured what appeared to be slow responses from government, police and security services (National Commission, 2004; 'Norway commission', 2011). Broadly speaking, this apparent lack of speed provides evidence of the terrorist's most cherished tactical weapon: surprise. It is also worth recalling that it was the tactic of coordinated attacks that put enormous strain on government, police and security responses at the time of both attacks. Moreover, although al-Qaeda is best understood as a terrorist move-ment, it is worth noting that leading al-Qaeda strategist Abu Musab al-Suri has long argued the benefits of inspiring lone wolf terrorist actions (Lia, 2007) of the kind undertaken by Breivik, albeit in pursuit of an opposite cause.

Breivik stands out, not just from other extremist nationalist lone wolf terrorists, but also from lone wolves in general by virtue of the time he spent in preparation for an act of terrorism. Preparation, in Breivik's case, might be usefully divided into three categories: thinking and writing about the political cause that warrants terrorist action; thinking and writing about the tactic of terrorism; thinking and writing about his actual plan of attack. In this respect he is on a par with strategists in al-Qaeda who also promote terrorist attacks in the United States and United Kingdom. To illustrate, inspired by Major Nidal Hasan, a military psychiatrist who killed 13 and injured 30 army colleagues in a spree killing at Fort Hood in November 2009, al-Qaeda propagandist Adam Gadahn called for Muslims to use similar ingenuity when planning attacks (Gadahn, 2010).

It is also worth noting that Hasan himself is understood to have come under the influence of al-Qaeda propagandist Anwar al-Awlaki (Sherwell & Spillius, 2009). So, too, did London student Roshonara Choudhry who was sentenced to life imprisonment for the attempted murder of her member of parliament Stephen Timms in 2010 after coming under Awlaki's online influence (Dodd & Topping, 2010). In truth, there is little difference in principle between these al-Qaeda lone wolf cases and those carried out or attempted in extremist nationalist circles. For Breivik terrorism was a tactic to be employed in the first stage of a long war against Muslims in Europe. From his perspective, it would be illogical and unreasonable if only one side used such a necessary tactic as terrorism.

Extremist Nationalist Political Violence

The political cause Breivik espouses is a wholly familiar and contemporary one, sometimes known as 'counter-jihad', which might best be characterized as belonging to the extremist nationalist movement in Norway with strong links to like-minded movements in the rest of Europe and the United States. A clear anti-Muslim sentiment sits at the heart of this political cause and Breivik is not the first European to adopt a terrorist tactic to promote it (Lambert, 2013). However, he is the first European to achieve international notoriety by adopting a terrorist tactic in pursuit of an anti-Muslim extremist nationalist political agenda. In contrast, in the United Kingdom, Martyn Gilleard, a violent extremist nationalist convicted of manufacturing nail bombs in 2008, singularly failed to register in the public consciousness in spite of his bid to attract attention and galvanize support. 'Be under no illusion,' he said in a prepared statement, 'we are at war. And it is a war we are losing badly ... I'm so sick and tired of hearing Nationalists talk of killing Muslims, of blowing up mosques, of fighting back ... The time has come to stop the talk and start to act' ('Nazi sympathiser', 2008). Interestingly, while Breivik shares Gilleard's frustration at the failure of extremist nationalists to take action, he also reveals a strong sense of leadership and genuine organizational ability to overcome it – qualities sorely lacking in Gilleard and others who have been convicted for similar offences in the United Kingdom (Lambert, 2013).

Gilleard is one of several unheralded individuals on the far right to be convicted for serious terrorist or terrorist-like offences in the United Kingdom in recent years. In an important report Gable and Jackson document cases involving individuals such as Gilleard, Terence Gavan and Neil Lewington who should not, they argue, be lightly dismissed as lone wolves and social misfits and instead treated more seriously as sharing the same extreme politics and propensity for terrorist violence

(Gable & Jackson, 2011). In the same way as Timothy McVeigh was able to utilize skills and contacts he had acquired in his US military service to build and detonate a massive bomb, so too was former British soldier Terence Gavan able to put his expert military skills to good use when manufacturing nail bombs with which to kill Muslims (Gable & Jackson, 2011).

With minimal help McVeigh was able to inflict more harm and damage with one bomb than four suicide bombers in London operating under an al-Qaeda flag in London 10 years later. If McVeigh and the social misfit London nail bomber David Copeland were adequate role models for would-be bomber Lewington, it should not be difficult to anticipate that Breivik himself has the potential to inspire followers in the violent extremist nationalist milieu (Gable & Jackson, 2011). It should also be noted that Tony Lecomber, a leading member of the British National Party (BNP), convicted for possessing grenades and petrol bombs in the 1980s, was reported in 2006 to have discussed plans to assassinate prominent British politicians, for presiding over 'the multi-cultural experiment' that the BNP, like Breivik, diagnoses as the root cause of the United Kingdom's ills (Gable & Jackson, 2011).

Cases of serious anti-Muslim, anti-immigrant and racist violence have often failed to attract significant government and media attention in the United Kingdom and across Europe. However, at the time of writing, a case has hit the headlines in Germany that suggests a much deeper malaise and is worthy of consideration in relation to Breivik's case (Wagner, 2011). In summary, during the last decade an anti-immigrant terrorist campaign by Beate Zschäpe, Uwe Mundlos and Uwe Böhnhardt, three members of the extremist nationalist National Socialist Underground (NSU), was wrongly attributed to the Turkish mafia. In addition, a member of the German security service was implicated as being involved in the conspiracy. During the investigation police discovered 'a hit list of 88 possible targets, including two prominent members of the Bundestag and representatives of Turkish and Islamic groups' (Pidd & Harding, 2011).

In consequence, 'investigators have been trying to establish whether the list included people the group was actively plotting to kill, or was simply a list of high-profile political opponents' (Pidd & Harding, 2011). According to press reports, 'two of those apparently targeted are senior politicians from Munich: the Green MP Jerzy Montag and the Christian Social Union MP Hans-Peter Uhl'. The case began in 1998, when 'two men and one woman from Thuringia went underground after the pipe bombs they were building went up in smoke'. For the next 13 years, they 'left a murder trail through Germany, killing a policewoman, eight Turks and a Greek, robbing banks, and probably a nail bomb, too' (Pidd & Harding, 2011). It will be difficult to pathologize Zschäpe, Mundlos and Böhnhardt and remove them from the political agenda of the extremist nationalist NSU in the same way that Breivik has been removed from the same extremist milieu because of a narrow focus on his mental health. For Lehr, the case also sheds light on a tendency for the German government to ignore far right violence – to be 'blind in the right eye' (Lehr, 2013) – a charge that might be made elsewhere in Europe. Again this helps to put Breivik's motivation, methodology and state of mind into a wider political context.

Quite possibly, Breivik was deluded to believe that he might succeed in prompting a civil war of the kind he envisages in *2083*. However, such a delusion is more a matter of scale and proportion than one that points to a fundamental disconnection with the real world. On the contrary, in *2083* Breivik shows the same kind of appreciation of the political world he lives in as many other extremist nationalists, some of whom have engaged in political violence for the same reason. In any event, he was not deluded about the substantial number of fellow Europeans who share some or all of his concerns about the 'Islamification of Europe'. Breivik might be deluded if he thought he possessed any of the charismatic or leadership qualities of Hitler. That said, there is already evidence to indicate Breivik's ability to inspire or nurture political violence at a local level. To illustrate, two men, aged 25 and 26, were charged in Västerås, Sweden in September 2011 for 'attempted murder in connection with attacks on two men of south Asian origin at the end of July 2011' in circumstances that revealed an appreciation of Breivik's actions ('Two men charged', 2011).

Clearly this is not the level of violence that Breivik intended his actions would inspire, although it is of the same kind. As Baron-Cohen reminds us, it is also reminiscent of the behaviour of Hitler's Brownshirts. One sobering fact is already crystal clear which helps put debate about his medical condition in context: Breivik's young victims on Utøya Island would still be alive today if they had been attending a nationalist anti-Muslim summer camp and not a left-wing multicultural celebration. For the sake of their memory Breivik should be taken seriously as a political terrorist. So too the immigrant victims of Zschäpe, Mundlos and Böhnhardt might be alive today if the German authorities had taken the threat of extremist nationalist violence as seriously as al-Qaeda inspired terrorism during the last 10 years. Without question, Breivik's politics would not have been marginalized in the same way if he had been inspired by al-Qaeda. In an effort to reduce more 'anti-Muslim', 'anti-multiculturism' terrorism from extremist nationalists in the future, it would be helpful if governments, practitioners and researchers began to take the threat more seriously. In terms of research this should include greater reliance on experienced, specialist terrorist interviewers such as John Horgan and Andrew Silke. Breivik and those like him cannot be fully understood by psychiatrist interviewers who have no specialist knowledge of terrorism.

Looking ahead, it would be prudent to assume that Breivik will seek to emulate Kaczynski as an effective political propagandist while in long-term custody. Early indications suggest that Breivik will not abandon the political cause he is committed to, especially when it continues to gain adherents across Europe. Just as Kaczynski has won plaudits from sections of the anarchist and radical environmentalist movements where he has become an inspirational figure in the field of 'leaderless resistance' (e.g., Campbell, 2001), so too might Breivik reasonably anticipate that he will be able to exert influence for his cause from his prison cell for a long time in the future. For the time being, however, he will have to contend with the fact that his opponents on the left are prepared to take him more seriously as a terrorist whereas many of his favourite 'counter-jihad' commentators are eager and determined to dismiss him as a madman.

Postscript: Breivik's Trial

Breivik's trial commenced on 16 April, closing submissions were made on 22 June and the court's verdict was delivered on 24 August 2012. Covering the trial for the *Guardian*, Mark Lewis reports the prosecution arguing that 'any doubt must favour an insanity judgement' and that in their opinion it was 'worse that a psychotic person is sentenced to preventative detention than a non-psychotic person is sentenced to compulsory mental healthcare'. Moreover, a prosecution lawyer added, 'the wishes of the defendant were an irrelevance'. The prosecution, Lewis notes, 'said the basis of their assessment was structured around the core delusion' that Breivik 'believes he is going to save us all from doom in the fight between good and evil. In this fight he believes he has the responsibility to say who will live and who will die.' Significantly, 'This responsibility is rooted in a senior position in a non-existent organisation' (Lewis, 2012).

For the prosecution the 'non-existent organisation' in question is the Knights Templar and Breivik's delusion can, on this account, be evidenced by 'trips to London and Liberia in 2002, which he claims were the founding meetings of the Knights Templar', but which the prosecution derided as failed business trips. Lewis reports that the prosecution suggested that, 'instead of causing fear, a tragic person emerges; a young man who in his struggle to be big becomes part of an imaginary network which lets him reach his unattainable goal'. However, it seems reasonable to suggest that, even if Breivik's claims about the Knights Templar network are found to be false, it does not follow that his attempts to add weight to his solo act of terrorism by inventing or embellishing links to a wider movement should be interpreted as evidence of delusion.

To the contrary, as leading far right scholar Matthew Goodwin argued during the trial:

> it is impossible to understand the actions of Breivik by treating him in isolation and divorcing him from the wider political context in which he was embedded. On day two of the trial, Breivik expressed his view that the atrocities in Oslo and on Utøya Island were necessary in order to 'save future generations' from Islam and multiculturalism. This survivalist rhetoric was similarly evident when Breivik was asked why he became emotional while watching his own propaganda video: 'Because I realised my ethnic group is dying', was his response. To underscore the point, he pointed to recent statements by Nicolas Sarkozy, Angela Merkel and David Cameron as evidence that our experiment with multiculturalism has failed.

It follows, for Goodwin, that Breivik is expressing 'vocabularies of motive' which 'are shared and cultivated by many within the far right':

> At one level, this sympathy can be seen in expressions of support for Breivik's ideas and warnings about the potential threat from Islam. Like these activists, Breivik appears strongly committed to his belief that Europe is facing a fundamental threat from Islam

and rising ethnic and cultural diversity; that ordinary native citizens have been forced into an apocalyptic-style battle for racial and cultural survival; that the established main parties are unable to protect this group, or are complicit in orchestrating threats to their survival; that only urgent and radical action can counter this threat and save the wider group; and that activists have a moral obligation to protect and (as they see it) ensure the survival of future generations. (Goodwin, 2012)

In emphasizing Breivik's coherent place within a wider far right discourse, Goodwin supports much of the analysis in this chapter. For their part, Breivik's lawyers 'admitted that Breivik was putting pressure on [them] to prove he had no personality disorders but said they would focus on proving his criminal responsibility' (Lewis, 2012). For Myhre, by declaring Breivik sane and 'convicting him as a terrorist', the court 'paved the ground for a political understanding of those shocking events on 22 July'. Equally, the verdict was welcome because it marked the end of 'a long trial process far too focused on Breivik's persona, and too little on the social and political climate that created him' (Myhre, 2012). Irrespective of the court's verdict, it seems safe to anticipate that Breivik will be understood by a small number of like-minded far right extremists (in various states of mental well-being) to have acted in support of a just and urgent cause. That will surely be a source of inspiration for Breivik as he contemplates a life as a prison writer in the same mould as Kaczynski – albeit lacking the Unabomber's academic and analytical skills. However, notwithstanding Norway's unimpeachable commitment to judicial integrity and transparency in respect of his case, it would be naive on Breivik's part to assume that he will be allowed to communicate with his target audience from a computer in his prison cell on exactly his own terms. His writing may well be subject to significant censorship and to restrictions on circulation.

At the conclusion of his trial Breivik evinced satisfaction that he had been declared sane and gave every indication of having the will and the capability to write in support of his anti-Muslim, anti-multicultural politics in prison. Unlike Kaczynski, however, Breivik is pursuing a political agenda that resonates with a significant minority of his fellow citizens and fellow Europeans. Whereas Kaczynski's extensive prison writing has only been avidly read by a fringe audience, Breivik might reasonably expect to attract the attention of the kind of readership he reckons would be necessary to extend his terrorist campaign and sow the seeds for the civil war he envisages in *2083*. If this seems fanciful it may be prudent to recall Baron-Cohen's comparison with Hitler's youthful composition of *Mein Kampf* while serving a prison sentence for political violence. While Breivik appears to possess none of Hitler's charisma and leadership skills, it would be wrong to dismiss his ability to impress unsophisticated audiences of the kind that inhabit far right milieus. Moreover, as in Breivik's case, psychiatrists may well have found elements of mental abnormality or mental instability had they examined Hitler during his productive literary spell of incarceration. By following Baron-Cohen's middle path we can begin to consider compatibility rather than incompatibility between the pathological examinations of individual terrorists such as Breivik and the far right political milieus that sustain them.

Notes

1   The findings in this report were later challenged by the findings of a second psychiatric
    report ('Norway killer Breivik', 2012). Both reports received detailed attention at Breivik's
    trial.
2   Breivik sheds some light on this question in evidence during his trial.
3   A spree killer is best defined as an offender who commits two or more murders 'without
    a cooling-off period; the lack of a cooling-off period marking the difference between a
    spree murder and a serial murder' (Morton & Hilts, 2008).
4   As noted in n. 1, a second court-appointed psychiatric report took an opposite view on
    the matter.
5   When representing Breivik at his trial, Lippestad appears to have developed a greater pro-
    fessional empathy with his client's perspective.
6   Derrick Bird was an apolitical spree-killer taxi driver who went on a shooting rampage in
    his taxi in Cumbria in June 2011, killing 12 people and injuring 11 more before shooting
    himself to avoid arrest ('Profile: Cumbria gunman Derrick Bird', 2010).
7   Thomas Hamilton, a lone gunman, went on a shooting spree at a school in Dunblane,
    Scotland, in 1996, killing 16 children and their teacher. Hamilton 'sprayed shots at random
    around the school gym in an attack that lasted just three minutes, but caused carnage in a
    class of five and six year olds. He then turned the gun on himself' ('1996: Massacre', 2008).

References

1996: Massacre in Dunblane school gym. (2008). On This Day 1950–2005. BBC.
    Retrieved 29 May 2014 from http://news.bbc.co.uk/onthisday/hi/dates/stories/march
    /13/newsid_2543000/2543277.stm

Ali, W., Clifton, E., Duss, M., Fang, L., Keyes, S., & Shakir, F. (2011, August). *Fear, Inc: The
    roots of the Islamophobia network in America*. Washington, DC: Center for American
    Progress. Retrieved 29 May 2014 from http://www.americanprogress.org/wp-content
    /uploads/issues/2011/08/pdf/islamophobia.pdf

Anda, L. G. (2011, 29 November). Norwegian disbelief at Breivik 'insanity'. *BBC News*.
    Retrieved 29 May 2014 from http://www.bbc.co.uk/news/world-15954370

Anders Behring Breivik may avoid jail after psychiatrists declare him insane. (2011,
    29 December). *Guardian*. Retrieved 29 May 2014 from http://www.guardian.co.uk
    /world/2011/nov/29/anders-behring-breivik-avoid-jail-insane

Anders Behring Breivik. (2011). *Guardian*. Retrieved 29 May 2014 from
    http://www.guardian.co.uk/world/anders-behring-breivik

Arendt, H. (2005). *Eichmann and the Holocaust*. London: Penguin.

Barber, M. (1994). *The new knighthood: A history of the Order of the Temple*. Cambridge, UK:
    Cambridge University Press.

Baron-Cohen, S. (2011, 1 December). Anders Breivik: Cold and calculating, yes – but
    insane? *Guardian*. Retrieved 29 May 2014 from http://www.theguardian.com
    /commentisfree/2011/dec/01/anders-breivik

Berwick, A. (2011). *2083 – A European Declaration of Independence*. Retrieved 29 May 2014
    from http://info.publicintelligence.net/AndersBehringBreivikManifesto.pdf

Campbell, D. (2001, 18 April). Anarchy in the USA: Profile of anarchist John Zerzan. *Guardian*. Retrieved 29 May 2014 from http://www.guardian.co.uk/world/2001 /apr/18/mayday.features11

Copsey, N. (2010). *The English Defence League: Challenging our country and our values of social inclusion, fairness and equality*. London: Faith Matters.

Dodd, V., & Topping, A. (2010, 3 November). Roshonara Choudhry jailed for life over MP attack. *Guardian*. Retrieved 29 May 2014 from http://www.guardian.co.uk/uk/2010/nov /03/roshonara-choudhry-jailed-life-attack

Dutton, K. (2011, 29 July). Guns and roses – The jilted, juxtaposed mind of Anders Breivik. *Psychology Today*. Retrieved 29 May 2014 from http://www.psychologytoday.com /blog/split-second-persuasion/201107/guns-and-roses-the-jilted-juxtaposed-mind -anders-breivik-0

Eagan, S, P. (1996). From spikes to bombs: The rise of eco-terrorism. *Studies in Conflict and Terrorism, 19*, 1–18.

Egerton, F. (2011). *Jihad in the West: The rise of militant Salafism*. Cambridge, UK: Cambridge University Press.

Gable, G., & Jackson, P. (2011). *Lone wolves: Myth or reality?* London: Searchlight.

Gadahn, A. (2010). Brother Nidal [Video with transcript]. Retrieved 29 May 2014 from http://publicintelligence.net/adam-gadahn-march-7-2010-video-with-transcript/

Goodwin, M. (2012, 18 April). Anders Breivik sees himself as a survivalist soldier. *Guardian*. Retrieved 29 May 2014 from http://www.guardian.co.uk/commentisfree/2012/apr /18/anders-breivik-survivalist-soldier?INTCMP=SRCH

Greenberg, G. (1999). In the kingdom of the Unabomber. Retrieved 29 May 2014 from http://www.garygreenbergonline.com/media/unabomber_letter.pdf

Hough, A. (2011, 24 July). Norway shooting: Anders Behring Breivik plagiarised 'Unabomber'. *Telegraph*. Retrieved 29 May 2014 from http://www.telegraph.co.uk/news /worldnews/europe/norway/8658269/Norway-shooting-Anders-Behring-Breivik -plagiarised-Unabomber.html

Hunsicker, A. (2006). *Understanding international counter terrorism*. Boca Raton, FL: Universal.

Jenkins, S. (2011, 26 July). The last thing Norway needs is illiberal Britain's patronising. *Guardian*. Retrieved 29 May 2014 from http://www.guardian.co.uk/commentisfree /2011/jul/26/norway-illiberal-britain-patronising

Kaczynski, T. J. (1995). *Industrial society and its future*. Retrieved 29 May 2014 from http://editions-hache.com/essais/pdf/kaczynski2.pdf

Kaczynski, T. J. (2010). *Technological slavery*. Port Townsend, WA: Feral House.

Kenney, M. (2007). *From Pablo to Osama*. Philadelphia: Pennsylvania State University Press.

Kenney, M. (2008). *Organizational learning and Islamic militancy*. Final Report. School of Public Affairs, Capital College, Pennsylvania State University. Retrieved 29 May 2014 from https://www.ncjrs.gov/pdffiles1/nij/grants/226808.pdf

Lambert, R. (2011). *Countering al-Qaeda in London: Police and Muslims in partnership*. London: Hurst.

Lambert, R. (2013). Anti-Muslim violence in the UK: Extremist nationalist involvement and influence. In M. Taylor, P. M. Currie, & D. Baldwin (Eds.), *Extreme right wing political violence and terrorism* (pp. 31–64). London: Continuum.

Laqueur, W. (2001). Left, right and beyond: The changing face of terror. In J. Hoge & G. Rose (Eds.), *How did this happen? Terrorism and the new war*. Oxford: Public Affairs.

Leader, D. (2011, 29 July). Anders Behring Breivik and the logic of madness. *Guardian*. Retrieved 29 May 2014 from http://www.guardian.co.uk/commentisfree/2011/jul/29/anders-behring-breivik-norway-madness

Lehr, P. (2013). Still blind in the right eye? A comparison of German responses to political violence from the extreme left and the extreme right. In M. Taylor, P. M. Currie, & D. Baldwin (Eds.), *Extreme right wing political violence and terrorism* (pp. 187–214). London: Continuum.

Lewis, M. (2012, 21 June). Anders Behring Breivik resists insanity claim by prosecution. *Guardian*. Retrieved 29 May 2014 from http://www.guardian.co.uk/world/2012/jun/21/anders-behring-breivik-insanity-claim?intcmp=239

Lia, B. (2007). *Architect of global jihad: The life of al-Qaeda strategist Abu Mus'ab al-Suri*. London: Hurst.

Michel, L., & Herbeck, D. (2001). *American terrorist: Timothy McVeigh and the Oklahoma City bombing*. London: HarperCollins.

Morton, R. J., & Hilts, M. A. (2008). *Serial murder: Multi-disciplinary perspectives for investigators*. U.S. Department of Justice; Federal Bureau of Investigation. Retrieved 29 May 2014 from http://www.fbi.gov/stats-services/publications/serial-murder/serial-murder-july-2008-pdf

Myhre, A. S. (2011, 30 November). Anders Breivik's hatred does not come from a delusional mind. *Guardian*. Retrieved 29 May 2014 from http://www.guardian.co.uk/commentisfree/2011/nov/30/anders-breivik-delusional-mind

Myhre, A. S. (2012, 24 August). Anders Breivik verdict: Now Norway must ask how it created a killer. *Guardian*. Retrieved 29 May 2014 from http://www.guardian.co.uk/commentisfree/2012/aug/24/anders-breivik-verdict-norway?intcmp=239

National Commission on Terrorism Attacks upon the United States. (2004). *The 9/11 Commission Report* (authorized ed.). New York: Norton.

Nazi sympathiser Martyn Gilleard jailed for 16 years. (2008, 25 June). *Telegraph*. Retrieved 3 June 2014 from http://www.telegraph.co.uk/news/uknews/2193160/Nazi-sympathiser-Martyn-Gilleard-jailed-for-16-years.html

Norway commission to investigate Breivik attacks. (2011, 27 July). *BBC News*. Retrieved 29 May 2014 from http://www.bbc.co.uk/news/world-europe-14317271

Norway killer Breivik is 'not psychotic', say experts. (2012, 4 January). *BBC News*. Retrieved 29 May 2014 from http://www.bbc.co.uk/news/world-europe-16416791

Norway massacre: Breivik declared insane. (2011, 29 November). *BBC News*. Retrieved 29 May 2014 from http://www.bbc.co.uk/news/world-15936276

Norway shootings: Anders Behring Breivik's YouTube video posted hours before killings. (2011, 24 July). *Telegraph*. Retrieved 29 May 2014 from http://www.telegraph.co.uk/news/worldnews/europe/norway/8657669/Norway-shootings-Anders-Behring-Breiviks-YouTube-video-posted-hours-before-killings.html

Norwegian gunman Anders Breivik is 'insane' and took drugs to be strong, lawyer says. (2011, 26 July). *Huffington Post*. Retrieved 3 June 2014 from http://www.huffingtonpost.co.uk/2011/07/26/norwegian-gunman-anders-b_n_909423.html

Ottersen, T. S. (2011, 27 July). Norway: Mad, bad or political terror? [Letter]. *Guardian*. Retrieved 29 May 2014 from http://www.guardian.co.uk/world/2011/jul/27/mad-bad-or-political-terror

Pidd, H., & Harding, L. (2011, 16 November). German neo-Nazi terrorists had 'hitlist' of 88 political targets. *Guardian*. Retrieved 29 May 2014 from http://www.guardian.co.uk/world/2011/nov/16/german-neo-nazi-terror-hitlist?newsfeed=true

Profile: Cumbria gunman Derrick Bird. (2010, 2 November). *BBC News.* Retrieved 29 May 2014 from http://www.bbc.co.uk/news/10216923

Rayner, G. (2011, 26 July). Norway massacre: Anders Breivik took drugs to make himself 'strong' before shooting. *Telegraph.* Retrieved 29 May 2014 from http://www.telegraph.co.uk/news/worldnews/europe/norway/8662603/Norway-massacre-Anders-Breivik-took-drugs-to-make-himself-strong-before-shooting.html

Rosenham, D. (1973). On being sane in insane places. *Science, 179*(4070), 250–258.

Schmid, A. P. (1983). *Political terrorism: A research guide to concepts, theories, data bases and literature.* Amsterdam: North-Holland.

Schmid, A. P. (2004). Frameworks for conceptualising terrorism. *Terrorism and Political Violence. 16*(2), 197–221.

Schmid, A. P. (2011). *The Routledge handbook of terrorism research: Research, theories and concepts.* London: Routledge.

Sherwell, P., & Spillius, A. (2009, 7 November). Fort Hood shooting: Texas army killer linked to September 11 terrorists. *Telegraph.* Retrieved 29 May 2014 from http://www.telegraph.co.uk/news/worldnews/northamerica/usa/6521758/Fort-Hood-shooting-Texas-army-killer-linked-to-September-11-terrorists.html

Silke, A. (2004). The devil you know: Continuing problems with research on terrorism. In A. Silke (Ed.), *Research on terrorism: Trends, achievements and failures* (pp. 57–71). London: Frank Cass.

Taylor, M. (2011, 1 September). More Britons face questions over links to Utøya killer Anders Breivik. *Guardian.* Retrieved 29 May 2014 from http://www.guardian.co.uk/world/2011/sep/01/britons-links-to-anders-breivik-utoya

Tietze, T. (2011a). Depoliticising Utoya: Anders Breivik as 'madman'. In E. Humphrys, G. Rundle, & T. Tietze (Eds.), *On Utoya: Anders Breivik, right terror, racism and Europe* [e-book]. London: Elguta.

Tietze, T. (2011b). Madness and Western civilisation. In E. Humphrys, G. Rundle, & T. Tietze (Eds.), *On Utoya: Anders Breivik, right terror, racism and Europe* [e-book]. London: Elguta.

Tietze, T. (2011c, 2 December). The Breivik diagnosis: Ideology wrapped in a straitjacket. *Drum.* Retrieved 29 May 2014 from http://www.abc.net.au/unleashed/3709600.html

Two men charged for Breivik 'tribute' attack. (2011, 27 September). *Local.* Retrieved 29 May 2014 from http://www.thelocal.se/36392/20110927/

Wagner, B. (2011, 16 November). Neo-Nazi terror cell shows Germany was fooled by the far right. *Guardian.* Retrieved 29 May 2014 from http://www.theguardian.com/commentisfree/2011/nov/16/neo-nazi-terror-cell-germany

Wilson, D. (2011, 24 July). The changes he saw all around him fed his warped sense of injustice. *Daily Mail.* Retrieved 29 May 2014 from http://www.dailymail.co.uk/news/article-2018118/Anders-Behring-Breivik-The-changes-saw-fed-warped-sense-injustice.html

Wright, L. (2006). *The looming tower: Al-Qaeda and the road to 9/11.* New York: Knopf.

Zerzan, J. (2002). *Running on emptiness: The pathology of civilisation.* Port Townsend, WA: Feral House.

11

Social Psychology and the Investigation of Terrorism

Karl Roberts

This chapter discusses the application of social psychological theory to the investigation of terrorism, focusing on group psychology, identity theory and methods of psychological assessment used within forensic psychology.

Terrorist Psychology

When considering terrorist atrocities, a common question is: Why do they do it? A frequent response is to suggest that, given the extreme nature of the violence, the perpetrators must be 'abnormal', 'mad' or psychologically 'different' in some way. When researchers have carried out systematic studies of terrorists, looking for signs of abnormality, little evidence for this has been found (e.g., Silke, 2003; see also Chapter 9 by Silke in this volume). Psychological abnormality does not appear to be a characteristic that distinguishes terrorists from other members of society. Given this, why do ordinary individuals carry out such acts? A promising line of recent research has identified the importance of social psychological factors such as group psychology and identity theory in the aetiology of terrorism (e.g., Arena & Arrigo, 2006; Horgan, 2005). This chapter will discuss the relevance of social psychological factors to terrorism and illustrate how they may be useful to investigators.

Groups

Group membership is an important part of human life, as we spend significant periods of time with others. Groups are sources of friendship, support and nurturance

---

Investigating Terrorism: Current Political, Legal and Psychological Issues, First Edition. Edited by John Pearse.
© 2015 John Wiley & Sons, Ltd. Published 2015 by John Wiley & Sons, Ltd.

and provide individuals with a sense of belonging. Throughout their lives individuals are part of a number of different social groups each with a different function depending on its context. The immediate family has a role in early learning, support and nurturance; other groups cater for friendship, religious and/or political needs. Group membership provides a number of rewards for individuals – material rewards such as money, food, shelter, and so on, and psychological rewards, such as companionship, meaning, social support and explanations for the way the world is and for an individual's feelings. Group membership can also provide a set of behavioural rules for how to behave across a range of different situations. Groups influence the behaviour of individuals in a number of ways – explicitly with rules and regulations and implicitly through processes such as conformity and obedience (Cialdini, 2001).

Groups have been important in the history of terrorism (Burleigh, 2008). There are obvious advantages of groups in terrorism both for the obtaining of material such as weapons and finance, and for psychological support such as ideological justification as well as the other psychological gains described earlier.

Group Development

When individuals form a group, regardless of whether it is made up of strangers or those with pre-existing links, the group goes through a series of stages in which the aims, objectives and roles of the members of the group are identified. These stages occur for all groups and are characterized by particular behaviours, attitudes and feelings within the group. Tuckman (e.g., Tuckman, 1965; Tuckman & Jensen, 1977) provided a model to describe the developmental stages of groups, identifying five stages: forming, storming, norming, performing and mourning (sometimes referred to as adjourning). Figure 11.1 shows the relationship between each of the stages of this model. The arrows show the relationships between stages and the direction of development from one stage to another. We will now consider group development and the implications this has for terrorist groups.

Forming

The first stage of group development is the *forming* stage when a group first comes together. This stage can be uncomfortable for all members, even if it includes individuals who have prior links with each other. At this stage, questions predominate: some will be asked directly; others are more implicit – Who are the other members? What do they want? How will they behave? At this stage the group has no structure and, often, vague aims. Where there is no clear leader from the start, individuals who are the most extrovert (outgoing, sociable and communicative) often assume the initial leadership of the group. If group members have a desire to remain together, the maintenance of the group is the most important objective at this stage, overriding all other concerns. In the context of this uncertainty and distrust, with initial leadership

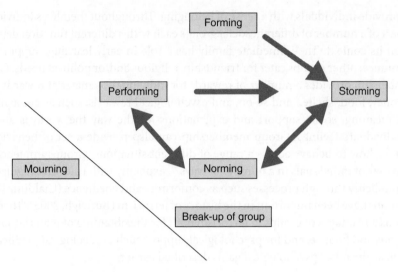

Figure 11.1   Tuckman's model of group development

often from the most voluble member and not necessarily the individual most qual-
ified, new groups are vulnerable to collapse during the forming stage. It has been
estimated that 95 per cent of nascent terror groups collapse within the first few weeks
or months of formation (Borum, 2004).

Storming

Should a group successfully negotiate the forming stage, it moves on to the storming stage. Here issues concerning the group's aims and objectives and the roles of
members dominate activities. This stage is characterized by disagreement, jockeying
for position and influence, and identification of authority. This is the most stressful
stage for members and may involve high emotion and anxiety. At the end of this
stage, assuming that the group remains together, roles are eventually allocated or
assumed. Importantly, the initial group leaders may not remain as leaders, and this
can lead to the formation of breakaway groups of those who disagree with the new
regime. The stresses of the forming and storming stages can be reduced if the group
is made up of those with pre-existing social ties. This is interesting, given the work
of Sageman (2004) who found that the majority of early members of al-Qaeda had a
pre-existing relationship with each other.

Norming

Following storming, the group has the task of identifying what it stands for. Questions predominate, such as: What do we do and what is expected of each member?

Here the group begins to develop a sense of identity. This may influence an individual member's own sense of identity; indeed some individuals for whom the group is of great importance will make their membership of the group a central part of their own identity (this will be discussed more fully later). In some cases the group exists because its members share a common set of aims and beliefs. This may help expedite this and earlier stages in group development. For the group to continue to exist, the majority of the members must accept the norms generated. Where members do not accept norms, the group is vulnerable and may slip back into the storming stage with a risk of collapse. The history of terrorism is replete with examples of groups failing to agree on their aims and objectives and moving into arguments and disagreements characterized by the storming stage (Burleigh, 2008).

Performing

If a group is able to negotiate the norming stage, the next stage is the performing stage. Here, based on its aims and objectives, the group must act. In the context of terror groups, the act can take many forms. It may involve fund-raising and criminal and other acts to gain access to funds and/or weapons in order ultimately to carry out terrorist attacks. It is important that groups ultimately perform, otherwise they are liable to collapse, because, if it fails to act to the satisfaction of its members, questions will arise about the point of the group. Failure to act can result in the group moving back into another norming or even storming stage. A terror group may fail to act because it lacks popular support or resources and so may reconsider what it is for. Some terror groups may evolve into political groups following a renewed norming stage, as did elements of the Provisional Irish Republican Army (PIRA), for example. A storming stage following a failure to act to the satisfaction of members may result in challenges to the leadership. The reappraisal of roles and breakaway factions may result. For example, in Northern Ireland the Real IRA and the Continuity IRA evolved partly out of dissatisfaction with the PIRA leadership's increasing acceptance of weapon decommissioning within the Northern Ireland peace process.

When groups perform, the acts are likely to be reviewed by the group: Were they successful? What went wrong? Is anyone to blame? Here the group may move back to a norming or a storming stage as the performance is reviewed, with the associated risks to the group's existence.

Mourning

In the event that a group breaks up, particularly when this was not a result of a membership decision, the final stage of group development may occur. This is the mourning stage where members may feel a sense of loss and sadness for the group – as if they are in mourning for it. Here former group members may experience a desire to rekindle the group and may take steps to contact other group members to re-create the group. For example, following the deaths and arrest of members, there were at least three reincarnations of the European Red Army Faction (Burleigh, 2008).

Using Tuckman's Model to Organize Intelligence and Predict Behaviour

The dynamics of group development can be applied to the investigation of terror groups. Observation of group member behaviour may allow the identification of the stage of development a group is in, so that predictions can be made as to the likely future behaviour of the group. For example, if surveillance indicates that argument and disagreements are a regular feature of the group interaction, it is likely that the group is in a storming stage and so may be trying to sort out its structure. Issues such as leadership and individual responsibilities will dominate, as may discussion of the group's aims or the apportioning of blame for failure, and so on. In such a case, the group is less likely to act in the near future. If surveillance indicates that roles have been clearly attributed, and that argument and discussion are minimal, the group may have completed its norming stage and is more likely to act in the near future.

Identifying the developmental stage may also suggest ways of disrupting groups. The storming stage is the most uncomfortable for group members and this is the stage at which groups are at their most vulnerable. The use of undercover infiltration of the group may be a useful strategy here, as the presence of a new individual will raise suspicion and the need for the group to reconsider roles. An undercover officer may also introduce challenging ideas that ferment disagreement, all of which will be likely to push a group into a storming stage and hence further away from acting.

A group is vulnerable following performing, as this is a stressful time for terror group members. There is extra police activity and public and media concern. At this time, in addition to other group members serving as a means of comfort and support for individuals, groups naturally reappraise their actions and, if these have been unsuccessful, consider why they have failed. Hence it is likely that there will be attempts by members to contact each other in the aftermath of a terror attack. This is useful for investigators, especially following failed attacks, as, if suspect and witness communications are monitored, they may be able to identify co-conspirators.

When a group has broken up, the members enter the mourning stage. Here there is anxiety at the loss of the group and a desire to re-create it. Individuals often cope with this by trying to contact or meet other former members. For investigators this is important for two reasons. First, attempts to contact each other can be monitored by police leading investigators to other suspects. Secondly, for individuals in the mourning stage, simply seeing other members of the group or being aware that they are nearby may rekindle the group ethos and the resolve of members. Therefore, if investigators wish to diminish the resolve and belief in the cause of group members, it is perhaps a strategy to avoid holding individuals at the same police station.

Social influence

Having considered the ways in which groups form, we will now consider the ways in which groups come to exert influence on their members. Two processes are particularly relevant: social conformity and obedience. We will consider each of these in turn and discuss the implications for terrorist behaviour.

Within Tuckman's model of group formation, to perform efficiently, groups need to have minimal disagreement and a clear set of aims and objectives to which members conform. The extent to which a group achieves this is referred to as the level of group coherence. Maximal group coherence is associated with maximal conformity of individual members and efficient performance. For example, consider a successful football team. Generally there is minimal disagreement between group members, a stable management and leadership structure, a shared set of goals that everyone understands and a settled squad of players each of whom knows their own role and is happy with it. Contrast this with an unsuccessful team, where disagreement is often rife, players wish to leave, managers resign and so on.

For all individuals within a group, the presence and behaviour of others can have a powerful effect on them. If an individual believes that the majority of the group members agree, they are more likely to modify their own views and to behave in accordance with the majority view (e.g., Asch, 1955). Normative social influence is the impact of group agreement on an individual and usually results in public compliance, that is, individuals doing or saying something without necessarily believing it. This appears to be related to a general desire to avoid confrontation and to a view that the majority is more likely to be correct (Cialdini, 2001). There is a difference between publicly conforming to the views of the majority and believing them. Those individuals most motivated to achieve the group's ideology will be most likely to believe in the group's views. By contrast, some individuals who publicly conform may harbour doubts while publicly acting in ways consistent with the group. How might individuals who publicly conform come to internalize the group's ethos more fully? There are a number of relevant processes here that are related to the nature of the group's leadership and the situation in which a group finds itself.

Social influence and leadership

The influence a group has over its members is increased if the group has a strong directive leader. Good leadership is characterized by leaders who are charismatic, have good social skills and are able to present consistent messages in a coherent manner. Good leaders often have experiences that are valued by the group members, which helps them be seen as credible. Messages given by a leader who is perceived to be similar in terms of attitudes, beliefs, background or experiences to other group members are also more influential. Leaders often go to considerable lengths to stress their similarity to their members, to convince them that they are just like you. The demands made of the group members by the leader should also be perceived to be reasonable given the context. A leader is also more influential where there are clear costs to not obeying a request, and where the costs are tangible, for example threats, or more esoteric, such as punishment from God (Messick & Kramer, 2005). Osama bin Laden, the founder of al-Qaeda, fits into many of these categories. He had credibility in the eyes of many followers, having fought against the Russians, been injured in combat and actively challenged the West. He held strong religious beliefs and was generally regarded to be very pious. The message he presented was consistent with a clear differentiation between the 'evil' West and the 'good' suffering Muslim community. Bin Laden eschewed the trappings of his wealthy family, using his money to support jihad against the West, living a simple, almost ascetic life, which served to illustrate his similarity to many of his followers.

As well as strong directive leadership, group consensus and the internalization of group norms are maximized where the prior beliefs of members are consistent with the group's beliefs; where members perceive the leader and other members to be similar to themselves; where group members are close to each other in time and space and meet regularly; where members perceive themselves to be different from non-group members; and where group membership is important to the individual members. Group consensus is further increased if the group perceives that it is under threat from outsiders and if it is separated or separates itself from other non-group members, for example, if the group members have no contact with former friends and/or family. Interestingly, group leaders often stress the group's difference from others and may expect individuals to reject their old lifestyle when joining the group. Football managers often utilize some of this to maximize coherence. For example, Sir Alex Ferguson and Jose Mourino insisted that their teams were 'hated' by others and treated unfairly; this served to distinguish their group from others and to increase the perceived threat within the group, which led to increased coherence.

Where there is high group coherence individual members begin to internalize the group's ethos and to act for the good of the group rather than for themselves. Under these conditions, groupthink (e.g., Janis, 1972) can arise. Groupthink is characterized by members sharing a feeling of invulnerability which leads to excessive optimism and encourages risk taking whereby members begin to discount warnings that challenge their assumptions and behaviours; members sharing an unquestioning belief in the group's morality, causing them to ignore the consequences of their actions; members begin to develop stereotyped views of outsiders and strong, often overt, pressure is applied on group members who disagree. When groupthink arises, any ideas that deviate from the apparent group consensus will be shut down; indeed, certain members will often appoint themselves as mind-guards who see their task as shielding the group from dissenting opinions. One of the outcomes of the development of groupthink is that groups can and do make irrational decisions and behave in ways that are not linked to external reality but to the group's particular idiosyncratic world-view.

Should groupthink occur within a terror group, it is perhaps more understandable why they may carry out what appear to be irrational and ultimately self-defeating acts. Groupthink impels individuals to act precisely because it serves the group, is consistent with the group's own morality and is not subject to reality testing against external criteria. By way of an example, consider the London 7/7 bombers. Many of the characteristics of this group of four individuals are consistent with the conditions for powerful group influences and for the emergence of groupthink. The group had similar religious beliefs and were all individuals who were members of minorities within the United Kingdom. The group became increasingly important in the life of each member and developed into a closed secretive group that began to distance itself from others. The leader of the group, Mohammed Sidique Khan, appears to have had many of the characteristics of the most influential leaders. He had trained in Pakistan, was intelligent and older than the other group members and perhaps had greater credibility as a jihadi. His suicide video demonstrates a clear conviction of the justification for his behaviour and an ability to communicate the message clearly and succinctly. The development of suicide bombing as the weapon of choice may have been partly motivated by the emergence of groupthink.

Implications for police investigators

For police investigators, being able to identify when groupthink is present is important when trying to assess a terror group for risk. Essentially, if the characteristics of groupthink are present, a group is at higher risk of acting.

Where groupthink has been established, individuals may well initially espouse the group ideology and philosophy and may use this to justify their actions to themselves and others. This might be useful for investigative interviewers in that allowing an individual to espouse their philosophy unchallenged may serve to develop rapport and may lead the interviewee to disclosures concerning other group members who are valuable to them.

Identity and Terrorism

Having considered the impact of group membership on individuals, we will now consider the psychology of the individual group members in more detail. Essentially this section will explore the concept of identity.

Identity

All individuals attempt to make sense of their world and of their place within it. The collected experiences and knowledge they have and the emotional values attached to them are contained within an individual's identity. Identity is made up of both thoughts and feelings about whom or what an individual thinks they are.

Identity is related to group membership and is essentially how individuals 'see' themselves. Identities suggest particular ways of being, of attitudes and behaviours in different situations impacting on modes of dress, lifestyle, social activities, beliefs, values, attitudes and goals. Individuals typically have many identities, for example, Muslim/Christian, father, husband, police officer/member of terrorist group/freedom fighter and so on, although some individuals may have only a small number of identities. The labels individuals attach to their identities are varied. For example, an outsider may refer to an individual as a 'terrorist', while that individual's identity might stress their role as a 'freedom fighter' or 'defender of the oppressed' (Stryker & Burke, 2000).

Competing identities

Of all the identities an individual has, some are compatible with each other while others are not. Where one has competing identities, this can cause problems. How does one manage if the requirements of one identity are completely at odds with those of another? Examples of this include one's identity as a father or a football supporter competing with the demands of one's work identity as police officer, lawyer, judge and so on.

Faced with competing identities, individuals have to identify strategies to cope. Some identities may be rejected in favour of other more compatible identities, for example, an individual may give up an identity as a 'political rebel' at university in favour of the demands of a job in the city. Sometimes identities are kept separate and never compete with each other, resulting in a secret identity – some members of terrorist groups are good at keeping their involvement in terrorist activities separate from other things they do. Often family members have no idea of an individual's involvement in terrorism.

The identities that are selected and rejected depend on the rewards associated with each. Islamist extremists often refer to the great rewards in Paradise as a result of following the Prophet's example, even when this causes personal hardship in life. The 'hard' identity is worth it as the eternal rewards are so great. Stern (2003) describes an Islamist extremist who justified his desire for martyrdom by likening his time on earth to a drop in the ocean relative to the eternity in Paradise were he to die a martyr.

Some individuals may become increasingly extreme and focused as they take on one extremist identity while rejecting others. Others may become less extreme as they find extremist views incompatible with the other important identities they have, and they may go on to reject terrorism/extremism (Horgan, 2005).

Different identities may require an individual to act in different ways in the same situation. For example, an individual may have extremist views and an identity as, say, a school teacher is incompatible with these views. This is a problem and requires active management on the part of the individual. It may be necessary to keep one's extreme views hidden. However, if the extremist views are very important, that is, highly salient, then they may 'leak out' and other individuals may be shocked to see the behaviours related to them. Sageman (2004) describes a group of males living in Canada who had developed into an extremist group. These men were invited to a wedding where they shocked the other guests by shouting extremist slogans. These individuals had allowed one identity to appear in the context of another, incompatible situation. This perhaps illustrates the importance of the 'extremist' identity to these men over other competing identities of brother, cousin, son and so on.

Implications of identity theory for terrorism investigators

In the use of identity theory, the first important practical question is: How does one assess levels of identity and strength of identity? There is likely to be an association between the number, strength and characteristics of different identities and an individual's behaviour. Hence, for investigators, the examination of intelligence records of an individual's involvement in different groups, the time and energy devoted to them, the degree of contact with others outside the groups and the level of influence an individual has in the group will give them a sense of the individual's different identities and of their relative importance. Those with the highest involvement in a terror group and the least contact with others are those who have fewer competing identities. They are likely to be most committed to the cause as they have effectively fewer other commitments or demands on them and fewer sources of challenge to the ideas embodied by the group. Individuals with other, competing identities that are important to them, for example, father, son and husband in addition to the terrorist identity, may find it more difficult to cope with the competing demands and challenges. This makes it harder for them to become embedded in the group and to begin to subscribe to its ethos. Such individuals will be more likely to see the errors and inconsistencies in the group's arguments and may feel some guilt and remorse for group actions. As a result of guilt and uncertainty, these individuals may well be more likely to wish to speak to investigators and may be potential intelligence sources. These individuals may also respond to interview strategies that, in part, identify other competing identities that are inconsistent with the terrorist identity.

Identifying the number and types of identity held by individuals may also be useful in the assessment of risk of violence posed by particular individuals. Those with fewer personally important competing identities are most likely to become more radical and to act out violently, as there are fewer psychological constraints on them related to other identities.

Identities contain behavioural scripts, that is, ways of behaving across a range of situations. In any situation, if an individual is made consciously aware of a particular identity they hold, that is, the identity is made salient, they are likely to behave in ways consistent with that identity (Stryker & Burke, 2000). For some individuals, particular identities are salient irrespective of the situation as that identity is of great importance to them; they define themselves in terms of the identity. Those most committed to a cause often fit into this category. Those with various competing identities will exhibit identities that the situation makes salient. The implication of this is that, if investigators are aware of an individual's different identities and some of the behavioural scripts associated with them, they can tailor their behaviour to make certain, more cooperative identities salient at the expense of other, more challenging identities. This might maximize compliance on the part of the interviewee and minimize the risk of confrontation.

As an example, if an individual perceives they are fighting a war, any investigator behaviour that signals to the suspect that they are a 'fighter' – perhaps a militaristic response from the police, torture or an interrogative threat-laden interview approach – will likely lead to responses that are governed by the 'fighter' identity, such as non-compliance, a counter-interrogation approach, and 'no comment' interviews. If the individual has another, competing identity, such as father, and he is close to his children, an approach that seeks to enhance signals of his parenthood – rapport-based, support and nurturing interview approaches – is more likely to make this identity salient and to produce more cooperative behaviour from the interviewee. This approach may also make salient any doubts or uncertainties the individual has about the terror group, which may help the flow of information. The use of special security measures with terrorist suspects while they are in custody – close guarding and invasive supervision – needs to be carefully considered. Such measures are used because of the 'high risk' classification of some suspects but are also likely to provide strong signals consistent with a terrorist or soldier identity.

It is important to note that an identity can be made salient by small as well as large behaviours. An ill-judged comment or gesture, the wording of questions and/or lack of respect for an individual's beliefs can be very influential in making an identity salient. The implication for investigators and interviewers is that, when individuals are arrested and in custody, care should be taken to manage the behaviour of those who come into contact with them to minimize the risks of such behaviour.

Theoretical debates in which interviewers try to challenge or change an interviewee's beliefs are likely to be unsuccessful. Explicitly threatening an identity in this way serves to make that identity salient. If the identity is important to the interviewee, this will further entrench the individual in the identity (Breakwell, 1983). If an identity is important, it is also likely that the individual will have spent time thinking about the ideas and behaviours associated with it and may have identified ways of defending it from attack. Finally, there is the issue of the credibility of the interviewer. A challenge to beliefs is more influential when it comes from a credible source. A police interviewer is unlikely to be seen as a credible source unless they are perceived by the individual to have expertise relevant to the identity.

Interviewer selection is important, as sensitivity to the contents of particular identities may lead to selecting interviewers with particular characteristics. For example, an individual will have a greater social influence on another if there is some perceived similarity between them. Investigators should therefore pay attention to the gender, age, race, appearance and attitudes of the interviewer to select those who may have greater influence.

Concluding Remarks

Groups are highly influential on individuals and are often instrumental in providing justifications that may form part of the motivation to act. Knowledge of these issues is important for investigators. Identification of the stage at which a group is functioning may contribute to risk assessment and may help to find ways of disrupting groups. Consideration of the group dynamics and behaviour of group members may in turn help investigators to identify different types of individual within a group who are likely to present different challenges when subject to investigation. Knowledge of different identities and of their relative importance to individuals may suggest different investigative approaches, for example in the targeting of intelligence sources and the design of interview strategies. This chapter has argued that the use of social psychological theory in counter-terrorism investigations provides a framework for organizing and analysing intelligence material that may have benefits for the investigation.

References

Arena, M. P., & Arrigo, B. (2006). *The terrorist identity: Explaining the terrorist threat*. New York: NYU Press.

Asch, S. E. (1955). Opinions and social pressure. *Scientific American, 193*, 31–35.

Borum, R. (2004). *Psychology of terrorism*. Tampa: University of South Florida.

Breakwell, G. (1983) *Threatened identities*. Chichester, UK: Wiley.

Burleigh, M. (2008). *Blood and rage: A cultural history of terrorism*. London: HarperCollins.

Cialdini, R. B. (2001). *Influence: Science and practice* (4th ed.). Boston: Allyn & Bacon.

Horgan, J. (2005). *The psychology of terrorism*. London: Routledge.

Janis, I. L. (1972). *Victims of groupthink: A psychological study of foreign-policy decisions and fiascoes*. Boston: Houghton Mifflin.

Messick, D. M., & Kramer, R. M. (2005). *The psychology of leadership: New perspectives and research*. Mahwah, NJ: Erlbaum.

Sageman, M. (2004) *Understanding terror networks*. Philadelphia: University of Pennsylvania Press.

Silke, A. (Ed.) (2003). *Terrorists, victims and society: Psychological perspectives on terrorism and its consequences*. Chichester, UK: Wiley.

Stern, J. (2003). *Terror in the name of God: Why religious militants kill*. New York: Ecco.

Stryker, S., & Burke, P. J. (2000). The past, present and future of identity theory. *Social Psychology Quarterly, 63*, 284–297.

Tuckman, B. W. (1965). Developmental sequence in small groups. *Psychological Bulletin, 63*, 384–399.

Tuckman, B. W., & Jensen, M. A. C. (1977). Stages of small group development revisited. *Group and Organizational Studies, 2*, 419–427.

12

Community Surveillance and Terrorism

Clive Walker and Simon McKay

In October 2007, West Midlands Police embarked on Project Champion (Thornton, 2010, p. 7, hereafter cited as *Project Champion Review*), a flawed and inaptly named operation to implement community surveillance in two areas of Birmingham where terrorist suspects were believed to reside. The police's venture was halted by a storm of local protests before it could be fully realized. But its conception, implementation, implications and demise will supply a core case-study for this chapter, especially since the subsequent full official inquiry offers transparency and important insights. By comparison, most surveillance operations remain deliberately concealed on grounds of national security or public safety, without even the assurance of independent monitoring or post-operative notification. Only occasional glimpses emerge, usually engulfed by great controversy, such as the secret Zircon spy satellite programme revealed by Duncan Campbell (Bradley, 1987a, 1987b), now eclipsed by the revelations of Bradley (Chelsea) Manning and Edward Snowden whose exposure of the global surveillance by intelligence agencies has received worldwide media attention.

Despite its notoriety, Project Champion is not a unique episode in counter-terrorism community surveillance. Therefore, in order to present a fuller picture of the counter-terrorism investigative technique of community surveillance, this chapter will initially provide an overview of other relevant community or mass surveillance tactics. This analysis will be contextualized within the analytical framework of 'all risks' policing, by which the risk of terrorism is perceived as so serious and so pervasive that police will treat anyone and everyone as a risk, whether or not any degree of specific suspicion exists. The chapter will also evaluate some of the dilemmas and consequences which flow from community surveillance in general and which prominently and damagingly arose in the particular scenario of Project Champion.

Investigating Terrorism: Current Political, Legal and Psychological Issues, First Edition. Edited by John Pearse.
© 2015 John Wiley & Sons, Ltd. Published 2015 by John Wiley & Sons, Ltd.

Overview and Context of Community Surveillance within Counter-Terrorism Strategy

Before Project Champion is considered, this part of the chapter will explain community and mass surveillance within counter-terrorism in a broader setting by providing an overview of the various formats which it might adopt and by providing a policy context.

Policy context

The current policy setting for community and mass surveillance is the UK government's counter-terrorism strategy (Home Office, 2006/2011, hereafter cited as CONTEST) workstream of Pursue, which aims to stop terrorist attacks. The more evident and publicized aspects of Pursue typically involve police arrests and criminal justice prosecutions (Walker, 2011a, chs. 4, 5), but the constant theme behind its manifold modalities is the importance of intelligence gathering (Gill, 2009; Walker, 2006). As a result, Pursue can also adopt the format of pre-emptive actions. The results of disruption, community assurance and further intelligence gathering are often opaque, though there may occasionally be individualized formal impacts in the guise of executive measures like control orders or deportations. Though prosecution is expressed to be the more legitimate and effective option (Walker, 2011a, ch. 6), and though lawyers' commentaries tend to be heavily skewed in that direction, non-criminal justice outcomes are in reality far more commonplace in counter-terrorism activity. They circumvent the negative lack of 'forensic certainty' for criminal justice purposes (Harfield & Harfield, 2008, p. 1), and they embody positively enhanced capacity for proactive and pre-emptive responses to the anticipatory risk of mass terrorism casualties or even the nightmare threat of weapons of mass destruction.

Next, the desire to negate apparently endemic and endless terrorist risk through pre-emptive interventions, rather than criminal justice processes, can be more fully explicated through the further concept of all-risks policing (Walker, 2009). This concept involves recognition of the 'new and urgent' (Garland, 2001, p. 12) imperative that terrorism risk must be intercepted at an early stage, as already indicated, and adds the acknowledgement that the source of the risk can emanate from anyone, whether 'neighbour terrorists' (Walker, 2008a) living in the backstreets of Leeds or external actors in Afghanistan, Pakistan or Yemen. In response, the security authorities must adopt a wide all-risks sweep to meet the anticipatory and pervasive threat. As a result, counter-terrorism laws have granted extraordinarily wide powers of surveillance, which are bolstered by other holistic responses to embedded terrorism risk such as contingency planning and resilience (Walker & Broderick, 2006). Hence, the operation of all-risks approaches results in anyone and everyone being treated as a risk. The reason for attention is not so much any defined suspicion applying to a given individual but the nature of a specified site, vulnerability or population set. A risk calculation is still present, but it shifts from the individual to the collective or to the potential target.

Overview of community and mass surveillance formats

The wide powers of surveillance within all-risks counter-terrorism can take many forms. Not all have arisen after 9/11; 'screening' was operated in Northern Ireland in the 1970s onwards (Hogan & Walker, 1989, p. 53). Nor do they all owe their existence to recent legislative grants, since many surveillance modes continue as informal tactics.

One of the most prominent formal legal power to facilitate surveillance has been stop and search exercises conducted under, until recently, section 44 of the Terrorism Act 2000 (Walker, 2011a, ch. 2). The widespread application of these powers, which required no reasonable suspicion on the part of any authorizing or operational police officer or confirmation of the authorization by the Home Secretary, occurred not only within defined localities, sometimes with concentrations of Muslim residents, but more often in locations such as central London and railway stations. Section 44 became highly controversial because of perceptions of disproportionate, discriminatory and ineffective imposition. The impetus for reform was heightened by an adverse decision (described later in this chapter) of the European Court of Human Rights in *Gillan and Quinton v. United Kingdom* (2010). The government responded by the Terrorism Act 2000 (Remedial) Order 2011, issued under the Human Rights Act 1998 (2011). Then, bolstered by the conclusions of Lord Macdonald's *Review of Counter-Terrorism and Security Powers* (2011), the Protection of Freedoms Act 2012, part IV, has replaced section 44 with section 47A of the Terrorism Act. Significant changes include: stricter tests for police authorizations and for the purposes of exercise; the maximum period of authorization is reduced to 14 from 28 days, with stricter oversight of both the time limit and geographical boundaries; and more detailed statutory guidance on the usage must be issued. These changes have seemingly alleviated one of the most troublesome chafe points in community counter-terrorism surveillance. During 2010–2011, stops were reduced by 91 per cent (to 9,652 in total) from the previous year's level (Home Office, 2011a, para. 2.1).

Aside from community-directed surveillance powers, many other counter-terrorism legal powers or tactics have sanctioned mass surveillance, in line with a truly all-risks perspective. The effect of 9/11 counter-terrorism has been 'to speed up and spread out' (Lyon, 2003, p. 1) surveillance techniques whereby 'successive UK governments have gradually constructed one of the most extensive and technologically advanced surveillance systems in the world' (House of Lords Select Committee on the Constitution, 2009, para. 1). Prime examples in this category include the legal powers of port controls under Schedule 7 of the Terrorism Act 2000 (entailing many of the same controversies as stop and search). There is also potential dataveillance through the compulsory retention of data traffic under European Directive 2006/24/EC (Maras, 2009), as implemented by the Data Retention (EC Directive) Regulations 2009 (Macdonald, 2011, p. 21), which after condemnation were replaced by the Data Retention and Investigatory Powers Act 2014. Other less formal, but equally invasive, powers include the collection and transmission of airline passenger name records (Council of the European Union, 2010; European Commission, 2011; House of Lords Select Committee on the European Union, 2010), the transfer of banking data by the Society for Worldwide Interbank Financial Telecommunication (known as SWIFT) under the agreement between the European Union and the United States of America on the processing and transfer of financial messaging data from the EU to the USA for the purposes of the Terrorist Finance Tracking Program, 2010 (European Commission, 2010), as well as international communications intercept networks such as ECHELON operated under the British–US Communication Intelligence Agreement 1946.

Of particular relevance to this paper, surveillance involving closed-circuit television (CCTV) has been promoted in the UK more than anywhere else in the world, with up to 4.2 million operative devices (JUSTICE, 2011, para. 4). CCTV has become especially rampant because it is sponsored not just through governmental agencies but also by becoming embedded in the architecture of private social space (Goold, 2003; Norris & Armstrong, 1999; Norris, Moran, & Armstrong, 1999). A crucial first step in the development of this approach occurred in the City of London, where CCTV was installed on a coordinated and pervasive scale to create a 'ring of steel' following bombings by the Irish Republican Army (IRA) in 1992 and 1993 (Coaffee, 2004, p. 276; Walker, 2004). In that site, technological developments also occurred, such as automatic number plate recognition (ANPR) and passenger recognition, applications which now envelop many major highways and conurbations. There is central collection through the National ANPR Data Centre, with 18 million reads per day and over 11 billion vehicle sightings stored (Association of Chief Police Officers, 2013). Even that level of sophistication might soon be surpassed by the introduction of police drones (Bowcott & Lewis, 2010; Minton, 2009, pp. 31, 139). These applications of CCTV have perhaps grown so prevalent because, as applied to transient populations like commuters, there is no identifiable settled community which feels intimately or collectively maltreated, and so the general population faces the danger of a 'sleepwalk into a surveillance society' (Surveillance Studies Network, 2006). However, these circumstances of indulgence did not apply to Project Champion.

Project Champion

Project Champion was conceived in late 2007 by the West Midlands Police primarily to bolster the work of the West Midlands Counter Terrorist Unit. The context for the operation was a perceived increase in terrorist activity in the Birmingham districts of Alum Rock and Sparkhill, including a failed attempt to kidnap and behead a Muslim soldier (*R v. Parviz Khan* [2009]; *R v. Nadim, Ali, and Mohammed* (2009)). The sole funding of over £3 million was applied for, via the Association of Chief Police Officers

(Terrorism and Allied Matters) executive (ACPO (TAM)), from the Home Office and approved in 2008. The equipment began to be installed in early 2010. The plan was to set up multiple overt ANPR cameras covering 106 traffic lanes, 47 covert ANPR cameras, plus 38 CCTV overt cameras and two covert CCTV cameras with a wide street view (*Project Champion Review*, p. 36).

A crucial question was how far the local communities were informed and assented. In April 2009 the police convened a Project Champion Briefing Session for local councillors and Safer Birmingham Partnership staff, where the crime reduction and community safety benefits of the scheme were explained. But members of the public and their local representatives began voicing objections in April 2010, claiming that they had been misled over the true purpose and extent of Project Champion. Work was halted in July 2010, when a review by Sara Thornton, Chief Constable of Thames Valley, was established.

The *Project Champion Review* affirmed that there were two purposes behind the initiative. There was a crime reduction purpose, but in truth 'What was missing was a plan to deliver on this intention' (*Project Champion Review*, p. 30). Therefore, Project Champion was really driven as a counter-terrorist operation, and any public consultation to make this clear was 'too little too late' (p. 32). The overall conclusion was that 'This thinking should have been challenged by strong ethical and strategic leadership right from the start and questions should have been asked about its proportionality, legitimacy, authority, necessity, and the ethical values inherent in the proposed course of action' (p. 35).

The *Project Champion Review* offered nine recommendations to the broad effect that greater account should be taken of human rights and equality values, that the police and police authority should strengthen oversight, and that police engagement with partners, community and elected representatives should form a key element rather than an adjunct (*Project Champion Review*, pp. 35–37). These points were accepted by the police authority, but the actual outcome was that all the cameras were rendered non-operational by September 2010 (p. 48) and were removed in May 2011 (Chief Surveillance Commissioner, 2011, para. 2.4).

Dilemmas and Consequences

Focusing on Project Champion as a case-study, several lines of critical inquiry about the value and ethics of community surveillance within counter-terrorism should be explored: effectiveness; the impact on community relations; legality and legitimacy; and accountability.

Effectiveness

Operational choices over surveillance methods entail different outcomes, both good and bad. For instance, surveillance can be covert or overt. Covert surveillance may secure the operational goals of pinpointing suspects whose activities are not yet to be interdicted so that a wider understanding of their projects and their confederates can be discerned. But covert surveillance can engender the disadvantage of community distrust rather than assurance, as in Birmingham. Similar arguments apply to the choice over the geographical focus of surveillance. On the one hand, all-risks policing demands a wide sweep but, on the other hand, such a wide sweep may prove beyond the practical capabilities and resources of policing and security authorities, a problem which was encountered in the investigation of the 7/7 bombings (Hallett, 2011; Intelligence and Security Committee, 2009).

Another important consideration relevant to effectiveness is that surveillance can be technologically based or collected through human agency. Project Champion suggests that technology is now prominent, and the operational rationale for its elevation appears to have been to avoid the risk of compromise (*Project Champion Review*, p. 8). The human infiltration of very localized and distinct communities was also found to be challenging in Northern Ireland. Even when 'supergrasses' and agents were recruited, the results were frequently problematic in terms of the quality of evidence or the ethical behaviour of agents and handlers (Bamford, 2005; Greer, 1995; Hyland & Walker, 2014; Moran, 2010). Yet, an overreliance on the allure of technology was criticized by the 9/11 Commission's *Report* as reducing the quality of intelligence (National Commission on Terrorism Attacks, 2004, pp. 77, 104, 415). Of course, 'Recruiting well-placed sources … remains difficult' for intelligence agencies in the context of the penetration of small friendship- and ethnicity-based informal terrorist groups (National Security Preparedness Group, 2011, p. 11). But there are reports that US police bodies, unencumbered by the legal injunction against domestic spying on the CIA (Executive Order 12333, 1981, para. 2.4(a)), have invested much greater attention in human intelligence (Appuzo & Goldman, 2011). Thus, it was reported in 2011 that the New York Police Department's Zone Assessment Unit has aggressively sought to gather intelligence from resident Muslim communities by the use of undercover officers to engage in social mapping and informants in cafes, bookstores and mosques. A similar mapping scheme in Los Angeles was shelved in 2007 after public criticism and the verdict of Mayor Villaraigosa that, "While I believe the department's efforts to reach out to the Muslim communities were well intentioned, the mapping proposal has created a level of fear and apprehension that made it counterproductive" (MacFarquhar, 2007, p. 31).

If Project Champion had been implemented, it would have generated a vast amount of data, but would the datasets have been effective in counter-terrorism? The disadvantages would be that the mass of data might serve to veil the few significant indicators of threat, as already noted in relation to the 7/7 inquiries. The pictures of the 7/7 bombers as they boarded a train at Luton for their journey to attack London commuters ('Timeline', 2006) is a poignant historical record not only of their wrongdoing but also of the ineffectiveness of technology to be any more than a dumb witness which is powerless to interdict their attack. In addition, the installation and operation of surveillance apparatus can serve as a constant reminder of the threat from terrorism, thereby amplifying rather than allaying community insecurities. Yet, CCTV footage may prove crucial. Even in the days of the Provisional IRA, Jan Taylor and Patrick Hayes were convicted of causing an explosion outside Harrods in January 1993, and they were detected through CCTV footage as they planted the bomb (*R v. Taylor, R v. Hayes*, 1995). More recently, pictures of the 21/7 London bombers undoubtedly assisted in their arrest ('Police hold four 21 July suspects', 2005).

In conclusion, effectiveness cannot be judged precisely without fuller disclosure of the state's innermost secrets regarding delivery and impact (Evans, 2008). As a generalization, human sources appear to be particularly effective against hierarchical and disciplined organizations, and infiltration in Northern Ireland probably achieved significant disruptive and destabilizing impacts (Moran, 2010, p. 17). The more heterarchical disposition of al-Qaeda offers less promising ground, and the police complained in 2007 of the lack of 'community intelligence' (Clarke, 2007). By contrast, scepticism has been most loudly voiced about blanket applications of data-mining (Brown & Korff, 2009; Committee on Technical and Privacy Dimensions of Information, 2008). There are also potential inefficiencies when ultimate decision-making about the application of surveillance is vested in inexperienced government ministers. At the level of individual or community surveillance, the judiciary can better ensure an independent, thorough and fair weighing of data and the full range of interests affected before security operations commence (Walker, 2010, 2011b). At the level of policy decisions, such as war and peace, democracy demands that politicians must retain the ultimate decision. Yet their involvement can come at the cost of the manipulation of intelligence for policy ends, as illustrated by the foundations for the invasion of Iraq in 2003 (Committee of Privy Counsellors, 2004; United States Senate Select Committee on Intelligence, 2004, 2008).

Community relations

Community relations can be treated as a bridging issue, with implications both for effectiveness (discussed in the previous section) and as affecting through claims of discrimination issues of legality (considered in the next section).

In the all-risks approach, policing is rarely applied evenly. While mathematical models of profiling might be used, they embody preconceptions. In addition, the applications of surveillance or stop and search powers can be perceived to be skewed (Choudhury & Fenwick, 2011; DSTL, 2010; House of Commons Home Affairs Committee, 2005, para. 153; Mythen, Walklate & Khan, 2009, p. 744), for example, through the influence of occupational cultures which in the case of the police are alleged to include racial bias (Gill, 2000, pp. 130, 249). These factors result in 'targeted governance' aimed towards 'risky' groups (Amoore & de Goede, 2005).

Because of these same factors, Project Champion is alleged to have been deeply resented by the affected local communities and to have damaged relations with the police, 'with many suggesting that the only solution is the removal of all the cameras' (*Project Champion Review*, p. 46; see also Awan, 2011). Evidence of community hostility included newspaper headlines recording public outrage and protest rallies (Authi, 2010a, 2010b). There were complaints from councillors that they had been misled, and even complaints to the IPCC by two Sparkbrook Respect Party councillors, Mohammed Ishtiaq and Salma Yaqoob ('City councillors', 2010, p. 5). Local MP, Roger Godsiff, tabled an Early Day Motion in the House of Commons, though it attracted just four other signatures (House of Commons, 2010). More mobilization of local opinion was garnered by web and media activities, especially those associated with the campaign group Birmingham against Spy Cameras (Jolly, 2010). The whole episode was later represented in a film, *Defeat of the Champion*, in 2011, which was controversially funded by the Iranian government-sponsored Press TV ('Iranian TV firm', 2011, p. 29).

Any trace of discrimination through racial profiling would be an evil in itself, but the adverse impact was made worse in this case by the impact on counter-terrorism effectiveness. The contemporary implementation of Pursue relies much more on community engagement than in previous campaigns to provide early warnings and intelligence, and it impacts even more within the innovative Prevent workstream (Home Office, 2011b). The concept of engagement between community and police is problematic even in non-political crime (Crawford, 1997), but when the community whose support is desired has the perception that it is an object of distrust, the police will face an uphill task (Briggs, 2010).

These failures in Project Champion have all had the further effect in the minds of some of giving some credence to the 'suspect community' thesis, whereby:

> a sub-group of the population … is singled out for state attention as being 'problematic'. Specifically in terms of policing, individuals may be targeted, not necessarily as a result of suspected wrong doing, but simply because of their presumed membership to that sub-group. Race, ethnicity, religion, class, gender, language, accent, dress, political ideology or any combination of these factors may serve to delineate the sub-group. (Pantazis & Pemberton, 2009, p. 649)

In its most coherent version, the thesis might sustain that the perception of an official 'suspect community' policy could conceivably arise 'through a host of readily available emotional, material and ideological resources' (Pantazis & Pemberton, 2011, pp. 1056–1057). However, hard evidence for any official policy or sanctioned practice in that direction is generally lacking (Greer, 2010). Aside from the difficulties in conceiving British Muslims as a single cohesive 'community' given their diversity in ethnicity, cultures, social and economic standing, and even religious beliefs, several factors underline that Project Champion does not reveal official action infected by Islamophobia against such Muslims as were resident in the affected districts of Birmingham. For instance, counterpart surveillance schemes have apparently not been replicated in all locations with high concentrations of Muslims. It has also been emphasized that all-risks measures more often depict the location (together with the population within or passing through it), rather than a population group, as 'suspect' (that is, suspected of being the object of an attack). Next, the project's motivation was rationally justified in view of detected terrorism in the area. Furthermore, given that surveillance was to be applied on a blanket basis in public places and not, for example, by secret cameras confined to Muslim meeting places, any impact on Muslims would be substantially diluted. Even so, a heightened impact on Muslims would still not have amounted to discrimination within the 'suspect community' thesis, provided the threat is being defined and addressed on objective and reasonable terms beyond race, ethnicity or religion. This point was sustained before the European Court of Human Rights in regard to the uneven impact on Northern Ireland Catholics of security laws and operations in the 1970s (*Ireland v. United Kingdom*, 1978, paras. 225–232).

Legality and legitimacy

The *Project Champion Review* identified the important flaw that 'there was very little evidence of consideration being given to compliance with the legal or regulatory framework' (*Project Champion Review*, p. 38). The Regulation of Investigatory Powers Act 2000 was recognized as relevant but without any sustained conclusions as to what it might have required (*Project Champion Review*, p. 37).

The legality of intelligence gathering through surveillance has primarily revolved around respect for human rights (Omand, 2010, p. 283). Privacy interests, recognized in Article 8 of the European Convention and enforced through the Human Rights Act 1998, are most engaged, though rights of expression and association are also pertinent. According to the Strasbourg-based European Court of Human Rights in *Klass v. Germany* (1987), the objective of defeating terrorism will count as a justified limit on privacy:

> Democratic societies nowadays find themselves threatened by highly sophisticated forms of espionage and by terrorism, with the result that the State must be able, in order effectively to counter such threats, to undertake the secret surveillance of subversive elements operating within its jurisdiction. (1987, para. 48; see further Council of Europe, 2005, p. 20; Council of Europe Committee of Ministers, 2005, Articles 2–5; Walker, 2008b, p. 73)

But that case equally reiterates the need for adequate and effective guarantees against abuses within covert action (*Klass v. Germany*, 1987, paras. 49–50). Governance and accountability will be considered in the next section.

The acquisition of photographic images derived from CCTV or other cameras located in public places does not, per se, necessarily amount to an interference with privacy either in the jurisprudence of the Strasbourg court, as in cases such as *Friedl v. Austria* (1995), or of the English domestic courts, as in *Wood v. Commissioner of Police for the Metropolis* (2009), a case discussed later. Provided the English courts recognize that there has been an interference with privacy, then there is usually no appreciable difference between the two jurisdictions. However, deep fissures have emerged over when Article 8 is engaged, as illustrated by several judgments.

Some of these judgments can be disposed of quickly since they do not relate to community surveillance, but they set the wider scene. Perhaps the most important has been *Campbell v. MGN Limited* (2004), involving the publication of details, including photographs taken covertly, of supermodel Naomi Campbell's attendance at Narcotics Anonymous. The House of Lords proved willing to extend the legal action for breach of confidence so as to protect a wider concept of privacy. For example, Lord Hope considered the 'touchstone of private life' to be whether the 'person in question had a reasonable expectation of privacy' (*Campbell v. MGN Limited*, 2004, para. 21). The tests to be considered are whether it is likely to be subjectively offensive to publish the information and whether the disclosure would appear objectionable if one were 'to put oneself into the shoes of a reasonable person who is in need of that treatment' (para. 98). It remains true that 'the taking of photographs in a public street must be taken to be one of the ordinary incidents of living in a free community' (*Hosking v. Runting*, 2003, para. 138), but, after *Campbell*, privacy interests exert important qualifications. Though a tort of privacy has not been directly recognized, protection against the mistreatment of private information has been further confirmed and refined (*McKennitt v. Ash*, 2006; *Murray v. Big Pictures (UK) Limited*, 2008; *Wainwright v. Home Office*, 2003).

This burgeoning protection of privacy rights has since been applied in the context of police surveillance, including within counter-terrorism. In *Gillan and Quinton v. United Kingdom* (2010), the European Court of Human Rights disagreed with the prior decision of the House of Lords (in *R (Gillan) v. Commissioner of Police for the Metropolis*, 2006) and found that searches of bags appurtenant to a stop and search under section 44 of the Terrorism Act 2000 amounted to a breach of privacy, especially because of the absence of effective legal restraints on the grant or application of that power. Next, in *S and Marper v. United Kingdom* (2008), on application from *R (S and Marper) v. Chief Constable of South Yorkshire Police* (2004), the Grand Chamber of 17 judges of the European Court of Human Rights, the judicial setting reserved on an exceptional basis for the most serious questions affecting the interpretation of the Convention, unanimously decided that the acquisition and almost indefinite retention of DNA profiles from both guilty and innocent subjects for police investigative purposes amounted to an interference with privacy, contrary to the majority opinion of the House of Lords.

The leading Strasbourg case to consider the human rights implications of CCTV in English law is *Peck v. United Kingdom* (2003, on application from the English case of *R v. Brentwood Borough Council, ex p Peck*, 1998). The applicant had been filmed by CCTV operators employed by Brentwood Borough Council as he walked down Brentwood High Street, armed with a knife with which he intended to commit suicide. The police were contacted, and they detained him under the Mental Health Act 1983. He was subsequently released without charge. The council published two still photographs of Peck in a press bulletin concerned with advancing the positive aspects of CCTV for community safety. These photographs were then reproduced by various local newspapers, local television and then national broadcasters. There had been some inadequate attempts to mask Peck's identity during the later broadcasts, but neighbours, friends and family told him they had seen him on television. The Strasbourg Court held that the mere monitoring of individuals in public places by CCTV did not in itself give rise to an interference with private life, but the systematic recording or creation of a permanent record of the data did so, and so a breach of Article 8 arose in this case. Although Peck was in a public street, there could be no justification for the considerable subsequent exposure of his behaviour under Article 8(2). It was accepted that the disclosure had a proper legal basis and was therefore in accordance with the law. However, any justification failed on proportionality grounds. He was not participating in a public event (unlike the applicant in *Friedl v. Austria*, 1995), nor was he a suspected criminal (as in *Murray v. United Kingdom*, 1994), a missing person or a public figure some of whose activities could be the subject of legitimate oversight (*Von Hannover v. Germany*, 2004). Discussion of the value of CCTV could be in the public interest but should have been achieved without revealing Peck's identity. Though a victory for privacy, and a reprimand for English legal laxity, the judgment represents a limited restraint for CCTV in that it engaged largely with the disclosure of surveillance data and not the initial surveillance per se.

The weight accorded to privacy was developed further by the Court of Appeal in *Wood v. Commissioner of Police for the Metropolis* (2009). Wood, a member of the Campaign against Arms Trade, was photographed leaving the annual general meeting of a company concerned in the organization of trade fairs for the arms industry. He had acquired shares in the company for the sole purpose of becoming eligible to attend the meeting. Associates of the claimant were also in attendance on the same basis, and some had previously caused incidents of a criminal nature at exhibitions and property owned by the company. The claimant himself had no previous convictions and had never been arrested for an offence. The Court of Appeal distilled the first issue in the case down to a relatively straightforward proposition: that the mere taking of an individual's photograph in a public street itself breaches no rights, 'unless something more is added' (para. 35). This 'something more' was later described as 'aggravating circumstances'. These included harassment, hounding and possibly assault (para. 36).

The second issue, the 'real issue', was 'whether the taking of the pictures, along with their actual and/or apprehended use, might amount to a violation' (*Wood v. Commissioner of Police for the Metropolis*, 2009, para. 38). The Court of Appeal did not see a difference between the act of taking the picture and its use and retention. But a distinction was drawn between the facts in *Wood* and leading Strasbourg authorities such as *Friedl v. Austria* (1995). In that case, photographs of the applicant were taken at a public demonstration and then stored, but the court was satisfied that privacy was sufficiently respected by assurances from the government that the subjects remained anonymous, and the photographs were retained for the sole purpose for which they were taken and not further processed. The limited storage purpose of future identification was crucial to the Commission in *X v. United Kingdom* (1973), also concerning the photographing of demonstrators. The court in *Wood v. Commissioner of Police for the Metropolis* unanimously concluded that Article 8(1) was engaged. Laws LJ held that justification under Article 8(2) also applied and dismissed the appeal, but Dyson LJ and Lord Collins upheld the appeal. The taking of the photographs was viewed by all judges as in the pursuit of a legitimate aim (the prevention and detection of crime). Nor was there significant disagreement over accordance with the law (but see *Wood v. Commissioner of Police for the Metropolis*, 2009, paras. 80–81 per Dyson LJ). Rather, the crucial point was disproportionality, the majority relying almost exclusively on the relatively recent judgment in *S and Marper v. United Kingdom* (2008). The interference was claimed to be founded on the aims of protecting the community from low-level criminality or the risk of public disorder. But no offence or disorder had been committed, at least on the part of the appellant, so there was no basis to retain the photographs at the time of the AGM or in the future. Even if there had been justification for keeping the photographs, based on the conversation the appellant had with one of the more active protagonists, retention would have been viable only for a few days after the meeting (*Wood v. Commissioner of Police for the Metropolis*, 2009, paras. 86–90).

To summarize, the development of both Strasbourg and domestic jurisprudence around Article 8 has elucidated some valuable principles on the ethical boundaries of surveillance. However, those boundaries are often highly contested and continue to cause fissures within the English judiciary and between England and Strasbourg. In those circumstances, legal certainty must be supplied by legislation. However, the main attempt to fill this gap, the Regulation of Investigatory Powers Act 2000 (RIPA), has given rise to a complex, partial and partially unsuccessful legal edifice, as documented by several extensive legal treatises (Colvin & Cooper, 2009; Harfield & Harfield, 2008; McKay, 2011; Williams, 2006). The Scottish counterpart, the Regulation of Investigatory Powers (Scotland) Act 2000, is very similar and so can be disregarded.

'Surveillance' is defined in RIPA, section 48(2), as including:

> (a) monitoring, observing or listening to persons, their movements, their conversations or their other activities or communications; (b) recording anything monitored, observed or listened to in the course of surveillance; and (c) surveillance by or with the assistance of a surveillance device.

Fundamentally, RIPA is designed to ensure that surveillance complies with Article 8 within surveillance work and expressly refers to concepts like 'private information' (as in section 26). Indeed, the revised Code of Practice on Covert Surveillance and Property Interference could not be clearer:

> Part II of the 2000 Act provides a statutory framework under which covert surveillance can be authorised and conducted compatibly with Article 8. However, where such surveillance would not be likely to result in the obtaining of any *private information* about a person, no interference with Article 8 rights should occur and an *authorisation* under the 2000 Act is therefore not appropriate. (Home Office, 2010, para. 1.14)

This represents a 'primitive analysis' (McKay, 2011, para. 5.28), but it is also now clear from the case of *Paton v. Poole Borough Council* (2010) that the Investigatory Powers Tribunal perceives the question to be more sophisticated:

> In considering and determining the complaints the Tribunal are not simply concerned with whether the outcome of the directed surveillance is a breach of the Complainant's Article 8 rights. They are concerned with the investigation and determination of complaints of alleged non-compliance with RIPA procedures for obtaining and granting authorisation. (*Paton v. Poole Borough Council*, 2010, para. 81)

The starting point in terms of RIPA's impact is section 26, which applies regulatory powers in Part II to two types of surveillance – 'directed' and 'intrusive'. In both cases, the surveillance must be covert, in other words, carried out under section 26(9) in a manner that is subjectively calculated to ensure that the target is unaware.

'Directed' surveillance, other than that which is an immediate response to events or circumstances that would make seeking an authorization impracticable, requires, under RIPA section 26(2)(a)–(b), the monitoring to be for the purposes of a specific investigation or specific operation and carried out in a manner that would acquire or is likely to acquire private information about a person (meaning any person, whether or not the intended target). 'Intrusive' surveillance within RIPA section 26(3)(a) is carried out in relation to anything taking place on any residential premises or in any private vehicle and involves the presence of an individual on the premises or in the vehicle or is carried out by means of a surveillance device.

It follows that in certain circumstances CCTV may be caught by the regime under RIPA, as was considered in *Rosenberg v. R* (2006). The appellant was convicted of drug-related offences and appealed because the trial judge had wrongly admitted into evidence CCTV footage passed to the police by her neighbours. The neighbours had erected what was described as an 'ostentatious' CCTV camera in their garden; it captured evidence of nefarious activities occurring in the appellant's front room – unwrapping packets of drugs in the house, handing objects to others and being shown how to use drugs paraphernalia (*Rosenberg v. R*, 2006, paras. 3, 21). This surveillance had not been authorized under Part II of RIPA. Yet, repeated contacts had been maintained between the police and the neighbours, a relationship described by the Court as one of 'complicity' (para. 22), and at one point the police had even warned about infringement of the appellant's human rights. The defence argued for the exclusion of that highly incriminating evidence as unfair under section 78 of the Police and Criminal Evidence Act 1984.

The Court of Appeal concluded that the surveillance could not be considered 'covert' for the purposes of section 29(9)(a): 'surveillance is covert, if and only if, it is carried out in a manner that is calculated to ensure that persons who are subject to surveillance are unaware that it is or may be taking place' (*Rosenberg v. R*, 2006, para. 20). Furthermore, even if the trial court had sustained a breach of Article 8, the judge would have been entitled, taking also into account the fairness of trials under Article 6, to admit the film footage:

> It is necessary in a democratic society for all relevant and probative evidence to be admissible to assist in the apprehension and conviction of criminals and also to ensure that their trial is fair. It remains necessary to engage in the exercise of reviewing and balancing all the circumstances of the case. In this case, they included intrusion, but intrusion which was openly practised, the complicity of the police in the surveillance, as described, and the seriousness of the crime involved. (*Rosenberg v. R*, 2006, para. 22)

However, this relatively short judgment did not consider European jurisprudence, such as *MM v. Netherlands* (2003) and *Van Vondel v. Netherlands* (2007), or the general saving for lawful conduct in section 80 of RIPA (see *C v. Police and Secretary of State*, 2006), or whether the police–neighbour relationship may have amounted to the deployment of covert human intelligence sources, which requires authorization under RIPA, sections 26(8) and 29.

Beyond the examples of covert surveillance within specific investigations or specific operations falling within RIPA, in which case the surveillance device may require authorization (as discussed in Home Office, 2010, para. 2.28), surveillance of a more untargeted and all-risks variety, such as through permanent and routine CCTV surveillance operated by the UK police on highways, is not unequivocally subject to specific legal controls whether under RIPA or otherwise. This legal abeyance has worried the Chief Surveillance Commissioner, but his angst has not been allayed by legal reform (Chief Surveillance Commissioner, 2006, paras. 14.1–5; 2008, paras. 2.3, 8.6).

Almost perversely, the position is slightly stricter for local authorities, which, under section 163 of the Criminal Justice and Public Order Act 1994, can provide 'apparatus for recording visual images of events occurring on any land in their area' for the purposes of promoting the prevention of crime. Similarly, the Local Government Act 1972, section 111(1), provides a broad power for a local authority 'to do anything … which is calculated to facilitate, or is conducive or incidental to the discharge of any of their functions'. The European Court of Human Rights in *Peck v. United Kingdom* (2003, paras. 66, 67) treated these grounds as a lawful basis for CCTV under Article 8. Local authorities have also become subject to tighter controls over their uses of RIPA, in line with recommendations in the report by Lord Macdonald (2011). By the Protection of Freedoms Act 2012, Part II, any invocation of directed surveillance must meet a seriousness threshold, and directed and intrusive surveillance (as well as the use of covert human agents) all become subject to magisterial pre-approval.

The use of CCTV and the processing of its product are governed by the Data Protection Act 1998. The Information Commissioner has issued a non-statutory CCTV Code of Practice (2008). The code recommends that police and local authorities clarify their responsibilities by agreement, though this is not a requirement (Information Commissioner, 2008b, p. 8). A further potential limitation of governance via data protection is that some aspects of data collection and storage might be protected from scrutiny by a national security exemption under section 28 of the Data Protection Act 1998. In the event of a challenge, a certificate from a minister of the crown provides conclusive evidence of the exemption under section 28(2) (*R (Secretary of State for the Home Department) v. Information Commissioner*, 2006). This course was followed in connection with cameras installed to facilitate Transport for London's congestion charging, not on their introduction in 2003 but after the system was extended in 2007 (Secretary of State for the Home Department, 2007). Presumably, by that time, counter-terrorism had been identified as a subsidiary but worthwhile purpose. If that course had been followed for Project Champion, then it would have reduced potential legal oversight but exacerbated community distrust.

Under the Protection of Freedoms Act 2012, Part II, there is to be closer regulation of all public uses of CCTV (which includes ANPR) through the issuance of statutory *Surveillance Camera Code of Practice* (Home Office, 2013). Its breach will not incur direct legal sanctions but can be cited as relevant evidence in related proceedings. The Home Office Code envisages a checklist before installation, public consultation and information and consideration of the length of data retention. A Surveillance Camera Commissioner (Tony Porter) was appointed in 2014 to oversee the scheme, taking over from the Interim CCTV Regulator announced in 2009 (Hansard, 2009). A National CCTV Oversight Body has also been established. It is an evident shortcoming of the new scheme that privately owned CCTV is not affected, as highlighted by the Joint Committee on Human Rights (2011, para. 109) and despite concerns by the Chief Surveillance Commissioner that 'many public authorities (including law enforcement agencies) are using private entities in one form or another (for example private investigators and ANPR product)' (Chief Surveillance Commissioner, 2011, para. 5.14). It is also uncertain whether the insertion of yet another specialist oversight commissioner into an already crowded field is the right approach – consolidation of existing commissioners would be far preferable, a point discussed later (JUSTICE, 2011, paras. 285–288, 407).

In conclusion, the statutory regime regulating surveillance in the UK has revealed multiple shortcomings, only some of which are remedied by the Protection of Freedoms Act 2012. Given these defects, it may be less surprising that one of Project Champion's fundamental flaws was the failure on the part of those involved to understand the concept, scope and application of the right to respect for private life. Not only are there substantive defects in the law, but it should be added that the curial testing of legal issues around surveillance can also trigger acute procedural conflicts between the interests of private litigants and the protection of national security. The Ministry of Justice's Green Paper, *Justice and Security* (2011), as implemented by the Justice and Security Act 2013, Part II, offers a solution for this conflict within civil proceedings in terms of enhanced 'closed material procedures' akin to those already applicable under the Special Immigration Appeals Commission Act 1997 or in the High Court in control order cases under the Prevention of Terrorism Act 2005. One hopes that this espousal of secrecy will be tempered by the experience of Project Champion and the realization that secrecy applied to the targeting of individuals or defined communities can, if not defined and executed in ethical terms, incur a heavy price in terms of legitimacy, for 'There is nothing more important to policing than its legitimacy in the eyes of the public' (*Project Champion Review*, p. 1).

Accountability

Accountability for intelligence gathering is 'beset by problems in relation to governance' (MacVean, 2008, p. 71) and these difficulties have grown more acute for two related reasons. One is that police tactics have melded with those of security agencies, for example, through the operation of police–security executive liaison groups to facilitate joint working (Intelligence and Security Committee, 2009, p. 8). Second, these tactics are increasingly applied not against exotic targets, such as Russian diplomats, but against locations or communities affecting residents (Hennessy, 2010, p. 371). Another problem is that security engages both public and private sectors within an 'intelligence community' (Omand, 2010, p. 299); the accountability of the public sector is hard enough to secure, but the imposition of standards favouring the public good within the expanding private sector (at venues such as shopping malls: *Appleby v. United Kingdom*, 2003) is even less advanced.

Even basic standards of constitutional governance – the reliance on express and clear laws rather than vague administrative discretions – have regularly been breached by surveillance practices as operated by the security agencies. Some remedies have been provided by RIPA, as well as the Security Service Act 1989 and the Intelligence Services Act 1994, but they have tended to affirm in law existing practices rather than to provide radically improved forms of governance or comprehensive coverage. Thus, there is still reliance on broad triggers such as 'national security'. That term was held to be sufficiently precise for human rights purposes in *Hewitt and Harman v. United Kingdom (No. 2)* (1993), *Esbester v. UK* (1993) and *Christie v. United Kingdom* (1994) but was rejected on fuller consideration in *Amann v. Switzerland* (2000).

So far as police oversight goes, the HM Inspectorate of Constabulary view is that the surveillance measures are running smoothly (2003, para. 3.39). However, the same body believes there is a need to clarify the accountability of ACPO:

> HMIC recommends that the position and status of ACPO should be clearly defined with transparent governance and accountability structures, especially in relation to its quasi-operational role of the commissioning of intelligence and the collation and retention of data. (HM Inspectorate of Constabulary, 2009, p. 151)

It will be recalled that the funding from ACPO (TAM) on a bid from the West Midlands Police was crucial to Project Champion, but its involvement was kept hidden from the public.

Much faith is placed in the work of the various judicial commissioners who audit surveillance measures under RIPA, Part IV, as well as those in the Intelligence Services Act 1994 and the Police Act 1997 (House of Lords Select Committee on the Constitution, 2009, para. 252). The Investigatory Powers Tribunal under section 65 hears individual complaints. Yet, there are many limitations in these systems. Most authorizations of surveillance are conducted by police superiors rather than through the 'best safeguard' of independent judicial authorization (JUSTICE, 2011, paras. 263, 407). There is also no provision for subsequent redress through notification of the operation to the subject, a device which is seen as desirable though not obligatory (*Leander v. Sweden*, 1987, para. 66; *Redgrave v. United Kingdom*, 1993). Nevertheless, the UK intercept rules have been upheld under Article 8 by the European Court of Human Rights in *Kennedy v. United Kingdom* (2010) as sufficiently clear and sufficiently supervised by the relevant commissioner and the Investigatory Powers Tribunal, though judicial review models are also approved (*Uzun v. Germany*, 2010). A contrary view is that these commissioners can only offer review as an afterthought and in selected cases compared to prior judicial authorization, while reliance on public complaints for triggering the Investigatory Powers Tribunal means that too few cases ever reach its doors (JUSTICE, 2011, ch. 9).

Oversight is also offered by the Intelligence and Security Committee under the Intelligence Services Act 1994, section 10. The committee, consisting of parliamentarians, examines the expenditure, administration and policy of the security agencies and has privileged access to information. Its performance has been considered wanting by the committee itself, which calls for reconstitution as a parliamentary body; a wider remit; withholding of information to be agreed by a minister; and more investigative and research resources (Intelligence and Security Committee, 2011).

Successive governments have recognized these shortcomings of the Intelligence and Security Committee (Ministry of Justice, 2008, para. 235ff.), which have become serially highlighted by inadequate investigations and reports into issues such as terrorism attacks, secret rendition and the reliance on intelligence obtained through torture techniques of foreign agencies. The *Justice and Security Green Paper* (Ministry of Justice, 2011, p. vii) contemplates not only reform of the Intelligence and Security Committee but also some reinvigoration of the equally limited constitutions of the Intelligence Services Commissioner, the Interception of Communications Commissioner and the Office of Surveillance Commissioners. However, the suggestions in the Green Paper are mainly tentative: an increased public profile and confirmation of a broader remit to include monitoring compliance with guidance on the detention and interviewing of detainees overseas (Ministry of Justice, 2011, paras. 3.43, 44). Correspondingly limited changes were made by Part I of the Justice and Security Act 2013. More radical would be their replacement by a consolidated and more proactive Inspectorate General (para. 3.45, Appendix I), but the government expresses more reserve about this model. As noted earlier, the Chief Surveillance Commissioner was able duly to record the demise of Project Champion in 2011 but played no part in scrutinizing its establishment, and the remote threat of retrospective audit by that commissioner was not even mentioned by any of the agencies or the *Project Champion Report*.

The courts are increasingly prepared to scrutinize surveillance activities and to judicialize intelligence matters (Kavanagh, 2011; Roach, 2009, p. 147; Walker, 2010, 2011b). The litigation surrounding Binyam Mohamed (*R (Mohamed) v. Secretary of State for Foreign and Commonwealth Affairs*, 2010), as well as several other cases arising from events in Guantanamo Bay or Iraq, has highlighted growing judicial defiance of executive arguments and warnings, but has also provoked an executive reaction towards proposed procedural restrictions on open justice in civil proceedings, as set out in the *Justice and Security Green Paper* and implemented by Part II of the Justice and Security Act 2013.

Conclusion

Security is 'at the heart of good government', and several factors have impelled policing and intelligence agencies in late modern societies towards techniques of surveillance which are emblematic of a 'protective state' (Omand, 2010, pp. 7, 9). One is the growing reliance of society on technology, which unlocks new possibilities for investigative techniques. Another is the growing capacities of computers to record and to analyse colossal amounts of data, well beyond the capacities of paper records. The transborder aspect of terrorism threats also encourages more sophisticated data gathering and transfer. As a result, the verdict of Andy Hayman, former Assistant Commissioner for Specialist Operations in the Metropolitan Police Service, is that 'Surveillance is key' (Hayman, 2009, p. 247).

It follows that the depiction of some locations as more at risk than others comes as no surprise. It is not even inherently wrong if rationally grounded: 'there can be no reasonable objection to areas being classified in this manner provided there is reliable evidence that they present particular risks' (Greer, 2010, p. 1179). The enhanced attention given by Project Champion to the selected locations in Birmingham conceivably had a rational basis in the successful prosecutions of 2007 and related intelligence. Yet, especially when surveillance is applied by design or by practice in ways that inevitably affect specified individuals or identifiable communities disproportionately, constraints must come more prominently into play, including rights to due process under Article 6 or, principally prominent in this survey, rights to privacy under Article 8. One rather bleak response to the prospect of such constraints is to assert that privacy is the terrorist's best friend (Posner, 2008) and consequently to seek limitations or even derogation. Untrammelled surveillance might be tolerable for brief periods in an emergency if public authorities could demonstrate tangible success from intrusions on privacy and could be trusted to act in a discerning and ethical way. But government departments have generally failed to meet these standards. They have failed to demonstrate positive results on a commensurate scale and have rarely commissioned studies (an exception being Gill & Spriggs, 2005). They have been repeatedly culpable of massive and careless losses of personal data (Cabinet Office, 2008). They have continually objected to constitutional and effective delimitations of surveillance powers, including those which endure over long periods. There remains the further danger that even weak controls over state agencies will be evaded by reliance on private providers (Balkin, 2008; Kerr, 2009).

The potential for harmful effects arising from surveillance should be countered with transparent and universal legal regulation which applies to all forms of CCTV and ANPR surveillance by public and private bodies (JUSTICE, 2011, para. 288); 'data minimization' at the outset (Information Commissioner, 2014, p. 8); greater attention to the quality of data being mined and to the premise behind any operation

(Cate, 2008); and a firmer application of judicial accountability over any intrusion into defined private lives.

Ultimately, the case-study of Project Champion suggests that community surveillance can be applied fairly and on a sustained basis only if the affected community is an active partner to the objectives and implementation of the surveillance. In this way, a new mind-set is required of counter-terrorism agents and police officers. The total abandonment of Project Champion may reveal that they are not yet ready to rethink or to bestow the level of trust demanded by this more ethical model of counter-terrorism.

Acknowledgements

The authors acknowledge the valuable insights of Professor Steven Greer, University of Bristol, but opinions expressed herein remain those of the authors.

References

Agreement between the European Union and the United States of America on the processing and transfer of Financial Messaging Data from the EU to the US for the purposes of the Terrorist Finance Tracking Program. (2010). Brussels: European Commission.

Amoore, L., & de Goede, M. (2005). Governance, risk and dataveillance in the war on terror. *Crime, Law & Social Change, 43,* 149–173.

Appuzo, M., & Goldman, A. (2011). With CIA help, NYPD moves covertly in Muslim areas. *Wall Street Journal.* Retrieved 2 June 2014 from http://www.ticklethewire.com /2011/08/24/with-cia-help-nypd-moves-covertly-in-muslim-areas-practice-raises -questions/

Association of Chief Police Officers. (2013, January). *The police use of Automatic Number Plate Recognition.* Retrieved 12 June 2014 from http://www.acpo.police.uk/documents /crime/2013/201303CBA-ANPR.pdf

Authi, J. (2010a, 11 June). Call to ditch spy cameras. *Birmingham Evening Mail,* p. 16.

Authi, J. (2010b, 29 June). Top lawyer to speak at demo over CCTV. *Birmingham Evening Mail,* p. 3.

Awan, I. (2011). Terror in the eye of the beholder. *Howard Journal, 50,* 199–202.

Balkin, S. M. (2008). The constitution in the national surveillance state. *Minnesota Law Review, 93,* 1–25.

Bamford, B. W. C. (2005). The role and effectiveness of intelligence in Northern Ireland. *Intelligence and National Security, 20,* 581–607.

Bowcott, O., & Lewis, P. (2010, 25 September). Use of spy in the sky drones for police surveillance rises. *Guardian,* p. 4.

Bradley, A. W. (1987a). Parliamentary privilege and the Zircon affair. *Public Law,* 1–3.

Bradley, A. W. (1987b). Parliamentary privilege, Zircon and national security. *Public Law* (Spring), 488.

Briggs, R. (2010). Community engagement for counterterrorism. *International Affairs, 86,* 971–981.

British–US Communication Intelligence Agreement. (1946). Kew: National Archives HW/80/4.

Brown, I., & Korff, D. (2009). Terrorism and the proportionality of Internet surveillance. *European Journal of Criminology, 6*, 119–134.

Cabinet Office. (2008). *Data handling procedures in government.* London.

Cate, F. H. (2008). Government data mining. *Harvard Civil Rights–Civil Liberties Law Review, 43*, 435–489.

Chief Surveillance Commissioner. (2006). *Annual Report of the Chief Surveillance Commissioner for 2005–2006.* 2005–06 HC 1298.

Chief Surveillance Commissioner. (2008). *Annual Report of the Chief Surveillance Commissioner for 2007–2008.* 2007–08 HC 659.

Chief Surveillance Commissioner. (2011). *Annual Report of the Chief Surveillance Commissioner for 2010–2011.* 2010–12 HC 1191.

Choudhury, T., & Fenwick, H. (2011). *The impact of counter-terrorism measures on Muslim communities.* Equality and Human Rights Commission Research Report 72. London.

City councillors: We were misled over CCTV cameras. (2010, 22 June). *Birmingham Evening Mail.*

Clarke, P. (2007). *Learning from experience: Counter terrorism in the UK since 9/11.* London: Metropolitan Police Service. Retrieved 2 June 2014 from http://www.policyexchange.org.uk/images/publications/learning%20from%20experience%20-%20jun%2007.pdf

Coaffee, J. (2004). Recasting the 'ring of steel'. In S. Graham (Ed.), *Cities, war, and terrorism* (pp. 276–296). Oxford: Blackwell.

Colvin, M., & Cooper, J. (Eds.) (2009). *Human rights and the investigations and prosecution of crime.* Oxford: Oxford University Press.

Committee of Privy Counsellors. (2004). *Review of intelligence on weapons of mass destruction.* 2003–04 HC 898.

Committee on Technical and Privacy Dimensions of Information for Terrorism Prevention and Other National Goals, National Research Council. (2008). *Protecting individual privacy in the struggle against terrorists.* Washington, DC: National Academies Press.

Council of Europe. (2005). *Terrorism: Special investigation techniques.* Strasbourg.

Council of Europe Committee of Ministers. (2005). *Special investigative techniques.* Rec(2005)10. Retrieved 2 June 2014 from https://wcd.coe.int/ViewDoc.jsp?id=849269&Site=CM

Council of the European Union. (2010). *EU External Strategy on Passenger Name Record (PNR).* 13986/10. Brussels.

Crawford, A. (1997). *The local governance of crime.* Oxford: Oxford University Press.

Criminal Justice and Public Order Act 1994, UK Public General Act. Retrieved 3 June 2014 from http://www.legislation.gov.uk/ukpga/1994/33/contents

Data Protection Act 1998, UK Public General Act. Retrieved 3 June 2014 from http://www.legislation.gov.uk/ukpga/1998/29/contents

Data Retention (EC Directive) Regulations. (2009). SI 2009/859. London.

DSTL. (2010). *What perceptions do the UK public have concerning the impact of counter-terrorism legislation implemented since 2000?* Occasional Paper 88. London: Home Office.

European Commission. (2010). *Proposal for a council decision.* COM(2010) 316 final. Brussels.

European Commission. (2011). *Proposal for a Directive in the use of Passenger Name Record data*. COM (2011) 32 final. Brussels.

Evans, R. M. (2008). Cultural paradigms and change. In C. Harfield, A. MacVean, J. G. D. Grieve, & D. Philips (Eds.), *The handbook of intelligent policing* (pp. 105–120). Oxford: Oxford University Press.

Executive Order 12333, United States Intelligence Activities, December 4, 1981. 46 FR 59941. Washington, DC.

Garland, D. (2001). *The culture of control*. Oxford: Oxford University Press.

Gill, M., & Spriggs, A. (2005). *Assessing the impact of CCTV*. Home Office Research Study 292. London.

Gill, P. (2000). *Rounding up the usual suspects?* Aldershot, UK: Ashgate.

Gill, P. (2009). Security intelligence and human rights. *Intelligence and National Security, 24,* 78–102.

Goold, B. J. (2003). *CCTV and policing*. Oxford: Oxford University Press.

Greer, S. (2010). Anti-terrorist laws and the United Kingdom's 'suspect Muslim community'. *British Journal of Criminology, 50,* 1171–1190.

Greer, S. C. (1995). *Supergrasses*. Oxford: Clarendon.

Hallett, H. C. (2011). *Coroner's inquests into the London bombings of 7 July 2005*. Inner West London Coroner. London.

Hansard. (2009). Hansard (House of Commons), vol. 502, col. 113ws (15 December 2009).

Harfield, C., & Harfield, K. (2008). *Covert investigation*. Oxford: Oxford University Press.

Hayman, A. (2009). *The terrorist hunters*. London: Bantam.

Hennessy, P. (2010). *The secret state* (2nd ed.). London: Penguin.

HM Inspectorate of Constabulary. (2003). *A need to know: HMIC's thematic inspection of Special Branch and ports policing*. London: Home Office.

HM Inspectorate of Constabulary. (2009). *Adapting to protest*. London.

Hogan, G., & Walker, C. (1989). *Political violence and the law in Ireland*. Manchester: Manchester University Press.

Home Office. (2006/2011). *Countering international terrorism*. Cm 6888 (2006), as updated by Cm 7547 (2009), Cm 7833 (2010) and Cm 8123 (2011). London: HMSO.

Home Office. (2010). *Code of practice on covert surveillance and property interference*. London.

Home Office. (2011a). *Operation of police powers under the Terrorism Act 2000 and subsequent legislation*. HOSB 15/11. London.

Home Office. (2011b). *Prevent strategy*. Cm 8092. London.

Home Office. (2013). *Surveillance camera code of practice*. London.

House of Commons. (2010). Project Champion and surveillance of the Muslim community in Birmingham. 2010–12 EDM 212.

House of Commons Home Affairs Committee. (2005). Terrorism and community relations. 2004–05 HC 165.

House of Lords Select Committee on the Constitution. (2009). *Surveillance: Citizens and the state*. 2008–09 HL 18. Government Response Cm 7616. London.

House of Lords Select Committee on the European Union. (2010). *The United Kingdom opt in to the Passenger Name Record Directive*. 2010–11 HL 113.

Hyland, K., & Walker, C.. (2014). Undercover policing and underwhelming laws. *Criminal Law Review*, 555–574.

Information Commissioner. (2008a). *Annual report 2007–08.* 2007–08 HC 670.

Information Commissioner. (2008b). CCTV code of practice. Wilmslow. Retrieved 2 June 2014 from http://ico.org.uk/Global/~/media/documents/library/Data_Protection /Detailed_specialist_guides/ICO_CCTVFINAL_2301.ashx

Intelligence and Security Committee. (2009). *Could 7/7 have been prevented?* Cm 7617. London.

Intelligence and Security Committee. (2011). *Annual report 2010–2011.* Cm 8114. London.

Intelligence Services Act 1994, UK Public General Act. Retrieved 3 June 2014 from http://www.legislation.gov.uk/ukpga/1994/13/contents

Iranian TV firm funds 'spy cam' documentary. (2011, 29 September). *Birmingham Post.*

Joint Committee on Human Rights. (2011). *Legislative scrutiny: Protection of Freedom Bill.* 2010–12 HL195/HC 1490.

Jolly, S. (2010, 23 June). Birmingham's spy-cam scheme has had its cover blown. *Guardian.* Retrieved 2 June 2014 from http://www.guardian.co.uk/commentisfree /libertycentral/2010/jun/23/birmingham-spy-cam-scheme

JUSTICE. (2011). *Freedom from suspicion: Surveillance reform for a digital age.* London: JUSTICE.

Kavanagh, A. (2011). Constitutionalism, counterterrorism, and the courts: Changes in the British constitutional landscape. *International Journal of Constitutional Law, 9*(1), 172–199.

Kerr, O. S. (2009). The national surveillance state. *Minnesota Law Review, 93,* 2179–2184.

Local Government Act 1972, UK Public General Act. Retrieved 3 June 2014 from http://www.legislation.gov.uk/ukpga/1972/70/contents

Lyon, D. (2003). *Surveillance after September 11.* Cambridge, UK: Polity.

Macdonald, K. (2011). *Review of counter-terrorism and security powers: A report by Lord Macdonald of River Glaven QC.* Cm 8003. London.

MacFarquhar, N. (2007). Los Angeles police scrap mapping plan, elating Muslims. *New York Times* (16 November), 31.

MacVean, A. (2008). The governance of intelligence. In C. Harfield, A. MacVean, J. G. D. Grieve, & D. Philips (Eds.), *The handbook of intelligent policing* (pp. 63–74). Oxford: Oxford University Press.

Maras, H-M. (2009). From targeted to mass surveillance. In B. J. Goold & D. Neyland (Eds.), *New directions in surveillance and privacy.* Cullompton, UK: Willan.

McKay S. (2011). *Covert policing law and practice.* Oxford: Oxford University Press.

Ministry of Justice. (2008). *The governance of Britain: Constitutional renewal.* Cm 7342. London: Stationery Office. Retrieved 12 June 2014 from https://www.gov.uk /government/uploads/system/uploads/attachment_data/file/250803/7342_i.pdf

Ministry of Justice. (2011). *Justice and Security Green Paper.* Cm 8194. London.

Minton, A. (2009). *Ground control.* London: Penguin.

Moran, J. (2010). Evaluating Special Branch and the use of informant intelligence in Northern Ireland. *Intelligence and National Security, 25,* 1–23.

Mythen, G., Walklate, S., & Khan, F. (2009). 'I'm a Muslim, but I'm not a terrorist'. *British Journal of Criminology, 49,* 736–754.

National Commission on Terrorism Attacks upon the United States. (2004). *The 9/11 Commission Report.* Washington, DC: United States Government Printing Office.

National Security Preparedness Group. (2011). *Tenth anniversary report card: The status of the 9/11 Commission recommendations.* Washington, DC: Bipartsian Policy Center.

Norris, C., & Armstrong, G. (1999). *The maximum surveillance society: The rise of CCTV*. Oxford: Berg.

Norris, C., Moran, J., & Armstrong, G. (1999). *Surveillance, closed circuit television and social control*. Oxford: Berg.

Omand, D. (2010). *Securing the state*. London: Hurst.

Pantazis, C., & Pemberton, S. (2009). From the 'old' to the 'new' suspect community: Examining the impacts of recent UK counter-terrorist legislation. *British Journal of Criminology, 49*, 646–666.

Pantazis, C., & Pemberton, S. (2011). Restating the case for the 'suspect community'. *British Journal of Criminology, 51*, 1054.

Police hold four 21 July suspects. (2005, 30 July). *BBC News*. Retrieved 2 June 2014 from http://news.bbc.co.uk/1/hi/uk/4727975.stm

Posner, R. A. (2008). Privacy, surveillance and law. *University of Chicago Law Review, 75*, 245–260.

Prevention of Terrorism Act 2005, UK Public General Act. Retrieved 3 June 2014 from http://www.legislation.gov.uk/ukpga/2005/2/contents

Protection of Freedoms Act 2012, UK Public General Act. Retrieved 3 June 2014 from http://www.legislation.gov.uk/ukpga/2012/9/contents

Regulation of Investigatory Powers Act 2000, UK Public General Act. Retrieved 3 June 2014 from http://www.legislation.gov.uk/ukpga/2000/23/contents

Roach, K. (2009). When secret intelligence becomes evidence. *Supreme Court Law Review, 47*, 147–208.

Secretary of State for the Home Department. (2007). Section 28 Data Protection Act 1998: Certificate of the Secretary of State. Retrieved 3 June 2014 from http://www.statewatch.org/news/2007/aug/uk-london-tfl-exemption-certificate.pdf

Security Service Act 1989, UK Public General Act. Retrieved 3 June 2014 from http://www.legislation.gov.uk/ukpga/1989/5/contents

Special Immigration Appeals Commission Act 1997, UK Public General Act. Retrieved 3 June 2014 from http://www.legislation.gov.uk/ukpga/1997/68/contents

Surveillance Studies Network. (2006). *A report on the surveillance society*. Retrieved 2 June 2014 from http://www.ico.gov.uk/upload/documents/library/data_protection/practical_application/surveillance_society_full_report_2006.pdf

Terrorism Act 2000 (Remedial) Order. (2011). SI 2011/631. London.

Thornton, S. (2010). *Project Champion review*. Kidlington, UK: Thames Valley Police. (Cited as *Project Champion Review*.)

Timeline of the 7 July attacks. (2006, 11 July). BBC News. Retrieved 2 June 2014 from http://news.bbc.co.uk/1/hi/uk/5032756.stm?ls

United States Senate Select Committee on Intelligence. (2004). *Report of the Select Committee on Intelligence on the U.S. intelligence community's prewar intelligence assessments on Iraq*. Senate Report 108-301. Washington, DC.

United States Senate Select Committee on Intelligence. (2008). *Report on intelligence activities relating to Iraq conducted by the Policy Counterterrorism Evaluation Group and the Office of Special Plans within the Office of the Under Secretary of Defense for Policy*. Senate Report 110-346. Washington, DC.

Walker, C. (2004). Political violence and commercial risk. *Current Legal Problems, 56*, 531–578.

Walker, C. (2006). Intelligence and anti-terrorism legislation in the United Kingdom. *Crime, Law and Social Change, 44,* 387–422.

Walker, C. (2008a). 'Know thine enemy as thyself': Discerning friend from foe under anti-terrorism laws. *Melbourne Law Review, 32,* 275–301.

Walker, C. (2008b). The pursuit of terrorism with intelligence. In J. Moran and M. Phythian (Eds.), *Intelligence, security and policing post-9/11* (pp. 54–78). Basingstoke, UK: Palgrave Macmillan.

Walker, C. (2009). Neighbor terrorism and the all-risks policing of terrorism. *Journal of National Security Law & Policy, 3,* 121–168.

Walker, C. (2010). The threat of terrorism and the fate of control orders. *Public Law,* 3–15.

Walker, C. (2011a). *Terrorism and the law.* Oxford: Oxford University Press.

Walker, C. (2011b). The judicialisation of intelligence in legal process. *Public Law,* 235–237.

Walker, C., & Broderick, J. (2006). *The Civil Contingencies Act 2004.* Oxford: Oxford University Press.

Williams, V. (2006). *Surveillance and intelligence law handbook.* Oxford: Oxford University Press.

Legal Cases

Amann v. Switzerland (2000) Application number 27798/95, 2000-II, Strasbourg: European Court of Human Rights

Appleby v. United Kingdom (2003) Application number 44306/98, 2003-VI, Strasbourg: European Court of Human Rights

C v. Police and Secretary of State (2006) IPT/03/32/H, 14 November 2006

Campbell v. MGN Limited [2004] UKHL 22

Christie v. United Kingdom (1994) Application number 21482/93, DR 78A, 119, Strasbourg: European Commission of Human Rights

Esbester v. UK (1993) Application number 18601/91, 2 April 1993, Strasbourg: European Commission of Human Rights

Friedl v. Austria (1995) Application number 15225/89, Series A 305B, Strasbourg: European Court of Human Rights

Gillan and Quinton v. United Kingdom (2010) Application number 4158/05, 12 January 2010, Strasbourg: European Court of Human Rights

Hewitt and Harman v. United Kingdom (No. 2) (1993) Application number 20317/92, 1 September 1993, Strasbourg: European Commission of Human Rights

Hosking v. Runting [2003] 3NZHC 416, affirmed on appeal [2004] NZCA 34

Ireland v. United Kingdom (1978) Application number 5310/71, Series A 25, Strasbourg: European Court of Human Rights

Kennedy v. United Kingdom (2010) Application number 26839/05, 18 May 2010, Strasbourg: European Court of Human Rights

Klass v. Germany (1987) Application number 5029/71, Series A 28, Strasbourg: European Court of Human Rights

Leander v. Sweden (1987) Application number 9248/81, Series A 116, Strasbourg: European Court of Human Rights

McKennitt v. Ash [2006] EWCA Civ 1714

MM v. Netherlands (2003) Application number 39339/98, 8 April 2003, Strasbourg: European Court of Human Rights

Murray v. Big Pictures (UK) Limited [2008] EWCA Civ 446

Murray v. United Kingdom (1994) Application number 14310/88, Series A 300A, Strasbourg: European Court of Human Rights

Paton v. Poole Borough Council (2010) IPT/09/01/C, 29 July 2010

Peck v. United Kingdom (2003) Application number 44647/98, 2003-I, Strasbourg: European Court of Human Rights

R v. Brentwood Borough Council, ex p Peck [1998] EMLR 697

R v. Nadim, Ali, and Mohammed (2009) The Times 10 March, p 4 (Central Criminal Court)

R v. Parviz Khan [2009] EWCA Crim 1085

R v. Taylor, R v. Hayes (1995) 16 Cr App Rep (S) 873

R (Gillan) v. Commissioner of Police for the Metropolis [2006] UKHL 12

R (Mohamed) v. Secretary of State for Foreign and Commonwealth Affairs [2010] EWCA Civ 65

R (S and Marper) v. Chief Constable of South Yorkshire Police [2004] UKHL 39

R (Secretary of State for the Home Department) v. Information Commissioner [2006] EWHC 2958 (Admin)

Redgrave v. United Kingdom (1993) Application number 20271/92, 1 September 1993, Strasbourg: European Commission of Human Rights

Rosenberg v. R [2006] EWCA Crim 6

S and Marper v. United Kingdom (2008) Application numbers 30562/04 and 30566/04, 4 December 2008, Strasbourg: European Court of Human Rights

Uzun v. Germany (2010) Application number 35623/09, 2 September 2010, Strasbourg: European Court of Human Rights

Van Vondel v. Netherlands (2007) Application number 38258/03, 25 October 2007, Strasbourg: European Court of Human Rights

Von Hannover v. Germany (2004) Application number 59320/00, 2004-VI, Strasbourg: European Court of Human Rights

Wainwright v. Home Office [2003] UKHL 53

Wood v. Commissioner of Police for the Metropolis [2009] EWCA Civ 414

X v. United Kingdom (1973) Application number 5877/72, D&R 45, p. 90, Strasbourg: European Commission of Human Rights

13

Thinking about Peace While Engaged in Counter-Terrorism

The Primacy of Intelligence

John G. D. Grieve

Introduction and Context

This chapter considers how intelligence was used by the Independent Monitoring Commission (IMC) in Northern Ireland and how it might contribute to winning the peace in the sense of winning hearts and minds during the later stages of counter-terrorist operations.[1] It argues that intelligence is necessary not just to pre-empt terrorist activity but also to win the hearts and minds of communities – a vital precursor to winning the peace. As Liddell Hart so elegantly noted, 'grand strategy looks beyond the war to the subsequent peace. It should not only combine the various instruments, but so regulate their use as to avoid damage to the future state of peace – for its security and prosperity' (1954, p. 336).

In the 1990s the national UK counter-terrorist strategy included the strap-line 'communities defeat terrorism' which was part of a wide-ranging set of tactical options for policing and public involvement (see, e.g., Grieve, Harfield, & MacVean, 2007, p. 97). In time this mutated into the Prevent strand of the UK government's CONTEST Strategy for Countering International Terrorism of 'Pursue, Prevent, Protect, Prepare' (Home Office 2006/2011). I will be using the experiences in the Northern Ireland Independent Monitoring Commission to support my arguments.

In considering the IMC role, I am also interested in a possible balance during the conflict between intelligence-led strategies for pre-empting terrorist activities by arresting or disrupting their perpetrators and the winning of hearts and minds by achieving community support and confidence. These decisions have a later impact for the peace process. I want to consider how a 'winning the peace' strategy can be supported by putting more intelligence – that is, information and analysis, 'intelligence designed for action' (Sims, 1993) – into the public domain. As Lord Butler (2004) wrote in his recommendation 37 (I hesitate to adopt his word 'recommendation' because of his use of the conditional 'if'): 'if intelligence is to be

Investigating Terrorism: Current Political, Legal and Psychological Issues, First Edition. Edited by John Pearse.
© 2015 John Wiley & Sons, Ltd. Published 2015 by John Wiley & Sons, Ltd.

used more widely by governments in public debate in future those doing so must be careful to explain its uses and limitations.'

It was convenient for the IMC to think that Lord Butler's (2004) timely description of the intelligence process as collection, collation, validation, analysis and assessment separated the latter three concepts, hence indicating that they can be carried out by the same person or group, particularly where expertise in a specialist area is needed and provided there is a separate auditing function. More significantly, Lord Butler explains that, because much intelligence is fragmentary or specialized, analysis has to be a conscious stage which 'assembles individual intelligence reports into meaningful strands[,] … reports take on meaning as they are put into context … analysis is also the process required to convert complex technical evidence into descriptions of real-world objects or events' (2004, p. 7). He also deals with the issue of dissent and the need for a record of the related discussions. Omand (2010, p. 119) uses the term 'elucidation', bracketed with 'access' and 'dissemination', as part of his version of analysis in the intelligence model. These two expert contemporary accounts have contributed to my thinking.

The context and chronology of the IMC role and of my argument follows experiences in conflict, post-conflict and peace in Northern Ireland and some early experiences with al-Qaeda precursor groups. There was a 30-year period of violence in Northern Ireland, a peace agreement in 1998, the Belfast or Good Friday Agreement, and then over a decade of late or post-conflict for all but not final peace (although there was for some) for reasons to be explained. This emphasizes the author's experiences as part of a policing, intelligence-led, community-oriented, rule of law, criminal justice paradigm of counter-terrorism, not the military paradigm. There is, however, some impact from the latter, perversely using elements of the military paradigm and the thinking of martial philosophers.

The argument here is that Lord Butler's conclusion that material could be put in the public domain to aid democratic decision-making could include intelligence and by extension this includes the processes and material prepared by the IMC which I would argue could and should form part of any contingency planning when working towards a peaceful resolution. Before moving on to that, I will consider how the IMC came about and its democratic international mandate and I will examine how that might fit into contemporary thinking about post-conflicts.

Northern Irish Peace Process: International Agreement and Domestic Legislation

After a series of attempts at peace agreements, 1998 saw a comprehensive agreement brokered by three governments, the British, the Irish and the American. In essence, there was to be power-sharing in a devolved government in Northern Ireland and decommissioning of arms by paramilitary groups overseen by an international commission. In 2003 the Irish and UK governments decided to hand over to another commission, the Independent Monitoring Commission (IMC),[2] the task of monitoring, analysing, reporting and making recommendations to limit the terrorist activities of the paramilitaries. Both the British and Irish governments passed domestic legislation to allow the IMC to work, not least with policing, security and intelligence agencies.

In the post-conflict period, which saw confrontations, there had been disruptive political disputes as to whether a paramilitary incident amounted to a breach of the ceasefire or 1998 peace process, with the consequent fear of a widespread return to violence. There were two Articles in the international agreement between the governments, of most relevance to monitoring paramilitaries and maintaining the momentum for peace: Articles 4 and 7. The IMC had other tasks in relation to the normalization of some policing activity and the military roles that are relevant to the shifts in the context described above. It also had a potential role in respect of complaints about some types of conduct by ministers and parties to the Northern Ireland Assembly that has never been used. It is worth considering the two articles in full.

Article 4.

In relation to the remaining threat from paramilitary groups, the Commission shall:

(a)   monitor any continuing activity by paramilitary groups including:

    i.   attacks on the security forces, murders, sectarian attacks, involvement in riots, and other criminal offences;

    ii.   training, targeting, intelligence gathering, acquisition or development of arms or weapons and other preparations for terrorist campaigns;

    iii.   punishment beatings and attacks and exiling;

(b)   assess:

    i.   whether the leaderships of such organisations are directing such incidents or seeking to prevent them; and

    ii.   trends in security incidents.

(c)   report its findings in respect of paragraphs (a) and (b) of this Article to the two Governments at six-monthly intervals; and, at the joint request of the two Governments, or if the Commission sees fit to do so, produce further reports on paramilitary activity on an ad hoc basis.

Article 7.

When reporting under Articles 4 and 6 of this Agreement, the Commission, or in the case of Article 6(2), the relevant members thereof shall recommend any remedial action considered necessary. The Commission may also recommend what measures, if any, it considers might appropriately be taken by the Northern Ireland Assembly, such measures being limited to those which the Northern Ireland Assembly has power to take under relevant United Kingdom law. (International Agreement between the Government of UK and Government of Ireland, 2003)

Article 13 is also relevant to the complexity of our post-Butler intelligence role, because it deals with confidentiality of IMC sources and imposes a duty on the IMC to ensure the security of people who talked to the IMC.

There are no direct precedents for late or post-conflict methods of how to create a commission with the tasks that had emerged during the implementation of a peace process. There are analogies to strategic arms limitation and monitoring, truce monitors and peace-keepers but no really close parallels. Innovative practice, however, showed there was much from which the IMC could learn, to use others' ideas and synthesize them with our own processes. The views of politicians, officials, commentators, critics, journalists, academics including historians, former combatants and everyone with whom the IMC initially came into contact provided the basis on which models could be built. There were many ingredients but no recipe. There was a wealth of dispute but no off-the-shelf menu.

Methodological Issues: Some Support from Other Public Inquiries

The IMC were therefore concerned with intelligence, in thinking about the wider nature of independence in governance, oversight and policing by comparing and contrasting similarities despite differences, and differences despite similarities, with other institutions and organizations set up to deal with post-conflict situations.

The *9/11 Commission Report* (National Commission, 2004) emphasizes unity of effort and sharing data across agency lines. Its recommendation proposes the resolution of legal, policy and technical issues to create a 'trusted information network' (2004, p. 418). This kind of trusted information network must be the objective of all intelligence efforts, including those of the IMC, and can be tracked through 50 years of public inquiries in the United Kingdom and elsewhere.

For example, the Audit Commission (1993, paras. 126, 127) makes the point much more specifically about intelligence: 'management should ensure that parochialism is not allowed to impair intelligence flows'. Moreover, it indicates at paragraph 73 that 'the core of police work is the linking of evidence from the scene with information about likely offenders' and goes on to consider possible contributions to that pool of information. Sir John May (1994, para. 21.26), in his final report into miscarriages of justice from the 1970s involving the IRA terrorist campaigns, looked at the sharing of information, specifically unused material, with the defence and trial judge. *The Stephen Lawrence Inquiry* report (Macpherson, 1999) described absence of understanding about the linked nature of institutional racism, community impact assessment, critical incidents and family liaison failures as blockages to intelligence flow. This is similar to descriptions familiar from Scarman (1981) to Bichard (2004).

> Where the offence occurs in the hours of darkness over a short space of time and the perpetrators disappear on foot into the locality, it then behoves investigating officers to act with speed and *intelligence*. Time is of the essence. With every passing hour. (Macpherson, 1999, Michael Mansfield, QC, closing speech, Stephen Lawrence Inquiry transcript, p. 11063, ll. 20–25; emphasis added)

In summary, there plainly has to be a *compendious and effective local intelligence gathering operation* in existence that can be accessed quickly by officers at any time, day or night, especially when those officers may not be familiar with the locality. The information itself should be categorised in such a way that it can be called up by reference to name, or description, or address, or offence, or modus operandi, or vehicle or associates. Computerisation must clearly have made this possible for the future. (Macpherson, 1999, Michael Mansfield, QC, closing speech, Stephen Lawrence Inquiry transcript, p. 11055, ll. 2–12; emphasis added)

The Victoria Climbié Inquiry (Laming, 2003, p. 322) examined the incompetence, not least the potential for conflict, through blurred roles that led to the failure to analyse or assess risks and missed opportunities in identifying and solving them. Lord Laming and his adviser John Fox pressed for open minds, an investigative approach and healthy scepticism among investigators that seemed to me to be relevant to the IMC.

During the Hutton Inquiry (2004), Richard Hatfield, personnel director at the Ministry of Defence, revealed that 'there are what is known in the trade as "compartments" which mean people are given access to particular lines of information because they need to know that and they are not given access to other lines of information'.[3] In Bichard (2004), almost the entire thrust of his criticisms about intelligence on dangerousness is about the effective use of joined-up information sharing between policing agencies. His conclusions go to the core of my argument.

Legal Assessment of the Validity of the IMC Role and Methodology

The IMC continuously reviewed how they were following the initial guidelines they had set themselves. After the first few reports,[4] its very existence was challenged by a political party, which led to the Secretary of State and the IMC being taken to the High Court in London, charged in part with prejudice and bias. The judgment provided a powerful examination and validation of the IMC intelligence-led methodology. At paragraph 133/4 of the judgment, the court concluded:

The IMC must nevertheless apply some defined criterion or evidential threshold for the purposes of fact-finding, since the process would otherwise be arbitrary and unfair; and where the facts relate to criminal conduct, the criterion or evidential threshold ought in our view to be a rigorous one. The letter makes clear, however, that the IMC does apply such a criterion, namely one of 'confidence'. The letter quotes a key passage from the Fifth Report which we have already cited in para 26 above: 'we will not say anything, or draw any conclusion, unless we have confidence in it'. In our judgment that criterion, if properly applied, is an appropriate one and gives rise to no procedural unfairness on the part of the IMC.

Mr Larkin took us to passages in the IMC's reports which, read in isolation, might be taken to suggest that the IMC applies a less clear-cut criterion than one of confidence.

In the First Report, for example, the language repeatedly used is that of belief rather than confidence (see the passages quoted at paras 27–28 above). On the other hand, when it comes to the findings of fact in the Fourth Report about the Northern Bank robbery, in relation to which [the complainant] is particularly critical, the language used is more emphatic. The report states that the information available since the robbery 'leads us to conclude firmly that it was planned and undertaken by the PIRA' and that some [of the complainants'] senior members 'were involved in sanctioning [it]' (see the passages quoted at paras 35–36 above). Looking at the reports as a whole, we see no reason to reject the IMC's clear statements that the commissioners will not say anything or draw any conclusion unless they have confidence in it.

The judgment went on at paragraphs 135 to 136:

> The adoption of such an approach is supported by the ruling on standard of proof issued on 11 October 2004 by 'The Bloody Sunday Inquiry' tribunal, chaired by Lord Saville of Newgate. Para 23 of that ruling reads:
>
>> In our view, provided the Tribunal makes clear the degree of confidence or certainty with which it reaches any conclusion as to facts and matters that may imply or suggest criminality of serious misconduct of any individual, provided that there is evidence and reasoning that logically supports the conclusion to the degree of confidence or certainty expressed, and provided of course that those concerned have been given a proper opportunity to deal with allegations made against them, we see in the context of this Inquiry no unfairness to anyone nor any good reason to limit our findings in the manner suggested. Thus, to take an example, we cannot accept that we are precluded in our report from analysing and weighing the evidence and giving our reasons for concluding that in the case of a particular shooting, we are confident that it was deliberate, that there was no objective justification for it, and though we are not certain, that it seems to us more likely than not that there was no subjective justification either. Of course we would have in mind the seriousness of the matter on which we were expressing a view, but that is not because of some rule that we should apply, but rather as a matter of common sense and justice. ([2007] EWHC 12 (Admin))

This was significant for us because in the IMC we had developed our process independently and had not been aware of the Bloody Sunday Inquiry ruling. The court went on to consider the IMC confidentiality clause:

> For reasons of confidentiality the IMC cannot set out the evidence on which its conclusions are based; and the question whether an opportunity has been given to [the complainant] to deal with allegations made against it is a separate issue considered below. Subject to those qualifications, however, the passage from the tribunal's ruling sets out an approach very similar to that taken by the IMC in relation to its own reports. As we have said, it is in our view an appropriate one. We do not accept that the IMC, given the nature of its functions, is required to adopt a more legalistic test than that adopted for The Bloody Sunday Inquiry. ([2007] EWHC 12 (Admin). Queen's Bench Division Divisional Court Case No. CO/9939/2005 delivered 19 January 2007)

This judgment confirmed that learning from other public inquiries was relevant to our work.

At the end of a conflict, consideration is given to what has been achieved; what follows a conflict may be as asymmetrical as the conflict itself. At a more strategic analysis level, this chapter is concerned with the concepts of order and security during a post-conflict process. This involves some elements of continuing confrontation but takes place before complete normalization.

For Liddell Hart this included thinking ahead, perhaps even earlier during the conflict or even in the pre-conflict confrontation phase, to the peace process and post-conflict period: 'grand strategy looks beyond the war to the subsequent peace. It should not only combine the various instruments, but so regulate their use as to avoid damage to the future state of peace – for its security approach ... and prosperity' (Liddell Hart, 1954, p. 336).

One of these instruments is intelligence. This is peculiarly appropriate when the policing paradigm for counter-terrorism is reconsidered at leisure in the post-conflict but confrontational world.[5] The challenge is to identify what can be done during a period of conflict to prevent some of the problems which may emerge during a peace process that could destabilize the situation. It was explained in the IMC final report thus:

8.9   It was clear from the beginning that to be effective we needed the fullest possible access to information from both official and other sources. There were two main aspects.

8.10 First, with the police and intelligence authorities North and South we needed to demonstrate we could handle material responsibly, drawing on it for our analysis but not putting things into the public domain in a way which compromised their work or the safety of individuals.* We believe that the way we handled this material in our First Report was key here. Fruitful relations with these authorities were established from very early on and we have been struck by how forthcoming they were with information and comment. However, we sought always to maintain a proper distance as well as a capacity to question, and in some cases to disagree, and our conclusions were always our own. While we relied on much more than just their material, theirs was an input without which it would not have been possible to produce reports of any depth and authority.

8.11 Second, it was essential that we had sources other than official ones and in our statement in March 2004 and subsequently we invited people to approach us in confidence. We needed personal and local perspectives and also information. We usually obtained it face to face on our premises or on visits around Northern Ireland. Though many approached us on their own initiative, we frequently took the initiative ourselves and asked to see people, individually or in groups, and believe it was important that we did so. We wanted to ask questions and to hear what it was like in local communities; what paramilitaries were up to in different areas and what the communities really felt about them; how real was the support or the fear; how the facts and views locally tallied with what we heard from official sources; what senior members of paramilitary groups themselves

---

* We were very careful to ensure the security of any material supplied to us on paper.

thought, and sometimes whether and how they were trying to manipulate us. Moreover, we wanted more than simply the grass roots view. We needed analysis and perspective as well, and found it in many conversations, including with senior figures and commentators in Ireland North and South.

8.12 The range of our non-official sources was thus very wide and from some countries in addition to the UK and Ireland. As we proceeded, some people who had initially been unwilling to see us became ready to do so. We gave a list of the categories in our Fifth Report which held good throughout our ensuing five and a half years.[6] Over the seven years we have met many hundreds of people, either individually or in groups. Their contribution was essential to our ability to make rounded assessments and to offer convincing reports. (IMC, 2011, pp. 24–25)

Policing, Intelligence and Counter-Terrorism in Northern Ireland, 1969–1999

It is not fashionable, as the Northern Ireland political process moves forward, to explicitly apply elsewhere the pre-peace agreement counter-terrorist policing lessons of Northern Ireland. The Royal Ulster Constabulary (RUC), it is argued by some, had developed into the most experienced and successful intelligence-led counter-terrorist police service in the world between 1969 and 1999 (Doherty, 2004; Ryder, 2000); for example, they originated the community impact assessment process. Former members of the RUC continue to be challenged and investigated, and their Special Branch and other intelligence organizations in particular are selected for criticism (McDonald, 2011). Public inquiries, trials and inquests all currently question the past role of policing, military, the state and its agents. Perversely, the alleged absence of current intelligence to pre-empt terrorist acts is also criticized (see McDonald, 2010, for an example). This ignores the numbers of residual terrorists arrested and charged with dissident terrorist activity (see, e.g., IMC, 2010a, 2010b).

The context, therefore, is not just the role of the IMC in the closing years of a 30-year campaign of violence but also a period of significant changes in wider UK policing that have affected the policing counter-terrorist paradigm. These have included a background of wider challenges to the police, the criminal justice system and the state itself and its powers, for example, the public inquiries by Lord Patten and his advisers into the future of policing in Northern Ireland, Lord Saville's Bloody Sunday Inquiry, Judge Cory's reviews of a series of murders, Lord Scarman's (first, second and third) public inquiries into policing in both Northern Ireland and London, the ongoing collusion investigations concerning the state and paramilitaries originally started by the Police Ombudsman for Northern Ireland (Brain, 2010; Grieve, 2007; Savage, 2007).

Outside Northern Ireland there were further public inquiries and that impacted on policing generally and also on the police paradigm for counter-terrorism. These included the Lawrence, Laming, Taylor, Hutton, Bichard, Butler and Morris inquiries.[7] They all touched on the independence and impartiality of police operations and decision-making. Courts, lawyers, defence and the Crown Prosecution Service (or the Public Prosecutor in Northern Ireland), the Regulation of Investigatory Powers Act 2000, surveillance commissioners and coroners have all emphasized the negative on occasion, pursued a need for change and criticized previous policing decisions and behaviour (Brain, 2010; Grieve, 2007; Savage, 2007).

There are general lessons from these inquiries. In all violent conflicts there is the potential for mistakes, errors and accidents, causes célèbres, miscarriages of justice, conspiracy theories where no conspiracies exist, and downright bad behaviour. Post-event and true conspiracies have been proved to exist in some arenas, but they are far less frequent than alleged. Where death is involved, they naturally become extremely emotive. The policing paradigm requires a robust lawful decision-making process to defend legitimate action, however audacious, examined by public inquiries with the benefit of hindsight in the post-conflict period.

There is also the wider context that post-conflict brings change, particularly where the peace process is negotiated, as in Northern Ireland; and that such change takes place in a new and modern world where a culture may place greater emphasis on diversity, where fragmentation, blurred boundaries and roles, and different alliances all impact on the way both past and present decision-making are viewed. Systems failures in public bodies may also create an environment that impacts on post hoc reviews.

On the other hand, internal cultural changes to policing organizations, such as those directed by the United Nations Code of Conduct for Law Enforcement (UNHCR, 2000) for professional ethics guidance, may be driven by committed concerned practitioners of the counter-terrorism policing paradigm in the same way as the military paradigm may be driven by a warrior ethos.

Three Models of Counter-Terrorism and a Hybrid Version

It has been argued by both English (2009) and Cronin (2009) that there are two paradigms for counter-terrorism, a police model and a martial model. I want to explore four variations on this: the police, policing and martial models and a combination of all three that appeared in Northern Ireland, a hybrid model. The police model means that the rule of law, particularly the power of the courts, is maintained without the use of the military, not even for military assistance to the civil powers (MACP in the UK). I prefer to adopt a policing model for reasons I will explore later but, in brief, the distinction is the inclusion of a wider model of policing that encompasses many other agencies and organizations as partners with the sworn police officers but not, for the purposes of this analysis, the military. The third version is the martial model, where the primary counter-terrorist agent of the state is the military. From these distinctions we can develop a further hybrid model, encompassing both policing and martial models. I have emphasized my experiences as part of a policing, intelligence-led, community-oriented, rule of law, criminal justice paradigm of counter-terrorism and a hybrid version of this, not the pure military paradigm.

This has clearly influenced my views. All four versions – police, wider policing, martial and hybrid – can be found in the Northern Ireland experience.

There is one important ingredient to this multi-agency hybrid policing model – the emphasis on intelligence as fundamental to all. In the *Twenty-Sixth and Final Report* the IMC recorded:

> 13.3   We identify the following, which together helped to establish confidence that we were independent, were telling it as we saw it and would stick to our task:
>
> - From the start we were *proactive* and determined to have a beneficial impact and to make the best possible use of our *powers, our capacities and our independence*;
> - We all made a sustained and very substantial commitment of time and effort;
> - Early publication of our scope, standards and criteria enabled us more readily to hold paramilitary groups to account, to demonstrate we were independent and to achieve consistency of reporting;
> - A blunt and consistent style of reporting combined with the rejection of terms we felt were inaccurate or misleading. Thus: frank descriptions of paramilitary crimes and their impact; 'victims' for all who suffered, including the communities with paramilitaries in their midst; no use of the term 'punishment beatings', which implied spurious legitimacy, but shootings and assaults; no 'ceasefire' because it was our responsibility to monitor all aspects of paramilitary activity and because the term ceasefire had been used by many groups as a shield to avoid scrutiny or criticism of their non-terrorist activities;
> - Defining our task broadly from the start, in particular to include all forms of paramilitary crime, which went hand in hand with our rejection of 'ceasefire';
> - *The breadth of our sources and the manner in which we analysed the information and views we obtained.* One reason for this breadth was our early declaration that our door was open and that we were keen to hear from people. Other factors were our confidentiality policy and growing public confidence in our reporting. (IMC, 2011, p. 39; emphasis added)

Two Models of Ending of Conflict

Richard English (2009) asks the question in the title of his book *Terrorism: How to Respond?* He answers the question using seven categories.

- *Learn to live with it.* There are presentational problems with this approach. However, there may be some contexts where a level of terrorist activity is the result of not over-reacting, avoiding over-militarization, emphasizing police primacy and waiting for the groups to implode. It might be argued that the absence of reporting of the terrorist incidents in Northern Ireland in any depth in the London press could be a manifestation of this category.
- *Address underlying causes where possible.* There are problems with this as well when there are groups like the dissident republicans in Northern Ireland whose

strategy is to undermine any peace efforts. For example, they attack nationalist or republican police officers and their associates who are involved in even-handed community or neighbourhood policing projects intended to promote public confidence. This too requires access to intelligence.

- *Avoid over-militarization: police primacy.* This goes to the heart of a counter-terrorism policing paradigm with the emphasis on the police. Recent Northern Irish experiences with dissident republicans suggest that a civilian police have dilemmas in fast response to a terrorist incident where they may be lured to their deaths. The military have additional resources, tactics and kit to respond to a variety of violent terrorist methods.
- *Intelligence vital.* This is at the heart of my arguments involving the policing paradigm and is closely related to the previous point. The key role of intelligence means more than just the tactics and technology of the secret covert world but relates to the core of my argument that intelligence as used by the police includes Lord Butler's recommendation that to put intelligence into the public domain as the governments did over weapons of mass destruction and Iraq required some thinking through and guidelines (Butler, 2004). This is one of the functions of the Independent Monitoring Commission: an emphasis not just on analysis, assessment and judgement in the intelligence process, but additional activity that involves educating customers of intelligence. There are issues about disclosure of policing methodology and operations, not just in the use of criminal justice systems but also in the education process, but this does not undermine the fundamental point. The IMC putting intelligence into the public domain is also related to English's last point about winning the intellectual arguments as well as the rule of democratic law.
- *Rule of democratic law: role of the criminal justice system.* This goes to the heart of informed decision-making in a democracy. To win hearts and minds to the rule of law, the criminal justice system and policing communities have to be given information.
- *Coordinate all measures, for example, financial investigation, technology deployed in counter-terrorism.* This category allows me to re-emphasize the multi-agency role of policing as opposed to pure police or martial paradigms.
- *Strong public arguments against violence; credibility of the instruments of the state.* This goes to the core of the IMC remit of placing analysis and assessment of the intelligence into the public domain and for the use of all. The chronology and analysis of both violence and confrontation is open to all across 26 IMC reports which challenge, make recommendations and comment on changes. You cannot engage in that debate without intelligence.

Audrey Kurth Cronin (2009) asks a related optimistic question: How does terrorism end? She considers six possible endings.

- *Decapitation – the state kills or captures the leaders.* This is not what happened in Northern Ireland. The leadership cadre was granted their freedom in the hope that they would play a role in the political peace process. Many of them did, as a result of the considerable leverage placed on the prisoner releases in the political process, in particular by the PIRA engineering department – considered by some to be their strategic and tactical leadership if not intellectual elite.

- *Negotiation – political solution discovered.* This is what happened in Northern Ireland (see Mowlem, 2002; Powell, 2008).
- *Success – they achieve their goals.* This is how Sinn Fein sold the peace process to their supporters, particularly the PIRA.
- *Failure – the terrorist groups implode, there is a backlash and the terrorists are marginalized.* The multiplication of sub-groups claiming to be the rightful inheritors of PIRA, the Continuity IRA and the Real IRA (in at least three manifestations) and others might exemplify this scenario.
- *Repression – the groups are crushed by the forces of the state.* This is problematic both in terms of an end to terrorism and as a motivator for another generation or cadre of terrorist.
- *Re-orientation – the groups become criminals or organized crime, or at worst the threat turns into (civil?) war.* There is considerable evidence of some shift to criminality in Northern Ireland. However, there is also considerable evidence of the creditable efforts made by the leadership of all the paramilitaries latterly to counter such criminality while going down the stable democratic political route to peace. In 1921 there was a civil war in the South following partition; there was none after 1999.

English and Cronin therefore provide a theoretical foundation for my arguments for the primacy of intelligence not just in pursuing terrorists but for contributing to the peace process.

Thinking about Peace in a Period of Conflict

Preparing for normalization is a key part of the intelligence-led policing paradigm during counter-terrorism or indeed any conflict or confrontation. As the fourth-century BCE Chinese military leader Sun Tzu observed, 'Generally in war the best policy is to take the state intact; to ruin it is inferior to this' (Griffith, 1963, p. 77). Considering Henry V's march from Harfleur to Agincourt, Juliet Barker (2005) notes his foresight in ordering that the penalty for the traditional plundering of an invading army was to be death. The lands through which his army travelled were to be his and the populace were to be his subjects; to do violence against them was illogical and would in any event sow the seeds of future conflict (Barker 2005, pp. 223, 410, 436, citing contemporary sources). Of course it is not easy to carry out the contemporaneous assessments and analysis that can aid such a judgement and decision-making as Patrick Beesly summarizes so elegantly and which I had identified during my period as Commander:

It is easy for all of us now, more than 40 years on to sift slowly through the relevant records, neatly arranged in chronological order, and ask ourselves, with the additional benefit of hindsight, why clues were missed, why appreciations were faulty, why incorrect decisions were taken. Those who have never experienced it should not forget 'the fog of war' factor, the atmosphere of urgency, the pressures, the strain, day after day, week after week, year after year, to try to solve the problems and complete the jigsaw puzzle – or rather puzzles because, in a world war, no single problem can be considered in isolation: there are dozens of them each calling for swift and most of them for immediate action. The more senior the individual concerned, the more likely it is that he [*sic*] will have to switch his attention at any time during the day – or night – from one end of the world to the other, from the land to the sea or to the air, from the tactical situation to the long-term implications, from the possible reactions of the enemy to the behaviour of allies. Nothing is simple, nothing is certain, but everything is important. (Beesly, 1990, pp. 317 – 318)

It is a fundamental principle of policing that public disorder or violence, let alone terrorism and war, is abnormal. A return to normality is part of any police commander's strategy. This is the foundation of my belief that thinking about peace during periods of conflict, indeed during warfare, is intrinsic to the police founding fathers' philosophy. Any conflict management or peace process that includes the seeds of the next conflict is, therefore, inherently unstable.

Leadership, Political and Paramilitary

This chapter is not arguing that the IMC role was leadership, although some have interpreted it in part as such. Rather, it was to provide, among other things, a spur to the paramilitary and political leaders to live up to their responsibilities. By providing intelligence to leaders and by putting it in the public domain, in particular, the IMC enabled them to challenge violent ideologies and political misinterpretation of their acts. It provided a public chronology and assessment. It is not possible for the strategy needed for winning hearts and minds to take place without educated champions and leaders being given usable information and intelligence.

Conclusions

The reason why the enlightened prince and wise general conquer the enemy whenever they move and their achievements surpass those of ordinary men is because of foreknowledge. (Griffith, 1963, p. 144)

In other words, the use of intelligence gives foreknowledge of how to win the peace. That is what taking the state intact also includes. Losing the peace would ruin it.

What does this contribute to our learning about how to use intelligence during conflicts, confrontations and the end of conflicts – about how not to lose the peace? The IMC philosophy of always being led by intelligence has helped my thinking about this; derived from the background of each of the commissioners was our opening statement about how we would go about our work. The intelligence process was rigorous and tested. The regular detailed reporting that put it in its entirety in the public domain was fundamental.

The decision of the two governments to give the role of preparing open intelligence reports, a trend noted by Butler (2004) in his recommendation 37, to an independent commission has, at the minimum, changed the debate from one about political direction, or spin of material in relation to alleged breaches of the ceasefire, to one about the skill and rigour of our information gathering and the objectivity of our reporting. Butler seems to imply that this could be extended to all periods, from pre-conflict, through conflict, to end of conflict. There is a possible problem here, however. The early identification of human rights as core principles was of great significance to us. How can such a process fit with a policing criminal justice paradigm?

Our process, as exemplified in the High Court action, as we refined each report, allowed us to test our principles and analysis, not least in a criminal justice paradigm. The method by which we explored analytic techniques and recent commentary (e.g., Butler 2004; Chapter 1 in this volume) offered us thinking and a methodology to avoid some of the areas that had been described as intelligence failures (see, e.g., George & Bruce, 2008) a frequently fruitful source for those looking for conflict through alleged conspiracies or to undermine effort to win hearts and minds. The High Court judgment again was helpful in that it justified our use of different levels of confidence in our material and in the methods of analysis we were using.

The IMC process of collection, analysis, preparation, assessment and publication, recording changes with the objective of normalization over six-month reporting cycles, was robust enough to survive even that legal challenge. This has built up an archive and chronology for use by all who are concerned or who tasked the IMC to effect the transition to a 'peaceful society and stable and inclusive devolved government in Northern Ireland' – to win the peace. These include those studying miscarriages of justice or conspiracy theories.

The final Twenty-Sixth Report of the IMC recorded:

12.1   In this Part we look at our contribution and the factors behind it. We do so with some hesitation. Self-evidently, no rounded assessment is possible so near the time. Moreover, many things relevant to such judgements, such as the records of the IMC and the candid views of the principal politicians, are not available now, and some may never be. We were part of a process which involved many people, parties and organisations. We do not want to take for ourselves credit that is due to others, whether the major figures in the process of change, institutions or the countless people who have worked for peace within their communities.* But notwithstanding this, we think it would be helpful to future discussion about the changes in Northern Ireland over the past seven years if we offer our thoughts as we close. What follows draws heavily on views expressed to us by a number of people from the UK, Ireland and the US. We are in their debt.

12.2   Any contribution the IMC has made has reflected where it is positioned. It is independent of the two Governments and came to be seen as such by all but a few ill-disposed observers. It has access to secret intelligence and can develop its own separate sources. It has to speak publicly, drawing in part on secret material but doing so in a way which did not compromise intelligence and police operations. It can say things which in practice would never be said by governments or by police and intelligence agencies.[8] It can develop a reputation for speaking candidly, as can be hard for governments, especially when tackling matters across the divide in Northern Ireland. This is a privileged but also a precarious position to be in.

12.3   We were struck throughout by the fact that, while our reports were not always welcome to everybody, there was no comprehensive challenge to our analysis of paramilitary activity at any stage by the media or the principal players. Persuasive attempts to undermine what we said could have reduced the impact we were able to have on public opinion. We note in this context the repeated public comments of Sinn Féin that they disapproved of the establishment of the IMC. However, many observers believe that the restoration of the Assembly and Executive in 2007 would not have been possible without the reports of the IMC. (IMC, 2011, pp. 38–39)

The IMC reports have been cited in analysis of developments, for example, by academics (e.g., Spencer, 2008, p. 232), politicians (e.g., Powell, 2008, pp. 239–240, 274, 276, 278) and the media (e.g., Godson, 2004, pp. 769, 771).

What are the lessons from the IMC that can be applied to a period of war, the military paradigm or preparation for normalization on the policing paradigm? One might be loosening the reporting and analysis controls over pre-trial publicity. With the current rules it is sometimes impossible to assess what is actually going on. The courts take an ultra-conservative line on what is publicized. This analysis is possible (just) in Northern Ireland, as I have explained.

Another application might be the independent reports of specific inquiries prior to the decisions, for example, a rigorous Chilcot-type inquiry by privy counsellors at the time of momentous decision-making, like going to war. Or a far earlier Saville Inquiry might have contributed to understanding the causes of continuing conflict.

---

* In addition to the public, religious and voluntary institutions suggested here, we noted in paragraph 1.11 of our Fifth Report in May 2005 some twenty three other bodies involved in monitoring what was happening in Northern Ireland; some were long standing bodies engaged in regular inspection but eight were specific to the peace process …

I have argued that the context is not just the closing years of a 30-year campaign of violence but also a period of significant changes in wider UK policing that have affected the pure policing counter-terrorist paradigm. These have included a background of challenges to the police, criminal justice system and the state itself and its powers; some of those challenges were specifically related to the Northern Ireland conflict and post-conflict. The context has also changed during the seven years of the IMC's existence. The dissident terrorists were most definitely not in a post-conflict mode. So the IMC found themselves reporting during a conflict, albeit one that did not resemble the conflict with PIRA. What follows a conflict can be as asymmetrical as the conflict itself.

For some years I have been arguing that educating customers of intelligence in the wider populace will help win the peace and that democracies need their constituents to make informed decisions. There are, of course, dangers and difficulties of exposing secret processes and sources. The main thrust of my argument is how to balance the need to lawfully succeed at operations, through audacious intelligence-led policing activity – not by deception or insidious penetration of communities, but by using intelligence to win hearts and minds. The final moves in the endgame of a conflict and peace process is the ending of confrontation and consideration of what has been achieved by all sides. This chapter has not only emphasized my experiences as a former counter-terrorist team leader, but has also explored the synergy of a policing, intelligence-led, community-oriented, rule of law, criminal justice paradigm of counter-terrorism in making peace, preventing violent extremism and winning hearts and minds. As the fourth-century CE Roman writer Vegetius observed, 'He who desires peace, let him prepare for war' (quoted in Mallinson, 2009, p. 573). What we are considering is a corollary to Vegetius: that the desire for peace should lead to preparations for that peace by using intelligence in the democratic process at an early stage in a conflict or confrontation.

Acknowledgements

I am grateful to my three former colleagues as IMC commissioners: Lord Alderdice, Joe Brosnan and Dick Kerr who, together with the joint secretaries, Stephen Boys Smith and Michael Mellett, once again did the thinking that led to my account, helped in the preparation and had the opportunity to comment on an early version of this chapter. It owes much to the thinking that went into our twenty-sixth final valedictory report in March 2011.

Notes

1   A version of this paper was given at St Antony's College, Oxford, on 27 May 2010, and I am grateful to the college and to Sir Hugh Orde, President of ACPO, for their discussion. See also Grieve (2011).

2 The IMC was set up in shadow form in September 2003, formally established in January 2004 and submitted its first report in April 2004. After that, it submitted 26 reports. The commissioners, of whom I was one, were nominated by the British, Irish and US governments, and were required only to report on events that bore on the IMC's period of existence.

3 The official website for the Hutton Inquiry has now closed but the transcript can be found on a number of other websites by searching for the Hutton Inquiry, for example, http://www.hutton.softblade.com/transcripts.php?action=transcript&session=2&witness=4 (retrieved 10 June 2014). This site was set up by an interested party who experienced difficulty following the transcript material on the official site.

4 All the IMC reports can be accessed via https://www.gov.uk/search?q=independent+monitoring+commission+reports (retrieved 10 June 2014).

5 For a discussion of this confrontation, conflict, post-conflict, further continuing confrontation, possible peace and normalization model see Smith (2005, p. 181).

6 The categories were: political parties; government officials; police; community groups; churches; charities; pressure groups and other organizations; former combatants, including ex-prisoners; representatives of business; lawyers; journalists; academics; victims; private citizens, individually and as families (IMC, 2005, para. 1.11; see also IMC, 2011, Annex X). Although this list held good for the rest of our time, we would add that we increasingly found ourselves sought out by journalists, academics and think tanks because of their interest in how we worked and what we had done. We hope this interaction was helpful to them; it certainly was to us.

7 For an account of the wide policing impact, not least in intelligence, of several of these examples, see later in the chapter and Grieve, 2007, p. 46–52.

8 Examples of things which we were able to say but which would be difficult for official agencies to articulate are: the important role of paramilitary leaders in guiding their organizations away from violence, and the need for them to remain in positions of authority over a period of transition; defining the criteria whereby paramilitary groups could be judged to be making progress towards giving up illegal activity and whether they had then actually stopped it.

References

Audit Commission. (1993). *Helping with inquiries: Tackling crime effectively*. London: Stationery Office.

Barker, J. (2005). *Agincourt*. London: Little, Brown.

Beesly, P. (1990). Convoy PQ17: A study of intelligence and decision making. In M. I. Handel (Ed.), *Intelligence and military operations* (pp. 292–322). London: Cass.

Bichard M. (2004). *The Bichard Inquiry report*. London: Stationery Office.

Brain, T. (2010). *A history of policing in England and Wales from 1974*. Oxford: Oxford University Press.

Butler, F. E. R. (2004). *Review of intelligence on weapons of mass destruction: Report of a committee of privy counsellors*. HCP898. London: Stationery Office.

Cronin, A. K. (2009). *How terrorism ends: Understanding the decline and demise of terrorist campaigns*. Princeton: Princeton University Press.

Doherty, R. (2004). *The thin green line: The history of the Royal Ulster Constabulary GC*. London: Pen & Sword.

English, R. (2009). *Terrorism: How to respond*. Oxford: Oxford University Press.

George, R., & Bruce, J. (2008). *Analyzing intelligence: Origins, obstacles and innovations*. Washington, DC: Georgetown University Press.

Godson, D. (2004). *Himself alone: David Trimble and the ordeal of Unionism*. London: Harper-Collins.

Grieve J. (2007). Behavioural science and the law: Investigation. In D. Carson, B. Milne, F. Pakes, K. Shalev, and A. Shawyer (Eds.), *Applying psychology to criminal justice*. Chichester, UK: Wiley.

Grieve, J. (2011). Monitoring the Loyalist paramilitaries. In J. W. McAuley & G. Spencer (Eds.), *Ulster Loyalism after the Good Friday Agreement: History, identity and change*. Basingstoke, UK: Palgrave Macmillan.

Grieve, J., Harfield, C., & MacVean, A. (2007). *Policing*. London: Sage.

Griffith, S. B. (1963). *Sun Tzu: The art of war*. Oxford: Clarendon.

Home Office. (2006/2011). *Countering international terrorism*. Cm 6888, as updated by Cm 7547 (2009), Cm 7833 (2010), Cm 8123 (2011). London: HMSO.

Hutton, B. (2004). *Report of the Inquiry into the Circumstances Surrounding the Death of Dr David Kelly C.M.G.* HC 247. London: Stationery Office. Retrieved 4 June 2014 from http://webarchive.nationalarchives.gov.uk/20090128221550/http://www.the-hutton -inquiry.org.uk/content/report/huttonreport.pdf

Independent Monitoring Commission (IMC). (2005, April). *Fifth report of the Independent Monitoring Commission*. Retrieved 12 June 2014 from http://www.justice.ie/en /JELR/IMCrpt5.pdf/Files/IMCrpt5.pdf

Independent Monitoring Commission (IMC). (2010a). *Twenty-third report of the Independent Monitoring Commission*. HC 17. London: Stationery Office. Retrieved 10 June 2014 from https://www.gov.uk/government/uploads/system/uploads/attachment_data/file/89952 /23rd_imc_report.pdf

Independent Monitoring Commission (IMC). (2010b, 4 November). *Twenty-fifth report of the Independent Monitoring Commission*. HC 565. London: Stationery Office. Retrieved 10 June 2014 from https://www.gov.uk/government/uploads/system/uploads /attachment_data/file/89892/twenty_fifth_report_of_the_independent_monitoring _commission.pdf

Independent Monitoring Commission (IMC). (2011). *Twenty-sixth and final report of the Independent Monitoring Commission: 2004–2011 – Changes, impact and lessons*. HC 1149. London: Stationery Office. Retrieved 10 June 2014 from https://www.gov .uk/government/uploads/system/uploads/attachment_data/file/89856/imc_26th_and _final_report_july_2011.pdf

International Agreement between the Government of UK and Government of Ireland. (2003). London: Stationery Office.

Laming, W. H. (2003). *The Victoria Climbié Inquiry*. CM5730. London: Department of Health. Retrieved 4 June 2014 from http://www.dh.gov.uk/prod_consum_dh/groups /dh_digitalassets/documents/digitalasset/dh_110711.pdf

Liddell Hart, B. (1954). *Strategy: The indirect approach*. London: Faber.

Macpherson, W. (1999). *The Stephen Lawrence Inquiry*. London: Stationery Office. See also nationalarchives.gov.uk search ref NT/2/57 pp. 11055 and 11068.

Mallinson, A. (2009). *The making of the British Army*. London: Bantam.

May, J. (1994). *Report of the Inquiry into the Circumstances Surrounding the Convictions Arising Out of the Bomb Attacks in Guildford and Woolwich in 1974*. London: Stationery Office.

McDonald, H. (2010, 16 April). Northern Ireland police left at risk by 'intelligence gap'. *Guardian*. Retrieved 4 June 2014 from http://www.theguardian.com/uk/2010/apr /16/northern-ireland-police-intelligence-gap

McDonald, H. (2011, 26 December). Nuala O'Loan calls for single body to investigate crimes of the Troubles. *Guardian*. Retrieved 4 June from http://www.theguardian.com/uk /2011/dec/26/northern-ireland-police-ombudsman1

Mowlem, M. (2002). *Momentum*. London: Hodder & Stoughton.

National Commission on Terrorism Attacks upon the United States. (2004). *The 9/11 Commission Report*. Washington, DC: United States Government Printing Office.

Omand, D. (2010). *Securing the state*. London: Hurst.

Powell, J. (2008). *Great hatred, little room: Making peace in Northern Ireland*. London: Bodley Head.

Ryder, C. (2000). *The RUC A Force under fire*. London: Arrow.

Savage, S. (2007). *Police reform: Forces for change*. Oxford: Oxford University Press.

Scarman, L. (1981). *The Scarman Report: The Brixton disorders*. London: Stationery Office.

Sims, J. (1993). What is intelligence? (Paper 1). In A. Shulsky & J. Sims (Eds.), *What is intelligence?* Working Group on Intelligence Reform, Consortium for the Study of Intelligence. Washington, DC: Georgetown University.

Smith, R. (2005). *The utility of force*. London: Allen Lane.

Spencer, G. (2008). *The state of loyalism in Northern Ireland*. Basingstoke, UK: Palgrave Macmillan.

United Nations High Commissioner for Human Rights (UNHCR). (2000). *Teaching human rights to police*. New York: United Nations.

Legal Case

[2007] EWHC 12 (Admin)

Index

Investigating Terrorism: Current Political, Legal and Psychological Issues, First Edition. Edited by John Pearse.
© 2015 John Wiley & Sons, Ltd. Published 2015 by John Wiley & Sons, Ltd.

This index was prepared by Neil Manley.